IMAGES OF
AMERICAN RADICALISM

IMAGES OF AMERICAN RADICALISM

By Paul Buhle
and
Edmund B. Sullivan

Art Young

"What's he been doin'?"
"Overthrowin' the govment."

Founded 1910
THE CHRISTOPHER PUBLISHING HOUSE
HANOVER, MASSACHUSETTS 02339

Library of Congress Catalog Number 94-69075

ISBN: 0-8158-0509-8

Second Edition-1999

We extend our very special thanks to Mimi and Abner Diamond, Scott McLemee and Penelope and Franklin Rosemont. They spent many hours digging through sources and providing art that we could not otherwise have obtained.

We thank Paul Andreas Rasmussen for his generous financial assistance.

We also wish to express our gratitude to Harold Walsh, Mary Murray, and Nancy Lucas at Christopher Publishing House for their patience and hard work.

PRINTED IN THE UNITED STATES OF AMERICA

Dedicated to the Memory of
Art Young, 1866-1943.

"Art Young by Himself."

Table of Contents

FOREWORD

In future years, this book will be used and treasured by scholars, not only in America but the world over. It is not simply another book on American radicalism; it is, as far as I am concerned, the best and most open-minded study of the subject that exists. It is put together in the best historical tradition, objectively and without malice.

The tremendous struggles of radical and socialist movements in America — a struggle for the well-being of all American working people — has been slighted or misrepresented in most American historical materials. This struggle has had a major role in the shaping of the United States. It has been maligned or ignored entirely since its beginnings in the colonial period. The thousands of brave and selfless people, men and women, who have given their lives to this struggle, have either been removed from history or mentioned with calumny and prejudice. Every social and compassionate advance in our history came out of the working-class and women's rights movement. There is almost no section of the American population, including those in the ruling class, both economically and politically, whose lives have not been altered and improved by these struggles.

Today, many scholars have turned to the radical movement as a historical subject, and for them this book will have enormous value. But its use goes beyond that. We are now engaged in a bitter battle to retain the social advances brought about by this long, hard fight for equality and social justice. The list of martyrs to this cause is a long one and it must be neither forgotten nor misunderstood. Paul Buhle and Edmund B. Sullivan have made a profound contribution to our understanding of our past. They deserve the gratitude of all people of good will.

Howard Fast

ACKNOWLEDGMENTS

This project initially grew out of a collaboration between the authors for an exhibition, "Voices of the Left, 1870-1960," at the University of Hartford's Museum of American Political Life in 1990-1991. We are grateful to President Humphrey Tonkin for permission to use several items from that exhibition.

We are also grateful to Ben and Beatrice Goldstein for the use of prints from their extensive holdings. Paul Richards, drawing on the extensive file of his father's superb camera-work, was most generous as was Gene Povirk of Southpaw Books, who made his wonderfully varied stock available to us. One author spent a few unforgettable hours with John Durham of Bolerium Books, selecting material to be photographed. Josh Brown of Hunter College's American Social History Project provided us with a solid foundation of illustrations for treatment of the nineteenth century labor movement. Fay Itzkowitz and Tobie Meyer translated material from Yiddish and Chinese, respectively. Labor historian and historical collector Scott Molloy not only supplied rare prints and photos, but also gave us the physical space to spread out materials while collating photography and text.

It would be impossible to acknowledge all those who have assisted us. But to those activists, artists, archivists, photographers whose work we have drawn from, or relatives of personalities illustrated in these pages and those otherwise genuinely interested in this project, we express our appreciation:

Dina Abramowicz, Mike Alewitz, Bernard Aspell, Barbara Bair, Rudolph Baranik, Lee Baxandall, Bettina Berch, Richard Bermack, Deborah Bernhardt, Janet Biehl, Joan E. Biren ("JEB"), Pamela Blackwell, Fay M. Blake, Jon Bloom, Grace Lee Boggs, Lorraine Brown, Alex Buchman, Mari Jo Buhle, Peter Buckingham, Ned Cartledge, Ronald Cohen, Oscar Campomanes, Gordon Chapman, Mary Chapman, Kim Chernin, Ward Churchill, Sarah Cooper, Carlos Cortez, Robert Crumb, Robert Cutter, Mary Cygan, Diana Davies, Eugene DeGruson, Dave Demarest, Rod Dresser, Steven Deutsch, Diane DiPrima, Greg Dowd, Howard Fast, Harry Fleischman, Kenneth Florey, Eric Foner, Marge Frantz, Harold Freeman, Dee Garrison, Barbara Garson, Chris Gavreau, Dan Georgakas, Shirley Golden, Tom D. Good, Van Gosse, Eric A. Gordon, Erica Gottfried, Gil Green, Alice Gronfeld, Ben Harris, Nathaniel H. Harris, Carolee Hazlet, Paul Hessell, Tony Hiss, Jim Hoberman, Jane Hodes, Anita Hoffman, Michael Honey, Maurice Jackson, Mary E. Janzen, Mike Konopacki, Bunny Botto Kuiker, Andy Lanset, Ring Lardner, Jr., Harold Levanthal, Ann Lipow, George Lipsitz, Priscilla Long, Michael Karni, Diana B. Kartsen, Ben Katchor, Harvey J. Kaye, Harry Kelber, Charles Keller, Jay Kinney, Denis Kitchen, Aaron Kramer, Timothy Messer-Kruse, Karen Kubby, Paul LeBlanc, Robert Lee, Ursula LeGuin, Jim Lorence, Lisa Lyons, Nora McCarthy, William McClenaghan, John McCormick, David McReynolds, Harry Magdoff, Manning Marable, Peter Marcuse, William Marshall, Elizabeth Martinez, Michael Meeropol, Sonia Meyers, James Michel, Robert Millar, E. Ethelbert Miller, Helen Mintus, Greg Mitchell, Jessica Mitford, Ralph Nader, Cary Nelson, Joanna Norman, Jim O'Brien, Lucy O'Connor, Walt W. Odets, Bertell Ollman, Roxanne Dunbar Ortiz, Daniel Ostroff, Nell Irvin Painter, Harvey Pekar, Lorraine Perlman, Ben Perry, Nancy Joyce Peters, Marge Piercy, Frederick Pohl, Carol Poore, Bill Preston, Richard Quinney, Peter Rachleff, Paul Andreas Rasmussen, Renqui Yu, Sid Resnick, Rick Rinehard, Trina Robbins, Lester Rodney, Spain Rodriques, David Roediger, Michael Rossman, Otto Rothschild, Annette Rubenstein, Bruce Rubenstein, Julie Rutherford, Bernie Sanders, Christine Schelshorn, Morris U. Schappes, Robert Shapiro, Mark Sharron, Irwin Silber, John Sillito, Ellen Shub, Katherine Kish Sklar, Art Spiegelman, Charles Schwartz, Nancy Sherbert, Linda Shopes, Judith E. Smith, Phil Stern, Elizabeth Stevens, Micki Beth Stiller, Lori Taylor, Lenore Templeton, Dorothy Thompson, Nick Thorkleson, Stuart Timmons, Rachelle Todea, Michael Topp, Mitzi Trumbo, Vincenza Uccello, Ruth Adlard MacLennan Uphaus, Rudolph Vecoli, Gene Vranka, Ted Watts, Alan Wald, Seema Weatherwax, Erik Weber, Rogert Wechsler, James Weinstein, Stan Weir, Cornel West, Alice Wexler, Pete Wilcox, Janet Walerstein Winston, Fred Whitehead, Frank Wilkinson, Kenneth Winetrout, Mary Witkowski, Alfred Young, Howard Zinn, Rebecca Zurier.

So, too, we thank those institutions which have been especially gracious with their time and materials: American Labor Museum, Botto House. Ansel Adams Publicity Rights Trust. Bibliomania. Bishop Museum, Honolulu, Hawaii. Bridgeport, Connecticut Public Library, Historical Collections. Chinatown History Museum, New York. Dorothy Day Collection, Marquette University. Florida State Archives. First Christian Church, Springfield, Illinois. Frame Center, Boston, Massachusetts. Friends of Camp Kinderland. Harburg Foundation, New York City. Hancock Shaker Museum, Hancock, Massachusetts. Historic New Harmony, Indiana. Hood Museum, Dartmouth College. Houghton Library, Harvard University. Immigration History Research Center, University of Minnesota. Institute on the Federal Theater Project, George Mason University. International Longshoremen's and Warehousemen's Union. Kansas State Historical Society. Library of Congress. Minnesota Historical Society. Moberly Area Community College. Montana Historical Society. Niebyl-Proctor Library, Berkeley, California. Oregon Historical Society. Oregon State University Library. Paper Tiger Television. Peace Collection, Swarthmore College. Pennsylvania State Archives. Prometheus Library, New York City. Schomberg Center for Research in Black Culture, New York Public Library. Smithsonian Institution, Museum of American History, Division of Labor History. Southern California Library for Social Studies and Research. St. Joseph College, West Hartford, Connecticut. St. Nicholas Croatian Catholic Church, Millville, Pennsylvania. State Historical Society of Wisconsin. Tamiment Library (Robert F. Wagner Archives), New York University. Transport Workers Union of America, New York City. University of Illinois Library, Edwin Rolfe Archive. University of Pennsylvania, Van Pelt Library. University of Washington Libraries, Special Collections. Utah State Historical Society. War Resisters League. Washington State Historical Society. Wayne State University, Urban and Labor Archives. Winterthur Museum, Delaware. Wolfsonian Foundation, Miami, Florida. YIVO Institute for Jewish Research.

INTRODUCTION

American Icons and
Meanings of Radical Memory

Images of American radicalism take their shape mostly from the radicals themselves. Egalitarians, feminists, environmentalists, rebellious non-whites along with their white supporters, unionists and other lower class (or upper class) dissidents, enemies of authoritarian state rulers and military-imperial schemes, they have been a persistent part of our history and our iconography. The nature of the images changes continuously with the available technology as well as graphic styles. But a similarity remains. The same or similar subjects have repeatedly been used to shame or cajole American society to live up to its own professed aims of liberty and equality. They continue to look out at us from photos, sketches and cartoons as heroes or as lonely crusaders — also occasionally as feared and hated figures from the mind's eye of the conservative or commercial press. They are crushed and discredited, but they rise again. Radical artists themselves also offer reverse-images of the mainstream: Iconoclastic pictures of a society whose leaders (and sometimes ordinary citizens) are full of self-deceit, prideful and arrogant where they should be humble.

Perhaps most interesting for this book's reader, all such images draw upon a collective visual legacy that has made its way into the American psyche. Consider, for example, the face of Henry David Thoreau, the naturalist and resister against imperial war who preached a doctrine of self-wisdom and restraint. He has been a minor hero for subsequent generations, but only during the 1960s, when millions of Americans opposed their tax money being used for a terrifyingly bloody war of conquest in Vietnam, did he re-emerge as a saint of

Courtesy: Archives of Labor and Urban Affairs, Wayne State University.

Josephine Conger Kaneko, editor of the Progressive Woman, at her desk, c. 1912. Note the photos of Debs, Marx, Elizabeth Cady Stanton, Mother Jones, and others in her workspace.

Photograph and Courtesy: Richard Quitney.

Demonstration at Internal Revenue Service offices, New York City, 1971.

Helen Keller, symbol of personal striving to overcome disability.

Mary "Mother" Jones, the miners' heroine, c. 1915.

non-compliance with wrongful authority. Like the socialist scientist Albert Einstein, Thoreau became a "poster personality" for buttons and banners seeking to evoke a collective attack of conscience.

Earlier and later examples abound, in a variety of media. Utopian, labor educator and early feminist Frances Wright, for instance, was known as the "female Tom Paine," after the American Revolution's great radical pamphleteer. In turn, generations of rebels were derisively called "Fanny Wrights." But Elizabeth Cady Stanton, unabashed leader of the nineteenth century world's premier woman suffrage movement and herself one of the most remembered photo-personages of women's history, placed a famous portrait of the always controversial Wright as frontispiece in the first volume of her documentary *History of Woman Suffrage*.

Walt Whitman also considered Frances Wright the embodiment of freedom, including his own. His poetry, he believed, captured that realm of individual self-expression which Wright symbolized. The famous portraits of the bohemian graybeard became for many the personification of the radical as the chronicler of democratic every-day life, the instinctive male feminist, and also the great mystic of the body's happy possibilities. Isadora Duncan, who in the 1910s all but invented modern dance, swore that she carried Whitman's famed volume *Leaves of Grass* with her everywhere.

Other images pass down to us over the decades, some so familiar that we could almost forget that in their lifetimes those depicted were long viewed as dangerous characters, vilified, spied upon, sometimes jailed. Eugene V. Debs won his martyrdom not only as tireless socialist candidate but by being imprisoned and pilloried in the press during the 1890s and again during the 1910s. His face inspired literally hundreds of portraits in every medium, from cigar boxes to parade banners. Coal miners, numbering at one time in the hundreds of thousands, made "Mother" Mary Jones — feared and hated by the mine owners and the yellow press — into an icon for her bravery in the face of state militias and company thugs. Readers by the millions still later owned copies of *My Life* by Isadora Duncan, treated in her lifetime as anti-patriotic and immoral.

Not all our reprinted images, by a long stretch, are those of political and labor leaders or even avant-gardists like Duncan. Especially after the rise of modern popular culture, radical heroes could often be movie stars, musicians, sports figures or simply unique figures who symbolically represented their causes in many different ways. Helen Keller, who skyrocketed to fame as the blind and deaf mute child grown into a formidable intellectual and humanist, surprised the middle class when she declared her sympathies for socialists and the Industrial Workers of the World. Immigrant neighborhood theaters during the 1920s and early 1930s often had only the single sign in front, "I Am Here Today," bearing a picture of the "Little Tramp." Everyone knew Charlie Chaplin was for labor and a better world, and they could easily see him make fun of society's wealthy parasites. Decades later, he chose his conscience over residence in the United States.

By the 1930s-40s, and still more by the 1960s and after, millions hummed or sang the songs of another beloved tramp, Woody Guthrie, who better than anyone else captured the misery, the humor and the hope of downtrodden in the Depression days. He was a "red" and no one truly concerned with American culture could completely ignore him or his politics. His rebel reputation brought a young folkie from Minnesota, Bob Dylan (nee Zimmerman), to the bedside of a physically failing Woody as the activist sixties were about to begin. Blues singer Billie Holiday had suffered blacklisting for her denunciation of southern lynchings, and anti-war spokesman Muhammed Ali had his title taken away. But they have been loved all the more for their pains.

Neglected or repressed images also return to life through media evocations. By 1982, most Americans had long since forgotten

Courtesy: Woody Guthrie Publications

Woody Guthrie in the FSA Camps, California, c. 1941.

Louise Bryant at Wellfleet, Cape Cod, c. 1917. Printed with the permission of Houghton Library, Harvard University.

Charlie Chaplin and Jackie Coogan in The Kid.

Courtesy: Library of Congress.

Martin Luther King, Jr., and Malcolm X, c. 1965.

Courtesy: Library of Congress.

about the once-famed bohemian couple who traveled to early Red Russia and wrote brilliantly for the press about what they saw and felt. That very year, actor-director Warren Beatty brought out *Reds*, the epic saga of John Reed and Louise Bryant. Beatty made them seem spiritually free — but caught in the contradictions of the age. The depiction renewed memories of the original Greenwich Village in the days when cheap rents were no myth, and of Provincetown, Massachusetts, which never quite lost its bohemian status and became a center of gay society.

Television and other films along with documentaries have brought back a wide swath of other heroes and heroines, from the African Americans seen in *Roots* (the mostly widely watched mini-series in television history); to fictional and non-fictional treatments of Martin Luther King, Jr.; to Spike Lee's *Malcolm X* to other film treatments of Guthrie, Chaplin, Duncan, lawyer Clarence Darrow, writer Jack London, a slightly fictionalized Abbie Hoffman, the martyrs Sacco and Vanzetti, Julius and Ethel Rosenberg, among many others. These characters so dramatically fictionalized or stylized will be found here, in the original.

The majority of this volume inevitably concerns radicals whose lives and activities remain little known. For that reason more than any other, the form of the documentation is for the most part frankly vernacular. Most of this material fits no art history categories that its craftsmanlike creators (unconscious of creating "art" in the first place) would have recognized and defies any ordinary "reading."

Not that we have shunned the fine arts. Some of the best American artists in a half-dozen mediums find their natural place here. But as Cary Nelson has argued in his important volume *Repression and Recovery: Modern American Poetry and the Politics of Cultural Memory*, 1910-1945 (1989), collective cultural memory must be expanded in order to encompass the forgotten challenges, the many qualities of lived experience now generally ignored. To evoke them demands a conceptual leap into the dark.

These challenges or aspirations may be seen best, very often, in every-day objects and styles rendered political, or in the old slogans and the political calligraphy now abandoned to the attics of political memory. Pamphlet and magazine covers, contemporary cartoons and caricatures, everyday objects of every description from banners to fund-collection boxes, snapshots of events and personalities, even children's books — all have valued roles here. Subjects from woman's rights and spiritualism in the nineteenth century to gay liberation and environmen-

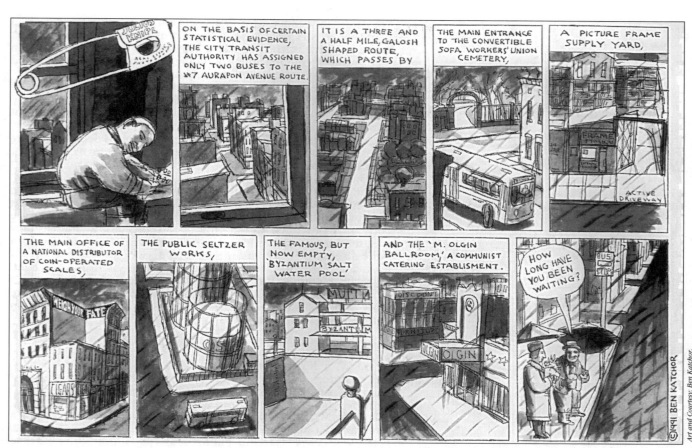

In the artist's invented landscape of Lower Manhattan, a restaurant is named for the famed Yiddish literary critic and Communist editor Moissaye Olgin, founder of the daily Morgen Freiheit *newspaper.*

talism in the twentieth have all inevitably inspired the production of artifacts, each subject and medium unique to itself and yet united to others by the invisible thread that, John Reed once insisted, connected Cubism and the I.W.W. The captions in *Images of American Radicalism* seek to record useful historical evidence and sometimes to classify the intention or changing technique involved with the visual document. A running narrative meanwhile suggests, in capsule form, the main lines of historical development. But the images themselves are intended to provoke a deeper and more idiosyncratic "reading" by way of the reader's own unique perceptions.

The effort of reproduction and classification is, inevitably, a self-conscious first step in a larger and more collective process. Alan Trachtenberg, author of *Reading American Photographs: Images as History, From Matthew Brady to Walker Evans* (1991), asks rhetorically whether any image can transform someone else's experience into our own. The answer is of course negative, but an ambiguous negative. We do certainly appropriate something of the experience this way, perhaps better or at least differently from any other means. Looking at a painting or a recent labor wall mural, a photograph of abolitionist Wendell Phillips or of civil rights leader Ella Josephine Baker can raise a wide spectrum of sensations and issues for the viewer. Through the power of imagination, it brings that viewer closer to the subject. If, as Walter Benjamin suggested, "the camera introduces us to unconscious optics as does psychoanalysis to unconscious impulses," the possibilities would seem limitless.

Trachtenberg also asks if we can approach any specific image

Abraham Lincoln. Drawing by Boardman Robinson for the cover of The Liberator, *February, 1919.*

Emma Goldman, the anarchist as a playful icon, c. 1975.

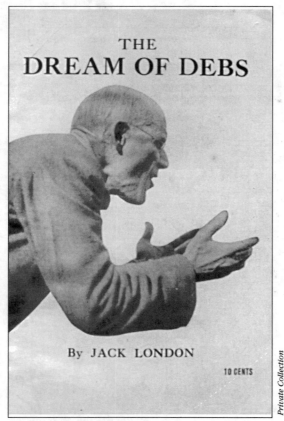

"The Dream of Debs," hero and martyr.

with the "innocence of a first encounter," *i.e.*, the uncalculated way that it was presumably first seen. Here the answer is yet more positive, although for a curious reason. The American media until recent decades, including mainstream books by noted historians and mainstream documentary or fictional films, have been so anxious to foreclose on the radical heritage that most of the images below will be simply unfamiliar to readers who have not spent a life time in social movements. The convergence (not to speak of the abundance) of images is therefore entirely new. Faces of Emma Goldman or Eugene Debs or Malcolm X, lithographs of notorious strikes and photos of AIDS protests coexist with the unfamiliar, forgotten or repressed. Seen in conjunction they inevitably take on new meanings.

The human story behind the images is, of course, the decisive context of *Images of American Radicalism*. It is not a story that we could exhaust, even if we wished to do so. New images are constantly produced and old ones reproduced, now increasingly post-modern collage style or even the imaginary landscapes of radicalism as it never quite existed. As we confidently offer a fresh angle of vision, we hope that our work will inspire thoughtful reconsideration, further graphic experimentation, and most of all a will to fight for a world that now more than ever needs the work of ordinary people of every kind to win its redemption from corruption, cynicism, and despair.

Further Reading

References to many books will be found below, at the end of each chapter. Perhaps the best general introduction to the larger subject is *The American Radical* (New York: Routledge, 1994), edited by Mari Jo Buhle, Paul Buhle and Harvey J. Kaye. The best general reference works are the *Encyclopedia of the American Left* (New York: Garland Publishers, 1990), edited by Mari Jo Buhle, Paul Buhle and Dan Georgakas; *American Reformers: An H.W. Wilson Biographical Dictionary* (New York: H.W. Wilson, 1985), edited by Alden Whitman; and *Labor Conflict in the United States: An Encyclopedia* (New York: Garland Press, 1990), edited by Ronald L. Filippelli.

Chapter One
Green Dreamers

AN EPHRATA SISTER

Utopian Imagination

Utopian Imagination

The radical, utopian tradition is near the tap-root of American society. The new civilization founded in North America by Euro-American colonists and their African-American slaves was, for a relatively small but important group of settlers, a divine mission in voluntary collectivism. These were the first self-conscious American socialists, and in many ways representative of radicals to follow. "Green" dreamers, they saw the new land as a paradise given to their trust by a higher power, not for conquest but for renewal of the human spirit. They scorned the spirit of the emerging competitive capitalism, repudiated slavery, suspected such accepted institutions as marriage, private property, militarism and patriarchy of widening unhappiness in the world. And they mistrusted the deepest impulses of the Puritan spirit: mortal fear of the forest and corresponding ethnocidal hatred toward Indians who inhabited unconquered nature. Green dreamers attempted to live out alternatives, both for their own souls' sake and as an example to others. Often they found their truest kindred spirits in the remnants of the hard-hit native tribes.

The communitarians' historical origins lay in the large traditions of Millenialism. The hopes for a new and sinless world aborning had been an undercurrent within Christian doctrine from its beginnings. Indeed, early Christian communal settlements crushed by Roman troops reflected still older traditions, including the Old Testament prophets like Isaiah who had railed against the accumulation of property and the abandonment of simple, godly ways of agrarian clans. These memories may, in turn, have retained vestiges of a common and mostly unwarlike Neolithic culture, preserved in the lives of many indigenous peoples before massive colonization.

Many generations passed after the corruption of Christianity through its grasp of institutional power, but the chiliastic tradition never died. Respected clerics, Meister Eckhart in the eleventh century and Joachim of Floris in the thirteenth, predicted the coming of a new joyous era, a "revolution" in the original sense of the term, which returned humankind to an innocent Beginning. Numberless prophets and alchemists nurtured a similar mystic vision in many cultures. "Beghards," roaming religious bands at the time of the Crusades, combined lay-preachers with noblewomen and aroused sections of the poor. Among the various Church orders Franciscans epitomized the impulse for voluntary poverty and a love of nature as the only true wealth, meant to be shared by all.

Increasingly desperate conditions exacerbated by class divisions and the growing power of a centralized State prompted violent uprisings. Beginning in the fourteenth century, the revolts swept across most of Europe. Urban artisans and the lower middle class, sometimes joined by peasants, overthrew the wealthy classes for weeks or months before being isolated and crushed. Yet things continued to worsen. Religious wars, mass suffering and the merciless repression of dissenters prompted artists like Albrecht Dürer to evoke the specter of Apocalypse from *Revelations* in the Bible. Communitarian religious uprisings in Central Europe during the Radical Reformation of the fifteenth and sixteenth centuries set the stage for the rise of modern utopianism when their leaders not only declared settlements free of kingly or priestly authority but also asserted their determination to return to a Biblical grace from which society (and religion) had fallen. They shared goods in common and honored labor as against the idleness of the lordly classes. They sometimes renounced the formal distinctions of marriage along with those of property, conducting themselves as "Free Spirits" acting with what they believed to be instinctive godliness.

These various rebels pushed medieval European soci-

Jacob Böhme in his study, c. 1620: As the carpenter's son created Christianity, the artisan-shoemaker reinvents dialectical philosophy. From an early Dutch edition of Böhme's works.

ety swiftly forward. Communitarian "Levellers" and "Diggers" in the English Revolution of 1640-60, for instance, supplied the human shock troops and the egalitarian ideology for the overthrow of royalist authorities, before being betrayed by the new rulers. In what is now Germany, during the first decades of the sixteenth century, Thomas Müntzer led one of the most dramatic rebellions anywhere, establishing a communal society and holding off kingly troops during 1525. In the end, the state, Church and their propertied allies returned to power, if never again quite so securely. The communitarian rebels left behind not only a precious legacy of sacrifice but also a wealth of images and symbolic objects for future generations to copy and build on.

The communitarians' emblems of struggle, devised by their artists and sympathizers, depicted the great conflict of good and evil as anticipated in the Biblical chapter of Revelations. The poor pressed down by the rich, driven to beggary and to martyrdom, here found their teachers in ancient and modern Jeremiads, their hope in common labor, and their guidance from the heavens. Like Dürer, they imagined an apocalyptic vengeance against the evil-doers. Their intricate carvings and illuminated Biblical texts depict a poor people's Christ and His servants glorifying in simplicity. One of their most popular symbols, the rainbow, offered to them heavenly vindication, a glorious promise of release from darkness and gloom.

The martyrs for Christian Communism also fertilized the soil of their philosophical successors. In Austerlitz, near the current German-Polish border, the communitarians had once been strong. There, amid surviving traditions, the simple shoemaker Jacob Böhme experienced mystic visions of oneness with Nature. During the early decades

In the popular portrayal of the Apocalypse, God's angels deal severely with sinners who have ruled the earthly domain, and crowned heads fall. The corresponding triumph finds the Woman in the Wilderness at the center of salvation. Taken from a series of woodcuts made by Albrecht Dürer.

*Profile of Johann Conrad Beissel, from J.F.
Sachse,* The German Sectarians of
Pennsylvania, 1708-1742, *Volume I (1899); A
page from Beissel's* Mystical Proverbs. *From
Sachse.*

of the seventeenth century, he composed a formidable theology of mystic eco-socialism heavily influenced by memories of Radical Reformation. According to his key text, *The Aurora*, God had given Man a great tree of Nature, but later the Merchant "cunningly deceived the simple ones," expropriating the tree to his own benefit, selling its fruits with false claims, turning the gullible into sinners striving after "riches and goods, after pride, pomp and stateliness...even as a swine tumbleth in the dirt and mire." When, with God's help, men were able once again to see the Tree of Life as it truly was, they "mightily rejoiced...and sang a new song...and so were delivered...[from] the hated merchant...as also [his] false wares," Böhme wrote.

Jacob Böhme's theosophy of the inner life, describing a realm of freedom to be rediscovered along a circuitous path, helped shape Romanticism and the German philosophy that produced Marxism. German-American immigrants of the nineteenth century, little knowing the distant origins of secular socialism, carried elements of Böhme's faith into their adopted homeland, founding some of the earliest labor unions, anti-racist newspapers and progressive schools. But his influence also came to American shores in a more direct way, through early religious communards.

As early as the 1690s a little group of Pietists, German colonists anticipating that the "last days" of earthly sin might close with the seventeenth century, formed a settlement on the banks of the Wissahickon River outside Philadelphia. They hoped their venture would literally lead them to a "Woman of the Wilderness," and named their society after her. In this world view, Sophia (after the Greek for "Wisdom"), who figured large in Böhme's writings, had been cast aside in the heavenly struggle between God and Satan, but represented the rightful mediator for humankind to recover from its own sinful nature and thus heal the split between man and woman. Sophia, embodying the purity of the New World, had been patiently awaiting her apostles. The colonists worked in common, prayed, and practiced celibacy among themselves in order to prepare for her arrival.

Johann Conrad Beissel, a former handicraft (or labor) leader of German bakers, sailed from Europe in 1720 to join the colonists, unaware they had dispersed. Already known as a leader of a mystic fellowship in the Rheinland, Beissel joined the Pennsylvania "Dunkard" pietistic sect, and in 1733 set out with friends to form the colony of Ephrata (the ancient name for Bethlehem), west of Philadelphia. There, a colony flourished almost to the end of the century. Ephratans created a school so renowned that children were sent from as far as Baltimore to attend it, and established a press that for a time was the most prolific publisher in the colonies. Their creative use of relatively primitive engraving methods to convey the transcendent possibilities of life was admired far and wide.

The Ephratans' architecture also reflected their way of thinking. Their high roofs and flat-topped dormers were built and framed without spikes or nails, as was believed of Solomon's Temple in Biblical days. Late medieval German in design, these structures carried the legacy of the craftsman who believed that the complexity and beauty of the design manifested God's will acting through the individual and group.

Their deeply artistic *way of living* gave them a sense of purpose and of being. Sizable cloister rooms boasted large hand-lettered charts with intricate designs, showing the mysterious ways of God. The Ephratans' landscaping, labyrinthine-designed bushes and low trees cut in a pattern to illustrate the enigma of human existence, expressed their concept of the complicated paths to be taken toward the inner truth of existence. More than seven thousand songs, some published in volumes by Benjamin Franklin's press in Philadelphia, echoed with a joy at nature's presence and beauty as guide to spiritual truth. Perhaps no group of this small size ever composed so much music, and it was played upon

America's first musical organ, imported from Germany for the Ephratans.

Their hymns, hundreds of them written by Beissel himself, also summed up their unique views. Celebrating a mystical feminism that exalted an androgynous future, they declared themselves against the steady drift of contemporary class society. Dispensing with marriage and property, and renouncing violence of any kind, they felt love for all others — emphatically including the endangered Native Americans. Frequent singing provided not only inspiration for worship, but also gave them recreation. Illustrations in their books give a sense of their yearnings and their faith, above all in Sophia, the guide toward their joyfully anticipated destiny.

Ephrata's colonists repeatedly experienced disappointment when various astrological signs (such as comets) did not usher in the New Age. Weakened by Beissel's own death, Ephrata dissolved, although its spirit lingered in the branch colony of Snow Hill, until after the Civil War. Ephrata's influence, along with that of other German-American Pietist colonies, continued in Pennsylvania folk-arts and poetry, an honored if increasingly misunderstood element of the "Pennsylvania Dutch" tradition. Scholars believe that utopianism blended into a deep reverence for egalitarian democracy and

Ephrata Colony buildings showing medieval design employed c. 1820.

Courtesy: Pennsylvania State Archives.

for the German immigrants' own special folklore.

This was, so to speak, the other path (or "lost highway" in Hank Williams's later country music parlance): The vision of an historical alternative, a belief that became the link between American radicals of nearly all kinds. In this case as in many others to follow, the compromise with reality also made a specific tradition of radicalism a part of mainstream folklore and later, American popular culture.

Among other eighteenth century colonies, none was so distinctive as the "Kingdom of Paradise" formed by immigrant German scholar Christian Priber, who arrived in South Carolina in 1735, divested himself of his worldly goods and made his way to the Cherokee lands. There he learned the native language and took up native clothes and hair style. In his "Kingdom of Paradise," both men and women, Indians and whites, were equal, material goods held in common, and marriage relationships dissolved at will. English traders worried when Priber advised the Cherokees to make no more concessions of land and when he protected them against the deception of traders. In 1743, English allies among the Cree Indians captured him, but he continued to expound his doctrines from a prison cell. In 1744 Christian Priber died, still imprisoned, his utopia disbanded and his plans for a vast Indian confederation of peace and cooperation totally lost. But his efforts, like those of other Pietists, at least made a strong impression on Indians, who regarded these unique individuals as utterly unlike other whites, rather people like themselves who did not regard the prospect of death with fear or consider the wilderness an enemy.

In his own way, Priber revealed the necessity for Indian peoples to articulate their entirely justified claims for freedom from domination. Pre-Columbian North America had been a continent of villages, widely varying in social forms but usually adapted ingeniously to the specific environment, and as a rule more cooperative and less systematically warlike than the societies that would displace them. The oldest continuously occupied community in the United States is Walpi, a homeland of the

New Harmony, Indiana: Labyrinth (arrangement of hedges), created by Harmony Society (Rappites) and restored by the New Harmony Memorial Commission. From Ross F. Lockridge, The Labyrinth *(New Harmony, 1941).*

communal Hopis (known as the "peaceful ones") in the mountains of today's Arizona. Their religious vision of the natural and supernatural flowing into each other had a more than curious resonance with the visions of the Pietistic communards, who wanted to escape the particular competition and cruelty fostered by European class society.

White colonization of North America increased destructive internecine warfare among Indian peoples and left ever fewer opportunities for cooperative lifestyles or applied ecology. Slaughtered or worn down by disease, their lands stolen, the survivors increasingly found themselves caught up in an expanding market economy where they abandoned traditional "thinning" methods of hunting to follow whites in the exhaustion of desired prey. By allying themselves with one white faction or another, they hastened their collective doom and closed out the earliest "socialism" that the continent had seen.

But some New England Indian tribes fought back with surprising success. In seventeenth century Rhode Island, white settlers were amazed to find a sophisticated agricultural and fishing society which viewed wetlands ("swamps") with the same degree of reverence as the English considered them the wild dwelling places of devils. Displaced by their new neighbors, their cornfields ruthlessly destroyed, the outgunned Pequots fought back and were slaughtered ruthlessly in 1637. Metacom or King Philip of the Pokanoket nevertheless led a series of surprise engagements (like later Mexican folk-hero Emilio Zapata, he would be known as "will-o-the-wisp") which made him the imagined genius behind Indian people's attacks across the region in 1675. [Plate 3] His forces were crushed less by whites than by Mohawks allied with the British. Yet Philip had given many Indians the determination to hold their ground somehow, as small segments of various tribes did in peaceful (or coerced) negotiations, surviving for later centuries. Only in the recent past have American historians ceased to consider Philip a cunning murderer, rather than a hero of his own culture. Elsewhere Indians who could make the transition successfully retreated into districts ever less desirable to whites, from the Florida swamps to the dry southwest. Among the whites who took their place, a stream of further communards were innocent, if anyone could be, of the crimes against an existing culture.

Moving from frontier to frontier and then back, "Father" George Rapp, a utopian patriarch, had led his followers from Germany to Pennsylvania in the early decades of the nineteenth century, then to Indiana, in various sites where they held property in common, prayed, and awaited the arrival of the Millennium. [Plate 4] Finding Indiana too swampy and malaria-ridden, the Rappites sold other utopians the property and returned eastward

The American Shakers

A Celibate, Religious Community

Coeval with the American Republic: First Shaker Family formed at Watervliet, N. Y., 1776; First organized Shaker Community established at New Lebanon, N. Y., 1788; Fifteen Shaker Societies in seven States of the United States of America.

Beginnings.

Founder, ANN LEE, of Manchester, England, (1736-1784). In religious revival of 17th Century, arose the "Shaking Quakers," or "Shakers," 1754. Nine persons from Manchester and Bolton, emigrated, May 1774, for the purpose of founding a Shaker Church in America. Eight remained faithful. They were ANN LEE, William Lee, James Whittaker, John Hocknell, James Shepherd, James Partington, Mary Partington, Nancy Lee.

FROM ANN LEE'S TEACHINGS.

Basic Principles of the Shaker Order.

VIRGIN PURITY, PEACE, JUSTICE, LOVE.

expressed in CELIBATE LIFE, NON RESISTANCE, COMMUNITY OF GOODS, UNIVERSAL BROTHERHOOD-- held to be the Divine Order of Society.

Resultant Beliefs and Practices Held as Ideals

TO BE ATTAINED IN THE INDIVIDUAL AND SOCIETY.

Equality of the Sexes, in all departments of life.
Equality in Labor, all working for each, and each for all.
Equality in Property.--No rich, no poor, Industrial Freedom,
    Consecrated Labor, Dedicated Wealth, A United Inheritance.
    Each using according to need.
    Each enjoying according to capacity.
Freedom of Speech, Toleration in Thought and Religion. Often persecuted,
    Shakers have never been known to persecute.
Abolition of all Slavery.--Chattel, Wage, Habit, Passion, Poverty, Disease.
Temperance in all things.
Justice and Kindness to all living beings.
Practical Benevolence. Thou shalt love thy neighbor as thyself.
True Democracy. Real Fraternity. Practical Living of the Golden Rule.

Religious Ideals and Worship.

All life and activity animated by Christian Love is Worship. Shakers adore God as the Almighty Creator, Fountain of all Good, Life, Light, Truth and Love,--the One Eternal Father-Mother.

They recognize the Christ Spirit, the expression of Deity, manifested in fulness in Jesus of Nazareth, also in feminine manifestation through the personality of Ann Lee. Both, they regard as Divine Saviors, anointed Leaders in the New Creation. All in whom the Christ consciousness awakens are Sons and Daughters of God. Spiritual man has, as his divine prerogative and highest destiny, to live in clear conception of and in active harmony with the Highest Good. The Life of the Spirit not the form of expression is essential.

Practical Issues.

Beautiful, comfortable Community Homes, in each a Christ Family.
Daily manual labor for all, according to strength and ability. "Hands to work and hearts to God." (Ann Lee)
Opportunity for intellectual and artistic development, within the necessary limits prescribed by the common good.
Sanitation, Health, Longevity.
Simplicity in dress, speech and manner.
Purity in thought, speech and personal habits.
Freedom from debt, worry and competition.

Government.

No Government without God, No Body without a Head.
The Head of the Shaker Order is Christ. The Visible Human Representative is vested in a

DUAL ORDER OF LEADERS.

Spiritual Leaders, of both sexes, a Ministry over Societies, Elders over Families.
Temporal Leaders, of both sexes, Trustees, Deacons and Care-takers, in charge of Business and Industrial Interests.

The Inner Life.

according to the Shaker Faith, is twofold, embracing
    Repentance--confessing and forsaking all sin;
    Regeneration--the growth and unfoldment in the individual of the Christ Spirit, through living according to the teachings and practice of Jesus Christ. As opposed to the common life of human generation and selfish gratification, this is held to be the Resurrection Life.

Physical development, mental growth and spiritual unfoldment form the only rational basis for a harmonious and happy existence; self-denial the corner-stone of the structure. The truths inherent in Shakerism are the underlying truths of God-life in all ages and the mission of the Shaker is to unfold and demonstrate these truths.

Private Collection

Shaker Broadside, c. 1840s.

to Pennsylvania, leaving behind one of the grandest hedge-row labyrinths anywhere. Considered by Rappites emblematic of their own harmonian spirit and the mysteries of God's purpose, it remained a place of public meetings until overgrown (and restored by sympathetic Indianans, generations later). Likewise, Rappite flower-cultivation was immensely impressive to visitors; flowers were considered symbols of the seed sprouted into the soul prepared for Resurrection. Displayed almost everywhere in season, in New Harmony and its Ohio successor colony, flowers decorated houses, yards, and workbenches. The Rappites' credo rejoiced that

> it has fallen to our lot, to live in the present important era, when the plans of God in the Creation, appear in all their harmony, symmetry, order and unity, and when everything in Nature, with incessant activity and renewed life, is pressing forward to a complete resemblance of the great Archetype.

Rarely articulated so well, this idea was present in the multitude of other religious-utopian experiments of the nineteenth century.

The Shakers left a deeper impression upon most Americans, in large part because their many colonies survived well into the twentieth century and because the furniture styles they pioneered became a standard fashion. Their dances, their hymns and their ideals of sexual equality reached a smaller group of intensely interested reformers.

Shakers (or "Shaking Quakers" as they were first called) traced their history to the Camisards, French Huguenots of the late seventeenth century who dressed in white smocks and prophesied divine revelation, even as they were tortured and killed by the authorities. Before dispersal, some made their way to England, where they touched enthusiasts in the heavily industrial town of Manchester. There, the Shakers disrupted religious services with spontaneous enthusiasm or "trembling." "Mother" Ann Lee, emerging as their leader, was confined to a prison cell for disturbing the peace. She saw a vision of carnal degradation and religious celibacy. Soon, she led her followers in whirling, jumping and gesturing, and in arguing that they could justify such acts in Biblical terms. Repeatedly persecuted in England, the Shakers resolved to seek tolerance in the New World.

They found little tolerance at first, as they settled in New England and upper New York State. Repeatedly thrown into prison for their free-form dancing in town squares, they expanded their ranks slowly at first. Mother Ann herself died in 1784 (although her followers insisted that her spirit remained present). For a time, her successors introduced formal order into the dance, but Mother Lucy Wright renewed spontaneous movements, known as "back" or "promiscuous manner." Ring dances, skipping, shuffling, free-form gesturing, all expressed a hopefulness about things to come. The body, seen as a microcosm of the universe, became a channel for cosmic forces.

Establishing their villages, Shakers carefully chose good land with reliable water sources. They became famed for their orchards and for their gardens which provided the food for villagers and also supplied the basis for herbal medicines which they packaged for sale to the outside world. Although Shakers used hides for boots and other necessities, eating meat created as a byproduct, they sought as much as possible to avoid cruelty to animals. (A song related: "Remember: He who made the brute/Who gave the speech and reason, found him mute; He can't complain; but God's omniscient eye/Beholds his cruelty. He hears his cry.") Humane mousetraps in Shaker barns captured rodents without injuring them.

Their famous textiles and furniture designs closely reflected their world-view, and the look of the heaven they expected to enter. Shakers believed that their domestic environment, their work, its products and even the tools used to produce them should all reflect the moral order. The simplicity of surroundings, the absence of knickknacks, and the variety of useful self-invented folding devices like serving tables provided great open space, in exceptionally airy and light rooms. Their patterns showed perfectly straight lines quite unlike the medieval bent of the Ephratans, furniture constructed with almost mathematical precision that carpenters believed to be the precise expression of their own religious commitment. Great effort went into perfecting each object, aged members often assisting in small ways. Clothing used the least quantity of material necessary and cooks measured out exact amounts. Long before architect Louis Sullivan proclaimed "form follows function," the Shakers had found their own way to this truth.

Above all, the Shakers had created a society or mini-society without waste. Space, talent, fruit, animal, all belonged to God, on loan only temporarily to Man's care. Continued recycling of buildings and various materials was not only proof of their adaptive genius, but of their faith. As an elder wrote, "if we were extravagant or wasted any useful thing, it was a loss to the Consecrated and in proportion to its value would prove a spiritual loss to our souls." Children were trained to pick up any useful item, needle, cloth, bit of thread, kernel of corn, offering anything extra as charity to the poor. Shakers felt similarly to everything that grew. While their neighbors consigned felled tree limbs and scraps to the fire, Shakers turned its branches into workboxes through a complex process of shredding wood while frozen in winter and weaving strips like cloth. They eagerly learned from nearby Indian tribes how to weave baskets from grass and how to make herbal medicines from bark.

Adopting orphans in lieu of sex and procreation, the Shakers gradually acquired a following of approximately six thousand. Their main source of notoriety, besides their designs and their dancing, was their social egalitarianism, equality of men and women at all levels of their society. The "gift to be simple," as an ideal and a way of life, appealed to egalitarianism and fellow love against the contemporary ills of slavery, landlordism, militarism — and the abuse of sexuality by men against women.

Hannah Cohoon's deservedly famous series of Shaker drawings explore a single major theme, the "Tree of Life" and its fruit. Inspired by her vision of a founder of the sect, this Tree obviously recalled Jacob Böhme's revelations, but also signaled to Shakers what they expected America could be: A community in which each individual glowed with his or her own light, but all remained

In the Shaker school, children were taught separately by sex in order to prepare them for later life; and Shaker women at washing, using appliances often very modern for the time, invented for the community as an extension of God's wisdom. From Charles Nordhoff, American Communism *(1876).*

connected in their equality. Insisting that "Mother Ann" Lee had visited her, Cohoon drew without any consciously labored skill; she had been instructed, she insisted, only by Nature's love. In like spirit, a full century before the Beatles' hymn to the 1960s, "All You Need is Love," the Shakers sang "More love, more love, Alone by its power/The world we will conquer; For true love is God./If ye love one another, Then God dwelleth in you,/And ye are made strong, To live by His word."

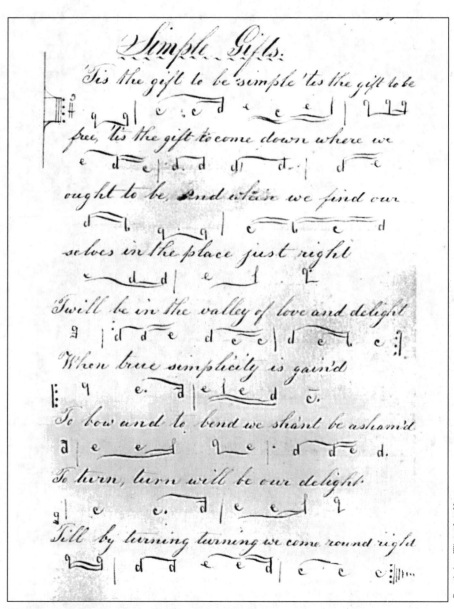

Permission: Winterthur Musum

The most famous or most enduring piece of Shaker music.

Whose Revolution?

Boston Massacre, engraving after a painting by Alonzo Chappel, 1868.

13

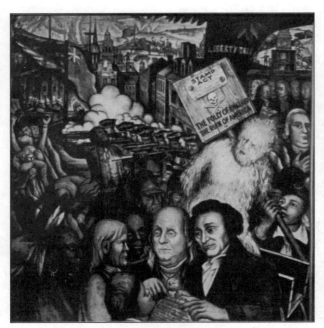

Revolutionary mural by famed Mexican muralist Diego Rivera: a section of a mural for the New Workers School, New York City, c. 1936, later dismantled.

Tom Paine, America's greatest radical pamphleteer. Engraving by A. Milliere, after George Romney.

Whose Revolution?

The American Revolution arose out of a complex set of relations between white settlers, black slaves, Indian peoples, and the British. If conservative in many of its phases, e.g., promising individual freedom for the individual accumulation of wealth, it was nevertheless extraordinarily radical in certain of its elements. Its radicalism had deep roots, including the century of antislavery agitation by Quakers and the sentiment of John Woolman who argued that "wealth is attended by power, by which...oppression...clothes itself with the name of justice..." Some segments of the powerless, those at the bottom of society, indeed demanded to be heard. Mass meetings of "mechanics" and others offset and occasionally overruled the influence of the upper classes. The "Jack Tar" sailors' strikes, slowdowns and protests against the British worried colonial leaders as well as royal authorities.

The Stamp Act Riots against new British taxes ruled out plans for quiet and dignified protest. The Boston Massacre of March, 1775, one famed incident among many less remembered ones, ensued when a rope maker challenged soldiers "Come O.... if you dare, fire and be damned, we know you dare not." Sons of Liberty put up Liberty Poles which soldiers tore down, or rioted to demonstrate their defiance of soldiers who paraded through the towns. According to the later portrait by Alonzo Chappel we can see the chaos of the scene and the possibly central role played by Crispus Attucks, the half-black, half-Indian sailor who died in the massacre and was arguably the first revolutionary martyr. An earlier print, made by Paul Revere from the work of a contemporary artist, was considerably less accurate but superior as propaganda, showing British soldiers firing on an unarmed crowd (and no Crispus Attucks in sight). For one of the rare times in American history, a radical uprising thus received the blessing of honored and official status, at the price of internal censorship. The image of victimization that it offered might be contrasted with contemporary engravings of Indian leaders, seen almost uniformly as fanatics and savages.

From a technical standpoint, Revere's memorable print was made possible by the efforts of the skilled engraver preparing wooden blocks. This propaganda was among the earliest of the mass-produced radical agitational styles that we can record in America. Unlike, for instance, the poetry or the illuminated Biblical texts printed in Ephrata, it was not devotional but instrumental. The finest and most memorable work in any medium, for centuries afterward, would draw on both traditions, finding artistic ways to merge the richness of life's possibilities with the necessity for tactical expression.

The Declaration of Independence, issued after a vote taken on July 2, 1776, was a remarkably radical document and almost as remarkable a visual impression for its time. It followed closely the vehement logic of Tom Paine's *Common Sense*, which helped crystallize the sentiment for an absolute break with England. The Continental Congress, meeting in a hall built by the carpenters' guild (*i.e.*, union) in Philadelphia, accepted Thomas Jefferson's draft of the Declaration, although it eliminated his condemnation of slavery. The compromise pledged common action in vivid paragraphs that spelled treason toward king and empire.

If pro-British Loyalists in colonial America generally accepted the permanence of social inequality and of "deference" of the poor toward the powerful, revolutionaries varied widely from economic aristocrats who wanted only national independence to egalitarians who wanted far more. The Declaration itself held "these truths to be self-evident, that all men are created equal," possessing "inalienable rights" including the right to alter or abolish a tyrannical government — a belief that later police and investigatory agencies would consider dangerously subversive. The delegates, almost uniformly men of power and position, needed the support of ordinary citizens. In that spirit they offered a radical possibility to all — all white men, that is.

The revolutionary Congress beseeched fellow Americans to "encourage frugality, economy and industry," to "discountenance and discourage every species of extravagance and dissipation" and to remember the "poorer sort" in the struggle ahead. This plea was far from radical, but it sustained a liberalism in which a more egalitarian vision could exist. Americans went on to defeat the British through often extreme sacrifice which naturally fell hardest upon the foot soldiers and other common people.

But tragically, a victory over the British was also a victory over the Indian peoples. Those who had made allies of the British suffered the most immediately. But tribes which fought bravely with the rebellious Americans were denied the territorial concessions promised in return for alliance. The successful consolidation of a national

Boston Massacre, engraving by Paul Revere, c. 1775.

TOM PAINE

The very soul of free thought, Tom Paine wrote the first radical best-seller, defended the French Revolution in England and died a champion of republican ideas and ideals.

Born to common people, Paine studied at a village school in his native Thetford, Norfolk. He apprenticed to his father, a corset-maker and a Quaker, then spent a year at sea. Over the next fifteen years, he had one failure after another, lost a beloved wife in childbirth, and became a debater in local Sussex politics. A move to London gave him the opportunity to attend scientific lectures and to meet freethinkers, including Benjamin Franklin. In 1774, at the age of 37, he left for America with a letter of introduction written by Franklin.

Paine intended to open a school. But after writing a few newspaper essays, he was made editor of the *Pennsylvania Magazine*. In that forum, he began to campaign for the abolition of slavery and to point to the oppression of women. In 1775, he committed himself to revolution, and in January, 1776, published *Common Sense,* his earth-shaking pamphlet. In less than a year some 150,000 copies were sold, spreading widely the doctrines of anti-monarchism and need for free elections. In 1777, Congress named him secretary to the Committee on Foreign Affairs in its negotiations with France. Attacked by conservatives and forced out of government, he saw his ideas adapted to the Pennsylvania Constitution. At fifty, Paine left the new nation for France, remaining abroad for fifteen years. Defending the French Revolution against British threats, he penned the *Rights of Man* in 1791, a classic statement on the rights of peoples to create their own institutions. In Paris, however, he barely escaped the guillotine. Returning to America, he was shunned by many old associates (including Thomas Jefferson) for his outspoken atheism and his attacks upon the growing patterns of wealth and poverty. He died in 1809, denied a spot in a Quaker cemetery. He lies today in an unmarked grave in the country of his birth.

Pulling Down the Statue of George III at the Bowling Green, New York City, 1776. Engraving by John McRae, c. 1860.

The Declaration of Independence, one of the most radical documents of the eighteenth century. During the McCarthy Era, civil libertarians would remove the masthead and attempt to obtain signatures based on the text of the document. They rarely succeeded.

government meant worse persecution ahead. By the turn of the century, expansion-minded settlers increasingly pushed Indians off their land or killed them outright.

Insisting that the land was "the common property of all tribes" and that no Indian people had the right to sell land "without the consent of all," the Shawnee Chief Tecumseh united Indians of many nations in today's eastern and midwestern states into a confederacy. He also enlisted British support during the War of 1812. "Why not sell the air, the clouds and the great sea as well as the earth?" he asked ironically.

His brother, the Prophet Tens-qua-ta-wa, meanwhile guided the effort to revitalize Indian religion in these regions. Having lost an eye in a childhood accident, Tens-qua-ta-wa fell into alcoholism but recovered after he experienced religious visions. Called "the One that Opens the Door," he preached a revival of traditional culture and the abandonment of alcohol and promiscuity. His followers from various tribes felt themselves strengthened spiritually against American expansionism.

This anti-imperialist revival meant likely trouble for aggressive white settlers. General William Henry Harrison, recognizing the Prophet's potential, destroyed the village of Prophetstown in 1811, dispersing his followers. Two years later Harrison's troops confronted the British in the Battle of the Thames, in Canada, where America's Indian allies slayed Tecumseh. Harrison called the fallen Indian leader "one of those uncommon geniuses which spring up occasionally to produce revolution." Harrison's leadership at the "Battle of Tippicanoe" (a standoff following an Indian attack in northern Indiana) was romanticized in "Tippicanoe and Tyler, Too!" a political slogan used to elect the former general as president in 1840. Battle-legends of "Old Tip" ironically helped keep alive the images of Tecumseh as a "noble savage" or at least a worthy adversary. The great vision of an Indian nation was not remembered so kindly.

Black slaves gained only slightly and mostly symbolically from the Revolution. Fearing that an appeal from the British would cause slaves to rise up, American rebels moved a few steps toward reform. All the states but Georgia and South Carolina banned the slave trade. A combination of self-interest and Christian idealism also led to the manumission of many slaves in the North, with thousands responding to promises made by politicians, of liberty to those enlisting in the Continental Army. These circumstances helped create a significant community of free blacks who formed their own institutions (incorporating "African" into many church names) and provided a community of mass support for the later abolitionist movement. But more slaves won their freedom through escape, some to the side of the British forces and some into the insular colonies of black and mixed Indian-black enclaves of remote swamplands. The moral compromises of the Constitution — which treated the slave as property, amounting to three-fifth of a human for proportional voting purpose — along with the profitability of slavery and the dominant racist mentality of the new nation guaranteed further generations of exploitation and misery.

Further radical phases of the American Revolution nevertheless followed the victory over the British. In 1786, Daniel Shays led a rural rebellion in Western Massachusetts on behalf of impoverished citizens. They raised popular militias and closed the courts, just as they had done during the Revolution. Similar disorders occurred elsewhere, crowds halting farm auctions and threatening to overthrow politicians in state legislatures. The "Shaysites" dispersed only after an armed confrontation at the Armory in Springfield, Massachusetts. Fifteen citizens were sentenced to death, two actually hung. Afterward, national leaders agreed on a strengthening of central governmental powers, as Secretary of the Navy Henry Knox put it, to "clip the wings of a mad democracy."

And yet while strengthening the potentially oppressive authority of the state, the new Constitution made important concessions. Along with potential coercion, it offered universal (white) male suffrage and a Bill of Rights, considered necessary to win state ratification of the Constitution. It was a bourgeois republic in which more rights could be claimed in another day, if not by Indians (not even considered proper "American" citizens of their own former territories) then by poorer workingmen — and also, if only potentially, by women and blacks. This context created, at least, a legal sphere where radicals could operate in some states and territories.

New or renewed conflicts arose in the 1790s with the specter of the French Revolution and of political partisanship at home. These events gave further indication of what lay in store for American radicals. Supporters of the French rebels and opponents to the "aristocratic" impulses of the elite formed Democratic Republican clubs in many cities. Their members met innocently, to toast their favorite

Pontiac, seen in hostile caricature. From an early engraving.

PONTIAC AND NEOLIN

The leader of Indians from at least eight distinct tribes and two language groups, Pontiac was perhaps the greatest of the first American radicals defending their way of life against dispossession and their peoples from annihilation.

During the middle of the eighteenth century, the Ottawa warrior made himself famous (or notorious) by his alliance with the French. He proved a key asset against the emerging British empire, which spread from today's Pittsburgh to Indiana. Pontiac and his followers finally made peace with the British in Detroit, hoping they would replace the French as trustworthy allies and suppliers of goods for lean times. But British officers demanded to be accepted as conquerors. As Pontiac called for braves to storm the Detroit garrison in retaliation, he evoked the message of the Lenape prophet, Neolin. The Lenapes had sought to make peace with the British earlier, but found it impossible because the British continually pushed them west and depleted their game. Neolin warned other tribes that the white men brought sickness and alcohol and promised that the deity would return game to the lands once freed of white control. In 1761, he predicted all-out war.

Together, the prophet and the warrior threatened white frontiers across the frontier of the 1760s. The British lost important forts to combinations of Ottawas, Chippewas, Wyandots, Senecas and others. Only after sustained and well-armed counter attacks, marked by massacres of Indian women and children, did the tribes pull back (as did the British, reforming their practices somewhat). Pontiac himself was killed by an Illinois Indian in 1766 and Neolin died obscurely. But "Pontiac's War" remained an important Indian memory. Healing the divisions among tribes in the name of a common independence from the new United States would be a great hope for the future.

world events and to organize among themselves. Federalists meanwhile directed a campaign of vilification against them, creating the first legalized "witch hunt" by enacting the Alien and Sedition Acts of 1799-1800. Many of yesterday's revolutionary leaders turned coward or conservative toward old friends and allies, refusing to defend a Thomas Paine against public attacks. Quavering liberals and reborn conservatives had already experienced all the revolutionary change and egalitarian rhetoric that they ever wanted and more. [Plate 6] Whatever their history and current political affiliation, they now supported property rights above all, much as backsliding ex-radicals would intermittently for the next two centuries.

A handful of intellectuals nevertheless pushed out in new directions. A small current of gender egalitarianism, partly in response to an English avant-garde, briefly surfaced. Young novelist Charles Brockden Brown, inspired by William Godwin's *Political Justice* (1793), produced *Alcuin* (1798), a fictional dialogue on the civil rights of woman. Brockden Brown himself, rapidly disillusioned with hopes of progress, quickly became the nation's first horror novelist. His *Wieland* (1799), the first uniquely American novel, described the psychological tremors of whites on the frontier, where freed from European cultural constraints they lost control of their rationality. Through Brocken Brown, psychological distortion and outright horror became an important literary medium of social criticism, destined to recur in many radical works of later generations. From the battlefield gore of Mark Twain's *Connecticut Yankee in King Arthur's Court* to the calculated disorientation of H.P. Love-

The slaying of Shawnee chief, Tecumseh, leader of Indian Resistance in the West, in 1813.

Courtesy: Library of Congress

TENS-QUA-TA-WA
or THE ONE THAT OPENS THE DOOR
Shawnese Prophet
Brother of Tecumthe

Courtesy: the Chicago Historical Society

Tens-qua-ta-na, Shawnee Prophet, lithograph by F. Barincou after a painting by James Otto Lewis, 1835.

JOHN CHAPMAN
("Johnny Appleseed")

One of the most beloved larger-than-life people, or living myths, of the American westward expansionism, Johnny Appleseed is completely unique. Unlike Daniel Boone or Kit Carson he never fought Indians or Mexicans and unlike the cartoonish Paul Bunyan he never conquered "wilderness" or cut down forests of trees. Unlike African-American hero John Henry, Johnny Appleseed did not even symbolize muscular strength, only a desire for peace and for planting apple trees.

The real John Chapman was born just two years before the American Revolution, during applepicking season, to a Massachusetts farm family. John evidently learned to read in school, and in 1797-98 he sought to make a living in backwoods Pennsylvania. There he planned to develop a nursery stock of apple trees, whose fruit would supply important sources of nutrition in many forms (especially over the winter) to eighteenth century Americans.

Rather than a businessman, Chapman became a local character: storyteller, bare-footed walker over large distances, and a reputed friend to Indians who helped him survive through an especially difficult winter. He took to traveling and planting his seeds through Pennsylvania and Ohio. At some point, he converted to the doctrines of Immanuel Swedenborg, Swedish mystic (and an unacknowledged disciple of Jacob Böhme) who preached the continuity of all existence through states of life and death. Swedenborg also preached "non-resistance."

Chapman was famous for traveling to isolated farm houses and villages carrying Swedenborg volumes he would loan, one day to return for lengthy conversations. He devoted the limited profits of his seed-sales to buying Swedenborg's books. He did not convince many pioneers, however, and in time he seemed to unsympathetic observers just an elderly, ragged sort of fellow uninterested in personal success. By the time of his death in 1845 he was also a frontier curiosity, with many stories about him. One settler claimed to have found Chapman playing with bear cubs as the mother looked on. Others told of him giving away his money to the poor, or recalled his particular kindness to children.

Later generations made Johnny Appleseed into a saint of agriculture and conservation, sometimes imaginatively associated — notably by the poet Vachel Lindsey — with Walt Whitman. Both men offered gentle alternatives to the barbaric side of expansionism.

craft's nightmarish creations, the "strange" offered keen insights beyond the censorial instincts of the bourgeois imagination.

JOHNNY APPLESEED.

"Johnny Appleseed" (John Chapman), mystic and pacifist settler. Earliest known portrayal, c. 1830.

Courtesy: Library of Congress

Repressive Legislation: Congressman Matthew Lyon, convicted in 1798 of violating the Sedition Act (after criticizing U.S. foreign policy), brawls in Congress with his opponents. From a contemporary print, "Congressional Pugilists." Artist unknown.

Freedom's Ferment

Freedom's Ferment

Eighteen forty eight was a year of revolution. In Germany and France, uprisings against tyrants inspired Karl Marx and Frederick Engels to write the *Communist Manifesto*. But across the seas that very year, events almost as thrilling unfolded. In Seneca Falls, New York, a convention of women issued a manifesto and established the first organized Women's Rights movement in the world. "My friends," pleaded reformer-novelist and poet Elizabeth Oakes Smith at a woman's rights convention four years later,

> do we realize what purpose we are convened? Do we fully understand that we aim at nothing less than an entire subversion of the present order of society, a dissolution of the whole existing social compact?

This rhetorical question applied not only to woman's rights, earth-shaking enough in itself, but to much else. For the next twenty-five years, woman's rights, spiritualism, abolitionism, temperance and peace agitation shared platforms and often the same speakers and audiences. Reformers of the 1830s to 1850s sought to interrogate nearly all aspects of collective and personal life, confident that the most apparently drastic changes would become possible. The "artificial" would fall away, permitting the natural or godly to rule. Challenged to justify the "Bloomer" costume of women's pants, named after clothes reformer Amelia Bloomer, the Rev. Samuel May could argue, "The structure of our bodies, each limb, each member, is undoubtedly the best that He could devise" and ask rhetorically, "is it not impious folly, then, to corrupt, abuse, or prevent the development and right action of the body?"

The constituency of the "Bloomer" costume, of woman's rights and the other reforms overlapped greatly with that of socialistic schemes. Indeed if enacted, their various schemes proposed a society so different that contemporary European ideas of "socialism" could scarcely encompass the total change. A vicious iconography of attacks upon women reformers customarily ridiculed their clothes as evidence of the wearers' purported "mannishness" (as if only men disguised as women could demand rights). Almost a century later, in 1944, arch-radical Yip Harburg and his collaborator Fred Saidy would stage *Bloomer Girl*, a musical-historical evocation of the need for great personal courage and for massive changes in current society.

William Lloyd Garrison and his newspaper, The Liberator. *From Lillie B.C. Wyman and Arthur Crawford Wyman,* Elizabeth Buffum Chace, 1806-1899, Her Life and Its Environment *(1914), and the Library of Congress.*

Shrewd observers of mid-nineteenth century America, radical or conservative, understood why such women and their allies seemed so terribly threatening. Like the German-American Pietists or the Shakers, but producing popular literature and acting within political reform circles, these perfectionists directly challenged the dire theology of Puritanism and its inference of Original Sin. Elizabeth Oakes Smith, in one of the evocative book-length poems of the day, *The Sinless Child* (1845), placed her protagonist at the frontier where she must instruct her mother who is held back by dogma:

> Dear mother! In ourselves is hid
> The holy spirit-land,
> Where Thought, the flaming cherub, stands
> With its relentless brand;
> We feel the pang when that dread sword

Courtesy: Library of Congress

Private Collection

United States Liberty Almanack. *Pamphlet-program of one of the first radical parties. With James Birney as its presidential candidate, it repudiated slavery in its platform, but left ambiguous the possible presence and civil equality of African-Americans in Western states.*

Courtesy: Library of Congress

Lucretia Mott, Quaker activist against slavery and war, an elder stateswoman of woman suffrage movement; and Lucy Stone, woman's rights pioneer who refused to give up her name in marriage to a fellow reformer, c. 1860.

SOJOURNER TRUTH

Symbol of the African-American woman's courage and resolve, Sojourner Truth was a complex figure, a religious radical and a proto-feminist activist. She was also perhaps the most powerful personal example of black and female equality that the nineteenth century offered.

Born in the 1790s in upstate New York as a slave named Isabella, she knew that her parents had lost other children to the slave trade. She spent her younger days on Dutch-speaking farms, repeatedly beaten to work harder and to show submission to her masters. She gained freedom in 1827 through a New York law and quickly joined the Methodist church, turning next to a "holiness" or Pentecostal sect. Moving to New York City, she renamed herself Sojourner Truth in 1843. There she became an itinerant preacher. Taking the advice of fellow perfectionists, she joined a utopian colony in Northampton, Massachusetts. Frederick Douglass's 1845 autobiography inspired her to write *The Narrative of Sojourner Truth*, which she sold at reform meetings for a quarter along with studio cards depicting her in a serene pose. She cut a remarkable figure at such meetings. Organizers counted upon her to draw a crowd by her reputation for bold appearance and oratory.

Her autobiography and her speaking talent attracted her to outstanding literary figures and leaders of the woman's rights movement. Harriet Beecher Stowe called her the "Libyan Sibyl" and Frances Gage dramatized an incident in which Sojourner Truth was supposed to have held up her powerful arm and declared "Ain't I A Woman?" Generations of readers thrilled to this speech, somewhat embellished by Gage. Living for a time in Washington, D.C., after the Civil War, she struggled to assist unemployed and impoverished blacks who had been helped little by formal emancipation. Along with a handful of woman suffragists, she opposed the Fourteenth Amendment in 1867 because it added the word "male" to the Constitution, and would permit black men to further tyrannize black women. She spent most of her later years at the utopian colony Harmonia, outside Battle Creek, Michigan. Sojourner Truth died in 1883, shortly after preparing a final edition of her story.

Courtesy: Museum of American Political Life

Sojourner Truth, c. 1865. In old age, she supported herself with the sale of these studio cards.

Inscribes the hidden sin,
And turneth everywhere to guard
The paradise within.
* * *
Unrobed, majestic, should the soul
Before its God appear,
Undimmed the image He affixed
Unknowing doubt and fear;
An open converse should it hold
With meek and trusting brow;
Such as man was in Paradise
He may be even now.

Born in paradise, children are free of history's burden. America's natural surroundings, Smith insisted, promised the same for those who would listen and learn. America's favorite writer (and Smith's close friend), Edgar Allan Poe, utterly pessimistic about the nation's claims to progress, regarded *The Sinless Child* as a great poem, depicting the women who might yet save the nation from itself.

The same degree of optimism in the possibility of radical reform stirred peace crusades, whose goal was nothing less than disloyalty of all citizens toward any government making war. John Humphrey Noyes, who publicly declared his independence from the government of the nation, sent abolitionist-reformer William Lloyd Garrison a stirring letter in 1837 urging loyalty alone to Christ and "Universal Emancipation from Sin." Garrison aroused readers in his weekly *Liberator* to join with the New England Non-Resistance Society, founded in 1838, which insisted that "Our country is the world, our countrymen are all humankind," and went on

> We love the land of our nativity only as we love all other lands. The interests, rights, liberties of American citizens are no more dear to us than are those of the whole human race...We register our testimony, not only against all wars, whether offensive or defensive but all preparations for war; against every naval ship, every arsenal, every fortification; against the militia system and a standing army; against all military chieftains and soldiers; against all monuments commemorative of victory over a fallen foe, all trophies won in battle, all celebrations in honor of military or naval exploits; against all appropriations for the defense of the nation by force of arms, on the part of any legislative body; against every edict of government requiring of its subjects military force.

"Christian Non-Resistance," destined to vanish in the Civil War, had a moment of grandeur during the United States conquest of Mexican territory. New England reformers lined up against the empire-building effort and Henry David Thoreau refused to pay taxes, publishing his famous essay "Civil Disobedience" in 1846.

Abby Kelley Foster, abolitionist.

Wendell Phillips, the "Great Soul" of the abolitionist movement, c. 1860. From Elizabeth Buffum Chace, 1806-1899.

The "ringleted exotic," immigrant Jewish agitator Ernestine Rose, who was a relentless advocate of woman's rights and black emancipation, c. 1860.

FREDERICK DOUGLASS

The quintessential African-American political figure of the nineteenth century, Frederick Douglass can be remembered as a pioneering editor, lecturer and agitator or autobiographer. But he is perhaps best remembered as an American whose radicalism transcended boundaries without leaving its own firm origins.

Born into slavery as Frederick Augustus Washington Baily in 1818 on Maryland's eastern shore, he escaped to freedom in 1838 and married his companion in escape, the free black Anna Murray. He had already studied the Bible, rhetoric, and whatever else came to hand. Never acknowledged by his father (almost certainly his owner), he had refused to bow to authority and at sixteen, physically overwhelmed a notorious "slave breaker." From then on, he remembered, he was his own man in whatever he faced.

Once free, he quickly became a mediator between black needs and white sympathies, mastering his approach to different audiences. He also became a committed radical, linking himself to William Lloyd Garrison's total rejection of anything less than absolute emancipation. His famed autobiography, *Narrative of the Life of Frederick Douglass, An American Slave, Written by Himself* (1845) made him an international celebrity, a reputation he expanded with two subsequent autobiographies and thousands of public appearances in the United States and abroad. On the lecture trail and at reform conventions, he frequently spoke for women's freedom as well, making himself one of the best-loved and best-hated orators of the age.

He also made himself the foremost black journalist. In *The North Star, Frederick Douglass' Paper,* the *Douglass Monthly* and the *New National Era,* published intermittently from 1847 to 1874, he created and cultivated an audience of free black readers and white activists crucial to emancipation agitation and to Radical Reconstruction. Especially in his younger years, he shrewdly varied his tactics and gathered new allies without losing sight of his goal.

Douglass easily emerged a triumphant figure during the Civil War, eloquently demanding the emancipation that Lincoln ultimately adopted. But the fragmentation of the reform forces afterward left him in a quandary. When one faction of reformers (including some of his closest allies) insisted that women and African-Americans had to advance together in gaining the vote, Douglass turned instead to those who insisted "The Negro's Hour" had arrived and demanded precedence over all other concerns.

Passage of the Fifteenth Amendment giving black males the right to vote bound Douglass to the Republican Party even as that organization steadily abandoned its progressive policies. Less radical than before or simply tied at once to a hopeless strategy of salvaging Republican idealism and to his own career advancement, he served in high appointed offices for much of the rest of his life. His turn to younger race leaders who sought to combat the growing tide of racial violence during the 1880s-90s was the dramatic last note in a life largely spent for democracy. He died in 1894, as southern Republicans launched "salt and pepper" tickets of fusion with Populist candidates in the literal last moment of nineteenth century liberalism.

In its own way the anti-slavery movement was the most absolute and perfectionist of any movement, certainly subversive to the leading principles of American economic and social history and unendurable to a large section of American society. It was also the most radical in its implications for the future. Elizabeth Oakes Smith readily gave up her writer's life in order to become an abolitionist agitator.

Behind the rise of abolitionist enthusiasm and southern resistance lay the specter of slave revolt. Slave Gabriel Prosser led an insurrection in Richmond, Virginia in 1800, organizing more than a thousand slaves under a banner of "Death or Liberty" and seeking support from the independent Black nation of Haiti. Found out at the last moment, the insurrection failed, Prosser was caught and hanged with 35 others. During the War of 1812, thousands of slaves escaped, and in various places attempted to lead insurrections, hoping that the British would help them. During meetings at the Sea Islands (off the Georgia coast), such verses were sung:

Arise! Arise! Shake off your chains
Your cause is just so heaven ordains
To you shall Freedom be proclaimed
Raise your arms & bare your breasts
Almighty God will do the rest.
Blow the clarion! A warlike blast!
Call every Negro from his task!
Wrest the scourge from Buckra's hand
And drive each tyrant from the land.

Black fugitives joined with Indians defeated in the Creek War, and reassembled by 1815 at the "Negro Fort" on the Appalachicola River in current-day Florida, drawing more escapees toward them. Headed jointly by a fugitive slave and a Choctaw chief, the embattled colony symbolized the complex inter-relationships and interracial blending of the groups. General Andrew Jackson set out to destroy them, and a navy ship soon did with shelling. During successive Seminole Wars from the 1810s to the 1830s blacks and Seminoles successfully defended themselves. Chief Osceola's warriors in the Second Seminole War, mostly black, then kept resistance alive until 1842. By that time, tens of millions of dollars had been spent for their extermination or dispossession. The heartless Indian Removal Act of 1830, urged by President Andrew Jackson, had made the final act inevitable.

In the meantime, the somewhat prosperous former traveling seaman and Charleston carpenter Denmark Veysey (along with a "conjure man," Gullah Jack) tried to rouse the slaves of

South Carolina to escape to Haiti in 1822. Only a few conspirators escaped arrest and hanging. In 1831, the most famous revolt of all, led by Nat Turner, spread through Southampton County, Virginia. Fifty-five whites and more than forty African-Americans perished in events that the South could not forget.

Abolitionism's popular support, among free blacks and radical reformers, demanded much even in the North. *Freedom's Journal*, the first African-American newspaper in America, was launched in 1827 in Boston. The paper announced that it intended "to vindicate our brethren when oppressed, and to lay the cure before the publick," a most unfriendly public in general. Brave activists of Garrison's American Anti-Slavery Society and other groups faced rock-throwing (occasionally also lynch-minded) mobs, broke numerous laws in hiding runaway slaves, and accepted the slander of inter-racial promiscuity from the Democratic Party press. Henry Garnet, destined to become a leading black abolitionist orator, completed his education at the Oneida Institute after the Noyes Academy in Canaan, New Hampshire, had been burned down around him.

Yet women reformers in particular flocked to the movement, seeing the parallel between slavery and their own voteless and powerless condition. Most of them stayed with Garrison after a division in the ranks, posing radicals (who accepted women's full participation) against moderates (who feared the consequences). Never were popular anti-reform images more cruel, more morally misguided than in scurrilous attacks on radical reformers. But the attackers were right in seeing that the slavery question went to the core values of human society at large and American democracy in particular. An America which accepted its full responsibility for denying equality to racial minorities and women would be drastically changed, unacceptably

Nat Turner, leader of the famed slave rebellion. From an early print.

Frederick Douglass

so for those with power and to many who wanted it. [Plate 8]

In the West, especially in Kansas, mob violence turned to gun-battles, massacres, and guerrilla warfare between pro- and anti-slavery factions. There, John Brown and his followers, drawn into the cycle of violence, decided that slavery could be overcome only through armed conflict. They therefore plotted a dramatic military campaign against the heart of slave holding. Hopeless from any strategic standpoint, the famous raid of Harper's Ferry, Virginia in 1859 dramatized the impossibility of compromise on the central issue of the age.

The Civil War, with its mobilization of

Courtesy: Library of Congress

Thomas Wentworth Higginson, a Civil War hero and author who led a Negro regiment in battle. Decades later, near the end of his life, he joined the Socialist Party.

Courtesy: Library of Congress

John Brown from an imaginative contemporary print of Brown in prison awaiting execution for his raid on Harper's Ferry.

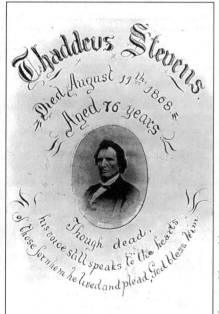

Courtesy: Library of Congress

Thaddeus Stevens, champion of Radical Reconstruction in Congress.

reformers around military victory and slave emancipation, crowded out other key issues. For a moment late in the War, Union military occupation of the Georgia Sea Islands (containing many Gullah blacks from Africa, never integrated into US society) seemed to promise a utopian experiment in black self-government. Army leaders, however, wanted firm rule and surplus crop production more than they wanted a transformation of Southern society. Like so much of the energy freed by the emancipation of slaves, including one or two other short-lived egalitarian colonies, the Georgia sea coast experiment was lost. But the possibilities of Reconstruction remained alive.

Radical Reconstruction, according to African-American scholarly giant W.E.B. DuBois, had been made inevitable by a black "General Strike" in the later stages of the war, *i.e.*, slaves fleeing their plantations with the approach of Northern armies. Set in full motion by the Northern victory and congressional action against the defeated South, Reconstruction offered Americans a singular moment of opportunity to achieve interracial democracy. Union troops, elected black officials and allied government agencies offered a measure of legal equality, minimal schooling and above all, hope to African-Americans. This noble experiment was undone by the corruption of Republican politicians and the terror of armed southern whites, but above all by a federal government unwilling to enforce laws minimally protecting black rights. The Compromise of 1876 followed inevitably, with removal of Northern troops and the end of all hopes for equality in the foreseeable future. DuBois concluded his famous narrative in *Black Reconstruction*:

> God wept; but that mattered little to an unbelieving age; what mattered most was that the world wept and still is weeping and blind with tears and blood. For there began to rise in America in 1876 a new capitalism and a new enslavement of labor. Home labor in cultured lands, appeased

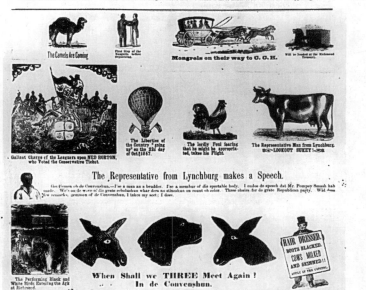

Above: U.S. soldiers evicting former slaves from their land after President Andrew Johnson pardoned Rebels and ordered their property returned to them. Below: Reconstruction era in which racists attacked new governments as "Black Vomit."

and misled by a ballot whose power the dictatorship of vast capital strictly curtailed, was bribed by high wage and political office to unite in an exploitation of white, yellow, brown and black labor, in lesser lands and breeds without the law. Especially workers of the New World, folks who were American and for whom America was home, became ashamed of their destiny. Sons of ditch-diggers aspired to be spawn of bastard kings and thieving aristocrats rather than of rough-handed children of dirt and toil. The immense profit from this new exploitation and world-wide commerce enabled a guild of millionaires to engage the greatest engineers, the wisest men of science, as well as pay high wages to the more intelligent labor and at the same time to have left enough surplus to make more thorough the dictatorship of capital over the state and over the popular vote, not only in Europe and America but in Asia and Africa.

DuBois had not captured the whole truth by any means; but he had seen the deep and subtle racial dimension to the changing class equation of American society. By crushing the radicals, America had lost its way.

Courtesy for both: Library of Congress

(Left) Defeated but never conquered: Chief Joseph, who led the Nez Perce across hundreds of miles of the northwest before surrendering to whites in 1877; (right) and Geronimo, a Chiricahua Apache, the last great leader of armed resistance in the southwest, defeated in 1886.

PSYCHOSOPHY

In Six Parts.

———

PART I.

THE SOUL IN HUMAN EMBODIMENTS.

———

MRS. CORA L. V. RICHMOND.

Spiritualism, an American Socialism

During the same historic year of 1848 with the European revolutions and the historic Woman's Rights convention, two young girls living near Rochester (and not far from Seneca Falls) heard a series of mysterious noises in their house. The news of Katie and Maggie Fox and their "spirit rappings" with messages from beyond the world of the living set off a wave of excitement that eventually created dozens of spiritualist newspapers, established hundreds of new church congregations (mostly converted *en masse* from Universalism, Unitarianism's twin) and inspired fervent believers, even in the United States Congress.

MISS MARGARETTA FOX.   MISS CATHARINE FOX.   MRS FISH.

Mrs FISH AND THE MISSES FOX,

THE ORIGINAL MEDIUMS OF THE MYSTERIOUS NOISES AT ROCHESTER WESTERN, N. Y.

Courtesy: Library of Congress

The famous Fox Sisters, Maggie and Katie, with their mother.

Experiments in mind travel seemed, given the scientific knowledge of the time, no less possible than electricity or heavier-than-air flight. Like Shakers before them, "sensitive" spiritualist individuals went into a trance state, either contacting spirits for loved ones or writing essays and poems while guided mysteriously from above. The emergence of a large audience for this activity played an especially important role for women who were the great majority of "mediums" and writers for spiritualist publications. They became the first large group of American *women* religious leaders and also the largest group of women public speakers. They were especially welcome speakers in African-American churches, which typically lacked a fixed, orthodox doctrine excluding "heterodox" currents.

Spiritualism had a special message for reformers. It made possible a vision of a cosmic oneness which reduced differences of race, sex and class to matters of near unimportance. Radicals and utopians of many kinds saw spiritualism as proof that a system of competition and destruction had no reason to last and could not last. They talked and sang about the "Good Time Coming."

Spiritualism had another, important link to hopes for a multicultural American democracy. As anthropologists have argued in recent decades, one overriding difference separates African and Western religion: Africans of many animist types feel a closeness of the dead to the living, a vagueness of the border. These traditions passed on to Afro-Caribbeans and African-Americans. For spiritualists, that vague border-

Andrew Jackson Davis, one of the foremost "philosophical" spiritualists and most radical.

trance state. In 1847 his volume, *The Principles of Nature, Her Divine Revelations and a Voice to Mankind*, appeared and a circle of writers close to Edgar Allan Poe helped publicize what Davis began to call the "Harmonial Philosophy."

Davis's political collaborator, Stephen Pearl Andrews, had come to radicalism as an anti-slavery lawyer in the South. He invented an early form of stenography, founded the Modern Times utopian colony on Long Island, and led an even more utopian literary scheme for world government called the "Pantarchy." Universology, as he described his doctrine, was like spiritu-

VICTORIA C. WOODHALL.
CANDIDATE FOR THE
PRESIDENCY OF THE UNITED STATES

Courtesy: Museum of American Political Life

Courtesy: Scott Molloy.

Victoria Woodhull as she looked to an artist and as Thomas Nast saw her, c. 1872.

Very Sincerely Your Friend
Cora L. V. Richmond

Courtesy: Charles H. Kerr Co.

Cora Richmond, popular writer and "phenomenal" spiritualist.

alism in reconciling all elements of the universe as part of one interrelated entity. Like Davis, he insisted increasingly upon a "philosophical" spiritualism, more political-minded and comprehensive than the mere "phenomenal" spiritualism of contacting souls from the Beyond. In 1870, Andrews met the third and most crucial of the secular socialist triumvirate: Victoria Woodhull.

Born in 1838, Woodhull (and her sister, Tennessee) had grown up within reform movements and self-improvement campaigns ranging from spiritualism to magnetic healing. Married at fifteen, she went on stage, left her husband and remarried a spiritualist-minded Union Army colonel. Then purportedly directed by a spirit to move to New York, she met and charmed the millionaire Cornelius Vanderbilt, who helped the two sisters to set up a stock-trading firm on Wall Street. Instantly successful because of their glamour and public appeal, the sisters announced in 1870 the publication of *Woodhull & Claflin's Weekly*, with their new acquaintance, Stephen Pearl Andrews, as editor.

Easily one of the most eclectic and exciting reform papers ever published in this country, *Woodhull & Claflin's Weekly* advocated women's rights, universal justice, free love, world government and several versions of spiritualism and socialism, all summed up in its motto — "Progress! Free Thought! Untrammeled Lives!" The *Weekly* also created a far-ranging social circle at Woodhull's picturesque mansion, the "Psyche Club House" known for intelligent conversation and for guidance by the spirits.

Woodhull & Claflin's Weekly declared itself a voice of the important socialist organization founded in Europe by Marx and others, the International Workingmen's Association. It also became the first English-language publication in America to offer readers Marx and Engels's *Communist Manifesto*. Grown familiar with the class of rich people, the paper declared them to be vampires upon the poor.

Socialists and other reformers could not help but be impressed by the dramatic panache of the sisters. In 1871, the Woodhull circle helped lead a massive New York demonstration, the largest the city had ever seen for any radi-

Woodhull & Claflin's Weekly, *socialist and spiritualist organ.*

Courtesy: Museum of American Political Life.

cal cause, honoring the fallen Paris Commune. A year later, Woodhull dramatically presented a petition to Congress in favor of woman suffrage, claiming that the law need only enforce woman's rights as citizens. Impressing President Grant, she received a serious hearing from the House Judiciary Committee and the admiration of woman suffrage activists. Meanwhile, Woodhull maintained her ties to spiritualism. She was elected an unprecedented three times as President of the American Spiritualist Society.

Her high point in self-dramatization marked a tragic end to her meteoric rise. In May, 1872, she accepted the nomination for Presidency on the Equal Rights Party ticket. The characteristic reform audience of "long haired men" and "short haired women with glasses" went wild at a rally in New York's Cooper Institute. She was the first woman, as well as the first socialist, to run for that office. But the currents of post-Civil War reform faded quickly. She could not possibly persuade Frederick Douglass, the famous ex-slave, to run as her vice-presidential candidate. Her followers turned to Liberal Republican candidate and sometime utopian-minded reformer Horace Greeley, or back to Grant, who vaguely promised action on woman suffrage.

By the time of the election, the Equal Rights party had disappeared. Woodhull herself sat behind bars for certain sexually-tinged passages in the *Weekly* considered indecent for public print. Within a year, she had entangled herself in a public scandal, accusing the nation's most revered (and one of its most politically conservative) ministers, Henry Ward Beecher, of involvement in an extra-marital triangle. With the death of her paper, Woodhull fled to England, married wealthily and renounced her former radical ideas.

Socialistic spiritualism did not die out entirely with the downfall and departure of Victoria Woodhull. A leader of the spiritualists predicted in 1879 that Spiritualism would yet "spring up unbidden in the very center of the socialist camp" because the

elements and tendencies of the two movements are such that a meeting and partial merging...is as much of a necessity, under natural law, as the attraction of bodies possessing chemical affinities...Both sides possess, in fact, nearly all of the activities now visible in the civilized world.

Courtesy: The Charles H. Kerr Co.

"Keep Your Brain Vibrating," an advertisement from 1902, shows that spiritualism had a continuing appeal past the turn of the century. The Progressive Thinker *billed itself "the Bible of the Future."*

New Visions of Utopia

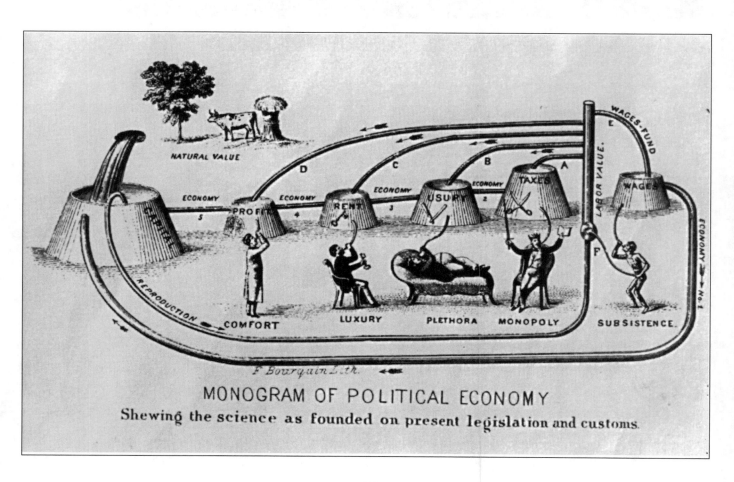

MONOGRAM OF POLITICAL ECONOMY
Shewing the science as founded on present legislation and customs.

OWEN'S PROPOSED VILLAGE.

Courtesy: Charles H. Kerr Co.

Courtesy: Charles H. Kerr Co.

Robert Owen's plan for New Harmony, Indiana and the main buildings of the North American Phalanx, near Red Bank, New Jersey, c. 1850.

New Visions of Utopia

Over the course of the nineteenth century the main vision of utopianism or socialism changed from religious perfection to progress through egalitarian, mostly secular social relations. Radical "progress" meant many different things, but definitely concerned the relationship of men and women to one another and of sexuality to both of them. Increasingly, such progress was envisioned to be achieved through the efforts of the individual or small groups until it could be realized among larger numbers.

By the second decade of the nine-

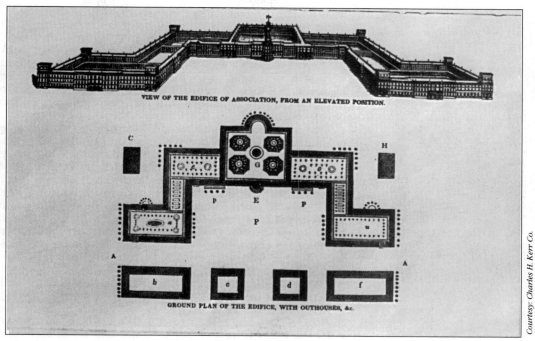

VIEW OF THE EDIFICE OF ASSOCIATION, FROM AN ELEVATED POSITION.

GROUND PLAN OF THE EDIFICE, WITH OUTHOUSES, &c.

Courtesy: Charles H. Kerr Co.

Plan for a Fourierist Phalanx, c. 1845.

THE

GOOD TIME COMING.

By T. S. ARTHUR.

BOSTON:
L. P. CROWN & CO., 61 CORNHILL.
PHILADELPHIA:
J. W. BRADLEY, 48 N. FOURTH ST.
1855.

PREFACE.

LIFE is a mystery to all men, and the more profound the deeper the striving spirit is immersed in its own selfish instincts. How earnestly do we all fix our eyes upon the slowly-advancing future, impatiently waiting that good time coming which never comes! How fast the years glide by, beginning in hope and ending in disappointment! Strange that we gain so little of true wisdom amid the sharp disappointments that meet us at almost every turn! How keenly the writer has suffered with the rest, need not be told. It will be enough to say that he, too, has long been an anxious waiter for the "good time coming," which has not yet arrived.

But hope should not die because of our disappointments. There *is* a good time coming, and for each one of us, if we work and wait for it; but we must work patiently, and look in the right direction. Perhaps our meaning will be plainer after our book is read.

3

The Good Time Coming, a novel by best-selling temperance author T.S. Arthur, warns against the contemporary enthusiasm for socialistic reforms.

teenth century, many more colonies had been launched, further and further to the West where open spaces and cheap lands beckoned. The New York Society for Promoting Communities organized in 1829 by Cornelius Blatchly, even attracted the interest of Thomas Jefferson. The former president considered a "communion of property" workable only within a small society, yet potentially the successful creator of "a state of as much happiness as heaven has been pleased to deal out to imperfect humanity." Robert Owen, the British philanthropist, addressed Congress, favorably impressing many members with his blueprint for a cooperative scheme of Western development.

Owenites led by Owen's son, Robert Dale Owen, sought to preserve the spirit of egalitarian enthusiasm but without compulsory religion and with a higher level of production. Lacking skilled workers and overloaded with intellectuals among the several hundred colonists, Owen's New Harmony (taken over from the Rappites' Indiana colony) lost money handily. Internal divisions also proliferated. It was said that when a puppet show opened with a charge for admission, Owen knew he had failed. By 1827, when Owen himself left New Harmony, the colony was doomed. Owenite ideals eventually reached wide audiences, from Pennsylvania to Texas, prompting many other efforts. Owen himself, in old age, became a spiritualist, in tune with many of his constituents. Yet no basically secular colonies, even those with a handful of spiritualists, could match the Pietistic German counterparts in durability.

Other secular European savants, Charles Fourier and Etienne Cabet, inspired efforts similar to Owen's New Harmony. Fourier secured the enthusiastic approval of famed journalists Horace Greeley and Albert Brisbane, held dozens of conventions during 1843-44 and more than 1,500 individuals, largely skilled workers, eager to join colonies. Many were formed, from the East Coast to Wisconsin. The most successful, at Red Bank, New Jersey, struggled through ten years of existence; most lasted less than a year.

Lacking sufficient material base and work-sharing arrangements, the "phalanx" (or plan for communal living) prompted confusion between the functions of family and group; women, often those most receptive to the ideals of Fourierism, were severely disappointed in the actual practice. Craft workers who sought to evade the consequences of economic recession found no solace in communal poverty. But at least one, Brook Farm, in today's West Roxbury, Massachusetts, attracted some of the leading reform lights of the day. Hardly successful in material terms, it provoked sometime communitarian Nathaniel Hawthorne to write *The Blithedale Romance*, about an almost more-than-human heroine whose tragedy is that the times are not ready for her. The melancholy Hawthorne probably thought that of the entire utopian movement.

Fourierism, nevertheless, had a wide impact upon American reformers in the 1840s-50s. Fourierists helped show reformers how political liberty could exist alongside extreme class division, and large classes make themselves "slaves of labor," deprived of the social and psychological gifts of cooperation. For Fourierists, as for the Ephratans and other communitarians, Americans had a different and better mission than empire-building. To "fulfill the law of love" demanded an abandonment of acquisitive individualism as the leading rule. Even the pro-slavery, Southern propaganda attack upon the miseries of northern wage labor owed something to Fourierist argument. In an entirely different realm of public life, Frederick Law Olmstead's marvelous plans for public parks, including New York's Central Park, had been inspired by his visits to Fourierist colonies, with the park as a melting point for city and country landscapes, a meeting ground of the communal spirit.

The revolutions of 1848, even more than the practical failure of its colonies, doomed Fourierism. Desperate Parisian working people and a fearful ruling bourgeoisie had sparked violent class revolt. Prominent French Fourierists joined or even led mobs storming government buildings, while American Fourierists felt repugnance at the violence. Seeking to separate themselves from this style of socialistic uprising, Fourierists merged themselves more and more with mainstream reform efforts. To the extent that they lost sight of their own ideal, their specific vision became less and less relevant.

On a much smaller and more obscure scale, Cabet's followers, several hundred

French men and women, attempted experiments with limited but genuine success. After seeking various locations, they settled firmly in Nauvoo, Illinois, a former Mormon village, in 1849. By 1854, the population reached 1,500, mostly French immigrants. The poverty-stricken village did not much resemble the happy vision of "Icaria" that Cabet had written about and for which he named the colony. After Cabet himself visited France and then attempted to retake control of Nauvoo, his erstwhile followers expelled him, a sign of their own independent-mindedness. Icaria and several offshoots nevertheless survived for decades. Virtually demanding marriage of each adult, Icarians sought to abolish dowries, unequal education of men and women, and any pressure of parents to compel unwanted marriage. All colonists cooked and ate in common houses belonging to the community, and all private homes were similarly modest; but these French immigrants had sought to preserve private life outside mealtimes, not to transform it. Ordinary people in many respects, Icarians expected less of utopianism than other utopians, and accomplished the goals of their lower expectations.

The colonists of Oneida, New York, offered a dramatic contrast. They were the only group to practice "complex marriage," each sex given free reign to as many partners as they chose, without any loss of honor. Spiritual father and Yale graduate John Humphrey Noyes compared his own version of Per-

Frances "Fanny" Wright, utopian and fearless supporter of socialism. From E.C. Stanton, et. al., The History of Woman Suffrage, Vol. I *(1881).*

FRANCES WRIGHT

"Fanny" Wright, in many ways a model of later American radicals, stood for free speech, woman's rights, African-American emancipation, free love, and socialism. For generations, radicals (and women radicals in particular) were scorned as "Fanny Wrights."

Born in Scotland in the last years of the eighteenth century, Wright was orphaned early and raised by rich, conservative relatives from whom she instinctively rebelled. In college at Glasgow, she penned a play exploring her utopian ideals, and traveled with the play to the United States. She returned in 1824 and after visiting the New Harmony utopian colony, became a convinced socialist. Wright purchased land in Tennessee for an experimental plantation where slaves might work the land and gain their freedom.

She moved to New York City after this utopian experiment failed. There, she joined Robert Dale Owen (son of British utopian, Robert Owen) in founding the Hall of Science dedicated to the public education of ordinary people. The two of them published the *Free Enquirer*, a socialistic paper with a working class audience. She and Owen espoused many reforms, but above all they hoped to create a new society through progressive education of young people in an egalitarian environment. By her force of personality, her advocacy of free thought uncluttered with religion, and her insistence upon women's emancipation, she startled and excited the public.

Often singled out for personal attack by conservatives, Wright left New York after the Workingmen's Party disintegrated at the end of the 1820s. She spent the rest of her life more obscurely, beset with personal troubles, and died in Cincinnati in 1852. She had nevertheless challenged, as perhaps no one before, the sexual oppression of women. The "female Tom Paine," she was regarded by suffrage leader Elizabeth Cady Stanton as a "saint of freedom."

THE KITCHEN. ONEIDA COMMUNITY.

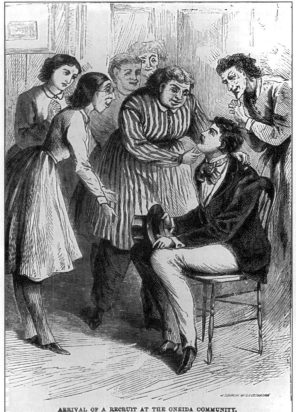

ARRIVAL OF A RECRUIT AT THE ONEIDA COMMUNITY.

John Humphrey Noyes's Oneida community satirically portrayed.

fectionism — "the immediate and total cessation from sin" — to temperance and abolition of slavery. Each demanded eliminating the *causes* of wrong-doing. The progression he envisioned for humanity went theoretically from a community of faith to a community of property, to a community of household, and finally to a community of affection. "Bible Communism," launched from Noyes' Bible School in Putney, Vermont, in the 1830s, therefore urged "spiritual affinity" over marriage ties.

Oneida theology resembled Shakerism in one important sense: The Shakers abolished the contradiction of monogamy and communality by ending all sexual behavior, while Noyes sought to abolish the same contradiction by allowing for multiple marriages. Convinced that the Kingdom of God had returned, at least among his followers, the sexes no longer had any obligation to earthly marriage ties — except that Noyes himself virtually insisted on approving each relationship.

Savagely attacked by the press for immorality, Noyes's Perfectionists argued all the stronger that the entire colony was part of a single, moral union, a complete marriage in which licentious flirting was banned (although a woman might flash her eyes to attract a male's attention), but all heterosexual relationships enabled through "perpetual courtship." The experiment successfully centered a common life and work for two generations. Perhaps the colonists' self-confidence and obsessive attachment to the sexual dimension blinded the members to the temptations of the evolving competitive society outside and even to the society's growing depredations against nature. While Oneidans lived quietly unto themselves, the trapping and killing of millions of beavers — creatures seen by Charles Fourier as the most associative animals on earth — was facilitated by Oneida member and inventor Sewall Newhouse's steel trap, which was manufactured at the colony under his direction. Ironically, spiritualists even took over John Humphrey Noyes's sexual-perfectionist Oneida Colony during its later years.

Colonies designed for African-Americans were also unique in their intentions. Scottish reformer and utopian Frances Wright, after a 1819 visit to the American South, proposed the creation of a community to train ex-slaves and supply means for their colonization outside the United States. James Madison and Thomas Jefferson, among others, enthusiastically supported her ideas. Wright's followers set out to create a secular colony, Nashoba, on 300 acres west of Memphis, Tennessee, where one hundred inhabitants would divide their time between schooling and manual labor. In 1826 a handful of slaves began work but faced a

land was the geography of their faith.

Rather than seeking the personal guidance of a savior, spiritualists tended to see the supernatural within the beauty and harmony of the natural world. They believed humans had been born good rather than sinful, reflecting the true image of God, and could save themselves by intelligent self-reflection. These beliefs, like the rejection of Calvinist images of Hell for sinners, encouraged a confidence in the possibility of change during this life. Spiritualists who died were spoken of as entering the "Summerland," "Passed to the Spirit Land," or "Translated." Spiritualism, already by the 1860s waning from its initial burst, regained enormous popularity in the wake of the Civil War with so many grieving over lost loved ones. Labor reformer Elizabeth Stuart Phelps's *The Gates Ajar*, an instant best-seller, tapped the aspiration, depicting Heaven as a summertime New England and its inhabitants spiritually close to those left behind. In the face of the continuous settlement of the frontier, Spiritualists also vigorously publicized the plight of Indians, who they viewed as spirit-peoples like themselves.

Spiritualism drew many remarkable radical characters. Popular author C.L. James, later a labor reformer, insisted "scratch a Spiritualist and you will find an anarchist." Free black Paschal Beverly Randolph, leading spiritualist, sexual theorist, Abolitionist and hashish-smoking visionary, was even founder of the Rosicrucian movement in the United States.

The connections between spiritualism and socialism were strong and continuous. Spirit "manifestation," voices and signs, were plentiful at the Christian socialist Hopedale colony in Massachusetts. Hopedale members created a newspaper called the *Radical Spiritualist*, propagandizing for "Spiritualism, Socialism, Anti-Slavery, Non-Resistance, Woman's Rights, Anti-Oath-taking and Office-hooding, Temperance, Vegetarianism, Anti-Tobacco (Tea, Coffee) and every other Reform which requires the practice of a higher life."

But the most important spiritual-socialists, by far, were the twin leader-philosophers of the spiritualist movement, Andrew Jackson Davis and Stephen Pearl Andrews, and the movement's most glamorous public figure, Victoria Woodhull. Davis, known as the "Poughkeepsie Seer," had been a sickly child, self-healed after attending a lecture on "animal magnetism." He began receiving "visits" from the spirit world and at age 19, even before the Fox Sisters' appearance and gave a series of public lectures while in a

Stephen Pearl Andrews.

Private Collection

Banner of Light, *leading spiritualist paper, 1840s-80s.*

Courtesy: Southpaw Books

Courtesy: Charles H. Kerr Co.

Private Collection

Private Collection

Robert Reitzel and his weekly Detroit paper, Der Arme Teufel, *champions of free thought.*

Moses Harmon, Free Love philosopher and publisher of Lucifer, The Light Bearer, *from Valley Falls, Kansas, 1883-1907, denouncing all loveless "marriage by compulsion."*

daunting dilemma of tilling poor swampy land ridden with the threat of malaria.

Unsuccessful economically, it also had little appeal to free blacks, placed socially below the handful of resident whites who could become members of the colony for $200 per year. Worse for publicity, its leaders made clear their hostility toward organized religion and marriage, emphasizing instead the right of individuals of whatever race to engage in sexual relations as they wished. An outcry against "free love" and against potential miscegenation overwhelmed all other discussion. After two years, its residents by now thoroughly impoverished, Nashoba became a mere association of individuals. In 1830, Wright abandoned the experiment.

WALT WHITMAN

The "great gray poet" (later generations called him the "great gay poet"), Walt Whitman practically reinvented poetic form. He also left behind a life exemplary in pursuit of freedoms of many kinds.

Whitman had a curious background as a devoted and even racist Democratic Party newspaperman. Growing up in Brooklyn, he apprenticed to a printer, taught school in the 1830s, and joined the staff of the *Brooklyn Eagle*. There he began to envision a freer America, far to the West, unbound by urban society's restrictions. Delegate to a national Freesoilers convention in 1848, he afterward grew disillusioned with politics and turned his full attentions to poetry. There, his interest in the utopianism and perfectionism of the radicals served him well, especially the visions of Quaker leader Elias Hicks who preached a code of "inner light" and individualistic conscience.

In *Leaves of Grass* and especially "Song of Myself," Whitman declared himself an unofficial observer of everything in creation. Especially did he insist upon a radical equality of all body parts and functions, promising a recuperation of the despised lower self through reconciliation with the soul. He struggled mightily against Victorian prudery, and placed himself unreservedly on the side of woman's sensuality. He also declared his faith in women's equality. His poetry often suggested, if it never stated outright, the validity of homosexual attractions (at least for men), making him a key figure for future generations of poets. His influence on "free verse" poetry is still larger, his example demonstrating a decisive shift from conventional meter to the long and unmetrical line. Never especially political after his younger years, he sometimes claimed to be more radical than all the radicals on account of his individualist views.

Courtesy: Library of Congress

Walt Whitman.

A scattering of other black colonies followed, in the United States and Canada. "Carthagena," for instance, a settlement of free black artisans and families occupying nearly 30,000 acres in Western Ohio, survived eight years amid hostile whites by mixing individual private property with heavy doses of community sharing. Other colonies never emerged from reliance upon charity and with it the guidance of white philanthropy. African-Americans could advance no better separated from the overpowering white society than by struggling within it. Less formally, dozens of informally organized, semi-cooperative colonies of mixed races existed of blacks, Indian peoples and usually some whites, from the rural South to the still uncolo-

Color Page – 1

Previous page, German currency from 1921 and above, Communist Party poster from 1925 commemorate the uprising led by Thomas Münzer. The black shadows on red background design, by Walter Hegeümunburg, was a 50 pfennig note for Frankenhausen; the sketch design by Karl Ullrich, was a 50 pfennig note for Muehlhausen. Issued during the hyper-inflationary period of the Weimar Republic, these bills had little monetary value but their appearance offered symbolic homage to radical history on the part of socialist government officials. The poster above, issued on Thomas Münzer Day (or the "four hundredth anniversary of class struggle in Germany") in 1925, was a linoleum cut by an unknown artist. Note the hammer and sickle, and the general descent of technique. Courtesy: Private Collection

Courtesy: Saint Joseph College, Rev. Andrew J. Kelly Collection

"King Philip" or Metacomet, the Pokanoket Chief who led an allied Indian force in 1675 to defend southern New England Indians against expropriation of their lands. Painting by Thomas Hart Benton, c. 1935.

Reinterpretation of the "discovery" of the Americas, 1992.

Father George Rapp, founder of the Rappites, c. 1830.

Hannah Cohoon, "Tree of Life," c. 1844.

"A Peep into the Anti-Federalist Club," 1793. Artist unknown. Thomas Jefferson and his Democratic Republicans are treated as objects of derision, unruly "Jacobins" to their Federalist opponents.

Color Page — 5

"The Bloomer's Complaint, a very pathetic song," published in Philadelphia, 1851. The lyrics dare men "to lecture, to scold, [but] she'll do as she pleases."

Color Page — 6

Frances Ellen Watkins Harper: poet, abolitionist lecturer and later a prominent novelist. Born in Baltimore of free black parents, Harper published her first volume while still in her teens. Among her better known works are Poems on Miscellaneous Subjects *(1854) and* Sketches of Southern Life *(1872). Irving Fromer, c. 1960, oil on canvas.*

Editor Horace Greeley popularized Fourierist ideas in the United States.

"Banditos," I.W.W. poet-artist Carlos Cortez's woodcut portrays nineteenth century Mexican-American rebels who resisted the expropriation of their land by "Anglos" through individual acts of banditry.

JOHN MUIR

Rarely considered a "radical" in his day, Muir has become one in ours. Firmly rejecting the economic system on non-socialist grounds, he has been lauded as a heretic of a society whose mainstream leaders have usually succeeded at the expense of the natural landscape.

Muir was born outside Edinburgh, Scotland in 1838, came to Wisconsin with his parents at age 11, and grew into the midwestern farming life. He spent his childhood leisure outside the house, escaping a mean father. An instinctive naturalist, he analyzed nature from the few written sources available. Muir precociously entered the University of Wisconsin where he learned science and envisioned a New England Transcendentalism transplanted to the frontier.

Muir, a committed pacifist, abandoned the United States for Canada to avoid the Civil War draft-call. He spent the next years wandering the upper Great Lakes region. After the war, he returned to society and fell victim to an industrial accident which blinded him for weeks. During this time, he experienced something like a spiritual conversion. He decided upon a tour of the wilderness, describing months of travel in his book, *A Thousand Mile Walk to the Gulf.* There he discovered or reinvented a kind of nature religion.

He gradually worked out a philosophy for himself which emphasized that Man's separation from Nature had rendered human experience and consequently the human outlook stunted and bigoted. Worse, from his viewpoint, this distortion had exposed the surviving wilds to depredations from evil intent armed with ever more powerful machines. In destroying nature, humanity destroyed its own best hopes, turning everything beautiful into ugliness and into opportunities for further greed. The desire to conquer nature had been the greatest error of all, spawning the further evils of war, poverty, and mass psychological ruin.

Muir settled himself at the end of the 1860s in the California natural paradise of Yosemite, which he struggled with all his energies and wit to save from destruction. He wrote frequently about Yosemite and other scenic vistas from the 1870s-90s, achieving a wide popular appeal. He aimed to create a vast system of "forest reserves," an idea later realized — in considerably reduced form — as the national park system, where large areas might be protected from malicious harm and above all from commercialization. He thoroughly disliked politics in all its forms. Theodore Roosevelt, who camped with him in Yosemite, posed for "photo opportunities," and agreed to expand the park system considerably.

From Muir, the "preservation" movement (as he named it) gained its purpose and logic. He personally founded the Sierra Club in 1892, destined to become the premier lobby for the environment. But he also urged another method of persuasion, not one of political urging but rather changing hearts one-by-one, through personal experiences in nature. As a self-willed tramp seeking his own freedom and more likely to side with animals than humans in any conflict. John Muir set an example that poets, scientists, teachers and millions of ordinary Americans still consider inspirational eight decades after his 1914 death.

Traubel assisted in the first volume published about Whitman, *Cosmic Consciousness* (destined to remain a classic in the field of mysticism). A few years later, Traubel found a religious sponsor for his weekly Whitmanesque magazine, *The Conservator*, published in Philadelphia for almost thirty years. Traubel also created the Whitman Brotherhood, which gathered famous and obscure Americans. Among them were the beloved socialist leader Eugene Debs, Helen Keller, champion of the handicapped, and humorist Don Marquis (creator of *archy and mehitabel*), coming together to honor the memory and realize or at least preserve the dead poet's vision. Largely through these efforts and the newer readership they encouraged, Whitman's status rose until he became known as America's greatest poet.

In Traubel, the transcendental idealism of Whitman — which fixed itself upon the free individual as the reflection of the "Cosmos" — became the collective possibility of the common crowd. Revising Whitman's individualist claims, Traubel recast the Grey Poet's images of divinity in human form. The idea of Socialism became, as the young Karl Marx had written in his own reflective moments, the "Answer to the riddle of human history which knows itself to be the Answer," not so much an economic system as a point of destiny always on the horizon. There, somewhere ahead, lay the future that the German-American Pietists and indeed all the Green Dreamers would have easily recognized:

I saw a thousand singers hand in hand,
Ages long the procession, the line unbroken
Vulturous pedantries swooping and
    threatening,
The masters, the prophetic strong voices,
    defiantly continuous, measure their
    tones with the infinite.
By these lips miracles: prison doors swung
    open, bonds of slaves vanishing, the
    blind seeing, the deaf hearing, silence
    given speech, the hungry fed, by no seen
    witness of grace.
This chorus is the rescue-dream of the
    innocent, it assuages the intermediate
    hours,
It is the open hand of nations and races, the
    light-beam bridging the abysses of stars,
    the dawn that withdraws gently the
    shadowy gray of death,
Knowing not offender and offended,
    knowing only man, woman, child,
    animal, life —

Of whom the song, of whom the singers chanting
  their ages long choral –
For whom the immortal line from perfect to perfect
  proceeding.

Further Reading

Herbert Aptheker, *American Negro Slave Revolts* (New York: Columbia University Press, 1943).

Russell Bourne, *The Red King's Rebellion: Racial Politics in New England, 1675-1678* (New York: Oxford University Press, 1990).

Richard M. Bucke, *Cosmic Consciousness* (New York: Dutton, 1969 reprint).

W.E.B. DuBois, *Black Reconstruction in America, 1860-1880* (New York: Harcourt Brace, 1935).

Donald Drew Egbert, "Socialism and American Art," in *Socialism and American Life*, I (Princeton: Princeton University Press, 1952), edited by Donald Drew Egbert and Stow Persons.

Lawrence Foster, *Women, Family and Utopia: Communal Experiments of the Shakers, the Oneida Community, and the Mormons* (Syracuse: Syracuse University Press, 1991)

Carl J. Guaneri, *The Utopian Alternative: Fourierism in Nineteenth Century America* (Ithaca: Cornell University Press, 1991).

Vincent Harding, *There Is a River: The Black Struggle for Freedom in America* (New York: Vintage, 1983).

Dolores Hayden, *Seven American Utopias: The Architecture of Communitarian Socialism, 1790-1975.* (Cambridge: MIT Press, 1979.)

Ulrike Heider, *Der arme Teufel, Robert Reitzel* (Buehl-Moos: Elster Velag, 1986).

Ich, Thomas Muentzer, eyn knecht gottes (Berlin: Henschelverlag, 1989).

Ross F. Lockridge, *The Labyrinth* (Westport: Hyperion Press, 1975 reprint).

Hal D. Sears, *The Sex Radicals: Free Love in High Victorian America* (Lawrence: Regents Press of Kansas, 1977).

June Sprigg, *By Shaker Hands* (New York: Knopf, 1975)

Andrew Weeks, *Böhme: An Intellectual Biography* (Albany: SUNY Press, 1991).

Alfred Young, ed., *The American Revolution Revisited* (DeKalb: Northern Illinois University Press, 1993).

Alfred Young and Terry J. Fife, with Mary E. Janzen, *We the People, Voices and Images of the New Nation* (Philadelphia: Temple University Press, 1993).

Environmentalist John Muir, c. 1872. Photo: C.E. Watkins.

Courtesy: State Historical Society of Wisconsin

Chapter Two
Class and Culture

The Republic of Labor

A Voice from the People!

—

Great Meeting in the Park!!

GEORGE HENRY EVANS.

Engraving of George Henry Evans, c. 1830.

The Republic of Labor

While utopian visionaries of various kinds sought escape mechanisms out of the class-divided and racist social order, working men and women of every race and nationality usually tried to make the best of life within its contemporary limits. At moments of extreme crisis, substantial numbers joined communitarian movements or rose up to defend themselves in violent class warfare. But more often, they adapted to institutions shielding them in one way or another from the worst effects of the emerging wages system.

Self-educated radical workers, usually master mechanics or craftsmen, had a self-conscious tradition to defend. Proud that their class played an important role in the Revolution, workingmen's associations initiated the first labor parades in American history around the time of the Constitution's ratification. On their parade banners they inscribed their deepest sentiments: "By Hammer and Hand All Arts Do Stand." For generations, the arm and hammer was their principal emblem (it was later officially adopted by the Socialist Labor Party).

But theirs was not an all-inclusive concept or claim. The "mechanic" of the eighteenth and early nineteenth centuries was a recognized member of a trade, operating within its rules. He lived and worked in the large cities such as Philadelphia, New York, Boston, Newport or Charleston, toiling in shipyards, construction sites, blacksmiths' or tailors' shops. By contrast, common laborers and household servants or slaves (either skilled or unskilled) were considered the bottom of the social ladder and their work received no recognition beyond meager payment. Women helped their husbands in skilled trades or engaged in low status "women's work" such as washing clothes or keeping bar. Indians were, of course, entirely out of this picture.

Changes in production steadily undermined the mechanic's dignity and his way of life. So long as a factory of twenty-five workers run by a master craftsman was still considered unusually large, the class system among white men had seemed fluid. But factories in many trades grew by the 1820s to hold dozens or even hundreds of workers, thus displacing craftsmen or driving them to the margins of the economy. For the unskilled worker earning a dollar a day or less — perhaps half that of the craftsman — price rises often drove families

PHILADELPHIA TYPOGRAPHICAL SOCIETY

Emblem of the Philadelphia Typographical Society, as drawn by William Blake's leading American disciple, John Sartain. Here, the universal ideals of this early craftsmen's movement are illustrated.

to the verge of starvation. By the 1830s work stretched to twelve-hour days, with entire families including even small children assisting in the shop. Meanwhile, the rapid growth of American cities caused the once-proud craft worker to suffer along with the poor, in crowded dwellings, with bad sanitation and outbreaks of infectious diseases. Long periods of mass unemployment, bursts of inflation, and continued uncertainties made many wonder what had been gained in the Revolution after all.

The steady decline in the overall status of labor prompted the birth of both utopian-minded and class-oriented labor movements. Court decisions prohibited labor groups from engaging in formal collective action or "conspiracy" to strike. But many organizations formed nevertheless during the early decades of the new century to represent workers' rights.

Socialistic beliefs first appeared at this time among American working people. Self-taught intellectuals among them derived from the British economic theorist David Ricardo the idea that the workday could be divided, conceptually, between the portion where workers earned their own wages and the other portion where capitalists skimmed the profits. As good republicans, they also held a view of Equal Rights as the proper fruit of the Tree of Liberty — an idea not so far removed from Jacob Böhme's (and the Shakers') Tree of Life. The trunk they envisioned as pushing up through corruption and greed, its branches spreading out into democratic suffrage. When a group of Lynn, Massachusetts, operatives in the 1820s petitioned a textile manufacturer to spare a very real tree near their factory, they expressed the double function of the image: its graceful beauty as part of their own daily lives and reminder of liberty's legacy.

Beginning in the middle 1820s, the movement of labor parties — the first ever seen in the world — spread from New York to Philadelphia, Baltimore and elsewhere. "Past experience," one of their newspapers declared, "teaches us that we have nothing to hope from the aristocratic orders in society; and that our only course to pursue is, to send men of our own description, if we can, to the Legislature." Their demands included free public education, more equal taxation, abolition of capital punishment and imprisonment for debt, and the destruction of economic monopolies. Attacked furiously in most of the mainstream press as "rabble," the "mob," "dirty shirts," "infidels," "rag tag and bobtail," their ranks were actually composed of mostly illiterate and decayed priests, painters, glaziers, bricklayers and typographers.

Advanced thinkers within the workingmen's parties envisioned something like a socialistic and non-racist society at large. Robert Dale Owen and Frances Wright often hosted in their Hall of Science popular radical speakers who sounded themes of free land in the West. They reasoned that land, like light and air, rightly belonged to no one and

The Four Traitors,*

Who most infamously sold themselves to the Dorrites, for Office and Political Power.

Let us not reward Traitors, but with just indignation abandon them as " Scape- Goats," to their destiny—forever.

Charles Jackson.   Samuel F. Man.   James F. Simmons.   Lemuel H. Arnold.
Providence.   *Cumberland.*   *Johnston.*   *South Kingston.*

"O, heaven, that such companions thou'dst unfold;
And put in every honest hand a whip
To lash the rascals naked through the world"

APOLOGETIC NOTE. At the present, dark, dismal and degenerate period of our history—when a man regardless of himself and his God, will sell his birthright for a mess of pottage—when an obscure individual like Polk, is elected to the Presidency, and a pompous, self-conceited man like Jackson, to the Gubernatorial chair—and other Dorrites, too contemptible to mention among men, are appointed to fill different offices under the general government—when Foreigners, ignorant, barbarous and uncivilised, as the wild ass of the wilderness, pour in upon us like the plagues of Egypt, scourging and desolating the land—when the murderer, with brazen front and seared conscience, his hands still dropping with human blood, stalks abroad, at noonday, unpunished—when there seems to manifest itself (among a certain, ignorant, low-bred Class of radicals, disorganisers, abolitionists assuming to be jurists, conscientiously afraid of the gallows, and vile, illiterate and decayed priests, a nuisance in society,) such a criminal and unhallowed sympathy for felons of every description. when we would do something for the public good, and attempt to stay the torrent of moral and political profligacy, which sapping the foundation, seems to threaten the overthrow of our most valuable institutions—when the law is trampled under foot with impunity—and every thing around is anarchy and confusion—to those who are disposed to cavil or criticise, and it is very easy to do so, we would say, that as the Originals could no be induced to sit for their portraits, without large sums of gold or pledges of high political trust, they were necessarily, with much difficulty, sketched from recollection; it cannot therefore be reasonably supposed, that their features are precisely exact; but if they had sat to the artist, the expression of their faces, being as variable as their characters, what might seem a good likeness to day, would cease to be so to-morrow; and this we deem a full and sufficient apology.

*The conduct of these men; two of them in particular, towards Governor Fenner, who fearlessly and nobly, sustained the State, through all its recent difficulties, is so treacherous, base and execrable, and is so well understood by the intelligent part of the community, that it needs no comment.

Courtesy: Library of Congress

Conservatives' attack on followers of Thomas Dorr, leader of the unsuccessful Dorr Rebellion in Rhode Island in 1842, who fought to overthrow the restricted system of suffrage. Most of his followers were Irish-Americans.

After the early wave of Workingmen's party organizations, labor groups as such were rarely involved directly in national politics. This 1844 Henry Clay campaign ribbon, probably from Philadelphia, is an exception.

should be at the disposition of the user — an idea different from the plan to expand private property by expropriating Indian land. With mass resettlement of the urban poor into seemingly endless Western acreage, wages would rise, unemployment would lessen, and the condition of those remaining in the East would improve dramatically. Echoing ideas of the medieval communist uprisings, they refused to accept claims of private property as final, at least in the use of natural resources.

A handful of radical writers like Thomas Skidmore, author of *The Rights of Man to Property!* (1829), believed that Indians and African-Americans also had a right to their own land, as well as full civil rights. All should unite to expropriate land and the emerging factories from their wrongful owners under the laws of democracy and nature. George Henry Evans, influential editor of the *Working Man's Advocate*, insisted similarly that the West had room for settlers and Indians tribes but no room for speculators. He attacked the Indian Removal Act of 1830, declaring that the states had "no more right to jurisdiction over the territory of the Cherokees than we have to be the King of England." Evans also bitterly attacked slavery, and gloried in the 1831 slave rebellion of Nat Turner.

Not all Workingmen's party supporters shared Skidmore's and Evans's generous and visionary ideas. On the contrary, many responded to the promises of amelioration from the Democratic Party. President Andrew Jackson, who often claimed to represent the impoverished classes, actually made little effort to aid the urban poor, while he ordered the mass dispossession of Indians and supported the Southern slavocracy. Nevertheless, Jackson's supporters successfully borrowed one "Workie" plank after another while conspiring to keep the real workingmen's parties off the ballot. Soon, the nation's first labor political movement disappeared and with it most of working class radicalism.

Labor's radical activity turned in other directions. The slow process of creating protest movements and building trades organizations took up much energy. Women reformers, Christian egalitarians, and workers themselves angered at their conditions all pressed for legislation limiting the work day to 10 hours. Idealistic labor radicals guided the formation of unions of carpenters, bakers, soap makers, printers, cabinetmakers and others from Boston to Baltimore in the East to Cincinnati and St. Louis in the West, numbering perhaps 100,000 members in all. In Philadelphia of 1835, weavers and their allies ignited the first inclusive (or "general") strike in one city. This action compelled the federal government to implement the 10 hour day in the largest of government navy yards the next year and in all public works by 1840.

Early unionization was virtually destroyed, however, in the severe depression that followed the economic crisis of 1837. Quickly, unemployment swept the trades, and many former labor activists grew more interested in socialistic solutions. The 1840s marked a high point of labor participation in utopian movements. Socialists inspired by Charles Fourier's writings joined mechanics at the New England Working Men's Association's founding convention in 1844, urging limitation of hours to ten per day along with more political freedom and access to public lands. They also invited women operatives, for the first time, to join workingmen's ranks officially. The Association quickly weakened, however, as the issue of slavery and the prospect of civil war overwhelmed competing reform interests.

In Philadelphia, the combined collapse of the hand-loom weavers' livelihood, nativist "Know-Nothing" hysteria and brutal racist response to abolition-

Labor's first best-selling author, George Lippard. From his novel, New York: Its Upper Ten and Lower Million *(Cincinnati, 1853).*

GEORGE LIPPARD

The second best-selling radical author (after Tom Paine), Lippard was also a crusading labor activist, and a notable spiritualist mystic.

Born in 1822 outside Philadelphia, he imbibed the lore of the American Revolution and the utopian colonies close to his grandfather's farm. After preparation for the Methodist ministry, he returned to Philadelphia as a legal assistant, repulsed at the dishonesty of the professions. There, at age 19, he began writing for the *Spirit of the Times,* mostly imaginative fiction attacking the hypocrisies of the wealthy and the churches. Audiences of poor readers loved his fiction, written in weekly installments. *The Quaker City; or Monks of Monk Hall: A Romance of Philadelphia Life, Mystery and Crime* (1844) was a wild success, based upon a real incident of a Philadelphian acquitted of murdering a gentleman who dishonored his sister. Over the next decade, it sold perhaps a half-million copies.

Following this success, Lippard wrote a series of novels based on patriotic and transhistoric legends of freedom struggles over the ages. In 1848, he founded a reform weekly, *Quaker City,* and the next year founded a semi-secret labor society, Brotherhood of the Union. The Brotherhood expanded to more than 140 chapters in 19 states and *Quaker City* attained a circulation of 10,000 as Lippard championed Fourierism, woman's rights, abolitionism, rights of Indian Peoples, and a drastic revision of capitalism. After the death of his daughter and beloved wife, Lippard lost heart, and died not long before his thirty-second birthday, in 1854. Lippard had done more in a few years than many great reformers achieved in a lifetime. The novels of the "American Eugene Sue" were read for generations after.

ism all limited reform activities. But Philadelphia was also a center for the heavily-pictorial "story" tabloids that gave the lower-class public the equivalent in serialized fiction of later radio or television for only a few cents. Here also flourished the popular theatrical figure of the "B'hoy," volunteer fireman and neighborhood tough guy eager for a fist-fight and resentful toward the rich (and usually just as resentful toward women's rights advocates or abolitionists). Caricatures of "Mose," this young Irish-American, appeared frequently in local theater programs and the story paper.

This set of class-drawn images by popular artists contrasted dramatically with the contemporary work of prestigious painters, illustrators or engravers, who all saw such lower class characters only as vicious idlers, unwilling to get an honest job and prone to mischief or violence. Unlike the European (especially French) artists who tried to encourage reform through showing the misery of urban dwellers, American artists tended to see the city itself as a source of corruption and its depraved inhabitants as proof of the degradation that expanded immigration had inspired. Genre painters and satirical caricaturists who sought a sympathetic lower-class character were likely to choose a "Down East" Yankee farmer of New England, a frontiersman, or even a slave working in the countryside or on the plantation.

THE HOME OF THE ASTOR HOUSE BEGGAR.

The Indignity of Labor: Beggers as seen by the press. From The Old Brewery and the New Mission House at the Five Points *(1854).*

Courtesy: American Social History Project, Hunter College

Author George Lippard, America's first best-selling radical novelist, created in words a very different picture of lower class life. Lippard described the rich as morally corrupt and the impoverished Philadelphia factory women (like his own sister) as possessing "more talent, more loveliness, more principle than all the darlings of aristocratic wealth." Lippard also envisioned the revenge of the repressed: in *Monks of Monk Hall* a servant dreams of a future Philadelphia with the stars and stripes replaced by a flag of chains with manacles, flying above columns of white and black slaves marching and chanting "Hurrah for Slavery." Suddenly dream turns to nightmare as dead soldiers from the Revolution rise out of their graves, plunging the city into Hell. Here again horror was used literarily against the pretensions of American progress.

Lippard's later novel, *New York: Its Upper Ten and Lower Million* (1853), depicted a radical, self-taught shoemaker learning socialism while working at his bench. He soon glimpsed the orgies carried on by the rich. The "Midnight Queen" of sexual debauchery turns out to be his own childhood sweetheart, earlier driven by trickery into licentiousness. He watches as the wickedest among them are placed on trial for economic exploitation by a subterranean "people's tribunal" and he pleads with the middle classes to help the poor. In the novel's conclusion, socialist Arthur Demoyne leads the masses from the East to the wilderness West, where a utopian hope remains.

Lippard's 1852 funeral in Philadelphia brought hundreds of public mourners, including those local radicals who loved him best: German-American workers

Women labor reformers were active in New England from the 1820s to the 1890s. Lillie Chace Wyman, daughter of abolitionists and woman's rights reformers, was active for decades as a labor journalist and short-story writer in Rhode Island. From Lillie B.C. Wyman and Arthur Crawford Wyman, Elizabeth Buffum Chace *(1914).*

Both, Courtesy: Scott Molloy

Women are seen as victims of poverty, of unions and of "communists," in drawings by Harper's Weekly's *famous cartoonist, Thomas Nast, 1871.*

Courtesy: American Social History Project, Hunter College

Illustration of a carpetweavers' strike in Philadelphia, shows women taking the lead.

Courtesy: State Historical Society of Wisconsin

Masthead of Le Socialiste, *organ of the French-speaking members of the First International in America, 1872.*

Courtesy: Scott Molloy

Early strike poster by textile mill workers in northern Rhode Island.

organized through the socialistic *Arbeiterbund* and associated fraternal societies. A considerable minority of German immigrants had learned their trades in the Old World as carpenters, weavers, cabinet-makers, cigar makers, bakers or tailors. In these trades, radicalism of various kinds flourished. Escapees from tyranny, carrying with them a rich tradition of communitarianism, they acted as a leaven within American labor and politics at large.

During the 1840s-60s, these German-Americans formed the shock troops of working class support for abolitionism, free land and other issues. In greatly disproportionate numbers, they marched off to the war against slavery and heroically spilled their blood to free the nation. But they did not favorably impress the growing legions of commercial artists who had watched their public meetings and social life with suspicion and fear.

Nativism played a key role here. If all but a few commercial engravers and painters had earlier ignored the urban poor or seen them as potentially dangerous, by the 1850s artistic prints of public meetings showed "foreigners" as suspiciously German, with their meerschaum pipes, beer mugs and thick mustaches. Soon popular artists had identified the immigrant types — drunken Irish, German anarchists and rapacious Jews — that the illustrated newspapers such as *Harper's* and *Frank Leslie's* and satirical magazines like *Puck* and *Judge* would use to vilify blue-collar radicals for the rest of the century.

Nevertheless, German-American radicals constructively laid the basis for modern-day unionism in many trades. When a National Labor Union formed for a few years after the Civil War, German tradesmen were among its staunchest members. They also made themselves the link between American workers and European socialists. They successfully nudged N.L.U. founder William Sylvis into direct contact with Karl Marx's International

Workingmen's Association in London. Sylvis had already concluded from his own experience that the wage system was at fault for poverty: "As long as we continue to work for wages...so long will be subjected to...all the evils of which we complain." He urged, instead, industrial cooperatives, a voluntary practice by which craftsmen could invest in their own equipment and prevent the downfall of their status. He had adopted an American version of German socialism.

This American style of socialism soon had a wide popular following. Ordinary workers composing "song-poems," often lengthy verse in their union newspapers, wrote hundreds of stanzas about the "true religion" of cooperation and the "false religion" of dog-eat-dog capitalism. Often they combined complaints of inequality with a vision of a harmonious cosmos whose teachings humankind perversely resisted. Iron-worker Michael McGovern, the "Puddler Poet" and Christian socialist, sometime union official and beloved versifier for forty years, typified those who insisted their beautiful world was destined for better:

> My church accepts the teachings of
>   The Nazarene of old;
> It places social truths above
>   Men's lusts and greed for gold.
> With heaven's glory beaming round
>   It's one great earthly pew,
> Where God's theologies abound
>   I grasp its truths anew.

One of the most respected labor reformers of the day, George McNeill of Massachusetts, carried a similar message. Leader of the International Labor Union, which brought Marxist trade unionists and Yankee reformers together at the end of the 1870s to unionize the underpaid (and largely female) textile work force, McNeill later published *The Labor Movement: The Problem of To-Day*, labor's exemplary effort at public explanation. He concluded:

> In this movement of laborers toward equity, we will find a new revelation of the Old Gospel, when the Golden Rule of Christ shall measure the relations of men in all their duties toward their fellows...Though the Mammon-worshipers may cry, "Crucify Him! Crucify Him!" the promise of the prophet and the poet shall be fulfilled...by the free acceptance of the gospel that all men are of one blood. Then the new Pentecost will come, when every man shall have according to his needs.

The Knights of Labor nearly approached that goal. Founded among carpet weavers in Philadelphia, the Knights spread slowly during the 1870s, and then took off with a sudden start in early 1885 when Western workers won a

THE GREAT MEETING OF FOREIGNERS IN THE PARK.—*Page* 197.

Workers seen as drunken "foreigners." From The Crisis, or the Enemies of America Unmasked *(1855).*

spectacular victory over the Southern Pacific Railroad owned by Wall Street manipulator Jay Gould (known popularly as the "worst man in the world"). By 1886, perhaps a half million workers of nearly every variety had joined the Knights. In many small industrial towns, they nearly replaced city government and were often seen by sympathetic local officials as the great democratic movement so long awaited. In a scattering of factories, Knights members seemed likewise to take over the day-to-day management of production, making decisions after democratic discussions.

This was the apex of labor republicanism, an ideal nurtured since at least the Workingmen's Party days in the 1820s. Extending the principle of self-government from voting to every day life, especially to the economic sphere, the Knights envisioned a free society as a republic of ordinary citizens. As a labor organization they represented not only the members of any particular trade but every worker in a district and, by extension, everyone willing to join (only lawyers and liquor dealers were constitutionally excluded).

The Knights of Labor easily surged past all previous labor movements by virtue of their membership including Mexican-Americans, African-Americans and women. In southern cities, especially industrialized Richmond, Virginia, blacks flocked into Knights locals as the first reform organization they could safely join since their abandonment by Northern troops and politicians in 1876. Naturally, they hoped that the Knights would dramatically change all Southern society and institute a cooperative labor system. In the Southwest, where whites increasingly grabbed land farmed by Mexicans for generations, armed uprisings had occasionally burst out and been brutal-

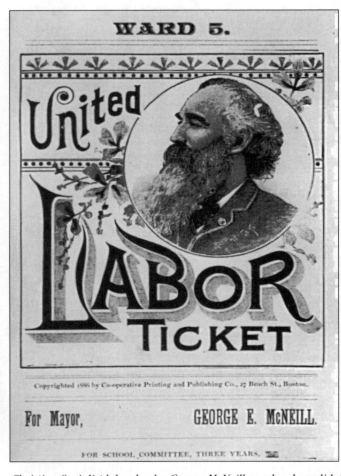

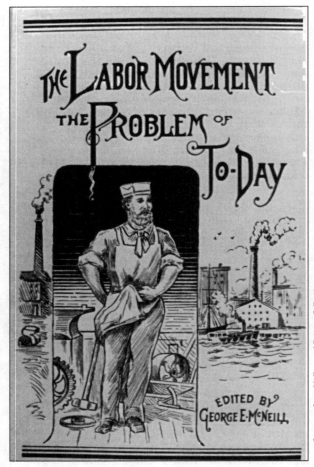

Courtesy: Scott Molloy and Private Collection

Christian Socialist labor leader George McNeill as a local candidate in Boston, 1886. His 1887 classic volume.

ly suppressed. The "Cortina War" in 1859, for instance, saw an army of 1,200 Mexicans temporarily capture the town of Brownsville, Texas. Many individual bandits, some of them rising to mythic status in the songs and memories of the people, expropriated Anglo property, avenged people wronged, and otherwise made trouble for the law.

In the 1880s the Knights offered a labor counterpart to *La Gorras Blancas* ("white caps," for their costumes) who mobilized across New Mexico to block the land-grabbing of the gringos and the railroads by cutting through fences and posting warning signs. Mexicano Knights, too, wanted much more than ameliorization of their working conditions: They envisioned a society organized along different lines with the return of "lost," semi-cooperative institutions.

While African-Americans and Mexican-Americans joined by the thousands, women joined by the tens of thousands, especially in the Northeast where whole factories of textile and rug operatives came over to the Knights with

THE TROUBLESOME RACE QUESTION

Courtesy: American Social History Project, Hunter College

"Knights Embrace All": Frank Farrell, "colored delegate," given a place of pride at the 1886 Richmond convention of the Knights of Labor, a most controversial move in the contemporary South. From Frank Leslie's Illustrated Newspaper, *October 16, 1886.*

Private Collection

Convention Ribbon of the Knights of Labor, at the Temple of Labor, Minneapolis.

TERENCE POWDERLY

Foremost leader of the Knights of Labor and symbolic conscience of labor republicanism, Powderly was also the most important Irish-American radical until Elizabeth Gurley Flynn and Mike Quill.

Born at midcentury in Scranton, Pennsylvania, Powderly worked on the railroads, joining the union at his first opportunity. The following year, he was elected secretary, later becoming president – and the first fired, for leading a strike. By 1874, after much traveling, he had become a Knight of Labor, rose to local leadership, went to summer school and became an organizer for the Knights and the Greenback Labor Party. He was elected mayor of Scranton in 1878 on the Labor Reform (some said, "Molly Maguire") ticket. The next year he succeeded Uriah Stephens as Grand Master Workman, becoming effectively the national head of the Knights.

His Irish Catholic background and political skills had helped him greatly. He was a regular reader of the *Irish World and Industrial Liberator,* also a member of the Ancient Order of Hibernians and Clan na Gael, the secret American branch of the Irish Revolutionary Brotherhood sworn to get the English out of Ireland by any means necessary. Irish Land Leagues, supporting the homeland movement, became the seedbed for future Knights of Labor locals. Americans of all types would join the Knights but Irish-Americans remained the primary body of membership.

By the early 1880s a general sense of unrest plummeted the Knights into public controversy and triggered a sudden increase of members. In many working class neighborhoods, portraits of Powderly (a strict non-drinker himself) could be seen in taverns and other public places. Indeed, probably no other American labor hero ever appeared in as many popular prints of various kinds. He spoke widely and incessantly against violence and also against the "wage system" as unjust, destined to be replaced by cooperatives.

Powderly was snared, however, in seething contradictions. Businessmen and the business press condemned the Knights as a weapon of anarchy. Despite some sympathetic bishops, deeply conservative Church leaders rightly suspected the Knights of radicalism and condemned (or refused to support) strikers. Eager to disprove them, and terrified at the outbreak of strikes in 1886, Powderly disavowed the Haymarket anarchists and drove radicals from the organization's leadership. In short order the Knights faded, and Powderly himself disappeared into obscurity. Others with whom he had worked closely, such as "Mother" Mary Jones, went on to lead movements in the twentieth century.

enthusiasm. Occasionally, as in Providence, Rhode Island, cooperative day-care centers appeared alongside Knights locals, administered with the assistance of Christian socialist ministers and their congregations.

For Irish-Americans, the largest single constituency of the Knights, their leader Terence Powderly became a supremely important national and international hero. His tours across the country aroused sympathy in many remarkable quarters. Frances Willard, President of the Woman's Christian Temperance Union, was said to keep a photograph of him on her desk, and people whispered that they were lovers (an entirely fanciful rumor).

Powderly inherited from his predecessors yet another quality of the Knights: A secret ritualism to bond members with each other. Like characters out of a George Lippard novel who envisioned a labor fraternity of all peoples, extending across the ages and meeting secretly from era to

Private Collection

This card picturing Terence Powderly, one of a series, shows him as the working people's saint.

MISS WILLARD IN THE DRAWING ROOM, THE COTTAGE, REIGATE, ENGLAND, 1895

Temperance leader and socialist Frances Willard. From her autobiography, Glimpses of Fifty Years, 1838-1889 *(1889)*

THE GOSPEL OF THE KNIGHTS OF LABOR.
"We work not selfishly for ourselves alone, but extend the hand of fellowship to all mankind."—*Mr. Powderly, at Richmond.*

"The Gospel of the Knights of Labor," by Joseph Keppler, Puck *, October 13, 1886. Contrary to his rhetoric, Powderly is shown offering the back of his hand to capital and "scab" labor alike.*

FRANCES WILLARD

Widely known as the Woman of the Century (that is, the nineteenth century), Frances Willard led the most powerful women's organization the world had ever known: the Women's Christian Temperance Union. She infused that nominally conservative organization with a reform zeal and herself grew into socialist convictions before her early death.

Growing up in Wisconsin Territory during the middle of the century, Willard was a tomboy and the daughter of a territorial legislator. She took a college degree at North Western Female College in 1859, taught at Gennesse Wesleyan Seminary, and returned to become dean of women and professor of English and Art at Northwestern University, which had absorbed the women's college. Abandoning an educational career, she became the chairwoman of the Illinois temperance movement.

She immediately indicated that her interests lay far beyond temperance, a convenient starting-place because it allowed women to gather without embarrassment or public attack. Elected president of the national W.C.T.U. in 1879, she popularized the "Do Everything Campaign," an appeal for fundamental reform based upon women's qualities and energies. An immensely popular lecturer, she avidly supported woman suffrage, joined the Knights of Labor (rumors falsely attributed to her and Terence Powderly, both unmarried, a secret romance), and sought unsuccessfully during the early 1890s to combine Populists, labor movements and temperance advocates into a great radical coalition.

She was moved intellectually by reading Edward Bellamy's *Looking Backward.* She urged W.C.T.U. members to join Bellamy Nationalist Clubs, telling them that "in each Christian there exists a socialist; and in every socialist a Christian." By the middle 1890s she urged socialistic principles upon the W.C.T.U. membership, declaring if she had her life to live over she would dedicate it to socialism. By this time, her health had begun to collapse, and she died in 1898. But socialist women organizers, many of them former temperance activists, could declare that Willard herself "preached the Debs doctrine" and that they merely followed her teachings.

Serialized romance novel of misery and love within the Knights of Labor. Many popular works at the time considered labor's plight, but few took women as the central characters. *From* Family Story Paper, June 30, 1884.

Courtesy: Scott Molloy

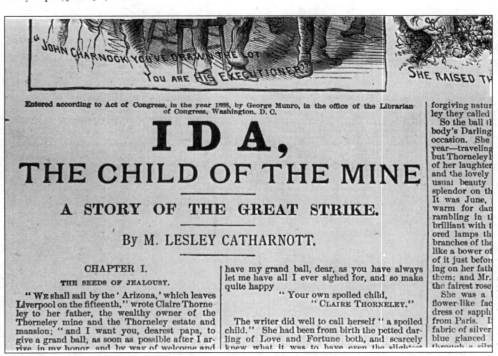

Courtesy: Scott Molloy

This serialized novel offers a familiar depiction of women and children as martyrs to labor conditions and conflicts. Fireside Companion, *September 29, 1888.*

era, the Knights drew mysterious symbols around new members, swore them to secrecy in oaths, and otherwise made them feel they had entered an inner sanctum. Many of them were members of Irish-American nationalist organizations and familiar with similar rituals. But for others, including racial minorities and women, the ritualism had a unique psychological uplifting effect. They had entered (as others later would join socialist and communist organizations) a great brother- and sisterhood. Like many lodge members of other types of organizations, they had their own ribbons and paraphernalia, their own special sense of mission.

Finally, the Knights and the hopes they raised made a fabulous if brief impression upon American popular life. Labor advertisements show that consumers could wear "Eight Hour" shoes, smoke "Eight Hour" cigars or go to bed on "Eight Hour" sheets, mirroring the Knights' demands for a shorter work-day. Deceased members had joined a "higher form of association." The Knights also created their own recreation halls for young people. Readers of "dime" novels and the mass culture press avidly followed serialized stories about the Knights. Whatever their failures, the Knights made themselves part of the emerging culture of modern society.

Strikes and Labor Processions

Strikes and Labor Processions

The lithography process, growing steadily more sophisticated by the Civil War, was used to great advantage for the popular literature about the war and the society emerging from it. Illustrators for newspapers and magazines developed cross-hatching and other techniques to manipulate the pen and ink and pencil drawings of artists (and so did artists themselves, in some cases). The distinctive style of the great Thomas Nast, the German-born illustrator for *Harper's*, was the epitome of mass culture artwork.

Increasing numbers of artist-technicians used a newer chalk process, either scraping a design onto a chalk-coated plate or using a liquid to draw directly on the plate. Finally, the photo-engraving or "line cut" — used widely by the 1880s — allowed the artist to work directly on cardboard, with the completed etchings then photographed and printed. As the technical costs of chromolithography (the use of metallic-based inks and certain refinements in the printing process) decreased, beautifully printed color images also became increasingly available to the average person. The familiar demeaning and scurrilous treatment of villains and scapegoats could now be presented in vivid color. Politicians and radicals continued to be favorite targets: the former as corruptors of the American dream, the latter as un-American subversives.

Women shoemakers in Lynn, Massachusetts strike over the declining conditions caused by employers' use of steadily more sophisticated shoemaking equipment. Frank Leslie's Illustrated Newspaper, *March 7, 1860.*

Courtesy: American Social History Project, Hunter College

These technical advances and the swift artistic adaptation that both inspired and followed them made possible detailed and panoramic images of large scenes, especially those with a sea of human faces. The eruption of labor's mass demonstrations and the organization of a labor movement offered the artist an opportunity usually available in America only for political campaigns and natural disasters. The resulting images were not always sympathetic. But they were usually attentive to the details of scene, such as banners and placards, frequently also to expressions and gestures. Altogether, they provided readers a welcome alternative to the stolid portrait with its implied personification of a large movement reduced to the image of a single personality.

Thus one can easily see the sheer visual respectability, for instance, given by the artist to mostly female shoemakers in 1860 in Lynn, Massachusetts who declared their determination not be made into wage slaves. That sympathetic image is exceptional among contemporary prints about labor issues in general but common when artists treated Yankee populations. However degraded by poverty or tempted by radicals, these common folk seemed to radiate a certain lower-class dignity, and in women and children a sympathetic pathos. Even the labor parade, undoubtedly full of the foreign-born, could be seen as an extension of the normal big-city parade scene, with marchers turning their benevolent and fraternal affiliations into rightful claims for justice.

During moments of perceived social crisis, a dark side to the lithographer's talent regularly emerged, usually with semi-racial undertones. The appearance of "hard times" after the Panic of 1873 brought a half-decade of severe crisis and great working class restlessness, including widespread demands for food and work. If likely to caricature railroad magnates as wicked manipulators, illustrated newspapers like *Frank Leslie's* and *Harper's* tended to portray an equally depraved and vicious Irish working class population. With still more meanness, they pictured brute or child-like Southern blacks deserving and even welcoming the return of white rule — Thomas Nast's support for Radical Reconstruction quickly became the exception.

"Communists," which generally meant German-American radicals, were seen by lithographers as conspirators raising the Red Flag against the Stars and Stripes, and urging the rabble to repeat the crimes of the 1870 Paris Commune. (For socialists everywhere, conversely, the Commune was the holiest of

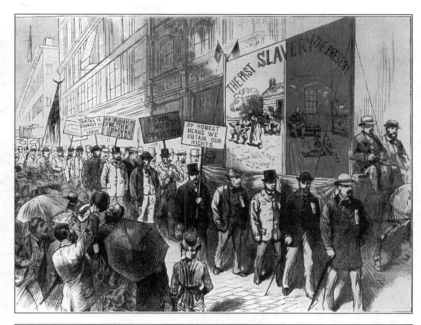

Both, Courtesy: American Social History Project, Hunter College

Labor's dignity is on display in these working people's parades. Frank Leslie's Illustrated Newspaper, *September 13, 1884 and September 30, 1871, respectively.*

nized West. Dependent upon an almost fugitive status, they were destroyed by the development of regional governments and formal property lines.

Free Love, interpreted in various ways, meanwhile permeated the new evocations of freedom in the last decades of the nineteenth century. Popularized by Victoria Woodhull, the idea of love free of legal ties appealed to "free thinkers" like Lois Waisbrooker, Ezra Heywood and Moses Harmon. They published periodicals like *Lucifer the Light Bearer*, mailed out pamphlets on birth control and endured the persecutions of the federal government and the Comstock Act (1873). Perhaps the most remarkable of these writer-editors was Robert Reitzel, publisher of the weekly newspaper from Detroit, *Der arme Teufel* (1884-1902). The most admired German-American literary stylist of the day, Reitzel was a former minister who turned to "free thought," condemning authoritarian religious authorities, anti-Semitism, nationalism and militarism. A charismatic traveling speaker, he also encouraged bohemianism and defended homosexuality (at the time, a very risky political act).

Walt Whitman, by contrast, only hinted of his own homosexual inclinations. But more than any other single figure of democratic optimism, he lifted popular expectation to a faith in American possibility to move ever further in the direction of freedom. Whitman found his radical amanuensis in his literary executor and chief promoter, Horace Traubel.

Son of a German-American craft worker and his Jewish wife, Traubel the boy met Whitman the aging figure on a street in Camden, New Jersey. They "grew into each other," as Whitman related, and by the time the poet entered his last months, Traubel was on hand, offering companionship and recording every word and gesture. In *The Beautiful Death of Walt Whitman*, Traubel observed that Whitman's exit from the world was marked by a keen awareness about his place in the universe. With two colleagues,

Courtesy: Library of Congress

Horace Traubel, Whitman's literary executor and publisher of The *Conservator. In the newspaper's Philadelphia office, c. 1900.*

In the most violent labor conflict to that time, railroad strikers and their supporters set fire to the roundhouse in Pittsburgh, Pennsylvania. Frank Leslie's Illustrated Newspaper, *August 4, 1877.*

memories, evoking images of immense courage and self-sacrifice). In real life, ordinary French working people had taken government into their own hand until crushed with great bloodshed. Few American socialists urged violent uprising of any kind.

In the economic wisdom of the post-Civil War era, the employer possessed the proper privilege and authority to change conditions of the work such as drastically lowering wages and laying off workers for long periods of time. In most commercial artists' eyes and pens, the employee had no legitimate protest other than leaving the job. Blocking the entrance to the work-site so that strike-breakers could not replace strikers was a denial of sacred property rights and individual rights (those of the strike-breakers, of course) as well. Respectable opinion took no particular notice of the support that the local small-business community often gave toward strikes against national corporations, or of the Christian spirit with which many strike leaders articulated their collective demands.

The great railroad strike of 1877 brought these impulses to a head. When shutdowns spontaneously broke out in West Virginia, sparking mass demonstrations against railroads and sometimes expropriations of train cargoes by hungry mobs, a caricature campaign went into high gear. Some artists were struck by the sheer grandeur of the scene, such as the burning of a round-house outside Pittsburgh or the

Courtesy: American Social History Project

Pennsylvania — Retreat of the Philadelphia troops through Pittsburgh, on their way from the round house to the U.S. Arsenal — "Reading prayers over the dying early on Sunday morning, July 22nd," Frank Leslie's Illustrated Newspaper, *August 4, 1877*

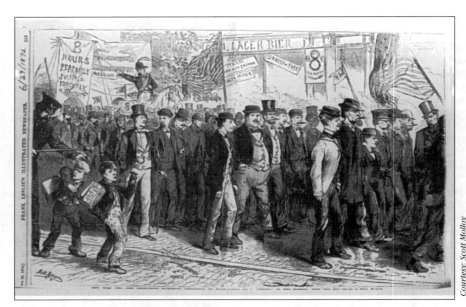

An Eight-Hour Day demonstration in New York City. Frank Leslie's Illustrated Weekly, *June 29, 1872.*

"King Debs," whose union followers peacefully shut down railroads west of Chicago. Harper's Weekly, *July 14, 1894.*

EUGENE V. DEBS

The closest thing to a folk-hero ever produced by the modern political Left, Eugene Victor Debs was named (by his French-born parents) after novelists Eugene Sue and Victor Hugo. He grew up in Terre Haute, Indiana, left high school to become a locomotive fireman, and won state office as a Democrat. As a national officer of the Brotherhood of Locomotive Firemen, he watched the conditions of the craft union railroaders decline and in 1892 he founded the all-inclusive American Railway Union. This union grew to 150,000 members before being crushed for supporting the Pullman Strikers in Chicago in 1894.

Spending his fortieth birthday in jail, Debs emerged a committed socialist and the greatest hero of American radicals since abolition days. For a few years he helped lead the Social Democracy of America, a utopian organization seeking to colonize the west, and then moved on with many of his followers to the socialist movement proper. In 1900 he ran for president, the first of five times, serving as symbol of an Americanized socialism. His "Red Special" touring locomotive, his famous heart-warming speeches, his sentimentalism and class-conscious courage reached far beyond the socialist and labor movements to middle America. But at best, in his 1912 race, only six percent of voters could bring themselves to abandon their regular affiliation and vote for him. Observers noted that millions of his immigrant and women sympathizers lacked the vote or were discouraged from participation.

Resisting the entry of the United States into World War I, Debs delivered a bold peace address in Canton, Onion, in 1918, knowing it could endanger him. Sentenced at age 63 to ten years in prison, Debs ran for president in 1920 from his jail cell. He received over 900,000 votes. Although released from prison the next year, he suffered from declining health. At his death in 1926, children and grown folks cried in the streets of urban neighborhoods, Jewish to Slovene, little Oklahoma hamlets, and most of all in his home town of Terre Haute. Neighbors who had never been socialists testified that the kindly Debs had been born, perhaps, a thousand years ahead of his time.

Army regulars marching on domestic enemies as they had on the Southern rebellion and on Indian uprisings. More often, though, they depicted half-human faces of Irish mobs with low foreheads and ape-like jaws, or they invented weapons such as guns and clubs when the real crowds had few or none. Soldiers were more far likely than civilians to be seen by the artists as the victims of armed conflict in which hundreds of unarmed Americans were actually shot at point-blank range and dozens killed.

After the passing of crisis and the emergence of rather conservative labor leaders, a certain visual calm returned. The newly formed American Federation of Labor's craft workers, especially those pleading their case with sober reasonableness, could again be seen sympathetically. The "girl striker," for the first time offered as a widespread image of youth entering life's fray, approximated in some small degree the reality of women's activity within the Knights of Labor. If hardly photographic in detail, contemporary lithographs captured details of clothing, also the sharp gender division between women strikers on the one hand and their male labor leaders on the other.

The craft unions themselves, in particular those non-German ones little influenced by socialistic ideas, naturally sought to consolidate their respectable image. Images of respectability quickly turned to conservative rage, however. The honorable and long-honored steel-rollers, craft laborers par excellence with the strongest craft union in America suffered a swift demotion. Prosperous and conservative, these Amalgamated Iron and Steel Workers unionists had not counted upon the determination of steel barons to replace them with cheaper labor as soon as technology made it possible. Mainstream magazines, frightened once again by economic depression and doubts

AN AWFUL BATTLE AT HOMESTEAD, PA.

The Homestead Strike, pitting state militia and private armies of the steel barons against formerly well-paid craft workers and their supporters, was a virtual civil war lost by labor's proudest union. National Police Gazette, *July 6, 1892.*

Courtesy: American Social History Project, Hunter College

about capitalism's future, rushed to condemn the strikers, as artists dipped their pens in acid to make strikers appear the source of violence and their supporting wives or daughters into Madame Defarge-style harridans urging bloody revolution.

NOTICE.

Desiring that our employees should understand the situation between the National Knit Goods Manufacturers' Association and the Knights of Labor, we submit the following statement:

The history of the labor question as it affects our industry briefly is, that operators in the various mills organized themselves together and joined the organization known as the Knights of Labor. Out of that organization there came unwarranted interference with the Knit Goods Manufacturers as to who should and who should not be employed in the mills. The Manufacturers, finding that such an association of employees apparently supported such interference, were obliged to associate themselves together for the purpose of mutual protection by all lawful means against such interference with the control and management of their business. In March, 1886, at Cohoes, N. Y., an extended discussion and negotiation of the questions at issue between the employees and manufacturers was had, which finally resulted in an agreement duly executed March 31, 1886, between the Executive Committee of the National Knit Goods Manufacturers' Association and the National Executive Committee of Knights of Labor represented by T. B. Barry, in which it was agreed as follows, viz: "The Manufacturers are at liberty to employ or not employ, discharge or not discharge whom they wish, whether they be Knights of Labor or not Knights of Labor, as they deem best."

That agreement, as we supposed, definitely settled the main principle for which the National Knit Goods Manufacturers' Association was formed and established the only rule upon which manufacturers can carry on their business; but to our disappointment, as early as September 1886, the said contract was broken and the principle thereby established was disregarded by the Knights of Labor at Amsterdam, who refused to work in the mill of Schuyler & Blood unless they could dictate who should work and who should not work in that mill, discriminating not only against non-union men but also against those who were Knights of Labor; and although the manufacturers have used the utmost endeavor to settle the said difficulty and have visited personally Mr. Powderly, the Grand Master Workman of the Knights of Labor, and the National Executive Committee of the Knights of Labor, including T. B. Barry, who negotiated the said contract, and have submitted to them the situation and the said action of the Knights of Labor in violation of their contract; whereupon it was fully admitted by the said authorities that the said action of the Knights of Labor was wrong and in violation of their agreement; and those authorities have so informed the Knights of Labor at Amsterdam and advised them through their local master workman, P. H. Cummins, to return to work and preserve their contract; still they refuse to work and insist upon their said unwarrantable dictation.

Now, although we greatly regret being obliged to sever our connection with any of our employees and have hoped that an amicable settlement of this issue might be effected for the good of all, still we cannot submit the control of our business to anyone besides ourselves, nor can we expose the operation of our mills or the direction of our business affairs to the interference of any outside association of persons or the individual members of such an association; therefore notice is given that on and after October 16, 1886, we will not employ in this mill or in its operation any person who is a member of the Knights of Labor, and any and all persons who at the time above stated are in our employ and who are members of the Knights of Labor and intend to or do continue to be such Knights, are hereby notified that they are discharged from our employment.

Dated Oct. 16, 1886.

TITUS SHEARD & CO.

A New York State employer breaks its agreement with the Knights and threatens to fire any members, 1886.

Labor Radicals and Reformers

THE MECHANICS' BELL.

The socialist movement, mostly German-American in composition, attempted to reach Irish-Americans on issues of English oppression.

Courtesy: State Historical Society of Wisconsin

Labor Radicals and Reformers

Images of radicals in the radical press itself presented an interestingly mixed message. At times, this press sought to protect the movement by establishing a legitimacy and even respectability; at other times and in other publications, radical artists threw off all guises in order to make revolutionary claims upon society as vividly as pictures could offer.

The development of both types of images was rooted in the experience and traditions of the German-American radicals. Their gymnastic societies (*Turnvereine*), politically progressive German-language schools, singing and theatrical societies constituted the first radical labor counter-culture. These institutions not only laid the basis for the modern labor movement but the modern socialist movement as well. The *Arbeiterbund* or Workers Union, founded by tailor-agitator Wilhelm Weitling and supported in Weitling's newspaper (*Die Republik der Arbeiter*, the first non-utopian socialist paper in America) was the first well-organized socialist labor group. They called a national convention of German-American labor in Philadelphia in 1850. Not surprisingly, the *Arbeiterbund* also served as a clearing house for German immigrant educational and cultural associations.

By the late 1860s and early 1870s, a younger generation of immigrants set themselves the task of spreading socialist ideas into dozens of German-American neighborhoods in cities like Chicago, Milwaukee, Cincinnati and Pittsburgh. Socialist papers like the *Vorbote* of Chicago achieved long life by cultivating union locals, leisure societies, and businesses such as breweries and cigar-makers which catered to their audience. For a long time, indeed, advertisements for beer or tobacco items made in unionized plants were the most "visual" aspect, beyond the masthead, of these publications.

During the 1870s Depression, when *Harpers* and other magazines and newspapers employed small armies of skilled craftsmen to recreate the tones of artistic pen-work in subtle shadings and with intricate cross-hatching, prestigious illustrators such as Nast cursed the same socialists in detail. Preying upon the worker's weakness, his empty belly and credulous expectations of steady work, they schemed for anarchy. In this respect the drawings of Nast, who was quick to see corruption in the era's politicians, reflected the mentality of the middle class at large: Skeptical but also intensely materialistic, concerned for social order, eager to believe the worst about the foreign born

Private Collection

Vorbote, *the first of the long-lasting weekly newspapers of German-American socialists, was founded in 1873 in Chicago.*

and eager for cultural images that reaffirmed its own prejudices. *Puck* and other pictorial magazines had somewhat more complicated versions of similar views. But German socialists were forever the "tramps" in these eyes and pens, guilty unless proven innocent.

German-American radicals had their own somewhat particularistic visions. Many of the craftsmen were losing their skilled positions to the growth of mass production techniques in American industry. They often felt a deep nostalgia for the relative freedom of pre-industrial artisans of centuries earlier. Their love for nature, cultivated by classic German authors, carried the same idea further. The Spring, with all nature reborn, brought hope into dark sorrows. Nature's wonders carried secrets which could free the soul, if only the confinement of class society's greed and selfishness could be shed — but not likely in their own lifetimes. Melancholy, a sense of the immigrant far from home, was also present; perhaps America had no place for them after all. German poetry rather than pictures mainly carried these impressions forward, although a thin stream of complementary visuals (in the annual *Pionier Kalendar*, the calendar of the daily *New Yorker Volkszeitung*) appeared, mainly reprints of Old Country scenes and events.

For moments, German socialists surged politically past these conceptual limits. During 1869-70, when they had joined with the United States branches of the International Workingmen's Association (or "First International" as it was later known), they successfully organized to provide international labor solidarity and socialist propaganda. Small sections of French refugees from the Paris Commune and various reformers

Courtesy: Ted Watts

The Tompkins Square Riot, 1874, provoked by extreme hunger and the brutal treatment of demonstrators by New York police, shown unsympathetically. Irish-Americans are notably caricatured as sub-human, a common treatment in newspaper illustrations of the 1860s-80s. Frank Leslie's Illustrated Newspaper, *January 31, 1874.*

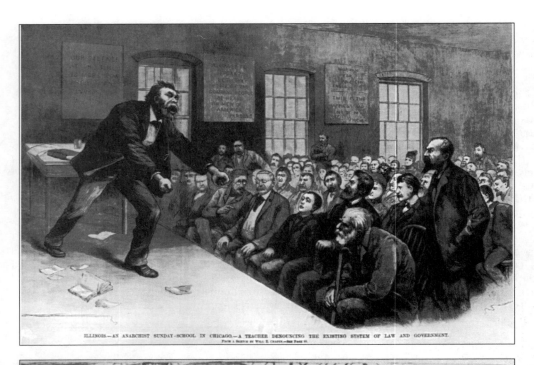

ILLINOIS—AN ANARCHIST SUNDAY-SCHOOL IN CHICAGO.—A TEACHER DENOUNCING THE EXISTING SYSTEM OF LAW AND GOVERNMENT.
FROM A SKETCH BY WILL E. CHAPIN—SEE PAGE 82.

NEW YORK CITY.—JOHN MOST, THE ANARCHIST, ADDRESSING A MEETING OF SYMPATHIZERS AT COOPER INSTITUTE, APRIL 6TH.
FROM A SKETCH BY A STAFF ARTIST.—SEE PAGE 102.

(Top) Hostile depictions of anarchists: an unknown Chicagoan, from Frank Leslie's Illustrated Newspaper, *March 16, 1889, and (Bottom) the thespian-agitator, Johann Most, from the same publication, April 16, 1887.*

Courtesy: American Social History Project, Hunter College and Scott Molloy

also joined, among others. New York house painter Joseph DeJacques coined the word *Libertaire*, and the presses of the French exiles, among the American First Internationalists, printed for the first time the composition, *L'Internationale*, destined to become the anthem of world socialism. But differences in political assumptions and perhaps just as much of styles proved overwhelming. The German-Americans' leaders could not tolerate Americans' emphasis on women's rights or on spiritualism. They had trouble also cooperating with the handful of militant Irish-American socialists, whose leader P.J. McGuire guided the massive 1873 march of the unemployed in New York City.

The First International fell into such internecine struggle in Europe that Karl Marx himself meanwhile urged removal of its headquarters to New York. There the world's foremost socialist institution died a quiet and obscure death in 1876. That very year, German socialists and an amalgam of American-born sympathizers united in the formation of the first modern Marxist-oriented group, the Workingmen's Party, which within a year transformed itself into the Socialist Labor Party (still in operation today). As a national movement, the Workingmen's Party and the S.L.P. were weak, but local bodies in New

Famous appeal to assemble to protest police misdeeds brought radicals to Haymarket Square and the resulting tragedy of Mayday, 1886.

Depiction of the Haymarket Riot inaccurately showed workers firing guns and radicals continuing agitation while the police advanced. Harper's Weekly, *May 15, 1886.*

Local socialists proudly hosted Marx's daughter Eleanor Aveling and her husband, Dr. Edward Aveling, during the couple's 1886 cross-country trip.

The later famed editorial cartoonist Frederick Opper early in his career lampooned anarchist principles. Captioned, "The only form of trial that would satisfy the Chicago Anarchists — a Trial By a Court of their Peers." Puck, *October 13, 1886.*

SHE WAVED THE RED FLAG.
MRS. PARSONS, THE WIFE OF THE CONVICTED CHICAGO ANARCHIST, ADDRESSING A SOCIALIST PICNIC AT SHEFFIELD, 1903.

Lucy Parsons as she looked to an imaginative contemporary artist and as she was drawn more realistically, with clearly non-white features.

Courtesy: Scott Molloy and the Charles H. Kerr Co.

York, Philadelphia, Cincinnati, St. Louis and Chicago flourished with their own press, labor connections and educational and fraternal apparatus.

The next and last great wave of German immigration (peaking at a half-million in the year 1882), reinforced the socialist movement, exciting further public fears and yet more outrageous caricatures against German-Americans. Anarchist and famed joke-teller Johann (or John) Most became an archetype for the bearded, raving madman who sowed disorder and urged mayhem. Most's image may even have been the original for the bearded Bolshevik of the comic strips, with a bomb in hand, thirty years or so later. In drawings of the 1880s he usually looked wildly animated, arms flailing.

Press excitement reached an apex May Day, 1886, when the workers of various cities promised a general strike for the eight-hour day. Attention properly focused on Chicago, known as "Little Paris," where revolutionary socialist (or anarchist) influence was centered in the German fraternal institutions. There, a pattern of anti-strike violence by police inspired a call for a rally in Haymarket Square. At the end of the rally, as the crowd began to disperse and Chicago police gathered menacingly, an unknown person threw a bomb, evoking confusion and unleashing a brutal police attack.

The arrest of six Chicago anarchists (all but one of them German-Americans) instigated police raids on radical offices across the nation and an unprecedented vilification of dissidents. The serialized story-press and an abundance of low-priced popular fictional volumes featured the newly created

LUCY PARSONS

One of the most extraordinary characters of an extraordinary era, Lucy Parsons epitomized the fearless enemy of exploitation.

Born in Texas, quite possibly a slave but definitely of mixed black, Indian and Mexican ancestry, she met and married Albert Parsons around 1870. Albert, a Confederate veteran who had been radicalized by race and class conflict, had already begun fighting for black and labor rights in the state. They moved to Chicago in 1873, and after opening a small dress shop when Albert was blacklisted, she became active in supporting tramps, disabled veterans and working women. She also gave birth to two children.

Lucy joined the anarchistic International Workingmen's Association (the "Black International") in 1883 and the Knights of Labor soon afterward. In 1885 she headed the anarchists' march on the newly-opened Chicago Board of Trade and on Thanksgiving day that year led a similar procession through city streets, defiantly ringing rich people's doorbells. She helped organize the general strike in 1886 for the eight hour day movement, putting special efforts into the mobilization of seamstresses, one of the worst-paid trades.

Lucy Parsons responded to the Haymarket bombing and arrest of Albert and his comrades by traveling widely to defend their innocence and their revolutionary goals. By 1892 she was publishing a short-lived newspaper attacking the rising tide of lynchings and the oppression of blacks. Later she became a member of Debs' socialist movement and a founding activist in the Industrial Workers of the World. By the 1910s she was once again speaking for the homeless and victimized in tours and lectures, taking up the cases, especially, of Tom Mooney and other imprisoned radicals. In 1927 the International Labor Defense made her a member of their national executive committee; in 1939 she joined the Communist Party. She died in a fire in 1942 and her possessions were seized by local authorities. In the 1960s anarchists republished, this time as a poster, her 1880s call to tramps to break into the houses of the rich and take the possessions for themselves.

detective genre, whose protagonists typically ferreted out anarchist plots and dispatched the foreign-born subversives to prison. The Pinkertons, accurately known in labor circles for strike-breaking and sheer brutality, thus emerged as righteous protectors of American law and order.

In the local labor press at this time, the so-called "revolution" might be in the price of hats and gloves advertised (at least according to shrewd and ironic advertisers). The Democratic and Republican parties were the hydra-headed monsters to be slain. And the leaders of labor — such as beloved printer John Swinton, an ardent sympathizer of socialism — were depicted as respectable gentlemen. Samuel Gompers, the cigar makers' leader who emerged from socialist training into leadership of the craft unions, was not yet ashamed to be among them.

Serialized sensationalism. Family Story Paper, *September 18, 1886.*

Anti-radical writers and artists such as Frederick Gratz saw the anarchists as foreign subversives eating away at the nation's vitals. Puck, *c. 1886.*

Courtesy: American Social History Project, Hunter College

Henry George, illustrated in Judge *magazine, 1886, urging workingmen to ignore attacks on him by New York Roman Catholic bishops.*

Private Collection

One of many labor or cooperative commonwealth party campaigns launched in 1886. Ironically, Greenwich and three neighboring towns were submerged forever in 1937 by the state of Massachusetts to create a water supply (now Quabbin Reservoir) for Boston.

HENRY GEORGE

Social theorist, reformer, political candidate and popular economist, Henry George gained an international following, especially among those of Irish descent. For a time during the 1880s, he seemed destined to provide a personal bridge between the German-American socialists and the Irish-American workers, often hostile forces within the American labor movement.

A self-educated typesetter and would-be writer in California of the 1860s, George rightly observed that the wealth of the new Anglo settlement was concentrated in a small number of fabulous land-holdings. From that observation, and his background in Irish-American life (where the memory of English landlords was a painful one), George drew wide conclusions. His *Progress and Poverty* (1879), a best-selling economic treatise, argued that all men had the natural right to apply labor to natural resources, that rent was parasitism, and that labor values rose to new levels with the increase of population. Therefore, a severe land tax (or "single tax") should be levied to free up economic initiative and assist the lower classes to make their own way. Rather than socialism, Henry George preached the more respectable anti-monopolism, but opened himself to more radical allies who shared some of his interests.

George established his fame on a lecture tour in England and Ireland during 1881-82, returning home for further successful tours orchestrated by the Irish Land League. The Land League, ostensibly a refugee organization to assist homeland rebels, served in many places as a nucleus for Knights of Labor branches a few years later. Among the many Irish Knights, therefore, George was a natural champion. In New York City, where craft unions were largely Irish and German, George emerged the natural candidate for a labor ticket in the 1886 mayoralty election.

Running against railroad magnate Abram Hewitt and the young Republican patrician, Theodore Roosevelt, George gave the United Labor Party and radicals across the nation hope for victory. Church authorities divided bitterly over the permissibility of Catholics supporting him, while the commercial press railed at him and his United Labor Party as dangerous radicals and business interests filled the coffers of his opponents. "Counted out" at the ballot box by Tammany Hall, he finished a near second to Hewitt, running far ahead of the future president.

George now considered himself constrained by his socialist allies, and maneuvered for complete control of the U.L.P. Instead the movement split, effectively isolating him. An unsuccessful candidate in other elections, George became a fading but symbolic figure inspiring many young radicals at the beginning of careers carrying them further left. Perhaps 100,000 mourners filed past George's casket at his death in 1897.

Pantheon of Labor's Heroes, 1870s-80s, including American Federation of Labor leader Samuel Gompers, a socialist in his early years, and John Swinton, socialist New York editor. From George MacNeill, The Labor Movement: The Problem of Today *(1887).*

Images prepared by local labor reformers, as in this Milwaukee poster of 1886, envisioned workers in a political coalition that could dismember monopoly.

"Less Corn and More Hell"

Courtesy: Library of Congress

Mary E. Lease, the Kansas Populist who warned hard-pressed farmers to "Raise Less Corn and More Hell."

Private Collection

The Greenback Dollar, symbol of agrarian reform plans to create cheap money for farmers to pay off their debts to banks and others.

"Less Corn and More Hell"

The unprecedented use of the photograph in magazines of the 1890s threatened the lithographer's livelihood and artistic accomplishment in both technique and subjective emphasis. Thanks to improved reproduction methods, a burgeoning popular magazine press expanded rapidly at lower newsstand prices. In those pages, the crowd could now be seen differently, with faces and even signs less prominent relative to the photographic composition of the scene as a whole. The appearance of a "documentary" style perfectly coincided with the armies of the unemployed spawned by the Depression of 1893 and with the spectacular growth and dissolution of the Populist movement.

In a deep cultural sense, agrarian unrest and the perennially related question of currency went to the heart of many Americans' collective self-image. Even for those whose families had long since moved off the farm, the concept of agrarian virtue and of the Western farmland as the defining edge of American civilization remained at the center of the national mythology. Farmers' protests at being deprived of the fruits of their labor therefore became an important part of the iconography of the late nineteenth century. So did the satiric caricatures of agrarian leaders urging cheaper currency to repay debts and weaken the power of the banks. The Patrons of Husbandry or "Grangers," launched in 1867, not only grew to 1.5 million members during the 1870s and established large cooperatives, but built cultural monuments to their energies by erecting Grange Halls across the nation. The Grangers' rapid organizational decline led to the appearance of the Farmers Alliance (or "Populists"), yet more politically aggressive.

Arising first in Texas and the plain states, the Populist movement found its most ardent fol-

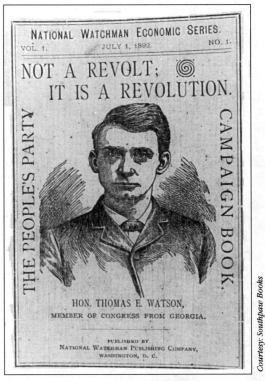

Tom Watson, who bravely defended black Populists in the South during the early 1890s, later became an arch-racist.

Courtesy: Southpaw Books

lowing in the South. Organized there into separate white and black wings, Populism managed to create far-reaching cooperative marketing mechanisms, and to generate a spirit of mass expectation that warring races might come together against the power of the planters and of northern investors. Only the worst abuses of voting laws and outright violence prevented a bi-racial Populist movement from taking power in Louisiana. As the rate of lynchings rose alarmingly, leading white southern Populists bravely declared themselves protectors of African-Americans.

Friendly critics of Populism might have predicted that any agrarian protest movement, however radical, would return to the currency question sooner or later. The amazing political energy of the People's Party, electing numerous Congressional representa-

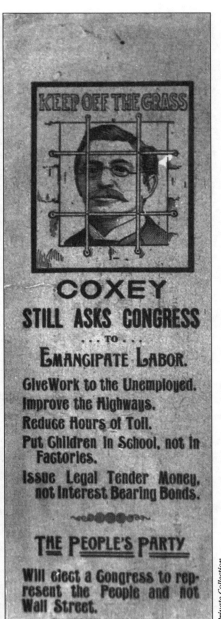

"General" Jacob Coxey, leader of the first national "army" of the unemployed to march on Washington. He was pictured in many places, including this Populist ribbon.

Private Collection

Courtesy: American Social History Project, Hunter College

Coxey's Army intensified Populist dissent, especially when Governor Lorenzo Lewelling of Kansas welcomed marchers. Frank Leslie's Illustrated Newspaper, *April 19, 1894.*

IGNATIUS DONNELLY

Radical politician and early science fiction author, Ignatius Donnelly is seen here with his 1900 running mate on the People's Party ticket, entrepreneur Wharton Barker. They received slightly over 50,000 votes, marking the practical end to Populism.

Yet Donnelly was far more than an eccentric. Born in 1831 the son of Irish immigrants, he moved west during the early 1850s, a partner in the newly-founded Nininger City, Minnesota. At 28, he was the state's Republican lieutenant-governor, and a brilliant orator. As a Congressman, he became increasingly concerned with poverty and the concentration of wealth. Disillusioned with the rightward shift of the Republicans, Donnelly was a natural leader for the new agrarian movements. A lecturer for the Grange, leading figure in the short-lived Anti-Monopolist Party and supporter of the Greenback Labor Party, he campaigned for measures like state-financed, free schoolbooks for children.

The defeat of political reform movements threw Donnelly toward a unique literary career mixing pseudo-scientific interpretation and science fiction-like novels. *Atlantis: The Antediluvian World* (1882) sought to demonstrate through evidence of folklore and mythology that the fabled island had actually existed. A companion volume, *Ragnarok: The Age of Fire and Gravel* (1883) argued that a great comet had caused a cataclysm recorded in the religious works of ancient times. He also attempted to prove that Shakespeare had not written the Bard's works. In his best-selling novel, *Caesar's Column* (1890), he treated industrial society as a "wretched failure" to "the great mass of mankind," and predicted a future so degraded that the slaves would throw off their oppression in a murderous rage, destroying civilization in the process. A more optimistic sequel, *The Golden Bottle* (1892), saw civilization saved by courageous women determined to win their equality with men.

The rise of Populism brought the "Sage of Nininger" into the forefront. He struggled to unite the farmers movements and the Knights of Labor, woman suffragists and temperance advocates, and wrote the unity plank of the famous St. Louis Populist convention which declared "we seek to restore the government of the Republic to the hands of 'the plain people' with which class it originated." Tragically, the Populist "fusion" with William Jennings Bryan's Democratic presidential slate and the subsequent rapid demise of the movement left too little room for his talent. He suffered a fatal heart attack only two months after the election of 1900.

Private Collection

Campaign button from 1900.

tives and a handful of leading state officials in 1888-94, led reformers of various kinds to hope for a merger of all energies into a single winning coalition. Populist governors' sympathetic support of the marching armies of unemployed workers gave substance to that hope. In their poverty and protest, the marchers seemed to come from city and farm alike, putting aside other differences. Few actually reached Washington, but they raised political consciousness greatly along the way.

Advocates of temperance, woman's rights, labor and agrarianism had struggled for unity at a St. Louis conference in 1892, and failed (due in part to differences over the liquor issue or women's rights, but also due to the distance between agrarian and labor demands). Henry Demarest Lloyd, prominent Chicago reformer, perhaps evoked the spirit of the times best with the observation that the "revolution" had already taken place in America, but that the businessmen were the revolutionaries. To undo that revolution required too much energy and unity.

Frustrated by the success of politicians in crushing the Populist third-party challenge, the People's Party endorsed Democratic candidate William Jennings Bryan in 1896 and attempted to place their own vice-presidential candidate, Tom Watson, on state ballots. Bryan and the Democrats, however, cared little for the radical demands for economic democracy that inspired Populism. Republican candidate William McKinley meanwhile used the currency question against Bryan to win urban voters who feared "soft" money meant inflation and unemployment. The first modern "machine" candidate, McKinley also had the war chest to outspend Bryan many times over, generating images of American power and prosperity and vanity campaign objects in unprecedented numbers.

The Populists, losing their independent identity, had meanwhile destroyed themselves. They left behind a legacy of protest that rural socialists transformed into a powerful movement in the Southwest and in scattered parts of the South.

Their stock of images, honest producers versus parasites and ordinary hard-working Americans versus bankers and financial swindlers, served the socialists well.

Henry Demarest Lloyd, Chicago reformer. A famed radical orator in defense of the Haymarket victims, he sought for a decade afterward to bring labor and farmers together in a broad-based Populist coalition. Independently wealthy as a result of marrying an heiress of the Chicago Tribune, *he has had a succession of radical descendants. His son, William Bross Lloyd, financed the first Communist Party convention and his granddaughter, Jessie Lloyd O'Connor, was a noted leftwing journalist.*

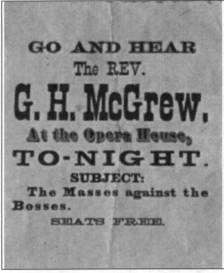

GO AND HEAR
The REV.
G. H. McGrew,
At the Opera House,
TO-NIGHT.
SUBJECT:
The Masses against the
Bosses.
SEATS FREE.

Courtesy: Bruce Rubenstein

Christian socialists spoke widely for the populist movement in the 1880s-90.

Courtesy: Kansas State Historical Society

A Populist group en route to a meeting in Dickinson Country, Kansas.

One of several original scenes in the "Garden of Eden," created by S.F. Dinsmore in Lucas, Kansas and still in existence. Here, "Labor" is crucified for the benefit of bankers, preachers, doctors and lawyers.

New Radical Beginnings

Edward Bellamy at about the time his famous novel, Looking Backward, *was published.*

Karl Marx's Wage-Labor and Capital *in Yiddish, one of the first Jewish socialist pamphlets published in the United States. From Morris U. Schappes,* The Jews in the United States *(1958).*

New Radical Beginnings

The renewal of radicalism amid Populist defeat could be seen, first of all, as the moment of Utopian novelist Edward Bellamy. His 1888 novel *Looking Backward* (the third best-selling American book of the nineteenth century, after *Uncle Tom's Cabin* and *Ben Hur*), brought utopianism up to date. It launched political movements, it inspired dozens of literary imitations, and most of all it encouraged tens of thousands of ordinary Americans to hope that something grandly cooperative lay not too far ahead.

Bellamy, a newspaperman from Chicopee, Massachusetts, wrote fiction from his early twenties concerning such matters as telepathy, hallucination and time-travel. He was deeply attracted to "outsiders," to dreamers like the spiritualists, and likewise to natural places surviving development, the "outside" of American civilization. He once proposed a national park extending in one strip from coast to coast, and exclaimed, "I wouldn't give much for a country where there are no wildernesses left." Cities would be smaller, nature closer, and the "true" frontier maintained not by government agencies in isolated western territories but by and for everyone in the future order.

Bellamy was also fascinated by current scientific potential. He shared, and brilliantly interpreted, a "science fiction" sense that swept over the public with the wonders of the telegraph (which the spiritualists believed, at first, would provide the ideal tool of departed souls to contact the living) or the Brooklyn Bridge, and the prospects for more wonders ahead. Social reformers of that time instinctively proposed all sorts of inventions and their cooperative uses. Commercial artists likewise often sketched "cities of the future" with clean, efficient public transportation and no poverty in sight.

In *Looking Backward*, the socialistic expectation is clothed in a delicate romantic fiction. A Rip Van Winkle-like sleeper re-awakens in the year 2000

RUSKIN BAND—1897.

to find America gone cooperative, with machines doing most of the physical labor. Freed for the cultivation of their individual talents and common pleasures like radio and tape deck-like musical systems uninvented in Bellamy's own time, the populace grows truly civilized. Comfort and security for all make possible an economy of happiness with universal high education, careers (or industrial service) from only the twenty-first to the forty-fifty year of life, guaranteed equal income to all, and an elaborate system of public honors to encourage excellence.

Reflecting on his own era, the time-traveler recalls the senseless cruelty of nineteenth century war and the economic exploitation and chaotic daily life in dangerous, ugly, planless cities. A romance with a young woman of the future, who is keenly

THE GRIST MILL AND SCHOOL CHILDREN.

Courtesy for both: Southpaw Books

Scenes from the Last Days of the Ruskin Cooperative. Although a financial failure, this Tennessee colony spawned The Coming Nation, *a popular socialist newspaper of the 1890s edited and published by J. A. Wayland. Its successor,* Appeal to Reason, *was the most popular socialist weekly in the history of the United States. From Isaac Broome,* The Last Days of the Ruskin Cooperative Association *(1902).*

conscious of her superiority to the repressed women of the past, illuminates in various ways the pleasant aspects of Bellamy's vision. The author showed hundreds of thousands of readers the triumph of love made possible in a happier world. By picturing this world as gained through rational agreement rather than by bitter and violent class conflict (as so many in the 1880-90s feared), Bellamy won over a frightened middle class desperate for a peaceful, cooperative use of industrial technology.

Looking Backward also prompted political-minded readers to form "Nationalist" Clubs, utopian-minded associations with some of the most beloved reformers of the nineteenth century. Thomas Wentworth Higginson of Civil War fame, woman suffrage leader Lucy Stone, temperance leader Frances Willard, the supposed father of baseball Abner Doubleday and others from prominent reform movements and families joined eagerly. (Thus long-time reformer and spiritualist Addie Ballou, herself descended from leading abolitionists, characteristically served as president of the San Francisco Nationalist Club.) For a few years the clubs flourished as educational forums. While some Nationalists including Bellamy turned increasingly to political agitation, others established what proved to be the last major utopian colonies of the nineteenth century.

Like their non-religious predecessors, these colonies faced difficult problems from their first day. Inhabitants generally discovered that inexpensive land had poor soil quality, and that skilled farmers were badly outnumbered by intellectuals. But several colonies had unique, memorable features. In Point Loma, part of today's metropolitan San Diego, followers of Bellamy had merged with Theosophists. They were mystic-minded searchers after truth inspired by the British Madame Blavatsky, who had wide contacts in European socialist circles. The Point Loma colony, with fantastic buildings and excellent educational facilities, flourished for decades due to funding from

Courtesy: Kathryn Kish Sklar

Florence Kelley, daughter of Radical Republican William 'Pig Iron' Kelly, converted to socialism and translated Engels' Condition of the Working Class in England, *joined the Socialist Labor Party for a time, and went on to lead the settlement house movement.*

Courtesy: State Historical Society of Wisconsin

Theresa Malkiel, a young Jewish garment-workers' leader during the 1890s and a fervent socialist. Later, she became an important labor supporter in the Socialist Party and author of Diary of a Shirt Waist Striker.

wealthy supporters and residents, especially baseball magnate Albert Spalding. Meanwhile the Ruskin Colony in Tennessee became the center for English-language socialist newspaper publishing with its weekly *Coming Nation*, read by tens of thousands. The Home Colony on Puget Sound, which lasted nearly twenty years, tucked itself away from developments. Its inhabitants, largely anarchists of working class background, believed earnestly if not religiously in nudism. Future Communist leader William Z. Foster also gained some of his key earlier supporters here.

These experiments exhausted American radicals' expectations of successfully guiding a society, by example, away from expansive capitalism, or of turning America into a paradise through encounter with a hidden mystic destiny. But they did not begin to exhaust the inner dream, fed by the hunger for transformation and the feeling that the contradictions between the reality and the rhetoric of American democracy could not persist.

Christian Socialists and romantic or pre-Raphaelite socialists took their inspiration from *Looking Backward's*

Courtesy of the State Historical Society of Wisconsin

Corrine S. Brown, a Chicago labor reformer, was a leader of the Illinois Women's Alliance, and later a prominent Chicago socialist.

Courtesy: Southpaw Books and Private Collection

Typical Morrisian images from the Comrade: *Walter Crane's most famous drawing on labor, and a contemporary illustration inspired by his work.*

Z. Libin (1872-1955), from a drawing by Bernard Gusso (1881-1957), in 1901.

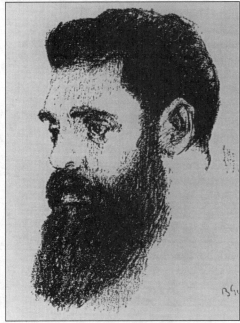

Morris Rosenfeld (lower left) and Morris Winchevsky (upper left) were popular socialist poets. Former capmaker Z. Libin (upper right) wrote short stories about ghetto misery; Jakob Gordin (lower right) was the father of the Yiddish theater. From the Groysser Kundes, c. 1911, and Morris U. Schappes, The Jews in the United States.

English counterpart, *News from Nowhere* by William Morris and the English socialists intellectual milieu. [Plate 19] In the Anglophile circles of American socialists in New York, Boston and such summer leisure spots as Newport, Rhode Island, "Fabianism" (the gradualist British style of socialism proffered by George Bernard Shaw, Sidney and Beatrice Webb) mixed easily with the artistic notions of Morris. Christian Socialism, a sister movement to Fabianism in Britain, found its American supporters chiefly in Bellamy's circles. A small stream of Christian Socialist publications, like *The Social Gospel* and the *Socialist Spirit*, found audiences prepared by the same ideas. The first artistic American socialist magazine, *The Comrade*, which began publication in 1901, was simultaneously British, Christian and William Morris-like.

The *Comrade* welcomed the new century but echoed older ones. Remarkably close to the German-American socialist yearning for a lost sense of common purpose, Morris's friend and comrade, Walter Crane (a visitor to the United States during the 1890s) artistically captured the dream of rolling back the ugliness of industrial capitalism and restoring the feeling of artisanship known to an earlier age. Socialists in Germany, considered the most politically advanced in the world, freely borrowed Crane's prints of Eden-like May Day celebrations; German socialists in America reprinted these images just as English-language socialists discovered them.

The rapidly evolving 1890s radical movement also had other, less utopian but equally vital currents. A branch of women activists in the Illinois Women's Alliance led by veteran urban reformer Corrinne Brown evolved into militant socialists. In the last few years of the century, some of the noted Yankee radicals of Boston and New York formed the Anti-Imperialist League, with William Dean Howells — the dean of American authors — in the lead.

Inspired by Jean Francois Millet's famous painting, Edwin Markham's poem about a farm laborer's misery, Man With a Hoe, *raced around the world after its 1899 publication.*

WILLIAM MORRIS AND AMERICAN MORRISANA

No European socialist, not even Karl Marx or Frederick Engels, inspired more touching American eulogies upon his death than did the British poet, designer and political activist, William Morris. From the Yiddish Marxist journal, *Di Tsukunft*, to Horace Traubel's literary weekly, *Conservator*, to the populistic *Coming Nation*, Morris was proclaimed as a giant of the times, an emanation of the future human being in the present.

An unparalleled designer who based himself upon patterns in nature (thus recovering a Celtic feeling for oneness with natural environment), Morris advanced the "Anti-Scrape" or conservationist movement among British opposed destruction of their countryside and historic buildings. He was also Poet Laureate, widely loved for his evocation of romantic and historical themes. Yet in the midst of a prestigious career, he committed himself completely to the socialist cause, editing and personally funding *Commonweal*, a weekly with a large impact upon British radicals and the small circles of English speaking socialists in the United States. Influenced by anarchism and by his own aesthetic views, Morris remained always heterodox in his socialism. His charming language and his obvious sincerity gave socialism a ready-made aesthetic, even if it proved inadequate to build a strong socialist political movement in England or the United States.

Some important American radicals had been directly shaped by Morris. Poet-activist Morris Winchevsky, "Zeyde" (grandfather) of Jewish socialist journalism had edited a sister Yiddish weekly in London and carried over many impulses to the United States. Reform intellectuals at the heart of Fabian socialism frequently visited abroad and brought back his ideas. Many others, mostly readers of Bellamy's *Looking Backward*, absorbed Morris's own very different utopian novel, *News from Nowhere* during the 1890s.

Morris's example had the most American impact, however, upon two particular currents. The group around *The Comrade* magazine drew their ideas about culture from Morris and their illustrations from the English artist Walter Crane, a member of the Morris circle. Morris and Crane together combined to offer the view of capitalism as a passing phenomenon. They offered the medieval past of collectivity and handicraft labor as a valid model despite all the negative features of material suffering and church oppression. The future, in their view, would bring humanity back to itself by returning it to learning from nature and to devising meaningful work for all.

The second current, around *The American Craftsman* magazine, sought to build an Arts and Crafts movement like that around Morris. It succeeded mostly by inspiring styles of furniture reminiscent of the Shakers in the spareness and use of natural design. But unlike the British example, these were made for mass production. Through the creations of Gustav Stickley and his imitators such designs continue to be popular with the American public today.

While jingoist and racist impulses ran wild in the commercial presses with abundant images of savages deserving extermination by the American military, these socialists bravely pointed to the real barbarism alive in the bloody suppression of self-sacrificing Filipino nationalists. A handful of anti-imperialists ardently declared themselves in full support of revolutions against racist American colonialism, just as would later generations of radicals.

Meanwhile, a Marxian socialist movement began to broaden and reshape itself. [Plate 21] The socialist current, dogged by internal conflicts and a political climate hostile to "foreign" radicals, made important headway among the new Jewish immigrants streaming into America from Eastern Europe in the late 1880s and early 1890s. Among these Jews, at least, socialist ideas were commonplace. The swift rise of a Yiddish-language

Courtesy of The Book Lover

"One day we shall win back Art again to our daily labor, win back Art, that is to say the pleasure of life, to the people"
WILLIAM MORRIS

William Morris as seen in the Comrade.

socialist and anarchist press created a prominent place for magnificent poets and agitators, even playwrights, within a few years. While German-American socialists had looked instinctively to the homeland for political cues and aesthetics, the new Jewish immigrants felt compelled to find new means of adaptation and organization, and a new language of socialism.

Jewish poets and short story-writers adapted current models of literary realism and naturalism to a rich fictional description of real-life misery of poor, oppressed, often tubercular Jews in American ghettos. But they also responded to a deep millenarian steak within Jewish culture. "Socialism" seemingly replaced the old idea of a Jewish homeland and a world redeemed by a messiah (some said Marx, the Moses of the working class, was the messiah's intellectual voice). Had they used pictures instead of words, their iconography would have recalled Mosaic versions of Radical Reformation themes in a coming socialistic Judgment Day.

By the middle 1890s, as the economy slumped to an all-time low and conditions in city slums grew desperate, radicals led fiery strikes in many trades and won over large numbers of unionists to socialism. A new English-speaking socialist leader from the Dutch Caribbean island of Curacao, the Sephardic Jew Daniel DeLeon, called for a revolutionized labor movement. [Plate 20] As former socialist Samuel Gompers guided the American Federation of Labor in an increasingly conservative direction, DeLeon's followers formed their own labor movement, the Socialist Trades and Labor Alliance. But it quickly failed. At the depth of the depression few workers could afford to join any new union. Besides, the strict DeLeon allowed local followers little room for autonomy and creative adaptation.

Private Collection

Leon Kobrin, known as the "Yiddish Zola," wrote heart-wrenching stories about ghetto life during the 1890s and after.

Courtesy: Charles H. Kerr Co.

Socialist Spirit, *a journal of eclectic spiritual socialism.*

Private Collection

Socialist Sheet Music.

LEON CZOLGOSZ, WHO SHOT PRESIDENT McKINLEY.
The above pictures are snap-shots of the assassin taken just after his arrest.

Courtesy: Library of Congress

Anti-Imperialist Assassination: Anarchist Leon Czolgosz, son of a prominent Buffalo socialist, assassinated President McKinley in 1901.

Courtesy: The Bishop Museum, Honolulu

Robert Wilcox, a half-Hawaiian anti-imperialist, helped lead an unsuccessful insurgency to overthrow United States domination of the islands by restoring Queen Lilliuokalani to her former throne.

Dissension now spread throughout the Socialist Labor Party. Poet-agitator Morris Winchevsky led a revolt of Jewish socialists against DeLeon's authoritarian rule. In the West, a final utopian movement formed by Eugene Debs was turning to political socialism and appealing to disaffected S.L.P.ers and disorganized, former Populists and Bellamyites among others. During the last years of the century, a variety of undogmatic socialists gradually came together. With Eugene Debs' 1900 presidential campaign, the isolation of the socialists from the larger society was finished — for now.

Further Reading

Alan Dawley, *Class and Community: The Industrial Revolution in Lynn* (Cambridge: Harvard University Press, 1976)

Amos Gilbert, *The Life of Thomas Skidmore* (Chicago: Charles H. Kerr Co., 1984 edition)

Frank Girard and Ben Perry, *The Socialist Labor Party, 1876-1991, a Short History* (Philadelphia: Livra Books, 1993)

Lawrence Goodwyn, *Democratic Promise: The Populist Movement in America* (New York: Oxford University Press, 1976)

Courtesy: Library of Congress

William Dean Howells, among the distinguished reformers who formed the Anti-Imperialist League in 1897 to protest American overseas expansionism.

Many populists and socialists protested American conquest of the Philippines. From The Comrade, *1901.*

Herbert Gutman, *Work, Culture and Society in Industrializing America* (New York: Pantheon, 1976)

Herbert Gutman and Donald Bell, eds., *The New England Working Class and the New Labor History* (Urbana: University of Illinois, 1987)

Clark D. Halker, *For Democracy, Workers and God: Labor Song-Poems and Labor Protest, 1865-95* (Urbana: University of Illinois, 1991)

Ulrike Heider, *Der Arme Teufel: Robert Reitzel* (Bühlmoos: Elster Verlag, 1986)

Dark Hoerder, ed., *"Struggle a Hard Battle": Essays on Working Class Immigrants* (DeKalb: Northern Illinois University Press, 1986)

Martin Keller, *The Art and Politics of Thomas Nast* (New York: Oxford University Press, 1968)

Peter C. Marzio, *The Democratic Art: Pictures for a 19th Century America* (Boston: David R. Godine, Publishers, 1979)

Celia Morris, *Fanny Wright: Rebel in America* (Urbana: University of Illinois, 1992)

MANILA—FILIPINOS IN ACTION—"FIRE AT WILL!"

DRAWN BY H. C. CHRISTY AFTER A PHOTOGRAPH OF INSURGENT TROOPS UNDER FIRE IN THE TRENCHES AT MALATE BEFORE THE SPANISH EVACUATION

Filipinos under Emilio Aguinaldo fought a bloody eight year war to resist domination by the United States.

Library of Congress

Bruce Nelson, *Beyond the Martyrs: a Social History of Chicago's Anarchists, 1870-1900* (New Brunswick: Rutgers University Press, 1987)

Daphne Patai, ed., *Looking Backward, 1988-1888: Essays on Edward Bellamy* (Amherst: University of Massachusetts Press, 1988)

David Roediger and Philip Foner, *Our Own Time: A History of American Labor and the Working Day* (Westport: Greenwood Press, 1987)

David Roedgier and Franklin Rosemont, eds., *The Haymarket Scrapbook* (Chicago: Charles H. Kerr Co., 1986)

Richard S. West, *Satire on Stone: The Political Cartoons of Joseph Keppler* (Urbana: University of Illinois Press, 1988)

Sean Wilentz, *Chants Democratic: New York City and the Rise of the American Working Class, 1788-1850* (New York: Oxford University Press, 1984)

The Comrade *recognized the power of the dream to inspire social action.*

Chapter Three
The Golden Age of Radicalism

John Sloan

TO US BELONGS THE FUTURE

Anti-socialist sheet music of the day. Photography: Steven Laschever

American Socialism

SOCIALIST RALLY

will be held at

OPERA HOUSE

To-Night

at 8:00 o'clock P. M.

Hon. J. Alex Bevan
and B. H. Rowberry,

will discuss the local Politics;
And will tell you what no other
member from the last Legislature dare tell about graft in
our Legislature.

Singing and dancing by the De La Mare
Sisters, and Good Music.

All are Cordially Invited.

Debsian Socialism

History buffs of American labor and radicalism often turn their attention from the movements of the nineteenth to those of the early twentieth century, and with good reason. The memories encased in artifacts are in many ways richer, the imagery more picturesque and more abundant, than almost anything to follow. During this era, Americans discovered socialism and millions found it (or at least its champion, Eugene Victor Debs) to their liking, even if they did not necessarily vote socialist or join the Socialist Party. The Industrial Workers of the World, widely hated and brutally crushed, nevertheless inspired a romantic vision of the rebel worker at the last frontier of American innocence. Avant-gardists for the rest of the century looked back on Greenwich Village of the 1910s as the most promising place and moment for radical artistic expression.

The "Golden Age" of socialism began with rise of Eugene V. Debs to national prominence and the emergence of grassroots socialism epitomized in *Appeal to Reason,* in its day the most widely-read weekly newspaper in the world. Founded by

The end of class struggles and class rule, of master and slave, of ignorance and vice, of poverty and shame, of cruelty and crime, the birth of freedom, the dawn of brotherhood, the beginning of MAN, that is the demand. This is Socialism.

Eugene V. Debs, America's favorite socialist.

Private Collection

Courtesy: Charles H. Kerr Co.

Charles Kerr, the prolific publisher of Charles H. Kerr books and the International Socialist Review.

Appeal to Reason or *"Little Ole Appeal,"* and Fred Warren, successor to J.A. Wayland at the *Appeal.*

former land speculator and utopian colonist J.A. Wayland, this paper had a circulation of 30,000 at the turn of the century and nearly three quarters of a million a decade later. Aimed mostly at the farmer or worker who had seen many disappointments in life, the *Appeal* had special popularity among the tenant farmers of Texas and Oklahoma, the railroad workers who had followed Eugene Debs, and reformers old enough to have learned about abolitionism or the early woman's rights movement from elder family members.

The *Appeal* had a deeply personal look. Editor Wayland addressed his readers personally, and often with sarcasm: "Work hard, get poor, talk rich, sneer at reform — and go to the poor house." His message was the degradation of the Republic and its redemption made possible by socialism. It was said that he could personally convert any passenger on a train while he traveled. He converted many ordinary people in the town of Girard, Kansas, where the *Appeal* was for decades the major business enterprise. The socialist movement which grew up around him had other favorite magazines, like *The National Rip-Saw* of St. Louis, which reached 150,000 weekly, mostly in the South. But readers liked the *Appeal* best, because it exposed the specific evils of capitalism (such as the dangerous additives in commercial meat-packing) and the larger moral decay. Back East, the *Comrade* was the first pictorial magazine of the American Left and one of the few ever to portray socialism as a way of life rather than merely an emancipating economic system. It drew inspiration from Walt Whitman and

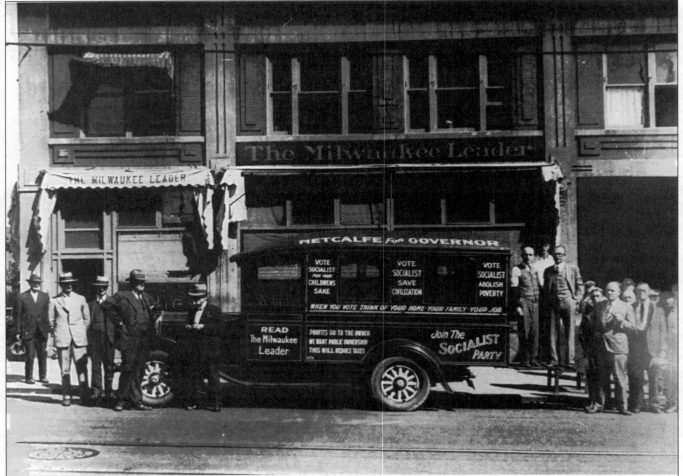

Socialist Party newspaper delivery truck.

American labor history revisited, from the Underhanded History of America, *written by James P. O'Brien and drawn by Nick Thorkelson (1974).*

Color Page — 9

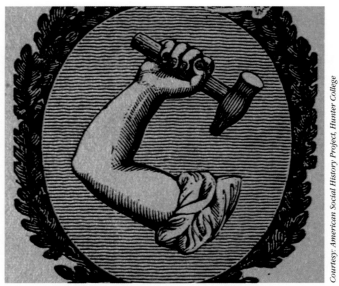

Labor's symbol from its earliest days: The proof of honest toil is a combination of strength and agility. The Union, *June 14, 1836.*

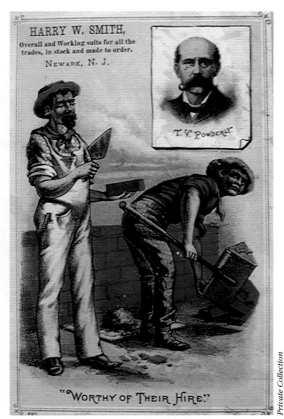

Terence Powderly was honored with many illustrations as suggested by this colorful trade card, one of a set, c. 1880s.

"The Strike," by the German-American artist, Robert Koehler, c. 1886. This painting is perhaps the best known fine artwork of nineteenth century labor conflict.

PUCK *caricatures, both by Joseph Keppler, satirize labor radicalism of the 1880s.*

"The Socialist," by Robert Koehler, c. 1886, is the first fine-art portrayal of a German-American agitator.

"I pay for all" expresses the farmer's view in this 1873 lithograph.

A popular print, c. 1873, with its message a self-evident claim of agrarian virtue, was widely used by Grangers and Populists.

A "Greenback" hailing Ben Butler's proposed "Cheap Money" monetary reforms as a panacea for various social problems. The backing of the card is an advertisement for Henken's ice cream salon in South Brooklyn, New York.

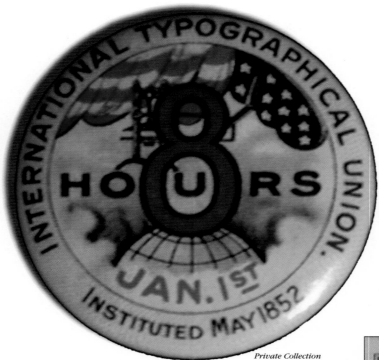

The Eight Hour Movement of 1886, led by labor radicals, succeeded in lessening the hours of many workers, without achieving its final goal. The International Typographical Union, oldest continuous labor organization in the United States, was a major force for the limited victory.

Social Gospel, *turn-of-the-century journal of Christian Socialism.*

The design of this beer tray advertises the virtues of the brewery union, which sponsored the German-American socialist press and contributed many activists to radical ranks.

Gymnastic associations, the Turnvereine, were also nineteenth century centers of socialistic education.

Color Page – 15

The woman suffrage movement bogged down during the late nineteenth century, with few victories except in sparsely populated Western states. Mean-spirited attacks like this one by Joseph Keppler in Puck *were typical of the time.*

The only known color portrait of Daniel DeLeon, by artist Fred Precht.

Color Page – 16

A Socialist Watch At an Anti-Trust Price

A Magnificent Watch for Socialists Only

The Genuine Burlington Special Admittedly the world's master piece of watch manufacture, with the beautiful emblems of Socialism SPLENDIDLY ENGRAVED ON THE CASE, BY HAND, direct to you on a staggering Anti-Trust Offer.

The Fight Is On! We are bound to win our gigantic Anti-Trust fight, even against the most overwhelming odds. We are determined that no price-boosting system, no "quiet" agreements to throttle competition, can or will stop us in our efforts to secure a fair deal for the consumer.
WE ARE DETERMINED to accomplish the introduction of our independent line of watches, even though we are obliged to fight a combination of all the other watch manufacturers in the country.
WE WON'T KNUCKLE DOWN to selling systems among dealers, or we have decided upon an offer so overwhelming in its liberality that it has completely revolutionized the watch industry of the country.

Special Offer to Socialists

THE MAGNIFICENT BURLINGTON SPECIAL, our very finest watch, direct to you at the ROCK-BOTTOM PRICE, less even than the regular wholesale price.

No Money Down We will gladly ship to you on approval. You pay nothing—you risk absolutely nothing—not one cent—unless you decide that you want the great offer after seeing and examining the watch.

$2.50 a Month and for the world's grandest watch! The easiest kind of payments at the Rock-Bottom —the Anti-Trust price. In ascore so that every Socialist will quickly accept this great introductory direct offer, we allow easy payments, just as you prefer.

Write for the Free Watch Book

You should not buy a worthless watch, just because it is cheap. Nor need you pay Trust prices now for a top-notch watch. The free Burlington Book explains. THIS BOOKLET will quickly convince you, too, that you DO watch an Anti-Trust watch—made in the Independent factory that is fighting the trust at best from by giving better quality and superior workmanship throughout, so as to quickly convince you that the Burlington watch is THE watch for the discriminating buyer, that it is THE watch for the man or woman who wants, not the largest selling brand, which everybody has, but the BEST watch, the watch boueht for a reason the BURLINGTON WATCH.
YOU WILL BE POSTED on INSIDE FACTS and galore when you send for the Burlington Company's free book on watches.

BURLINGTON WATCH CO.
Suite 2732, 19th St. and Marshall Blvd.
Chicago, Ill.

Burlington Watch Co.
Suite 2732.
19th St. & Marshall Blvd.
Gentlemen: Please send me the free watch book and prepaid your free book on watches and explanation of your $1,000 challenge, and explanations of your cent-a-month offer on the Burlington Watch.

Name ....
Address ....

Helen Keller's "Out of the Dark"

"A person who is deaf and blind from infancy may be taught a few of the fundamental things of life, but he can never hope to attain to a realization of the social problems."—So said a very learned person when Miss Helen Keller went to college. But he did not know.

In her new book Miss Keller tells how, step by step, she has been led out of her isolation into full social consciousness—how at last she has come to "touch hands with the world."

She has become an enthusiastic Socialist and is absorbing through finger reading, the many-thousand-worded works of Karl Marx.

A COPY FREE

The first edition of this book was sold out two weeks before Christmas, but the publishers have sent another shipment that will now enable us to carry out our offer of giving a copy to every comrade mailing us $2.00 for two yearly Review subscriptions, or four six month subs. Miss Keller has never seen the sunlight nor heard the spoken word, but her book is like a song of Hope—Socialism, the Hope of the World!

Send $2.60 and we will send TWO yearly subscription cards and TWO copies of "Out of the Dark."

THE BEST BOOK TO LEND TO YOUR FRIENDS!

CHARLES H. KERR & COMPANY
118 W. Kinzie St., CHICAGO, ILL.

INTERNATIONAL SOCIALIST REVIEW *Jan. 1912* 383

Free Offer to Socialist Comrades and Locals

Does YOUR Local keep Open Headquarters? Would not a Phonograph do more to attract an indoor crowd than anything else? The $25.00 Disc Talking Machine shown in this cut is in our opinion the most thoroughly satisfactory Phonograph yet produced. Up to Dec. 31 we offer it FREE (together with three musical records) to every Local or comrade selling 250 copies of the INTERNATIONAL SOCIALIST REVIEW, and remitting for them at 10 cents each. We make the same offer to Locals or comrades sending $25.00 for 25 yearly, 50 six-months or 100 three-months Review Subscription Cards.

Just the thing for the young soap-boxer. Our Phonograph can be so adjusted as to carry the sound to a large crowd. Open and close your meetings with the

MARSEILLAISE

and other revolutionary songs and pieces. The more entertaining you make your meetings, the larger they will be.

All standard disc records including the Columbia can be played on this instrument.

We shall later be able to supply our prize winners with HAYWOOD records at 65 cents each.

Consider our offer. Move to accept it at your next Local meeting. Send us $25 or $10 or $5 for Reviews or subscription cards at retail prices and start selling them. As soon as you have paid $25 we will ship the musical instrument shown in the cut. We have tested it thoroughly and can recommend it.

Nothing in the way of Socialist literature sells so easily as our Fighting Magazine. Any Local can easily earn this premium in a single month. The greatest offer ever made to the Socialists of America. Tell us what you think of it.

Charles H. Kerr & Company

118 West Kinzie Street   -   -   -   Chicago Ill.

Socialist Pennants

extra special in quality: crimson felt bearing the word SOCIALISM in artistic lettering; sell them at your meetings; decorate your local with them: regular price, sent by mail, without canes, 15 cents each; 2 for 25 cents. For $2.00 we will send by prepaid express 1 dozen pennants with bamboo canes. Address R. B. Tobias, 118 West Kinzie Street, Chicago, Ill., second floor.

Int'l Socialist Review, Sept 1911

Socialists! Move With the Movies!

It is said that American Workers spend Five Hundred Million Dollars annually in twenty thousand Picture Theatres. The Social Revolution must be represented! A company is now being organized to manufacture Socialist films. More capital is needed. One Dollar will make you part owner of this company. Let your money work for Socialism while it is working for you. BIG PROPAGANDA! Shares $1 each. Send money at once with full name and address, stating number of shares wanted. Information and references for stamp. Address

CHAS. L. DRAKE, Sec'y, Room 303, 167 W. Washington St., Chicago, Ill.

BE A SUCCESSFUL SOCIALIST SPEAKER

How would you like to have the comrades say of you "After he had talked five minutes you couldn't have DRIVEN people out of the hall"? That's what they said of me at Ann Arbor, Michigan University, after I had studied and practiced the WINNING METHOD. Don't go blundering along, losing your crowds and failing to convince. Study a method that means absolute SUCCESS. Used by lawyers, orators and leading socialist speakers. Build up your argument till it is simply irresistible. Start somewhere and get somewhere. I will teach you how. Send 2c stamp for press comments and testimonials, with circular describing the method.

SAMUEL W. BALL, 6442 Bishop St., Chicago

Socialist advertisements. From various issues of the International Socialist Review, *1910s.*

JACK LONDON

The most popular and most radical "adventure" novelist of the 1910s, Jack London was an ardent socialist and Wobbly. He was also a socialist mystic of sorts, with a science fiction sensibility that provided a radical twist to the futurology of emerging pulp fiction.

London was born in Oakland, California, in 1876, son of an unmarried astrologer and spiritualist, and the Bay Area's famed literary bohemianism played a large role throughout his life. Raised in poverty, he used his own small boat to raid the oyster beds owned by the railroad investors. Narrowly escaping criminal charges, he headed for the Alaska Gold Rush. After a year, he returned home to write stories of the North, including *Call of the Wild,* the national best-seller of 1900. His "dog stories" of courage and brutality made him famous, but he also penned a steadily growing volume of stories and reportage about poverty and the evils of capitalism. His science fiction-style novel, *The Iron Heel,* depicted a future society run by a master class of totalitarians.

An ardent follower of Eugene Debs, London lectured, raised money, helped found the Intercollegiate Socialist Society to reach young intellectuals, and made himself available in many other ways to the socialist movement. Affected by the melancholy of a working class writer uneasy in a middle class environment, he also drank heavily. He sometimes emphasized racial themes, which left him ill-prepared to grasp the significance of the First World War and the contemporary changes in the working class, as well as in American culture at large. At the time of his early death, in 1916, he had given up most of his hope for socialism, although he remained a dedicated supporter of the Industrial Workers of the World. The Russian Revolution, which he did not live to see, ironically produced regimes so entranced with his work that Jack London's translated writings were famous across the world decades after he had been nearly forgotten in the United States.

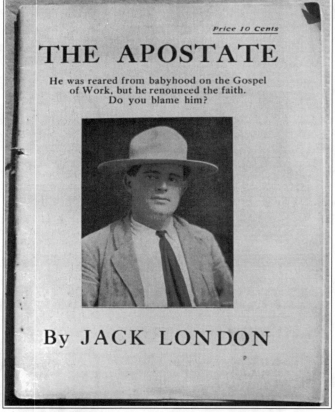

Jack London, "A Famous Rebel Thou Art," from C. de Fornaro's Mortals and Immortals: Caricatures *(1911), and* The Apostate, *c. 1910.*

Mark Twain, Socialist.

All, Courtesy: Utah State Historical Society

John Osborne
Fin. Sect.

J.T. Lavery
Cor. Sect.

Thos. Watkins
Treas.

H.B. Cromar
President

Chas. M. Vinson
Grand Marshall Labor Day Parade

Prominent Utah Socialists Rev. Franklin Spaulding and William Brown Thurston, and officers of the socialist-led State Federation of Labor. In heavily Mormon Utah, many socialists came from Mormon backgrounds or from the mining camps where socialist ideas were popular.

William Morris and was determined "to mirror Socialist thought as it finds expression in Art and literature [and] to develop the aesthetic impulse in the Socialist movement." It declared editorially,

The fires on the old alters are dead. The religion of to-day is impotent; the Art of to-day is parasitic; the life of to-day is stifled. Into the miasma of commercialism is coming the breath of a new ideal. Men are growing conscious of the fact that present social forms are passing. They are beginning to understand that they can take hold of the world and fashion it anew after their desires, and it is in this instinct of creation that they become like unto gods.

Socialism, in the *Comrade's* drawings, is the sunlight of the future gleaming into the present, illuminating beautiful men and women half-clothed and innocent of cruelties. In the glimmering, one could see the coming together of eighteenth century beliefs in perfectibility, nineteenth century confidence in scientific perfection, and American democratic optimism. Nathaniel Hawthorne's socialist son Julian predicted "the time will surely come when heaven's first law will rule our daily lives and deeds, and the world we live in will be like noble words set to mighty music." *Comrade* enthusiast and poet Edwin Markham envisioned the common man and woman awakening from centuries of lethargy to the promise of reform. At the fringes of *The Comrade* and of the socialist cause, an Arts and

Crafts movement formed as an extension of William Morris' English leadership. *The American Craftsman*, published during the first sixteen years of the new century, focused on the decorative arts, from the medieval guilds' work to Morris' studio to Shakers and to Native American arts, the last a great favorite of *Craftsman* editor (and former stonemason) Gustav Stickley. Unlike the British, who created beautiful items for a few homes, Stickley aspired to produce "democratic" furniture, known for its "mission" style of determined simplicity.

The Socialist Party, founded in 1901 by Debs and others, could not fulfill the expectations of those who saw an entire transformation of civilization just ahead. It did not become a serious competitor to most Democratic and Republican officeholders, although it elected hundreds of local officials, an occasional state legislator and two Congressmen. Many cities, mired in the typical political corruption of the time, also looked to socialists for cleaner, more efficient government. Socialists won what they could, but employed electoral opportunities mainly for a massive educational campaign about the evils of the competitive system and the possible alternatives.

The socialist press carried much of the weight of this effort and created or reprinted most of the movement's basic iconography. Several hundred tabloids including a few dozen dailies appeared, in more than twenty languages, and many union newspapers or magazines regularly endorsed socialist programs and ideas. Active socialists sold these papers at street-corners where "soap-box" speakers provided popular entertainment of day, and at labor meetings, strikes, picnics, concerts, door-to-door to neighbors and to strangers. In the Southwest, farmers and small-town folks took a few days off between crops and gathered for entertainment and education under the large tents usually reserved for religious revival meetings. Skillful orators also told jokes, sang songs and played musical instruments to make their presentations more lively.

Socialists could also count on some of the most popular, beloved writers in American fiction. The tremendously popular Jack London devoted all his spare energies to the Cause. Upton Sinclair, whose best-selling novel of stockyards life *The Jungle* (1905) reminded readers of family degradation and of unsanitary working conditions, was serialized first in *The Appeal To Reason*. Like London a very popular platform speaker for socialism, Sinclair turned

Both, Courtesy: Southpaw Books

The "Red Special," famed chartered train that Debs and his running mates took across the country in election years.

Courtesy: State Historical Society of Wisconsin, and from the Groysser Kundes, 1911

Victor Berger, sent to Congress from Wisconsin in 1913, is shown trimming political corruption from Uncle Sam's beard. Emil Seidel, shown in his machine shop, was the first socialist elected mayor of Milwaukee, Wisconsin, in 1912.

out volume after volume, including one about Socialist party life, *Jimmie Higgins* (1917). Other socialists and those influenced by socialist ideas wrote sensational novels about the degradation of women under capitalism, and their search for personal as well as political emancipation. Among poets, Hoosier James Whitcomb Riley delivered a 1900 campaign poem for his intimate friend Eugene Debs, Carl Sandburg began his career as a reporter on a socialist newspaper, and Vachel Lindsay's "Why I Vote the Socialist Ticket" was a ringing defense of Abraham Lincoln's tradition revisited in socialism:

> I am unjust, but I can strive for justice
> My life's unkind, but I can vote for kindness.
> I, the unloving, say life should be lovely.
> I, that am blind, cry out against my blindness...

All this had a very American ring. In Oklahoma, where socialists achieved the highest proportional vote, in any state, of more than 15% in 1912, they reached tens of thousands of impoverished tenant farmers with their message of redemption. They promised to return what capitalism had stolen. Editor-humorist Oscar Ameringer guided an unprecedented agitational campaign uniting Native Americans clinging to their reservation, African-Americans and whites who had fled the post-Civil War South, miners and industrial workers. But the heart of Socialist territory was the small town where the *Appeal to Reason* was the best-read political paper and merchants hung red flags in their windows. There, socialists amused and inspired themselves as they sang from former Populist leader Tad Cumbie's radical hymnal (to the tune of the old favorite, "Longing for Home"):

> They have given our lands all away
> To the railroads and rich men you see,
> And force us and children each day
> To work for the landlords each day,
> Working each day, working each day,
> Work for a landlord each day.

Quickly, the socialists moved to consolidated their strengths. Small-town or rural socialist branches made up of railroad workers, teachers and ministers' wives and even businessmen gathered to study economic theory and the evolution of society. Big-city immigrants or socialists of varied backgrounds in the mining camps established centers for workers to gather after work and on Sundays. The exchange of ideas and skills helped them lead their workmates into unions and into the party. [Plate 24]

Their very success led to contradictions. By 1908, Socialists held thirty-five elected offices in eight states. Four years later, more than 2,000 held office. Typically, they went after labor support on economic issues like control of public utilities and

LITTLE BOY BLUE

LITTLE Boy Blue, come blow your horn;

It's the chance of your life, as sure as you're born;

You can vote to be caught in the spider's webs,

Or vote to be free with Seidel and Debs.

ROCKABY BABY

ROCKABY Baby, your home's in the slum;

Your dad's out of work and has gone on the bum;

The wolf is a' gnawin just outside the door—

It's a dam fine system— let's vote 'er some more.

SIMPLE SIMON

SIMPLE SIMON met a renter on election day;

Said Simple Simon to the renter, "How will you vote, I pray?"

Said the renter to Simple Simon "Just like other fools---

I'm votin' for a boss to own the land and all the tools."

All, Private Collection

Democratic party which supplied jobs and tolerated corruption. Large parts of the old slave South, both black and white, remained untouched by socialists, who had no good answer for the dilemmas of racism. Even women, who formed fifteen percent of the party and had their own popular press and agitational bureau, had trouble breaking through the conservatism and political apathy of the housewife and working girl. Ardent participation in the national woman suffrage movement, crucial in some states to passage of the amendment, made a strong impression of socialist sincerity but won few members.

In 1912, Eugene Debs' premier presidential campaign reached almost every state with his "Red Special" train, meeting huge audiences who considered him a savior. He captured nearly a million votes, but only six percent of the popular poll, disappointing enthusiasts who expected him to challenge the major candidates. Exhausted and aging, Debs would not run again until 1920 — and then from a prison cell. The Socialist party, which sunk into a decline from its 100,000 members in 1912 would rebound along with its municipal campaigns. But never again did it seem to be advancing steadily, inevitably, toward victory.

The images of the Socialist party in these early years go straight to the backbone of the movement: its press. Not only did these papers and magazines provide images of the party and its leaders at work; they also created an unprecedented arena for the adaptation of European radical graphic styles, and for the home-grown caricaturist or cartoon-strip artist. Cartoonist Ryan Walker even ran, for a few years, his own school for radical cartoonists in Michigan. To most readers, though, Art Young was their favorite. Raised in Wiscon-

Socialist Nursery Rhymes, from the Ripsaw Mother Goose *(St. Louis, 1912), by Ryan Walker.*

Henry Dubb, a favorite socialist cartoon strip drawn by Ryan Walker, was about the worker who could never understand his own interest.

sin, a leading cartoonist in the commercial press already during the 1880s (where he supplied the best-known caricatures of the Haymarket martyrs), Young had worked with Thomas Nast and become known for his reformist temperament when he converted to socialism around 1910. From then on, he epitomized the Middle American awakened to capitalism's many injustices. His old-fashioned drawing style perfectly fitted the sensation of a society which left a simpler past behind and plunged into modern insanity — unless it could choose something better than individual and collective greed.

By one who was once a chattel slave freed by the proclamation of Lincoln and now wishes to be free from the slavery of capitalism. From the dedication to a pamphlet by Rev. Woodbey

Rev. George Washington Woodbey, the most prominent African-American socialist before the 1910s. A prolific writer on "Bible Socialism" his pamphlets included The Bible and Socialism: A Conversation Between Two Preachers *(1904). Arrested and severely beaten several times as a "soap box" speaker and advocate of free speech in San Diego, Woodbey disappeared from prominence in 1915. His later fate is unknown.*

OSCAR AMERINGER

REVOLUTIONARY HUMOR ARCHIVES

Illustrations by ART YOUNG

Oscar Ameringer, the "Mark Twain of American Socialism," was a beloved radical humorist, editor of a half-dozen newspapers, and leading socialist lecturer in Oklahoma during its socialistic peak of the 1910s. His Life and Deeds of Uncle Sam *(1909), a satirical history of the United States, sold a half-million copies in various languages. From* Cultural Correspondence.

Wisdom of the Poor Fish

The Poor Fish *says*: There never was such prosperity. People are living in more expensive quarters than ever.

Private Collection

The Poor Fish, Art Young.

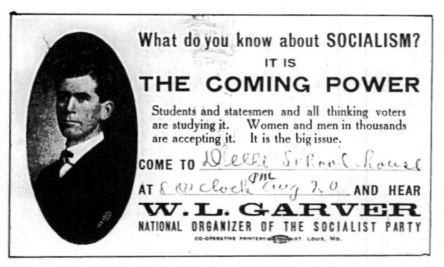

Well trained speakers brought the message of Socialism to many small towns.

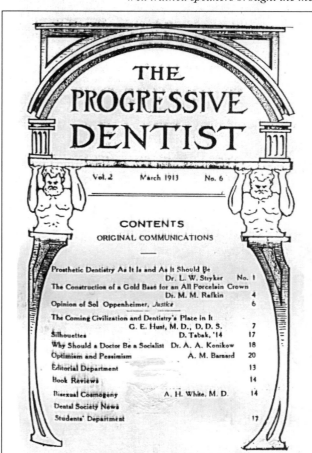

Unintendedly humorous to our eyes, The Progressive Dentist *was typical of socialist magazines appealing to the emerging middle class.*

Roosevelt Exposes Socialism. Republican President and Progressive candidate in 1912 Theodore "Teddy" Roosevelt promised to exterminate socialists, if need be, to keep order.

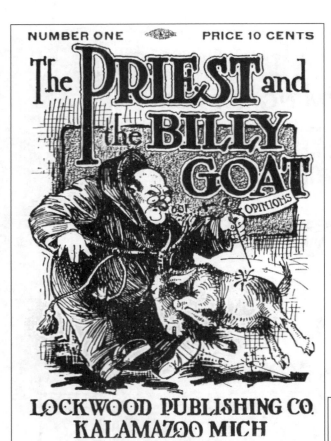

Socialist humor magazine published in Kalamazoo, Michigan, took on different names, including The Prophet and the Ass and The Billygoat.

If you want the omelet you must break the egg. —Chicago Socialist.

Wisdom of the Poor Fish

The Poor Fish says things will probably come out all right in the end, but he doesn't expect to live to see it.

Art Young, from Good Morning, 1921.

מ אַ י ר ל אָ נ ד אָ ן : פּיער זאָבען מוזט איהר אין זינען האָבען, אויב איהר
ווילט זיין אַ סאָציאַליסט : איהר מוזט זיין עהרליך, אינטעלינענט, קלאַסענבע-
וואוסט און אַ גוטער קומפער (אין צייט פון קאמפיין).

Meyer London, who was elected to Congress from New York's heavily Jewish East Side in 1914, lost his seat in 1918 and won it again in 1920. From Groysser Kundes, 1911.

Catholic Church officials, like Southern Protestant leaders, issued hundreds of anti-socialist broadsides in the early twentieth century. Ethnic variations, like this Slovenian one, were among the most fanciful.

"They're going to make slaves of the Russian People."

OF COURSE NOT

CAPITALIST (at the Writers' Club): "Boys, never mix propaganda with your art."

STILL AT IT!

Art Young drawings from Good Morning, *1921-1922.*

The Wobblies

WILLIAM D. HAYWOOD

"Big Bill" Haywood, one-eyed Wobbly from the West, was the symbol of the rough-and-tumble labor movement dedicated to industrial unionism and socialism.

Born in Salt Lake City, the son of a Kentucky miner and a South African-born woman, Haywood early went to work as a miner's helper and there learned the doctrines of radical unionism. By the 1890s, after abandoning a homestead, he rose to union leadership in Silver City, Idaho. A brilliant administrator, he came to Denver in 1901 to be secretary-treasurer of the Western Federation of Miners, a militant organization faced with constant threats of mine company violence. Haywood carried his six-foot frame and two hundred pounds (also a revolver) on legendary organizing drives, and wrote with equal courage in the socialistic *Miners Magazine,* which he edited. In 1905, he was one of the founders of the Industrial Workers of the World. For two years, he took little role in the I.W.W., instead defending himself against trumped-up murder charges of having planned the bombing murder of a former Idaho governor.

Successfully defended by Clarence Darrow, Haywood emerged a working class hero and wide-ranging lecturer. Organizer-at-large for the I.W.W., he was on hand for the successful Lawrence, Massachusetts, textile strike and other historic but less successful battles. He also spent time in Greenwich Village, beloved by bohemians for both his rough appearance and his keen intelligence. Asked by reporters why he could eat meals and smoke cigars that rich friends gave him, he replied, "Nothing is too good for the working class." He was also supposed to have said that he "had never read Marx's *Capital* but had the marks of capital" all over his body.

As secretary-treasurer of the organization, he led the I.W.W. to its greatest success and stability, mostly among western loggers, miners, and farmworkers. Then came World War I and Haywood's arrest on the Sedition Act, followed by a sentence of 20 years. Rather than face these consequences, and ailing with diabetes, he jumped bail and fled for Russia. There, he spent his time with Americans, in part planning the creation of an International Labor Defense and writing his autobiography, *Bill Haywood's Book,* one of the most beloved radical volumes. He died in 1928 and was buried in the Kremlin wall.

The Wobblies

Founded at a 1905 convention which western miners' leader William D. "Big Bill" Haywood declared to be the "Continental Congress of the Working Class," the Industrial Workers of the World (or "Wobblies" as they quickly came to be known) revived the dream that the Knights of Labor had lived out for a moment, of a new society within the old one, preparing its members through education, discipline and solidarity for an all-encompassing economic democracy. With its few thousand members, the new movement had slim prospects to accomplish this goal. Yet the decline and the timidity of the American Federation of Labor, representing only the skilled "aristocrats of labor" and relatively few of those, posed an urgent need for a true union movement. [Plate 30]

The inevitable growth of the new class of unskilled workers, drawn to the cities or to American shores by the rapid expansion of the economy, pointed toward the need for industrial unionism. Common membership for every worker in the same and similar industries would bring solidarity and a renewed idealism to labor. Later movements accomplished this goal in most major industries during the late 1930s and 1940s, long after the I.W.W.'s virtual disappearance. But the grand vision had been present from the beginning. Delegates to the first convention included a wide spectrum of political and labor leaders, from Eugene V. Debs to Haymarket victim Albert Parsons' widow Lucy Parsons, former local leaders of the Knights of Labor, current Socialist party unionists and many others.

Perhaps the most controversial delegate was Daniel DeLeon, who brought his small Socialist Trades and Labor Alliance into the I.W.W. as a body. Out of his earlier failures, he had gained an important insight. Advanced in industry if backward in radical politics, the United States offered the ideal spot for ordinary workers to take history into their own hands. Administered properly, economic democracy no longer required a political state, with Congressmen and presidents. All this could now be bypassed, for a government that provided necessary services without profit and left citizens otherwise to their

Courtesy: Scott Molloy

Newspapers affiliated with the American Federation of Labor, especially but not only in the West, were often known for their aggressively racist determination to eliminate the non-white competition for jobs.

own freedom. The I.W.W., DeLeon insisted, represented a new stage of human civilization. No wonder its enthusiasts called it the "Greatest Thing on Earth." The blueprint of future government, known as "the Wheel" or "Father Hagerty's Wheel of Fortune," was reprinted on circulars thousands of times, and embossed upon a chart for street and hall lectures. [Plate 35] Generations later, the Socialist Labor Party still used a version of the chart for pamphlets and propaganda meetings.

Fired up by this ideal, Wobbly agitators became within a few years almost mythical figures of American labor. They pioneered the "sit-down strike," by which workers remained in their places at work rather than leaving the job-site and opening up the possibility of replacement by "scabs" or strike-breakers. The first of these strikes took place in Schenectady, New York in 1908, and by the 1930s had become industrial unionism's chief tactic.

Only the solidarity of all workers, they insisted, could break through the barriers of privilege within labor organization, as well as outside. The Wobblies denounced as "union scabs" those AFL members who abided loyally by contracts which commanded them to continue working in a factory whose other workers had gone on strike. Unlike the exclusionary A.F. of L., Wobblies determinedly organized African-American timber workers, appealed to Asian-Americans, offered solidarity to Chicano anarchists, and led many important women's strikes. They also staged dramatic "free speech" fights to defend the right to speak on street corners where local

Courtesy: Dan Georgakas

Unlike the A.F. of L., the I.W.W. prided itself on its inclusiveness. These Japanese-American Wobblies had their own group in the San Francisco Bay Area.

relief for the unemployed; they spread their appeal to middle class voters on moral issues such as political corruption. In a few places, above all in heavily-German Milwaukee, they managed to create an admirably efficient city government and perpetuate a political machine able to reach constituencies in more than a half-dozen languages in a few hours.

But for the most part, Socialist victories were followed by defeats. Republicans and Democrats formed "fusion" tickets to eliminate the outsiders, often promising a reform coalition better connected to clean up corruption. Worse, Socialists suffered the disillusionment of their working class voters, who hoped that a victory would bring a dramatic change in their lives. Socialists rarely had a majority on city councils. But even with greater influence they could hardly challenge capitalism from the local venue. Daily newspapers continued in capitalist hands and they raved demagogically against socialist officials as a threat to city life. Industries threatened to leave or shut down rather than pay raised taxes.

Greater than all these problems, in a national sense, were divisions among the working and middle classes. The poorer classes, who might have supported socialist candidates, mostly did not vote. Catholics, especially Irish Catholics, remained sturdily loyal to the priests who warned them against "atheistic" socialists, and to the

Courtesy: Tamiment Library, New York University

Successful mostly in heavily blue-collar, one-industry towns, these candidates suffered many reversals in 1913 and after. Some briefly returned to office during 1918-20. Seymour Stedman, Debs' 1920 running mate, is pictured at the lower left.

Ralph Chaplin, Wobbly poet-artist-editor, shown with Solidarity *in his days at the editorial helm.*

This socialistic publication of the Western Federation of Miners was an early supporter of the Industrial Workers of the World.

DON'T BE A SCAB

DON'T GO TO THE MINING CAMPS OF SO. DAKOTA

Where members of Organized Labor are Locked Out because they refuse to scab and sign the following pledge:

"I am not a member of any labor Union and in consideration of my employment by the HOMESTAKE MINING COMPANY agree that I will not become such while in its service."

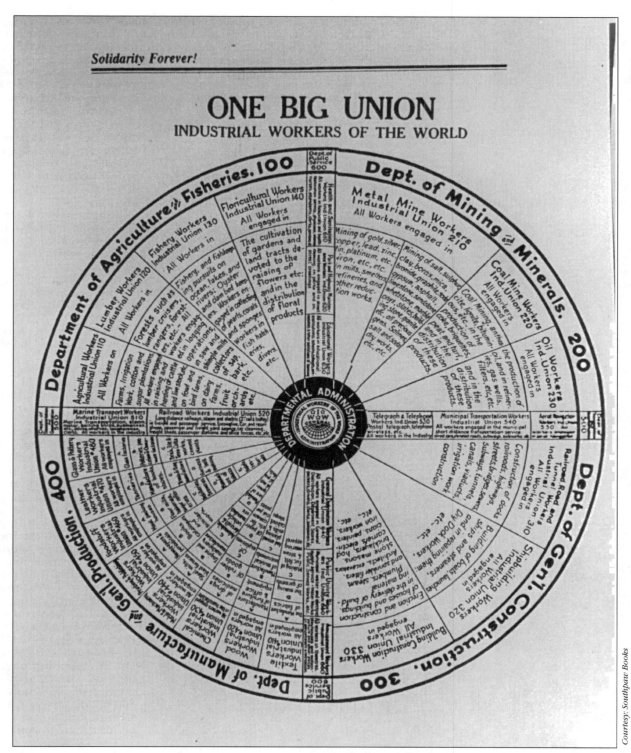

Often referred to as "Father Hagerty's Wheel of Fortune," for the former priest who promoted the idea of a chart describing the functional basis of present industry and future economic government.

officials denied underdog populations their First Amendment privileges.

Wobblies organized most effectively in the Western frontier districts, where I.W.W. halls offered the migratory agricultural worker, the timber worker or miner the only alternative to the local tavern, whorehouse or Salvation Army. They also commanded many of the railroad freight cars which migratory workers rode from job to job. On the streets of Western towns, Wobbly lecturers standing on "soap boxes" would appeal to workers to believe in themselves; competing with the Salvation Army for listeners, they would sing satirical music mocking capitalism and ministers who supported the system. To the tune of "Sweet Bye and Bye" they intoned:

> Long-haired preachers
>   come out every night
> To tell you what's wrong
>   and what's right
> But when you ask them
>   for something to eat
> They will tell you in
>   voices so sweet:
>
> You will eat, bye and bye,
> In the glorious land above
>   the sky
> Work and pray, live on hay,
> You will eat in the sky
>   when you die (that's
>   a lie).

At this edge of the American Dream, where migrants fleeing hard times found they had reached the geographical limit, the Wobblies also offered something more intangible. I.W.W. writers frequently expressed love for the natural world surrounding the tramping worker drawn to the beauty of the land and appalled by early cross-cutting of timber and other destructive, wasteful corporate moves. Like the German-Americans of the nineteenth century, the I.W.W.'s immigrant members in particular viewed picnics in the countryside and hiking society events as advanced glimpses of the better society to come.

The I.W.W. stirred enormous hatred from employers, religious institutions, the press and the A.F. of L.

Buying California Products
Patronizing California Movies

The State is Quarantined Against Hoof and Mouth Disease.

It Sends Workmen to Jail from One to Fourteen Years for Organizing Labor Unions.

Put it on the Unfair List.

Don't Buy its Canned Goods or Fruits.

Give its Movies the Cold Shoulder.

Boycott All California Products!

Courtesy: Southpaw Books

After 1910, Wobblies found many of their strongest supporters among migrant farm workers, mobilized in the Agricultural Workers Organization.

The Shame of California
BY HENRY GEORGE WEISS

This is the shame of the orange state
  That sits by the western sea
Where the tide comes in through the
    Golden Gate
  And the great ships go out free;
This is the crime of a sunny clime
  That I write for the years to read,
So the babes unborn can visit their scorn
  On the fruits of the System's greed.

Now the land was fair, and the land was
    broad,
  And rich in timber and soil,
But the Masters came and they fenced it all
  From the hands of the men that toil;

With only the right that spoilers have,
  And ruthless to maim and kill,
The seal of their brand was set on the land
  And held it to their will.

They reaped the fruits they had never
    sowed,
  They pillaged the forest glade,
From the sweat of slaves beneath the goad
  Were their ill-got dollars made;
And their power grew as their fortunes
    grew
  And bought laws served them well,
And in fifty years the state was theirs—
  And they turned it into hell.

MAY, 1925

Twenty-seven

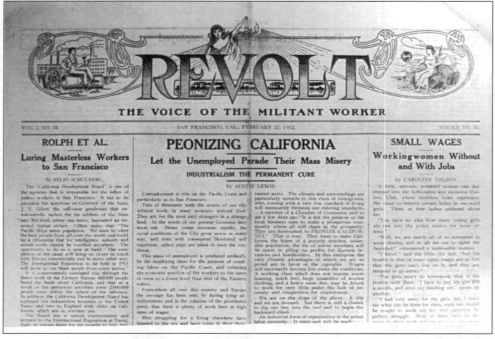

This California paper was sympathetic to the I.W.W. and devoted to mobilization of workers through mass strikes. Austin Lewis, translator of Engels's Anti-Duhring, *was among its major contributors.*

union leaders. Known as the "I Won't Work" or "I Want Whiskey" brigade, Wobblies represented a nightmare of revenge, like the images of African-Americans in southern novels. Along with internal conflicts, this hostility sharply limited the organization in its first years. But in 1909-11, without notable I.W.W. incitement, mass strikes of foreign-born workers broke out across the East. Although the I.W.W. reached only 100,000 members at its peak, it exerted an influence far beyond those numbers.

The most dramatic success took place in Lawrence, Massachusetts, a major textile center not only for the United States but for the world. Here, at least twenty-five

Typical local Wobbly hall — this one in St. Louis — where itinerant workers received food, shelter and education.

nationalities of workers, mostly unskilled, moved against repeated wage cuts in January, 1912. The A.F. of L. denounced the walkout as a "revolution." But I.W.W. organizers took charge of the strike, by establishing a democratic representation of each major group on the strike committee, staging dramatic parades (at which a famous sign appeared: "We Want Bread and Roses, Too"), even sending hungry children away for their safety to sympathizers in other cities.

The strike raged on for a month, with pressures building on both sides from around the nation. These immigrant strikers seemed, to many authorities, to represent all the underpaid immigrants in the nation; their strike might set off an earthquake of activity, even revolution. Judges ruled consistently against strikers' rights, while police and the militia meted out physical punishments. On the other side, labor organizations of all kinds, Italian immigrants and others along with socialists sent support. In late February, the strike was won, up to twenty percent pay increases with many additional benefits. Eugene Debs called it "the most decisive and far-reaching ever won by organized workers." Textile-mill owners across the East raised their workers' wages. Charismatic strike leaders Joe Ettor and Arturo Giovannitti, imprisoned on false charges, won their legal vindication months later. Youthful agitator Elizabeth Gurley Flynn became a national symbol of working women's courage and skillful mobilization.

The I.W.W. could not follow up this victory in the East. It lacked the resources to maintain a strong union local even in Lawrence, where it seemed to become a legendary memory. A great strike by textile workers the following year in Paterson, New Jersey, was beaten back after large parades and a star-studded benefit supporters' performance in Madison Square Garden. The I.W.W. retreated largely to its Western branches, where its Agricultural Workers Organization mobilized itinerant crop-pickers, and its timber and extractive workers held onto established loyalties.

Courtesy: Charles H. Kerr Co.

"Mr. Block," a favorite Wobbly cartoon character and object of a famous satirical song.

During its post-1913 decline, however, and only a few years before its violent suppression by the United States government, the I.W.W. etched some of its most memorable symbols on the consciousness of American labor and rebel traditions. Artist-poet Ralph Chaplin or perhaps Seattle unionist and propagandist Walker C. Smith was thought to have decisively popularized the "sabo-tabby" or Black Cat, an I.W.W. warning that employers crushing their workers could expect small acts of sabotage on the job. The name came partly from the French word *sabots,* or wooden shoes, identified by French anarchosyndicalists with sabotage. But unionists had long carried out such practices without naming them. I.W.W. sabotage was, in any case, nonviolent, and often along the lines of underpaid waitresses telling cus-

Private Collection

Even after the organization was dismembered by government attacks, the I.W.W.'s magazines remained an important political and educational influence in working class life.

Courtesy: Charles H. Kerr Co.

The I.W.W. also survived locally as an open forum for views unpopular within the Left. This leaflet for a Joseph Giganti lecture also illustrates the common use during the 1920s-50s of the mimeograph for notices, pamphlets and small circulation periodicals. Joseph Giganti, a former journalist and opera columnist for the Italian language Left press, was expelled from the Communist party during the 1920s but remained active in the Trotskyist movement.

Elizabeth Gurley Flynn during the Paterson Strike.

In later decades, the I.W.W. was mainly active among agricultural workers and in the struggles of the unemployed.

Favorite symbol of Wobbly threat to sabotage production, the "Sabo-Tabby" threatened non-violent action until working conditions improved.

tomers that the food was less than fresh. The "Sabo-Tabby" was a reminder that even powerless workers could make a boss's life difficult.

The iconography of the advancing proletariat was another important Wobbly adaptation. In this case an Art Nouveau or William Morris-style vision of a new world was often seen as dawning. So much did the I.W.W. believe in the power of the ordinary person to change society that the image of a worker folding his arms (borrowed from European themes of the non-violent, general strike) promised to usher in a utopia. On the other hand, the Wobblies' satirically playful malice toward the backward worker eager to please the bosses was legendary. "Mr. Block," the Blockhead worker, like the Socialist variant "Henry Dubb," could not be educated. He did not enjoy being abused, but he invited abuse by his anti-unionism, his racism, and his pure stupidity. Wobbly drawing styles of these satirical frames were, for the most part, straight out of the "funny papers." But the form had been successfully subverted.

In all, Wobblies were perpetual romantic outsiders and superb self-promoters. Adept at ridiculing the boss and equally adept at formulating catchy slogans for solidarity among workers, they hurtled themselves fecklessly into settings where they seemed certain to end up martyrs. In their faith that democracy could sweep away all the obstacles of wealth and power, they appeared the most wild-eyed idealists. But in their main message, that ordinary people could challenge authority on a day-to-day basis, they represented the American spirit at its best.

Joe Hill. Drawing by Carlos Cortez.

The I.W.W. often published the same, basic pamphlets in several languages, including Italian, Polish, Greek, Russian, Croatian and in this case, Bulgarian.

Rising of the Masses

THE ADVANCING PROLETARIAT.

Rising of the Masses: The Great Strikes, 1909-1919

The I.W.W. call to industrial revolt coincided with the spreading impulses in a variety of other industrial and ethnic groups whom the I.W.W. could not reach successfully. The most important non-I.W.W. industrial union was the Amalgamated Clothing Workers, founded as a dissident group of operatives in men's clothing from the conservative and timid United Garment Workers. A series of organizing drives after 1909, especially a decisive 1910 strike in Chicago, effectively unified different groups (notably Jews, Italian and Slavs) under a common program of immediate improvement and a Wobbly-like dream of radical industrial democracy. Even some former I.W.W. leaders, including Arturo Giovannitti, found space for themselves.

Ferment within the mainstream A.F. of L.'s heavily Jewish unions, such as the International Ladies Garment Workers Union, upset the staid bureaucratic atmosphere and made the unionization of the unskilled a moral crusade here, too. The "Uprising of 30,000," mostly young, unskilled women garment workers in the New York area, was a strike in 1909 under the auspices of the I.L.G.W.U. and greatly aided by women socialists and the Women's Trade Union League, an alliance of women reformers. Their courage and example stirred the more experienced, largely male cutters and others toward all-out mobilization. Amalgamated Clothing Workers and I.L.G.W.U. activists, in turn, along with the United Capmakers and others, provided neighborhood backing for Socialist candidates who seemed to reach nearer electoral victory with every New York election. Socialists in office or close contention encouraged unionization, often represented unions

As seen variously by the Jewish Groysser Kundes, working class self-confidence soared during 1911-13.

(as did lawyer Morris Hillquit, a frequent Socialist candidate, and Meyer London who was elected to three terms in Congress).

Wartime conditions in Europe changed the labor movement's prospects dramatically. Production raced forward with European orders, and immigration was practically cut off. Under these circumstances, many workers felt free to quit their jobs, confident they would find others; and even stubborn employers found new reasons to negotiate. From 1915 to 1919, each year saw a new peak in the record number of U.S. strikes in a single year. Not only unskilled workers, but also craft unionists (their jobs undergoing rapid change, due to further mechanization and closer management supervision) organized new locals and went on strike. For the first time since at least the Knights, workers in very different categories practiced "solidarity" with each other.

Radicals faced a great opportunity, but not as they had expected. The closer the United States moved to war, the more dangerous it became to talk or write about socialist ideas. But at the same time unions could be formed or taken over, even within the generally conservative American Federation of Labor, by radicals concentrating on industrial organizing. They found that American-born workers and many immigrants, also, remained skeptical of radical ideas but welcomed radical leaders. This paradox helped explain the presence of radicals in many union offices and newspapers.

At its apex in 1919, the strike wave led to a General Strike of Seattle workers, in which the city lay quiet for a week, practically governed in day-to-day economic affairs by the strike committee. Elsewhere, a nationwide steel strike of many nationality groups was led by a radical unionist and future communist, William Z. Foster. And in the stockyards of Chicago, notorious for its

The Shirtwaist Strike, famed "rising of the 20,000," and the subsequent role of women needle trades workers inspired their fellow employees. International Socialist Review, *1909 and* Groysser Kundes, *1911.*

Courtesy: American Social History Project, Hunter College, and Private Collection

conflicts between black and immigrant workers, radicals had successfully promoted an alliance to bring the races together. These were almost economic revolutions, and in many places May Day and Labor Day, 1919, saw giant parades of unionists proud to assert their dignity as the productive sector of American society.

It did not entirely explain the joy and expectation with which workers of every variety participated in strikes and demonstrations during these years, or the nature of the demands they made at their workplace. As many observers reported, Labor Day parades suddenly seemed more festive, as if the participants were waking up to life. As famed radical journalist John Reed noticed, workers also expected more opportunities for industrial democracy at work, the possibility of making decisions about how their jobs would be done to make them more interesting and fulfilling.

Perhaps the most striking images

A cover of the Groysser Kundes *mourns the tragedy of women workers killed in the Triangle Shirtwaist Fire of 1911, an event which helped spur efforts of the philanthropic Women's Trade Union League to organize them into unions.*

of these years are amateurs' photographs. The *International Socialist Review,* after its conversion into a popular-format magazine in 1909, invited its readers to submit their work and many reporters provided the shots accompanying their articles. Indeed, the *Review* may have been the first major American magazine to encourage the amateur photographer. These photographers captured a range of subjects, from the great individuals (the countless photos taken of Debs, or "Mother" Jones) to the crowds at cataclysmic events. Elsewhere in the socialist press, the easily afforded equipment available made camera-work a standard and permanent part of the strike scene.

Socialist electoral victories and successful strikes combined to make for an optimistic Mayday. Groysser Kundes, *1911.*

Both, Courtesy: Library of Congress

Two views of the famous "Bread and Roses" Lawrence, Massachusetts, textile strike of 1912.

(Right) Socialists in Alaska, from the International Socialist Review. Socialistic and Wobbly influence peaked in territorial Alaska when thousands of miners turned to the Left.

SOCIALIST HALL.

The Growth of Socialist Sentiment in Alaska

Int'l Socialist Review, Jan. 1912

(Below) The deportation of workers from Ludlow, Colorado (not Lowell, as labeled inaccurately) marked one of the most violent labor events of the 1910s, the Ludlow strike and "Massacre" — with federal troops shooting dozens and brutalizing hundreds of miners in a kidnapping that took the prisoners deep into the desert.

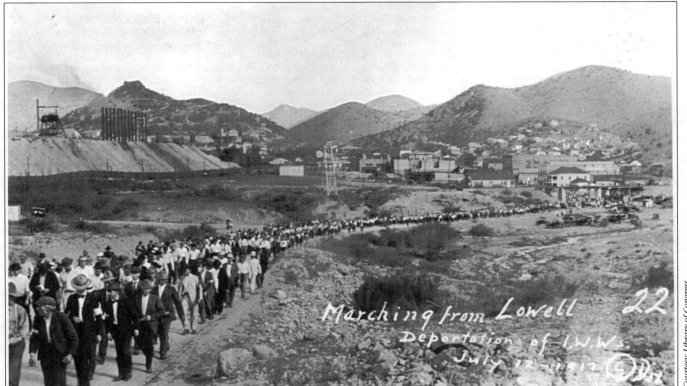

Marching from Lowell   22
Deportation of I.W.W.
July 12 - 1912

JOHN REED

Journalist, romantic, avant-gardist and revolutionary, John Reed remains the great symbol of the early twentieth century writer and romantic. In some ways, Reed the person does not quite live up to the legend. He remained a dilettante in the political life that he sought for himself, and he hardly took the time to think through the implications of his furious journalism. As the 1981 film *Reds* dramatized he possessed many negative virtues as a husband of an equally avant-garde talent, Louise Bryant. That said, Reed has never been surpassed as a radical journalist and as a connecting point between bohemianism and middle America.

Born in 1877 in Portland, Oregon to a prosperous family, the sickly Reed was sent East for finishing school and went on to Harvard. His father, a conscience liberal and a federal prosecutor of timberland fraud, meanwhile ran for Congress on the Progressive Party ticket in 1910 before his sudden death two years later. This family reformism had little immediate effect upon young Reed, who devoted his energies to typical school activities, including a season as a Harvard cheerleader.

But Reed's determination to be a serious writer, at this moment in American history, radicalized him quickly. Moving to New York in 1910, he found that he could make a living only by devising superficial essays for superficial commercial magazines – with one important exception. *Metropolitan Magazine,* which leaned toward structural reform and frequently opened its pages to talented socialists like Reed. He found his spiritual home, however, in the pages of the *Masses* magazine. Here, he could write playfully or in deadly earnest, poems, sketches, book reviews and short stories.

He pioneered a twentieth century style of strike reportage during the Paterson, New Jersey, textile strike of 1913. Thumped by a cop and recalling his experiences in jail as part of the story, he put himself into the picture. Earlier journalists (few of them radical) had also "lived" their experiences in the Wild West or urban slums. But they rarely felt the sympathy for the lower classes or enmity toward the rich to shape their work in realistic, yet dramatically rendered reform prose. Reed threw himself into the actual strike support, and his energies proved crucial in creating a Pageant in Madison Square Garden (featuring the strikers themselves) which marked the high point of strike enthusiasm. Tragically, the sympathy and excitement created could not sustain the strike against overwhelming odds. Reed's favorite labor radicals, the Industrial Workers of the Works, had been beaten.

But he moved on to other and even greater excitements. When the Mexican Revolution broke out in 1910, *Metropolitan* and the *New York World* sent him across the border. Then as now, the great majority of American reporters on foreign missions wrote about "revolutionary" subjects from the materials available in State Department and United States intelligence offices, or they ventured out only to tell the story that the prosperous classes (like their American backers) wish to be heard. Instead, Reed rode with the revolutionaries, struck up a friendship with Pancho Villa, and marched with soldiers en route to a decisive battle. Contrary to the usual practice of bemoaning chaos and property damage, Reed drew literary vitality from his sympathies for the revolutionary *joie de vivre.* The hostile attitude of the United States government, down to the invasion of Mexico by liberal president Woodrow Wilson (halted only by United States concerns for greater dangers in Europe), confirmed his attitudes and his methods.

Back in Greenwich Village between assignments, Reed and his intimates (including his wife, Louise Bryant) tried to live the freedom that they espoused for humankind. In their work for the *Masses,* he and Floyd Dell, Max Eastman and others successfully won over the finest artists and many of the best writers to depict the collective life of the urban masses. Meanwhile they wrote plays (and acted in them), engaged in love affairs and met great strike leaders. They pioneered psychoanalysts and became world-class bohemians. Despite the claims to sexual equality, sex and everything else was less equal for women – but far more equal than elsewhere in society, a fact of the greatest importance to Reed personally.

But all this began to come to an end with the United States entry into War. The federal government suppressed the *Masses,* putting its editors and artists on trial. Reed, sent to the battle front, found himself unable to write stirring prose about trench warfare with no ideals but incremental advance and real meaning but military regimentation and mass murder.

Reed's journalistic instincts and a series of lucky accidents found him in the middle of the Russian Revolution. He saw only one party, the Bolsheviks, which embraced the Soviets and seemed determined to push to a revolutionary conclusion (rather than supporting the continuation of the punishing war, as did the short-lived Menshevik government). For a short time an employed as propagandist for the Soviet Foreign Ministry, he returned to the United States and was arrested, and had his papers seized. Recovering his documents legally, he penned *Ten Days That Shook the World,* the finest book of revolutionary journalism to that date, and one of the finest examples of journalism about revolutionary crises written in any language in the entire twentieth century.

Reed could not translate this journalistic or literary triumph into the revolutionary politics to which he aspired. Always lukewarm toward the Socialist Party, he threw himself into the formation of a Communist movement out of the battered socialist fragments. But he had little talent for this kind of political leadership. His essays for otherwise obscure papers, like *Revolutionary Age* of Boston, show some of his hidden strengths, such as a careful observation of American workers seeking to puzzle out their own path to change (through control of their workplace rather than the expected revolutionary uprising). But these insights counted for little in the charged factional atmosphere where connections with (or behavior inspired by) the Russian Communist leaders counted most.

In flagging health but still combative, Reed traveled to Moscow to argue for the positions of his Communist Labor Party, the most "American" of the revolutionary factions. He could not have won, nor would he likely have lasted in the later American Communist movement. A free spirit, Reed looked to his own conscience and his immediate impulses to guide his way. He belonged to the 1910s, and his death from typhus (due in no small part to the American-sponsored blockade that deprived the Russians of medical supplies) in 1920 froze his image in time. Thereafter, Reed might signify to Communists the brilliant cartographer of the Bolshevik victory, but he signified to others the romance and the promise of a time lost in blood and disillusion.

STORM BOY

John Reed, drawn by Masses *artist Art Young, responded to the 1913 Paterson, New Jersey, textile strike by helping to create a fund-raising pageant in Madison Square Garden.*

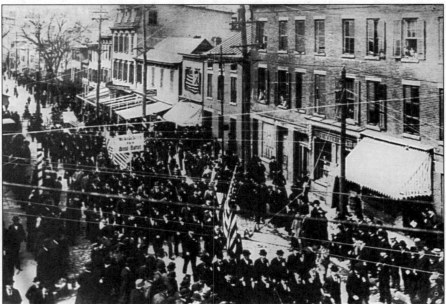

The Paterson Strike of 1913, a major incident in I.W.W. history, also allowed Italian-American anarchists and members of the small Socialist Labor Party one last burst of activity and attention. Defeat left all the activists crestfallen. Picture from the International Socialist Review.

MARCH, 1913   PRICE TEN CENTS

The INTERNATIONAL SOCIALIST REVIEW
THE·FIGHTING·MAGAZINE OF·THE·WORKING·CLASS

New Shoes for the Striking Coal Miners' Children—Mother Jones on the Right

LATEST NEWS FROM GREAT STRIKES

Courtesy: Southpaw Books

Coalminers strike with help from Mother Jones.

Two heroes of the Lawrence Strike, talented organizers Joe Ettor and Arturo Giovannitti.

In A Prison Cell Because They Are Loyal To Their Class

TWO NOBLE FIGHTERS IN THE STRUGGLE OF TWENTY FIVE THOUSAND STRIKING TEXTILE WORKERS WHOSE WAGES AVERAGED LESS THAN SIX DOLLARS PER WEEK.

Our Fellow Workers
Arturo Giovannitti & Joseph J. Ettor

INTERNATIONAL PRINTING CO.

Private Collection

The Labor Advocate

VOL. 3, NO. 6. EXPIRATION NO. 110.   PROVIDENCE, R. I., OCTOBER 3, 1914.   TWO CENTS—50 CENTS PER YEAR

NO 12-HOUR DAY for STORE GIRLS!

What Socialist Officials Did In Haverhill

Ex-Mayor John C. Chase Tells of Successful Efforts of Socialist Administration to Aid Workers in the Massachusetts City.

OPEN - AIR MEETINGS

PAWTUCKET
Sunday, Oct. 4
Speaker, JOHN DUFFY

WOONSOCKET
Sunday, Oct. 4
Speaker, E. W. THEINERT

OLNEYVILLE
Sunday, Oct. 4
Speaker, S. H. FABSEL

MARKET SQUARE PROVIDENCE
Saturday, Oct. 3
Speaker, E. W. THEINERT
Sunday, Oct. 4
Speaker, E. MORRISSEY

RIVERPOINT
Tuesday, Oct. 6
Speaker, E. W. THEINERT

LONSDALE
Tuesday, Oct. 6
Speaker, E. MORRISSEY

CENTREDALE
Tuesday, Oct. 6
Speaker, THOMAS DILLON

CENTRAL FALLS
Wednesday, Oct. 7
Speaker, JOHN DUFFY

MANVILLE
Thursday, Oct. 8
Speaker, THOMAS DILLON

BROAD AND WEYBOSSET STS., PROVIDENCE
Friday, Oct. 9
Speaker, DR. JAMES P. REID

DOYLE MONUMENT
Thursday, Oct. 8
Speaker, SAMUEL H. FABSEL

FIGHT CONTINUES AGAINST SATURDAY NIGHT WORK IN DEPARTMENT STORES

Girls Threatened with Instant Discharge if They Attend Organization Meetings.—Hired Spies Busy in Service of Store Proprietors.

Outlet and Dimond's Condemned at Open-Air Meeting

Attempt of Samuels Bros. to Pose as Philanthropists Shown Up as Rankest of Hypocrisy. Speakers Declare Nothing Can Prevent Organization of Store Girls.

The Dick Military Law as a Means of Conscription

Workingmen in United States May be Forced Into Military Service, Just as Are the Men of European Countries.

LOCAL DEMOCRATS USE PRINTED MATTER WITHOUT UNION LABEL

Eighth Ward Politicians Show Just How Friendly They Really Are to Organized Labor.

PAWTUCKET POLICE PREVENT SOCIALIST OPEN-AIR MEETING

Declare Permit Must be Obtained.—Local Comrades Will Insist on Right of Free Speech.

Courtesy: Scott Molloy

A.F. of L. support for women's organizing was rarely enthusiastic, but sometimes blossomed locally during the wartime wave of labor solidarity.

Courtesy: Taminent Library, New York University

This all-time popular labor defense poster reflected fund-raising activities across New England and elsewhere for the Lawrence strike leaders.

Private Collection

The dramatic strikes of 1919 included a number by women needle-trades and textile workers, shop clerks and others. The Liberator *magazine celebrated the events with this 1919 cover.*

Courtesy: Hood Museum of Art, Dartmouth College

The struggle and persecutions in Colorado inspired some of the most dramatic political art of the day, such as this drawing by John Sloan.

Beautiful Bohemia

"You wasn't in the breadline Las' Night." "Nah — They Don't Use the Union Label."

Courtesy, all: Rebecca Zurier

In clockwise order from lower left, drawings from the Masses: Robert Minor, "O Wicked Flesh!" a comment on the censorial Comstock Law, October-November, 1915; John Sloan's feminist "True Story of Adam and Eve," and Glenn Coleman's evocation of working class urban life, "Class Consciousness," both from March, 1914.

Beautiful Bohemia

Another virtual revolution, perhaps even more important for the future, also took place with the help of various radicals. A cultural transformation began during the early 1910s in Greenwich Village, New York, where equality of the sexes and sexuality before marriage became the intellectuals' credo and their pursuit of happiness. "Flappers," young women excited by the jazz music and the idea of personal freedom, could be seen in many urban districts, carrying out the practices of the intellectuals, even if ignorant of the fine points. Books by Sigmund Freud and others, focused on sexuality, also circulated widely for the first time.

These events did not only take place in New York environs, of course. Midwestern bohemians like Henry M. Tichenor, St. Louis editor-publisher of the socialistic free thought magazine, *The Melting Pot,* gave their own literary interpretations of free love. The *International Socialist Review* and the Charles H. Kerr Company from Chicago sent out thousands of copies of *Love's Coming of Age,* a treatise on romantic affection by British homosexual Edward Carpenter. The *Masses,* the American Left's finest illustrated magazine, similarly made available various works on sexology, which small-town readers could examine and absorb. Little leftwing bohemian neighborhoods flourished in the North Side of Chicago (around the famed Dill Pickle Club), Seattle, San Francisco and doubtless elsewhere. All this seemed at the time rather daring, certainly disapproved by conservatives and most religiously-inclined Americans. The bohemians enjoyed twitting them, and the look of the avant-garde had burning youth and feminism closely emblazoned on it.

Unique, individual women associated broadly with the radical movement were able to stamp their image on the times. Emma Goldman, the anarchist writer and speaker, became a very popular figure for adulation and for ridicule in the press, known for her advocacy of "free love," her promotion of the avant-

The Unemployed

A STORY BY JAMES HOPPER IN THIS NUMBER

Courtesy: Southpaw Books

EMMA GOLDMAN

Reviled and feared in the conservative press as she was beloved by her radical following, Emma Goldman seemed a larger-than-life symbol of free love, anti-militarism, atheism and homosexual rights. From her entry into the American anarchist movement in 1889 to her deportation in 1919, she was easily one of the most controversial Americans of either sex.

Born into a lower-middle-class Jewish family in Lithuania in 1881, Emma Goldman grew up lonely but inspired by a devoted female teacher. She wished at first to study medicine. But the family's financial status forced her to go to work, surrounded in St. Petersburg by a climate of anti-Semitism and by the legends of the revolutionary anarchist-terrorists who assassinated the Czar. She carried this strong memory to the United States, as she emigrated with her sister to Rochester, New York in 1885.

There, she worked in a sweatshop and married a fellow Jewish immigrant. Like a small but dynamic fraction of recent immigrant Jews, she was transformed by the Haymarket events and the martyrdom of anarchist leaders. Leaving her husband and job, she traveled to New York. Immediately she fell in with the notorious German-American anarchist editor-agitator Johann Most, known for his defense of terrorism, his theatrical performances and his Rabelaisian humor on the lecture trail. Within a few years, Goldman had become a female counterpart to Most, rhetorically flaunting bourgeois laws and standards as if to challenge her audience to do likewise.

Goldman worked out her own intellectual system during the 1890s, mixing the cooperative visions of Prince Peter Kropotkin with the individualist anarchism of Henrik Ibsen and others. She decided that revolutionary emancipation must honor individualism, emphatically including the subjectivity of women. An extraordinary view for even the radical movement of the 1890s, it marked her as a "character," *sui generis.*

She also scoffed at electoral politics, even socialist electoral politics, and urged direct action including vengeance against capitalist oppressors. With her lover Alexander Berkman, she therefore planned in 1892 the unsuccessful assassination of steel magnate Henry Clay Frick. Berkman served fourteen years in prison for this action and Goldman repudiated terrorism. But she spent a year in prison, 1893-94, for telling people that during a severe depression they should seize the food they needed to keep their families from starving.

After her release, she devoted herself in lectures and essays on a wide range of social questions. She insisted upon erotic life as a creative force, troubling socialists who — frequently accused by conservatives of plotting free love — often sought to maintain a Puritanical appearance to their movement. She denounced the bondage of conventional marriage and the power of the patriarchal husband and father over wife and daughters. She demanded the availability of birth control, especially for women. And she became a public interpreter of European avant-garde cultural currents in theater and literature.

The assassination of President McKinley by an anarchist comrade from Buffalo in 1901 drove the anarchist movement underground for years. Yet Goldman emerged — rejoined by Berkman in 1906 — the publisher of an anarchist magazine and a beloved or notorious lecturer to public audiences of all kinds. Through *Mother Earth* magazine, Americans learned about European anarchist currents, personalities and ideas. Meanwhile, Goldman herself became a Greenwich Village personality of major stature, author of well-received books on politics and culture, mentor to civil libertarian Roger Baldwin (founder of the American Civil Liberties Union), and the idol of aging working class immigrant anarchists.

The entry of the United States into the First World War darkened her path in two ways. Proclaiming the right of civilians to resist induction, she drew a prison sentence of two years in 1916-17. Meanwhile, if she had no fondness for the Socialist party and little actual contact with the I.W.W., she felt almost immediately alienated from their joint successor, the American Communist movement. She insisted upon the Bolsheviks' right to make a revolution. But she felt only revulsion at the Communist state and left Russia in 1921, becoming a virtual pariah in the Left for her increasingly shrill rhetoric of anti-communism and anti-Marxism.

Goldman never again found her way. Permitted to return to the United States only if she would testify against American Communists, she refused on principle. Living in Britain, later Canada, she wrote her controversial autobiography, *Living My Life* — which concerned her search for love as much as her search for revolution — and in old age threw herself into one last spectacular campaign. Defending the Spanish anarchists who had seized Barcelona and many provinces, she toured the country torn by civil war and raised money abroad for them. The Spanish Communist attack on the anarchists, and the suppression of them both by Franco's fascist forces, deprived her of immediate campaigns and deepened her bitterness against communism. She died in 1940, not quite forgotten, and was buried in the Waldheim Cemetery of Chicago with the Haymarket Martyrs. A little over a quarter-century later, a garbled version of her thoughts appeared on a popular feminist sweatshirt: "If I can't dance, I won't join your revolution." Although an inaccurate representation of her actual phrase, it had been true to her sentiments.

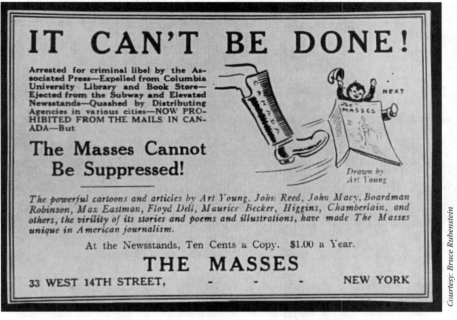

Masses *responds cheerfully to attempts at wartime repression, 1917.*

Anarchists and bohemians: Emma Goldman's magazine Mother Earth, *preached free thought while editor Sh. Yanofsky of the anarchist Yiddish* Freie Arbeter Shtimme *(caricatured in the* Groysser Kundes*) published some of the most experimental Yiddish writers of the day.*

ART YOUNG

Harry Godfrey

'HE STIRRETH UP THE PEOPLE'

JESUS CHRIST

THE WORKINGMAN OF NAZARETH
WILL   SPEAK
AT   BROTHERHOOD   HALL
— SUBJECT —
— THE RIGHTS OF LABOR —

The Masses, 1913

The Profiteer: "I'm as good a friend of labor as the next man — but there's no denying the fact that workingmen do spend their money foolishly"

Courtesy: Bruce Rubenstein

Art Young, dean of the Masses *artists, and some of his work. From* Art Young: His Life and Times *(1939).*

garde theater, and her hostility to socialist electoral strategies. Margaret Sanger, the chief pioneer of birth control activism, began her public access with a socialist press column and went on to found her own movement with its strongest following in Greenwich Village. The dancer Isadora Duncan offered an ideal that thousands of self-made heroines imitated by defying moral and aesthetic standards around them. Socialist intellectuals saw themselves as the formulators and articulators of the "modern" tendencies, and defenders of wide availability for then illegal birth control devices.

But it was the quality of the artists' images in the *Masses* which made the greatest impression at the time and left the most lasting memory. When the artists took over the magazine in 1912, they leaned way from didactic and propagandistic illustration common in socialist magazines to the wry humor and detailed print-work in European satirical magazines like *Simpliccimus* and *L'Asiette au Beurre,* but also toward encouraging artists to experiment with their own styles. The most important technical innovation, the use of the coarse crayon, had not been employed extensively in any United States publication. Borrowing from the French artist Honore Daumier, they sought to offer raw appearing glimpses of the lower classes in daily life and in moments of crisis. Unlike nineteenth century American prints which typed the poor as coarse or pathetic, these images were drawn from life. Rather than neat and finished, the style looked invitingly incomplete and subjective.

The results were stunning beyond all previous American (and perhaps any other) leftwing magazine experiments. The readers and artists seemed less "separate" from each other than they did in commercial magazines, closer to the proximity of J.A. Wayland and the rural audience he had addressed directly and intimately. Art looked artless, an avant-garde provocation to the existing art world as well as an invitation to the readers to look at the society around them.

Courtesy: Hood Museum, Dartmouth College

Portrait by John Sloan of Floyd Dell, avant-garde literary critic, revolutionary editor and playwright who took over as managing editor of the Masses *magazine, enticing writers on psychology, feminism and free love into its fold. In later decades, Dell became a leading writer on sex and morality.*

Private Collection

The Groysser Kundes *ridicules Jewish Forward editor Abraham Cahan for popularizing a Yiddish translation of August Bebel's famed volume* Women and Socialism *as if it were racy literature.*

In fact, the artists of the *Masses,* like John Sloan and Maurice Becker, helped invent the "Ashcan" school sweeping New York with unromanticized or stylized images of modern big city life. They went far to break with the historic prejudices of American artists against the city, mirroring in some ways the avant-garde milieu around master photographer Alfred Steiglitz and the transformation of the photograph from didactic instrument of reform to a vision of how urban life might be seen. If socialist drawings had traditionally seen working people as terribly oppressed or about to awaken, *Masses* art captured their real-life vitality and capacities to be themselves and (at least implicitly) to create a world from their lives and their hopes.

Much of the *Masses* art remained determinedly socialistic, and world war hardened the political determination of leading artists. Others resigned, leaving the magazine less experimental and more propagandistic. By 1917, *Masses* cartoons and editorials led to its suppression and the arrest of its leading figures. Out of that suppression came a new magazine, *The Liberator,* which believed also in the

Courtesy: Southpaw Books

Brainchild of St. Louis socialist philosopher and humorist H.M. Tichenor, the Melting Pot *circulated widely in the plains states and the South.*

Courtesy: the Prometheus Library, New York

December 1930   Twenty Cents

BIRTH CONTROL REVIEW

Woodcut by Dorothy Owen

Volume XIV, No. 12   Two Dollars a Year

Courtesy: Southpaw Books

The Birth Control Trial in New York City. Several Poor Mothers Brought Their Large Families to Aid Mrs. Margaret Sanger in Court. The Photograph Shows Mrs. Sanger and Mrs. F. L. Byrne in Front of the Court of Special Sessions in Brooklyn, Also Mrs. Rose Haltern, with Her Six Children, Ranging in Age from 16 Months to 10 Years.

Courtesy: Library of Congress

Women socialists like Antoinette Konikow (top left) and Margaret Sanger launched the birth control movement. Publisher of the anarchist Woman Rebel, *c. 1912-13, Sanger later published the politically staid* Birth Control Review.

Private Collection

spirit of cultural rebellion, but placed its main hopes in the Russian Revolution's consequences. Frequently beautiful, it was printed on cheaper paper, with a heavier dose of traditional political-style cartoons and an increasing sense of being an American support mechanism for Bolshevism. Everything had changed.

The cultural rebellion had meanwhile permeated considerable parts of immigrant and minority race circles, prompting new imagery with some of the same changes. Jewish intellectuals, writing in Yiddish, determined to promote their own modernism, with a literature and artists' style open to the most experimental, radical expressions. Arturo Giovannitti attempted a kind of syndicalist or bohemian version of Italian Futurism in his short-lived magazine, *Il Fuoco.* Meanwhile in Harlem — so bubbling with life that it became the black metropolis of the world — black artists and writers moved in what young socialist leader A. Philip Randolph called the "New Crowd." As he ran for office, he published *The Messenger,* a political-cultural monthly with a flair (and some jazz reportage) if not the *Masses'* artists. Unfortunately, time was running out on these experiments.

In retrospect, avant-gardists of every kind had failed to anticipate the depth of intolerance in the fabric of the society they promised to transform, but their hopefulness carried an element of naivete which perhaps made their easy-going confidence possible. As they woke up to the emerging horrors, the very shock of recognition made them more articulate and creative in words and design than anyone to follow.

Maurice Sterne, Untitled, from The Masses.

Private Collection

The "Divine Isadora" Duncan as seen by Abraham Walkowitz. The artist, a well-known figure among the Greenwich Village circle of the 1910s and already a famous artist of New York scenes, drew a series of Duncan sketches from memory after seeing her dance. From the New Masses.

Van Wyck Brooks, an editor of The Seven Arts, *the leading radical aesthetic journal during World War I.*

Successor to the repressed Masses, The Liberator *was more political and after a few years, less artistic.*

ISADORA DUNCAN

Inventor of "Modern Dance," feminist extraordinaire, opposed to all hierarchies and all hatreds of the body, Isadora Duncan is one of America's most authentic culture heroes. She had little interest in politics as such, but she instinctively aligned herself with the possibilities of social revolution similar to the revolution she sought in human life.

Born in 1877 and raised in the San Francisco Bay area by her freethinking mother, Duncan was exposed to poverty but also to utopian socialist ideas and the physical culture movement. She discovered for herself, in her teens, the fundamentals of her emerging style. Rebelling from the standard Victorian dance performances, which vacillated between pretentious ballet imitations and girlie shows, she focused upon the liberated body, starting with her own. Abandoning formal choreography, she expressed herself through such gestures of daily life as running, walking and skipping, extended into an upward movement.

Duncan adopted two important literary or cultural sources of her inspiration. Walt Whitman, whose *Leaves of Grass* she carried with her continuously, helped her understand that within any one individual, the multiple qualities of humanity could be found. She felt therefore that dancing was for her a collective act of the race, even when conducted alone. Second, she adopted an almost fanatical devotion to Greek civilization, unashamed of the body and proud of fusing its splendor with the highest ideals of culture. This relocation in a classic persona fortified her rejection of Victorianism and gave her an alternative vision.

Isadora received early success as a dancer, although largely in Europe rather than in the more prudish United States. Educated European young people fell in love with her, and the avant-garde of the Continent crowded her recitals. Returning periodically to America, she took part in (and also inspired) the artistic and political modernism of the 1910s. Intellectuals saw in the "divine Isadora" the personal realization of their strivings, her will to overcome staid tradition not only in theory but in living practice. Her admirers included the *Masses* group, notably the painter John Sloan, whose fluid and realistic portraits captured, for many who did not see her, Isadora's muscular fusion of spiritual and bodily freedom.

Excited by the 1905 Russian Revolution, she inspired a veritable legion of performers at the socialist Rand School and the anarchist Modern School. She became a controversial defender of the Russian Revolution of 1917, accepting an offer to establish a school of dance in Moscow in 1921. Her new style, influenced by Russian nationalist idealism, rendered struggles against oppression and into freedom via a story, personally choreographing dance versions of "The Internationale," Ireland's "Wearing of the Green," and funeral marches for Lenin. These earned her steadily less popularity in avant-garde circles, and she deepened her isolation by attacking the popular jazz culture. In a particularly disastrous tour, she returned to the United States in 1922-23, intimidated by federal interrogation at Ellis Island, threats of the Ku Klux Klan and editorial attacks by leading newspapers.

Isadora Duncan had become a sort of caricature of modernism before her tragic death in an automobile accident in 1927. But she had already left a lasting monument in modern dance. She had not diminished her vital political commitments: her Paris apartment doubled for the European headquarters of the Sacco-Vanzetti Defense Committee. Her autobiography, *My Life,* which reached print only after her death, remained extremely popular for decades, especially among women readers. Two films of her life, including a stunning performance by Vanessa Redgrave, inspired new generations' interest during the radical 1960s and after.

BRANDON TYNAN IN "EQUITY"
Strike of the Actors Equity
Association Aug, 1919.

Actors striking in 1919 added drama to their appeals for public support.

Courtesy: Congregational Church of Springfield, Illinois

Vachel Lindsay, famous free-verse poet of Springfield, Illinois, aligned himself with the Socialist party and tried to formulate an American radicalism.

*Alice Paul celebrates passage of the
Nineteenth Amendment at National
Women's Party headquarters.*

*Inspired in part by women's cultural
emancipation, the woman suffrage movement
revived during the 1910s and swept to victory
in 1919. Led by Alice Paul, radicals of the
National Woman's Party initiated "militant"
tactics and sensationalist spectacles to dramatize their cause, while socialist suffragists
exerted decisive influence in many locations,
especially New York and the far West.*

IL FUOCO

CIO' CHE NON VIVE NON ARDE

דער גרויסער קונדס

דער סאצערנער בעפרייער

Marx, the Wonder-Worker, leads the children of Israel through perils to Paradise.

Karl Marx the Liberty-giver. Marx becomes Moses leading the masses through the Red Sea of capitalism. Refashioned after a cartoon in Puck *by Joseph Keppler showing America as the haven for the world's impoverished. From* Groysser Kundes, *1912.*

Immigrants/Race Minorities

By 1912, the radical movement had begun a subtle change in another dramatic sense: from native-born to European immigrant. To a far lesser but important extent, it was also changed by the movement of African-Americans to northern industrial cities, the response of Mexican-Americans to the Mexican Revolution, and of Asians to the events in their homelands. A development as natural as the appeal of fast-growing American industry to Europeans eagerly escaping Old World poverty, these tendencies brought a welter of new voices into the Socialist Party and the radical union movements. They also broke down any lingering hope that American radicalism could remain free of the internal conflicts that wracked Europe and the rest of the world.

The change did not happen all at once. German-Americans had already become, by the turn of the

Courtesy: Photo preserved by Kate Dobronyi (seated in front of standing woman), bequested to Aaron Kramer and made available by him.

A banquet of old-time German-American socialists in New York City's Labor Temple, c. 1907, honoring famed German socialist Karl Liebknecht.

century, "*alte Genossen*" or "old heads," somewhat weary of throwing themselves against the apparently unyielding stone walls of American life. Still, these aging craft workers and their wives remained, in parts of New York and New Jersey especially, one of the most tenacious constituencies in the Socialist Party, faithfully attending every event, singing socialist music in their choral groups, determinedly supportive but understandably pessimistic right to the end.

The new immigrant constituencies had none of this weariness,

Courtesy: Immigration History Research Center, University of Minnesota

Italian immigrant support their newspaper, La Parole *(the Word) in Paterson, New Jersey, a hotbed of anarchist sentiment from the 1890s to the 1910s.*

Courtesy: Charles H. Kerr Co., and Carlos Cortez

This ad for Regeneracion, *organ of the Mexican-American anarchist Magon brothers, demonstrates the growing internationalism of the United States socialist press. Ricardo Flores Magon is seen here by I.W.W. artist Carlos Cortez.*

Courtesy: Florida State Archives

Ybor City's Cuban-Spanish radicals were a major force in Florida's labor and radical communities, c. 1910.

Ivan Molek, Slovenian-language socialist editor of the Chicago daily Prosveta *for decades, was also a beloved novelist. From Mary Jugg Molek,* Immigrant Woman *(1980).*

Toveritar *(The Female Comrade), subtitled the "only Finnish women's journal in America" was published by socialists and for decades edited by novelist, poet, playwright and historian Helmi Mattson.*

but also in many cases little organization. Among the Eastern Europeans streaming into the United States during 1890-1915, radicals first formed small groups of Hungarians, Poles, Russians and others, but especially among Italians and Jews. Others followed in immigrant nationalities as small as Bulgarians (known for their satiric theater groups), Armenians (famous for their logistic support of other nationalities), Latvians (dogmatic supporters of Russian revolutionaries) and East Indians (who formed the Communist Party of India in Seattle and San Francisco).

Anarchist Italians published especially important newspapers and led strikes from Paterson,

New Jersey, as early as the 1890s; an extreme group among them sent textile weaver Gaetano Bresci back to Italy where he successfully assassinated King Humbert in 1900. (Leon Czolgosz, son of a Polish-American socialist in Buffalo, assassinated President William McKinley the next year.) Italian radical orators, said to be so charismatic that they could provoke riots with their words, stamped their presence on the American labor scene. But most Italian-American radicals felt uneasy around political socialists, too anarchistic to believe in the possibility of electoral victory over capitalism, hoping instead for an all-encompassing revolutionary strike wave as the only possible road to workers' control. The several thousand organized Italian-American socialists — a tiny fraction of all Italian-Americans — joined the independent Italian Socialist Federation, which disdained the Socialist Party as insufficiently anti-clerical.

Most other immigrants groups were more sympathetic towards political education and electoralism. But they attached their vision of socialism to organizing *unskilled* workers, the overwhelming majority among themselves. For instance, Hungarians worked in the mines and heavy industry of the East and Midwest; Slovenes similarly industrialized with their fellow South Slavs, the Croats, in Pennsylvania, Cleveland and Chicago. Even small groups such as Greeks felt the desperate need for representation of the most oppressed in their communities. For them, the Industrial Workers of the World proved a savior. Italians, Hungarians and a handful of other groups published their own I.W.W.-oriented newspapers. Russian immigrants established a combination of job employment agency and fraternal society, the Union of Russian Workers, with 10,000 members loosely attached to the I.W.W.

Mexican-American anarchists carried on an extraordinary agitation in the southwest. Ricardo Flores Magon

(K.A. Suvanto's caricature of himself.)

Finnish-American radical cartoonists published several magazines of their own, most notably Punikki, Vapanteen *and* Lopotossu, *over the decades from the 1910s to the 1930s. Their outstanding artist, A.K. Suvanto, was equal to the best of radical cartoonists in any language.*

Finnish cooperatives sponsored musical groups and much amateur theater during the 1910s-20s.

Two leading Yiddish radical literary personalities. Chaim Zhitlovsky, a social revolutionary, was a mystic Zionist and a spell-binding lecturer on many subjects. Moshe Nadir was a favorite ghetto humorist, poet and literary figure for decades. From: Morris U. Schappes, The Jews in the United States *and Noah Shteinberg,* A Bukh Moshe Nadir *(1926).*

A leftwing Yiddish humor magazine, published by Sam Liptzin, honors the memory of beloved Yiddish writer Sholem Aleichem, who died in the Bronx.

The Jewish People's Chorus of Chicago, about 1948, Eugene Malek, conductor (second row, center); this was the first Jewish workers' chorus founded, and is oldest affiliate of the Jewish Music Alliance.

Jewish radicals' enthusiasm poured into dozens of choral, drama and social groups of the 1910s-50s, dozens of Yiddish periodicals, and a short-lived experiment in cooperatively-owned housing in the Bronx Cooperatives, on Allerton Avenue, which opened in 1926 (and continued as a charged political community for decades longer). From Dienst fur Folk: Almanakh fun Yiddish Folks Ordn *(1947);* The Coops *(1977) and YIVO Institute for Jewish Research.*

A massive outpouring of the Yiddish-speaking Left, in honor of beloved Communist newspaper editor Moyisse Olgin at his death in 1938. Mother Bloor is at the right of the coffin. From Dienst fun Folk.

社會主義の為めに
片山潜

FOR THE CAUSE OF SOCIALISM
SEN KATAYAMA

Courtesy: Charles H. Kerr Co.

Sen Katayama, a leader of the Third International, had worked as a dishwasher and editor in United States of the 1910s, while developing support for creation of a Communist movement in Japan.

and his two brothers guided a faction of the Mexican Revolution, led a 1911 armed attempt to seize Baja California, and urged an anarchism based in the relatively egalitarian ways of life before the Anglo colonizers came to the West. Despite continual legal persecution, the Magons' newspaper *Regeneration* and their Wobbly connections fed organizations of Mexican Americans from Texas to Fresno, California.

By the time World War One broke out in Europe, these tendencies had already been far advanced. But the war's various effects on the American labor movement placed industrialized immigrant groups in a pivotal situation. It did not move most of them much beyond the tasks of creating socialist organizations and local clubhouses, newspapers and unions. Finns and Jews were exceptional for many reasons. Both groups experimented with their language as they could not in Europe and took great pride in their American-based publications and theatrical forms. Both had large numbers who shunned religion and sought a cultural substitute. Both had radicals at the center of their culture's artistic core, so that socialistic publications and events carried the best work of their creative talents. Finns, mostly isolated in rural areas, lived culturally through their "hall culture" where they gathered for every kind of event. Jews, concentrated in the big cities, especially New York, had the critical mass for many kinds of expression. Finnish radical humor magazines — to take a point of contrast — never got far beyond political didacticism, whereas Yiddish humor magazines borrowed heavily from commercial humor styles, but with their own content.

Jewish theater took on a new dimension in the 1920s with the founding of "ARTEF," the Jewish Art Theater. Experimental as well as political drama, with often highly expressionist sets, Artef plays drew an audience of radicalized Jewish workers. From Tsen Yor Artef *(1937).*

War and Revolutions Afar

Pennsylvania A.F. of L. leader and socialist state legislator James H. Maurer addresses an anti-war rally in 1916.

War and Revolutions Afar

The coming of world war cast a shadow over all hopeful developments. Since 1910, Europe had been ripe for conflagration. The Socialist parties and syndicalist unions had vowed a General Strike to halt military mobilization. But when the flare of conflict was touched off in 1914, the great majority of European socialist and labor leaders enlisted themselves in nationalistic aims. Only a minority of intellectuals, pacifists, and Left socialists, including V.I. Lenin's Bolshevik party in Russia, directed supporters to appeal to workers across national boundaries, to halt the war and turn it into a class war against the ruling cliques.

War preparations became a political issue in the United States, but both Republican and Democratic presidential candidates in

"Come On In America, Blood's Fine." This famous cartoon by artist M.A. Kempf prompted government charges against the Masses *in 1917 and against the cartoonist, who fled to Mexico.*

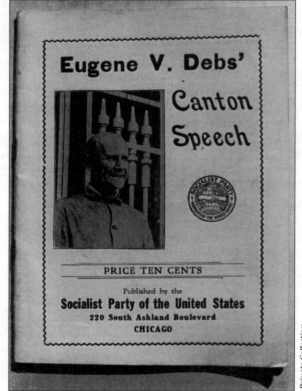

Eugene V. Debs'
Canton
Speech

PRICE TEN CENTS

Published by the
Socialist Party of the United States
220 South Ashland Boulevard
CHICAGO

The famous and courageous speech which, as Debs expected, brought federal charges against him.

The messages on the front and back of this unusual ashtray are superb examples of socialist advertising.

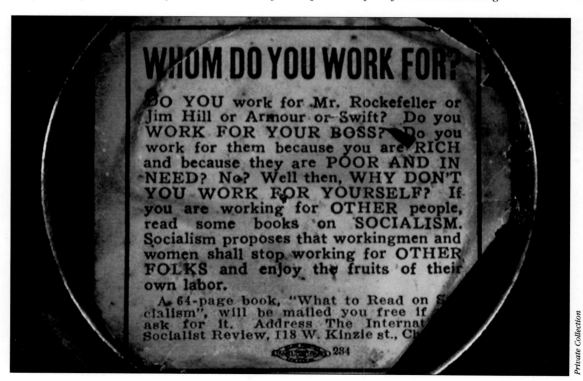

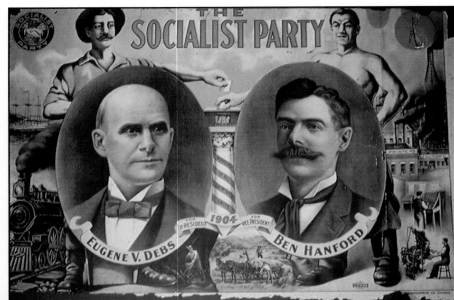

A selection of American Socialist Party buttons depicting Eugene Debs, 1904-1920. Pictured at the lower right is one of the famous "convict" buttons issued during his presidential campaign when Debs was confined in a federal penitentiary.

Clarence Darrow, the great people's advocate, ran an unsuccessful campaign for mayor of Chicago in 1902.

Color Page – 18

"The Tree of Evil," 1912. A widely popular print. Theodore Roosevelt, the trust buster, saws ineffectually at a branch as Karl Marx points out to a worker that its roots must be destroyed; otherwise the lifeless bodies of workers will continue to nourish it.

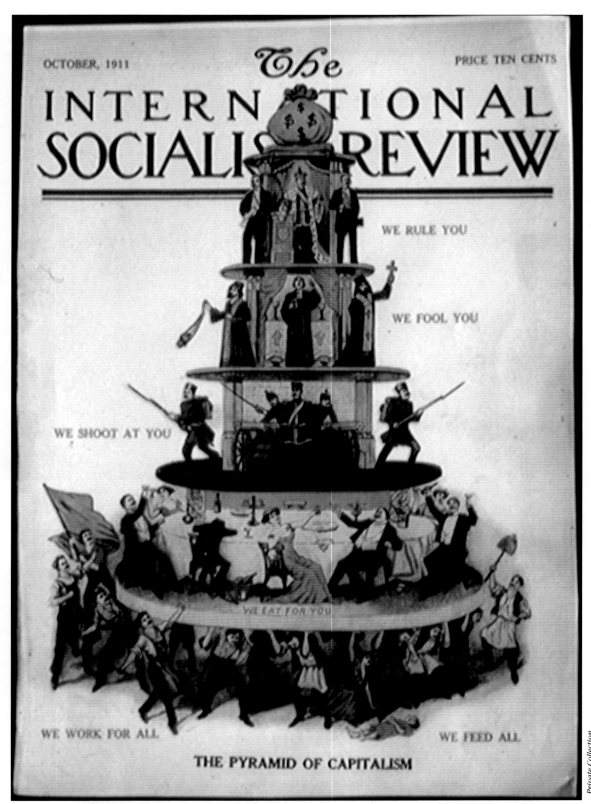

The "Pyramid of Capitalism" a popular international socialist drawing.

During the Western Federation of Miners Strike of 1899-1900 against Standard Oil-owned mines in Coeur D Alene, Idaho, federal troops were brought in to force the striking miners into a makeshift stockade known locally as "the bullpen."

FOR PRESIDENT

EUGENE V. DEBS

Presidential campaign poster, 1920.

KARL MARX PIN

PRICE. 25 CENTS

THE RED FLAG

THIS is an exact duplicate of the Socialist pin worn for years by Karl Marx, and now in the possession of Capt. French. It was given by Marx to Engels; by Engels to John Spargo; and by him to Comrade French.

WILSHIRE BOOK COMPANY
Clearing House for all Socialist Literature
200 WILLIAM STREET · · NEW YORK

An enameled socialist pin whose meaning is explained on the accompanying card.

Color Page – 23

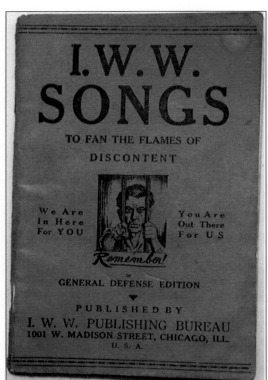

One of many editions of the famous Little Red Song
Book. *This example was published in 1918.*

*"Put Your Shoulder to the Wheel," a stylized version of
Father Hagerty's "Wheel of Fortune."*

The *"Rebel Girl,"* Wobbly musician and composer-agitator
*Joe Hill's tribute to women labor activists, was modeled
on Elizabeth Gurley Flynn, c. 1915.*

Art Young's autobiography, one of the best in
American radicalism, recalled the glory days of the
Socialist Party's 1910s optimism.

1916 promised to keep America out of the military conflict. American Socialists meanwhile bravely denounced war as a consequence of the business race for profits and the politicians' greed for glory, and warned of its terrible consequences. Only the mainstream socialists of a few nationality groups, such as Poles and Slovenes, favored war as a means of gaining independence for their homelands. Some prominent Jewish anarchist and socialist-zionist leaders also hailed the war, but the vast majority of Jewish radicals stuck to their anti-war principles.

Pressure on the socialists grew steadily in 1917, as the United States edged close to war entry. Leading liberal intellectuals, such as philosopher John Dewey, jumped aboard the militarization bandwagon, using the *New Republic* magazine and government propaganda agencies to wage an all-out slander campaign against war opponents. At St. Louis, a socialist convention went on record against United States participation, despite warnings that repression would follow. Soon, Eugene V. Debs was arrested (and finally imprisoned, until 1923) for an anti-war speech in Canton, Ohio. President Woodrow Wilson directed his Attorney General A. Mitchell Palmer to monitor and suppress, if necessary, the opinions expressed in publications. Hundreds of Socialist newspapers, especially those in rural districts, were successfully repressed when the Post Office banned one issue or more, then denied them Second Class mailing permits on the basis that they had failed to keep up to schedule. Socialist public meetings were banned "for health reasons," headquarters broken up by mobs with police looking on, and arrests or deportations of immigrants widely threatened.

Understandably, the socialist response waxed melodramatic, bordering on hysterical warnings of civilization's doom. Socialists, anticipating Naziism and the Holocaust, accurately pointed out that this war would lead to another and worse one. Drawings in the *Masses* portrayed bloodbaths, orators aroused crowds, and perhaps most dramatically, thousands of Harlem residents marched in a "silent parade" to protest both the war and the rising tide of racial violence against African-Americans.

At the height of the "Red Scare," the Wobblies suffered the worst. "Criminal Syndicalism" laws made I.W.W. activity almost automatically illegal. Employers in the west leaped at the opportunity to call in U.S. Army troops to crush strikes and to brutalize

NO MORE WAR!

This cry is being raised throughout the world.

In England, France, Germany, Austria, Holland, Switzerland, Czecho-Slovakia, Hungary, Portugal and Sweden men and women are uniting, on the anniversary of the Great War, to voice their demand that there shall never again be such a cataclysm of murder and destruction.

Statesmen and diplomats, financiers and conferences, will not end war. War will never be abolished until you men and women, you fathers and mothers, you workers, you who pay the price of war in sorrow and suffering, in disease and death, in unemployment and poverty, raise your voices to say that there shall be

NO MORE WAR

Men and women of New York City will express their opposition to war on

Saturday Evening, July 29th, 1922

BY A

TORCH-LIGHT PARADE and MASS-MEETING

ARRANGED BY

THE WOMEN'S PEACE SOCIETY
THE WOMEN'S PEACE UNION of the WESTERN HEMISPHERE
THE FELLOWSHIP OF RECONCILIATION

and other organizations. The parade will form at Union Square at 7:30.

Come and join us in an imposing protest against war!

MARCH WITH US FOR PEACE!

Declare your willingness to march in the No-More-War Parade by signing the attached slip. Do it now!

I expect to march in the No-More-War Parade on July 29th.

Name

Address

Telephone Number

Return to Miss HENRIETTE HEINZEN, *Parade Secretary*,

WOMEN'S PEACE SOCIETY

Vanderbilt 3522   Room 1101, 505 Fifth Avenue, New York.

There will be a special Men's Section.   We need volunteer workers.
Women are asked to wear white, if possible.   Can you help?

Pass this word on

Courtesy: Swarthmore College Peace Collection

Feminist efforts joined socialist anti-war energies as United States leaders prepared for future armed conflict.

or get rid of rank-and-file leaders. Subjected to mass trials on their past statements rather than any deeds offered as proof against them (in fact, the I.W.W. did not actively oppose the war, instead throwing its energies into organizing), hundreds of Wobblies were given long sentences. Their sometime allies, anti-war anarchists, suffered next worst. Hundreds from an Italian-American anarchist group, supporters of the newspaper Cronoca *Sovversiva,* were seized and many deported. Mexican-American leader Ricardo Flores Magon was wrongly convicted under the Espionage Act and sent to Leavenworth federal prison where he died mysteriously (probably murdered). His once-important newspaper *Regeneracion* died, too, as his followers returned to Mexico or regathered in Los Angeles.

Amazingly, the Socialist Party fought back effectively against this repressive climate. Calling for free speech and a negotiated end to the conflict, the party made new headway in dozens of communities, raising its membership to nearly 100,000 and electing hundreds of new local officials on anti-war platforms. Especially among German populations, as in Milwaukee and rural Wisconsin, this appeal struck a chord. But public disillusionment in the war spread across ethnic groups and geographical areas. The People's Council for Peace and Democracy, a wide coalition with Amalgamated Clothing Workers' chief Sidney Hillman among its leaders, refuted both conservative and liberal claims to patriotic legitimacy by making peace the highest claim to democracy.

Already, however, an earth-shaking development far from the United States foredoomed any long-term revival of the Socialist Party. Russian workers and peasants, suffering terribly in the war, had risen up to demand a new government. Following the collapse of Czarism, moderate socialist Alexander Kerensky took the helm but sought to continue the unpopular war effort. Bolsheviks hailed the revolutionary workers' councils or "Soviets" as the basis of a completely new order, and offered the masses "Peace, Bread and Land." This Russian Revolution swept aside Kerensky. The Soviets seemed, to American enthusiasts, very much like an I.W.W. come to power. At the very least, they concluded, a form of socialism had won somewhere in the world. European leaders shuddered at the growing revulsion at the war and the fascination with Russia, backing a "White Terror" on its borderlands. Yet despite popu-

Courtesy: State Historical Society of Wisconsin

Socialists gained office on anti-war platforms in many cities during 1917-20. This is a particularly vivid example of courage in the face of repression.

Courtesy: Bruce Rubenstein and Tamiment Library, New York University

The Bohemian twosome of John Reed and Louise Bryant, their memory returned to the limelight in Warren Beatty's classic 1982 film Reds, *were real-life journalistic heroes.*

Private Collection

The Liberator *for October, 1921 sees Leon Trotsky, a commander of the Red Army, as a revolutionary champion.*

lar unrest, the ruling groups held onto power everywhere but Finland and Hungary — sometimes with the help of pro-war socialists. Discredited, the Socialist International collapsed, as the Russians called for a new world body of revolutionaries, a "Third International."

Now constituting more than half of the American Socialist Party, immigrants placed their hopes very largely upon the Bolsheviks who, they hoped, would emancipate their homelands. They might have transformed the party. But the Bolsheviks decreed a break-up, not a takeover, of the old parties, for Bolshevik-style organizations everywhere. As agents of the new Bureau of Investigation (soon to the become the FBI) infiltrated the contentious political factions, would-be American

Private Collection

Revolution Emerging from War, seen by the Groysser Kundes. *The Jewish humor weekly welcomes the Russian Revolution (in a Phrygian cap) as a happy outcome of a terrible war.* Groysser Kundes, *1917.*

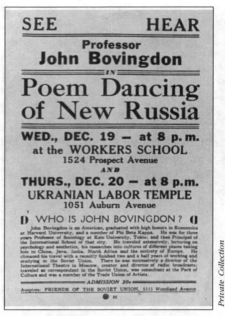

Especially before the consolidation of Stalin's rule, Red Russia seemed to many travelers extremely hopeful, with many possibilities for artistic expression.

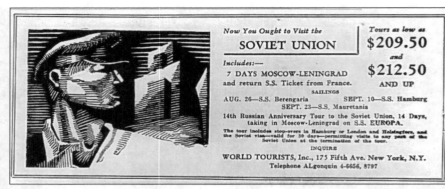

Bolsheviks turned on one another, each group claiming to hold the "true" revolutionary position. "A few slogans," one of the leaders observed a few years later, "have served like hallelujahs at a revival meeting," but instead of fearing hellfire, the combatants feared "being the minutest fraction under one hundred percent Bolshevik." In this confusion, socialist leaders expelled entire state branches of the party and the Socialist Party virtually ceased to function. On the Communist side, a Communist Party launched in 1919 eventually merged with a rival Communist Labor Party founded the same year, and later factions, creating a unified Workers (Communist) Party of perhaps 30,000 members in 1922. The Communists had captured large sections of some immigrant radical groups (especially Finns and Jews, but also Hungaians, Ukrainians and others). But they had left behind nearly all American-born radicals and most of the geographic scope of pre-1920 radicalism across the Midwest, South and Southwest.

Black socialist activists tapped into yet a third revolution of the age: Black Nationalism. The First World War and the thirst of smaller nations for self-determination rejuvenated an old African-American impulse toward independence of white rule. West Indian-born socialist and nationalist Cyril Briggs published *The Crusader* from 1918 to 1920, calling for separate black states in the United States. Veteran socialist and street-speaker Hubert Harrison launched the Liberty League of Negro-Americans, demanding black self-defense against white violence escalating into lynch mobs and riots from Texas to Chicago.

Both Briggs and Harrison drew upon energies roused by Marcus Garvey, Jamaican-born Black Nationalist who published the widely-circulated *Negro World* from New York and directed the Universal Negro Improvement Association. The Garveyites, for a time, had a following in virtually every American black neighborhood. Garvey himself was no socialist, but during the late 1910s he encouraged black radicalism guided by immigrant West Indians.

Feared by most white Americans and defended by

Soviet flyers were greeted with the excitement of a Communist version of "Lindy" (Atlantic solo flyer Charles Lindbergh, Jr.), pilots of the future.

few, militant black radicalism could be suppressed effectively. Bureau of Investigation director J. Edgar Hoover himself guided the persecution of Garvey's organization (including the deportation of Garvey). Industrial unionism and labor radicalism were the next victims. By the early 1920s, what was called the "American Plan" of non-unionism had almost wiped out all the organization of unskilled workers achieved in 1919, and the radical influence within it. But as with bohemianism, various moods and memories survived. These were not necessarily expectations for collective rebellion in any near future, but more likely a sensation of unease with the dominant American culture, sometimes a desire for ethnic self-defense, sometimes for personal escape or for artistic alternatives to the mainstream. Here lay the nexus of politics and modern art, including a range of ethnic cultural projects (such as experimental modernist theater in the Yiddish language) which successfully leaped over the gap between avant-garde tastes and a working class audience.

The mood that remained after the radical wave had passed was inevitably vicarious. Hope grew for a new civilization in Russia that could survive and someday outlast the revival of world capitalism under American leadership. Such hope was not particularly realistic. But like the little pockets of avant-garde and ethnic cultural radicalism, the images of the "New Russia" gave many radicals a needed psychological mechanism for survival. If not the industrial working class, then perhaps oppressed peasant peoples of Asia, Africa or Latin America would ally with Russia and help slay capitalism through their desperate struggles for national liberation. Thus Communists, along with Christian Socialists, took up the campaign to defend the original revolution of Augusto Sandino, a spiritualist who rose to power in Nicaragua before being crushed by U.S. forces. The instinct for solidarity with the victims of U.S. corporations and American Marines would remain deep in radicalism long after Communism lost its importance.

The World Tomorrow, *a Christian Socialist monthly, opposed imperialism and racism.*

Augusto Sandino's Revolution, supported by the American Left, is crushed by United States military invaders.

Courtesy: Schomberg Collection, New York Public Library

Hubert Harrison, a native of the Virgin Islands who joined a Harlem branch of the Socialist Party in 1909 and served as a prominent lecturer, organizer and journalist until his resignation from the party in 1914. In 1917 he launched the Liberty League of Negro Americans and in 1925 the International Colored Unity League, both radical nationalist organizations.

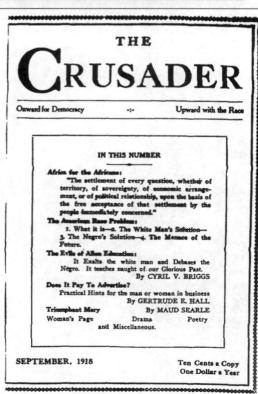

Courtesy: Library of Congress

The Crusader, *a radical Black Nationalist magazine with socialist sympathies, was something new to America.*

Farmer Labor Movements

Farmer Labor Movements

The effort to create a farmer-labor movement or party after World War One came out of the socialist collapse and the widely felt need for more popular control over government institutions increasingly central in day-to-day life. The first move was made in North Dakota, through the newly formed Non-Partisan League. Veteran socialists there wisely realized that lifelong Republicans had been outraged by the overpricing and assorted swindling of farmers by banks, grain dealers and railroads. They resolved to enter the Republican primaries with a disciplined movement, holding preparatory local meetings where everyone interested could openly discuss the issues. Their platform demanded state ownership of key agencies like banks and grain elevators, and insisted that all Non-Partisan League nominees keep discipline in State House politics rather than changing their vote in return for lobbyist dollars.

Regional activists tried to reach out to a national audience.

In 1917, the N.P.L. achieved dramatic success. Three quarters of the Republicans and nearly all the Democrats elected were in the N.P.L. caucus. By 1919, when they also controlled the governorship, N.P.L. supporters pushed through a host of important reforms, including advanced versions of workmens' compensation, income and inheritance taxes, limits to legal injunctions on strikes, and a rigorous mine-safety law. Never had democratic action worked so quickly in American politics, perhaps because the resistance was so weak. After defeat in the 1922 elections, however, the N.P.L. drifted rightward and by the 1930s tended toward a nativist version of isolationism.

Nevertheless, the example of the N.P.L. spread to neighboring Minnesota. Large milling and mining interests there, and the size and complexity of the working class, dictated a different strategy. The World War had been unpopular, especially among German-American populations, and Minnesota Congressman Charles A. Lindbergh won wide approval for denouncing the United States government's participation. Fearful government leaders banned N.P.L. public meetings, and ordered the arrest of a visiting North Dakota N.P.L. leader on sedition charges.

After some hesitation at forming a new party, Minnesota farm leaders and a handful of labor representatives fielded a Farmer-Labor slate in 1922. Henrik Shipstead was elected to the Senate, and the F.L.P. emerged overnight the second-strongest party of the state. At the local level, the Farmer-Labor clubs were more democratic than any mainstream political organization in state history. A somewhat similar process unfolded in Wisconsin, where the Progressive Party leader, Senator Robert M. LaFollette, had alienated the wealthy and relatively conservative wing of Progressives (originally liberal Republican good-government reformers drawn to Theodore Roosevelt) by vigorously opposing the War. Although Wisconsin socialists continued to win many local elections, a larger wing of radical constituents both rural and urban swung over to LaFollette and to a radicalized Progressive movement. In both North Dakota and Minnesota, the familiar theme of the "producing" classes (farmers and workers) versus the bankers and middlemen evoked images of "real America" and faith in the possibilities of a broadened electorate ("the people").

A preliminary effort to launch a national Farmer Labor Party in 1920 had meanwhile emerged mainly from the Labor Party of Illinois, along with some sister state labor parties, and a fraction of the former Progressive party supporters of Theodore Roosevelt from the 1912 campaign. Only a handful of important agrarian organizations (including the N.P.L.) supported the party, and LaFollette himself declined the nomination. Parley Parker Christensen, a progressive Utah lawyer and counsel for imprisoned Industrial Workers of the World, ran for president in competition with the jailed Socialist Party candidate Eugene Debs. Christiensen's running mate, Max S. Hayes, had been a Cleveland socialist leader and newspaper editor since the 1890s. Despite limited funds and an atmosphere of severe repression, the F.L.P. gathered more than a quarter-million votes in just eighteen states where it gained ballot status.

Many political reformists and even AFL leaders, struck by an increasingly conservative national politics and the aggressively anti-union "Open Shop" campaign, proposed a larger third party campaign in 1924. Communists meanwhile entered farmer-labor activity from the Northwest to the Midwest, often successfully recruiting local leaders and sometimes converting organizations to their positions. By early 1923, when the A.F. of L. had

Courtesy: State Historical Society of Wisconsin

"Fighting Bob" LaFollette in his last and most glorious campaign, running for the presidency in 1924.

ROBERT M. LaFOLLETTE

"Fighting Bob" LaFollette, Wisconsin governor, Senator, anti-war activist, 1924 presidential candidate and founder of the state's Progressive Party, was the grassroots radical *par excellence.*

LaFollette grew up on a farm and then in Madison, Wisconsin, in the 1860s-70s. Entering the University of Wisconsin, he became a champion orator and met his future wife, an ardent woman's rights enthusiast. As a practicing lawyer and Republican politician, he gained election to the House of Representatives where he defended African-American and Indian rights but otherwise distinguished himself very little. During the 1890s, as he realized the Republican party had abandoned its abolitionist heritage and become a tool of big business, he set out to create his own base of support within and outside of it. He began to challenge the railroad' political power, campaigning ceaselessly among ordinary Wisconsinites.

Winning the governorship repeatedly, he championed the consumer and developed the "Wisconsin Idea," a commitment to honesty and scientific research in government. Wisconsin became a model "progressive" state with regulation of child labor, public utilities, and workmen's compensation. As Senator beginning in 1906, he challenged Republican conservatives and founded *LaFollette's Weekly* (later renamed *The Progressive*) in 1909. His drive for a reform presidential candidacy was stopped by Theodore Roosevelt, the militaristic conservative who nevertheless shared many progressive supporters of LaFollette's. The two split sharply over the approach of war: Roosevelt welcomed the invasion of Mexico and beat the drums for "preparedness"; LaFollette bravely resisted militarization and intervention.

By the 1920s, his new Progressive Party successfully defeated Wisconsin Republicans, and the corruption of the Harding administration exposed the need for reform. But those supporting his farmer-labor coalition in 1924 were too few, although the Socialist party threw all its flagging energies into the campaign. He took five million votes, but carried only Wisconsin. A year later, LaFollette died. His farmer-labor coalition survived in the Wisconsin Progressive party for more than a decade, and the *Progressive* magazine remains a bastion of free-thought from the heartland.

timidly pulled back from promising support and many reformers concluded that the time was not ripe, radical farmer-labor leaders lost heart.
Communists and a handful of allies (including Mother Jones) pushed ahead
to form a Federated Farmer Labor Party, which virtually disappeared
before the election. Meanwhile Robert LaFollette had agreed to run on the
Progressive Party ticket, conducting a dramatic coast-to-coast campaign
without, however, creating a national third-party movement that might
have played a great role in the 1930s.

LaFollette's death in 1925, the confusion created by Communist maneuvering, and a general sense of political reaction placed Farmer-Laborism in
a strictly limited focus. A League for Independent Political Action formed
in 1928 by prominent reformers including W.E.B. DuBois and John Dewey
stirred trade unionists in the early and middle 1930s to call for a national
third party. But Franklin D. Roosevelt's consolidation of his influence on
labor in 1936 eclipsed this tendency. Farmers dumped milk, sat-in at state
legislatures and sometimes intimidated banks to relent on selling bankrupt
farms, but had no hope of launching a national party,
either. Small groups of socialists and communists
played heroic roles in supporting such farm actions,
but never regained the radi-

*Charles "Red Flag" Taylor, 1922. A three hundred
pound, charismatic organizer of the farmer-labor
movement in Montana, Taylor was editor of the*
Producers News, *for a time the most lively newspaper of the farmer-labor movement. He was also
a secret communist while serving as a Republican
state legislator in the 1920s.*

Parley Parker Christensen, presidential candidate of the Farmer-Labor Party in 1920, meets with Lenin in Moscow, c. 1922.

cal bases across large parts of rural America.

Farmer-Labor politics returned, at last, to weakened regional roots. While the Wisconsin Progressive Party shifted toward the center, the Minnesotans moved further Left. Elected to office by steadily wider margins, the F.L.P. promised in its 1934 platform "immediate steps...to abolish capitalism in a peaceful and lawful manner." Business interests in the state and nationally kept up a ferocious attack on the Minnesotans, and they had no chance to institute their proposals of taking over factories, mines and utilities by the people. By 1938, state Republicans broadcast claims that "Jewish Red Conspirators" secretly ruled the F.L.P., and the new House Un-American Activities promised an investigation — not of the anti-Semitic attacks but of the farmer-laborites! Following an overwhelming defeat to Elmer Benson, the final F.L.P. governor, the party drifted toward merger with the state Democrats.

By 1944, even the Communists agreed, and the leading spirit of that merger was Hubert H. Humphrey, who had been their quiet ally. In the next few years, Humphrey purged the F.L.P.'s Left, including Minnesota supporters of the 1948 Progressive Party. The power of federal patronage and the demagogic politics of the Cold War virtually wiped out all third-party insurgency except at the local level.

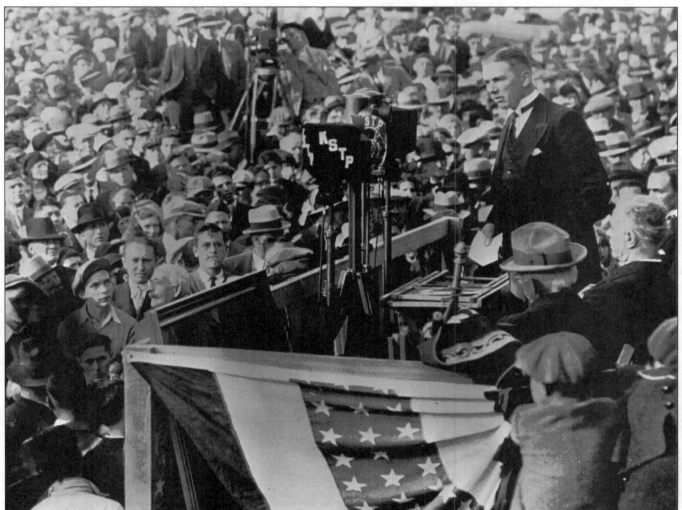

Courtesy: Minnesota Historial Society

Minnesota Governor Floyd Olson addresses a Farmer-Labor party crowd, 1936.

*Election card of Ruth Adlard, Christian Socialist and Ohio farmer-labor candidate,
c. 1937.*

Almost the last of the imagery of the united rural-and-urban "producing classes" against the monopolists also disappeared after the ferocious liberal-conservative attacks on Henry Wallace (whose family had for generations published *Wallace's Farmer* in Iowa) and his running mate Glen Taylor, the singing cowboy from Idaho. More and more farms had by then been snapped up by agribusiness, and surviving small farmers fought a lonely economic struggle just to hold on.

Further Reading

Mari Jo Buhle, *Women and American Socialism* (Urbana; University of Illinois, 1982)

Paul Buhle, *Marxism in the United States: Remapping the American Left* (London: Verso, 1991 Edition).

Ralph Chaplin, *Wobbly: The Rough-and-Tumble Story of an American Radical* (Chicago: University of Chicago Press, 1948).

James R. Green, *Grassroots Socialism: Radical Movements in the Southwest 1895-1943* (Baton Rouge: Louisiana State University Press, 1978)

Michael Karni and Douglas Ollila, eds., *For the Common Good: Finnish Immigrants and the Radical Response to Industrial America* (Superior, Wis.: Tyomies, 1977).

Joyce Kornbluh, ed. *Rebel Voices: An I.W.W. Anthology* (Chicago: Charles H. Kerr Co., 1988 Edition)

Colin M. MacLachlan,

*Farm workers resettled. Singer Woody Guthrie is introduced to the well-kept grounds of Shafter, a
Farm Security Administration camp near Bakersfield, California, 1941.*

Anarchism and the Mexican Revolution: The Political Trials of Ricardo Flores Magon in the United States (Berkeley: University of California, 1991).

Robert L. Morlan, *Political Prairie Fire: The Nonpartisan League, 1915-1922* (St. Paul: Minnesota Historical Society Press, 1985 edition)

David Montgomery, *Workers Control in America: Studies in the House of Work, Technology and Labor Struggles.* Cambridge: Cambridge University Press, 1979).

Nicholas Salvatore, *Eugene V. Debs: Citizen and Socialist* (Urbana: University of Illinois, 1982).

Elliot Shore, *Talkin' Socialism: J.A. Wayland and the Role of the Press in American Radicalism, 1890-1912* (Lawrence: University Press of Kansas, 1988).

James Weinstein, *The Decline of Socialism in America, 1912-1925* (New York: Monthly Review, 1967)

Art Young, *Art Young: His Life and Times,* edited by John N. Beffel,

This well-remembered "proletarian" novel by communist Ben Field, with an introduction by Erskine Caldwell, sought to capture the "feel" of agrarian struggles.

Ella Reeve "Mother" Bloor, c. 1938. A former urban organizer and Connecticut woman suffrage leader, Bloor became a leader of Communist rural agitation during the Depression, organizing branches of the United Farmers League and supporting farm "holidays" (non-payment of mortgages and non-delivery of goods), as recounted in her autobiography.

(New York: Sheridan House, 1939).

Rebecca Zurier, *Art for the Masses: A Radical Magazine and Its Graphics, 1911-1917* (Philadelphia: Temple University Press, 1988).

Courtesy: Minnesota Historical Society

Meridel Le Seuer. The literary voice of the farmer-labor spirit, she was the daughter of suffragist Marian Wharton (creator of the first Little Blue Books) and Arthur Le Sueur, once the socialist mayor of Minot, North Dakota. Meridel dropped out of high school, lived on a commune with Emma Goldman, acted in silent films, was jailed in 1927 defending Sacco and Vanzetti, and became during the 1930s an important proletarian novelist. Her stories of Midwestern poverty and women's struggle for life have gained wide recognition in recent years.

Courtesy: Minnesota Historical Society

Former Minnesota farmer-labor governor Elmer Benson with Philip Murray (far left), Sidney Hillman and Leo Kryzcki, urging wartime unity, c. 1944. Benson remained an important progressive figure for decades after his gubernatorial term. Note the National Citizens Political Action Committee poster by Ben Shahn in the background.

Chapter Four
The Old Left

Typical caricature of radicals during the Red Scare mixes racism and anti-immigrant prejudice. Drawing by Rodney Thompson, c. 1917.

Facing Repression

Courtesy: Library of Congress

Defender of I.W.W. leaders and other victims of repression, Clarence Darrow (standing) was a fabled figure of Free Speech.

Facing Repression

Repression of the radicals, whether organized by legal authorities or carried out by rightwing vigilantes, was at least as old as the Alien and Sedition Acts or the wars of extermination against Indians. But the intensity of repression during the First World War created a mood and a distinct movement which became part of radicalism thereafter. The repressive mood, generally anti-Semitic with an undertone or marked emphasis of racism, was advanced by the tabloid press and opportunistic politicians (including ostensible liberals determined to prove their tough-mindedness). It had been ignited by the massive strike movement of 1909-13, which seemed to threaten mass disorder, and by the sheer internationalism of the activists. But it caught fire with a series of extraordinary arrests during 1914-16.

Earlier, after two explosions

SOME "LIVE ONES" WHO ARE BACKING UP "JUSTICE."

Courtesy: Charles H. Kerr Co.

Avid supporter of industrial unionism and mass strikes of immigrant workers to achieve that goal, the weekly Justice *was attacked in 1912 by legal authorities in Pittsburgh.*

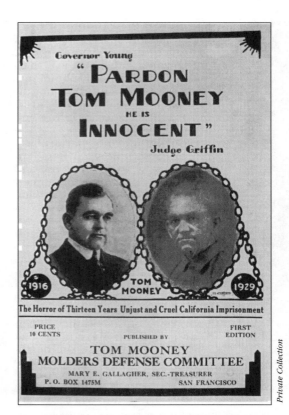

Robert Minor, "The Lynching of Tom Mooney," crayon c. 1917-18, portrays Mooney as a scapegoat for capitalism's crimes.

A Representative sampling of material related to Tom Mooney's incarceration and the cause celebre that it became.

A long-delayed civil liberties victory is celebrated in 1939.

Courtesy: Library of Congress

Silent Protest Harlem, 1917. The famous Silent Parade, protesting the evils of war and racist violence, was the most noteworthy African-American public event in the United States to that time. Participants impressed onlookers with their dignity, neither shouting slogans or singing, in the usual fashion of parades.

had ripped the printing plant of the anti-union *Los Angeles Times* in October, 1910, John J. McNamara and his brother James were charged with the bombing. Both members (John an important local figure) of the International Association of Bridge and Structural Iron Workers, they were solid and not particularly radical craft unionists. But Clarence Darrow led the defense and William D. Haywood threatened to call a general strike nationwide during the trial; large crowds in every city outside the South rallied to defend the brothers. Job Harriman, the leading Los Angeles socialist, ran for the mayoralty on a plea of their innocence. Shortly before election day, they admitted to their guilt. James McNamara received life imprisonment, his brother fifteen years, and Job Harriman was humbled in the polls, the death-blow to all hopes for an elected socialist mayor.

By contrast, I.W.W. songster Joe Hill, arrested in Salt Lake City

Courtesy: Immigration History Research Center, University of Minnesota

Radical Italian organizer Anthony Capraro, deported from Lawrence, Massachusetts in 1919 during a determined strike by mostly Italian textile workers, was nearly beaten to death by employers' thugs.

SCOTT NEARING

Courtesy: Southpaw Books

Scott Nearing, fired in 1917 from his faculty position at the University of Pennsylvania for opposing World War I.

in January, 1914, was charged with a murder in that city although he had neither criminal record nor motive, nor did any witness identify him. But the ultra-conservative Mormon church and the Copper Trust seized the opportunity to make a lesson of an I.W.W. agitator. The A.F. of L., the Swedish government and Woodrow Wilson among others appealed on Hill's behalf as lawyers disproved the "frame-up." None of this availed, however, and Hill was executed by a firing squad on November 19, 1914.

"Railroading" radicals to jail suddenly became more popular. Tom Mooney, labor activist, was arrested the following year when a bomb exploded killing ten persons during the San Francisco Preparedness Day Parade. He was actually guilty of being a leader of the California Federation of Labor, a dedicated and influential socialist. He edited the militant journal *Revolt*, had been known to advocate sabotage, and was earlier acquitted of dynamiting property of the Pacific Gas and Electric Company. Warren Billings, previously convicted of carrying dynamite onto a passenger train, was arrested with him shortly after the bomb went off. Testimony against them was almost certainly perjured, and a federal commission later described the purpose of the charge as simply putting a labor activist away. Union members and radicals flooded the statehouse with appeals, and for two decades, Mooney and Billings earned the status of labor's martyrs, mentioned on almost every possible occasion. (A weary landlord in the Bronx was reputed to have told angry rent strikers in 1931, "I can turn up the heat and fix the plumbing but I can't get Tom Mooney out of jail.") In 1939, New Deal governor Culbert Olson pardoned both. Mooney died within eighteen months; Billings went on to become a vice-president of the Watchmakers Union.

The terrible persecution of the Industrial Workers of the World turned that movement from aggressive organizing (by then, mostly in the Western states) to full-time defense of political prisoners. Many "class war prisoners" who remained in jail after 1920 felt abandoned by the apathy of the public and the labor movement. The legal defense movement had by that time changed dramatically in its purposes and strategies. Socialists and Wobblies thought that the masses of American workers would soon rise up and protect their own from hostile authorities. Radicals after 1920 felt far more isolated and endangered, even when they successfully created activist movements for defense of political prisoners.

Communists organized their movement in America against the backdrop of the young Russian Revolution and fading American radicalism. "Americanism" and "Socialism" (in the Russian model) emerged from

A Wobbly cartoonist mocks the Red Scare mentality common among American businessmen during the late 1910s and early 1920s. From the Industrial Worker, *c. 1919.*

Courtesy: Charles H. Kerr Co.

The General Defense Committee's widely distributed publication was a very effective fund raiser.

Private Collection

Wind up the Season with the

DEFENSE PICNIC
of the
NEW YORK DISTRICT—INTERNATIONAL LABOR DEFENSE
SUNDAY, AUGUST 30th

All Out!   *Show Your Solidarity!*
with the

Striking Miners   The Scottsboro Negro Boys
Mooney and Billings   The Paterson Victims
The Alabama Share Croppers
and

All Victims of Capitalist Justice

and HAVE ONE GRAND TIME
from Morn till Midnight

Take I.R.T. Subway to 177th Street, then Unionport car up to end of line.
Busses will meet you there.

PLEASANT BAY PARK — UNIONPORT, BRONX
ADMISSION 35 CENTS

*Seattle and New York picnics, 1919 and 1935. Defense
Committees held social events across the country to raise legal-
defense funds for imprisoned radicals.*

World War One the two great contending principles
in the world at large. So long as U.S. prosperity held
out, radicals could not hope to win over the consumer
with his Ford and his high expectations — even if
Communists could not usually admit it to themselves
White Americans also tended to see themselves as the
race aristocracy of the planet. By the early 1920s the
Ku Klux Klan actually captured several state governments, despite desperate and sometimes successful
socialist fights against them. Prejudice toward immigrants, especially but not only Jews, was also intense.
Thus the radical ranks, mostly newer immigrants and
far-seeing intellectuals, often considered themselves
aliens or outsiders in an unfriendly America.

This mood reshaped American radicalism, from politics to aesthetics. Having failed to spread revolution
into Europe and the United States, Lenin and his successors turned their main attention to the regions
where white colonialism hung heavily upon dark peoples, worsening age-old sufferings. Communists committed themselves, as socialists and wobblies before
them had never previously done, to helping emancipate the colonized peoples. So did many non-com-

munist radicals, especially Christian socialists. On the home front, Communists relied upon the resentments and yearnings of the ethnic immigrant groups treated badly in American society; and they pointed themselves toward the worst-treated, African-Americans, as the natural constituency for revolutionary change. With the optimism of the old socialist and wobbly days used up, radicals seemed to need the crutch of a socialist model somewhere else in the world — even if they had to believe their own myths about it. The Soviet Union became that crutch but legal defense also became a constant struggle.

The International Labor Defense, founded in 1925 by Communists and their supporters, specialized in representing political activists, unionists, immigrants and non-whites. Its main founder, James P. Cannon, stressed the importance of "mass defense" or "mass protest" rather than passive reliance upon legal efforts alone. Its first great campaign, to spare the lives of Sacco and Vanzetti, was undercut by the conflict between anarchist and communist supporters in local defense committees. By 1930, the I.L.D. had rightly become famous for defending the rights of African-Americans.

The campaign around Angelo Herndon, a 19-year-old black communist organizing an interracial hunger march in Atlanta, Georgia, began with his arrest (on "attempting to incite insurrection," a death-penalty offense) in 1932. Black attorney (and later prominent communist) Benjamin Davis, Jr., challenged the constitutionality of Georgia laws, while the I.L.D. built a massive protest against his conviction and sentencing to 20 years on the chain gang. In 1937, the Supreme Court threw out the Herndon case, ruling the Georgia insurrection law was unconstitutional.

But this case and its able defense paled before the case of the

Courtesy: Washington State Historical Society

Bill Haywood visits with the Chaplin family and friends shortly before he jumped bail, during 1921, to spend the rest of his life in Russia. He was buried in the Kremlin Wall close to John Reed.

Both, Courtesy: Bruce Rubenstein

A pamphlet recounting the armed attack on Wobblies in Centralia, Washington in 1919 and a card commemorating the Wobblies behind bars.

"Scottsboro Boys," nine young black men falsely accused of raping two white women on a freight train in Alabama, in March, 1931. All but one sentenced to death, they turned to the I.L.D., which built an unprecedented campaign with international demands for the defendants' release. Communists won the respect of black churches, lodges and societies in their ardent support, while for the Left at large, Scottsboro became a favorite theme of drawings, songs and plays. After internal confusion and failure to win a new trial, the I.L.D. cooperated in securing the release of four and lengthy sentences for the other five. Among the important precedents established, the Supreme Court ruled in 1935 that the defendants could not be represented if blacks were barred from jury rolls. More important, the inspiration of the interracial defense movement helped promote the formation of a civil rights movement in the 1940s-50s.

From an aesthetic standpoint, the main images of "Labor's Martyrs" had been established in the late nineteenth century, with the sudden death (ironically, in a duel over a woman later married to a prominent editor of the *New Yorker Volkszeitung*) of beloved young German socialist leader Ferdinand Lassalle, and the appearance of death-iconography, statuettes and portraits of him (later Karl Marx and Frederick Engels) ubiquitous in the German-American movement. The martyrdom of the Haymarket victims dramatized the role of the persecuting State. Immigrant Jewish radicals added their young poet, David Edelshtot, dead from tuberculosis but alive in his songs of sufferings within cruel capitalism. Wobbly iconography with its brave character

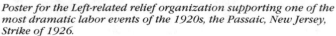

Courtesy: Prometheus Library

Poster for the Left-related relief organization supporting one of the most dramatic labor events of the 1920s, the Passaic, New Jersey, Strike of 1926.

Courtesy: Museum of American Political Life

Eugene Debs is released from Leavenworth following his pardon by President Harding in 1923. His health never recovered.

behind bars ("We are in Here for YOU — You're Out There for US!") sought to identify the hero-victim with the viewer. Communist journalists' treatment of racial cases magnified the horror of the standard repression imagery ("Boss Terror Increasing Daily") to portray the South as an armed camp of racial sadism.

The heightened need to raise money for defense causes prompted a format that mixed the picnic atmosphere or musical concert entertainment with somber speeches and near-hysteric appeals. Successors to religious martyrs and suffering saints, the radicals' heroes and heroines lived on in memory; some of them were lucky enough to actually outlive confinement and march with their rank-and-file saviors in radical-sponsored events. Whatever Communism's cruelty in Stalin's Russia, victims of American capitalism probably owed more to American communists than to anyone else (except, in some cases, the socialists' Workers Defense League) for building a mass movement to support them.

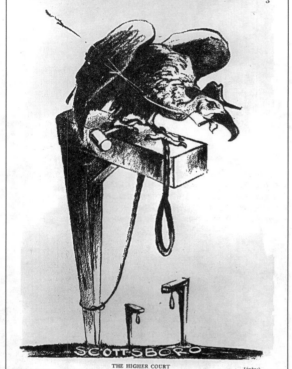

THE HIGHER COURT

Courtesy: Museum of American Political Life

Courtesy: Scott Molloy

Companies of Italian-language actors touring to raise funds through local performances marked an artistic high point of the Sacco-Vanzetti defense activity.

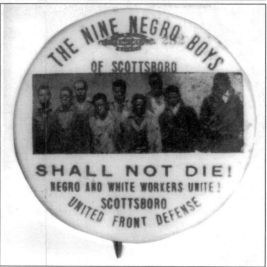

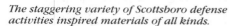

Private Collection

The staggering variety of Scottsboro defense activities inspired materials of all kinds.

Private Collection

Vigilante violence, supported by landowners and local officials, marked struggles of southern Californians in the 1920s-30s. Spanish translations were aimed at Mexican-American workers.

Photo and Courtesy: Harold Freeman

Angelo Herndon, a young African-American who organized a hunger march in Atlanta in 1932, was arrested and charged with "attempting to incite insurrection," a capital offense. After years of mobilizations and protests, the Supreme Court overturned the state law in 1937, and that year Herndon marched in New York's May Day Parade.

Courtesy: Robert F. Wagner Archives, New York University (Charles Rivers Collection)

Ruby Bates (left), the supposed victim of the Scottsboro Boys, went on tour renouncing charges and supporting the defendants. Here she is accompanied by Alice White, in Schenectady, New York, 1932. Photograph by Charles Rivers.

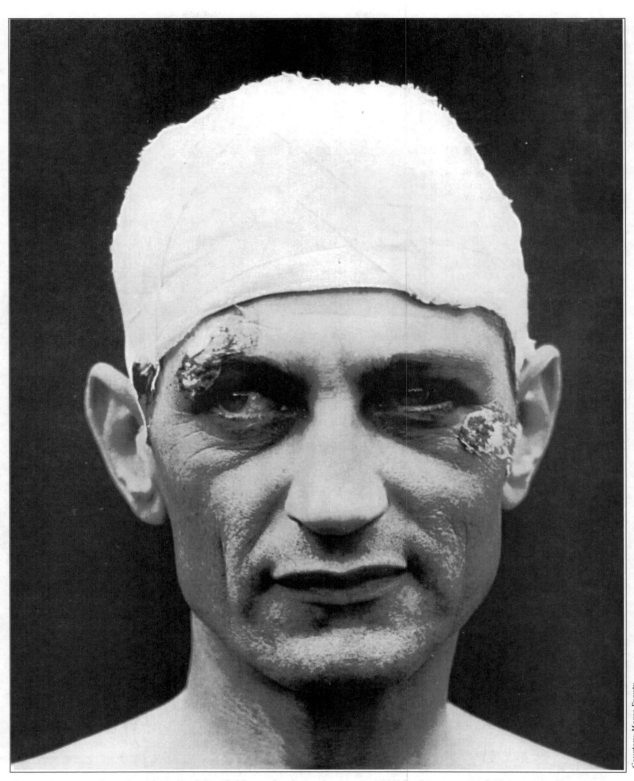

A prominent southern Jewish radical, Joe Gelders, after being beaten in 1937 for his support of African-American causes.

LITTLE BLUE BOOKS

Two of the hundreds of Little Blue Book titles among thousands of more general works. Produced by Emanuel Haldeman-Julius, the last publisher of the *Appeal to Reason,* from Girard, Kansas, most of them were 3"x5", sellng for as low as a dime. Together, they constituted a "university in print" for the self-education of free-thinking common people.

Responding initially to the appeals for inexpensive textbooks from the nearby Socialist People's College of Fort Scott, Kansas, Haldeman-Julius created in 1919 a package of fifty booklets selling for $5 per set. These literary classics and socialist tracts proved instantly popular with *Appeal to Reason* readers. Mass production techniques allowed Haldeman-Julius to lower prices and expand publication. With the collapse of the *Appeal* in 1923, he turned his full attention to the booklets and his own free thought monthly. Shakespeare, Greek and Roman plays gradually gave way to joke books and how-to manuals. But Haldeman-Julius also published original works by W.E.B. DuBois, Bertrand Russell, Clarence Darrow and James T. Farrell, as well as then-controversial birth control manuals, attacks on religion and repressive institutions, including the F.B.I.

Gradually, the audience of the Little Blue Books became more rural, but always remained the pocket-poor reader rich in imagination. Although production ceased with the founder's death in 1951, the books remained available until a catastrophic fire in the old *Appeal* building on July 4, 1979.

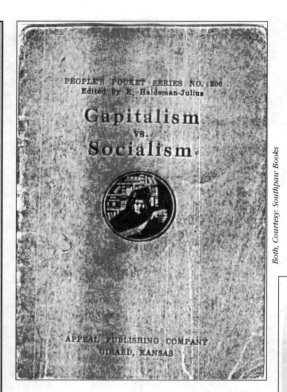

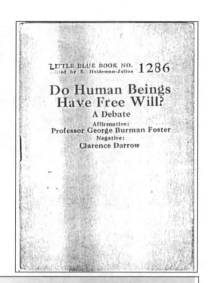

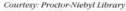

Courtesy: Proctor-Niebyl Library

In the mid-1930s, always controversial author Theodore Dreiser led a delegation to investigate the Harlan County, Kentucky "mine war."

MRS. INA WOOD (Picture taken during her trial)

Typical defense appeal of the 1930s.

Communism and anti-Communism

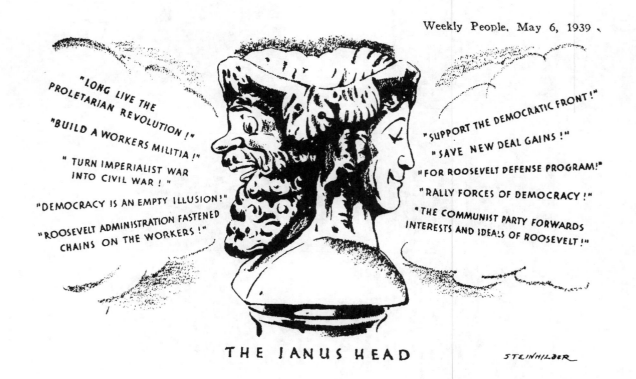

Weekly People, May 6, 1939

"LONG LIVE THE PROLETARIAN REVOLUTION !"

"BUILD A WORKERS MILITIA !"

" TURN IMPERIALIST WAR INTO CIVIL WAR ! "

"DEMOCRACY IS AN EMPTY ILLUSION !"

"ROOSEVELT ADMINISTRATION FASTENED CHAINS ON THE WORKERS !"

"SUPPORT THE DEMOCRATIC FRONT !"

"SAVE NEW DEAL GAINS !"

"FOR ROOSEVELT DEFENSE PROGRAM!"

"RALLY FORCES OF DEMOCRACY !"

"THE COMMUNIST PARTY FORWARDS INTERESTS AND IDEALS OF ROOSEVELT !"

THE JANUS HEAD

STEINHILBER

The Vanguard, Chinese language paper.

Three of the dozens of U.S. publications in more than twenty languages supporting the Soviet Union. The Workers Monthly *absorbed the* Liberator *in 1924 and was itself merged into* The Communist *in 1928 (which, under the name of* Political Affairs, *is still published today). Rodo Shimbun, (Labor Newspaper) edited by Karl Yoneda, had a circulation of a few hundred among Japanese-Americans, mostly on the West Coast, and folded with the coming of World War II when Yoneda himself was confined to the Manzanar detention center.*

Communism and anti-Communism

Reliance on Russia and the Bolshevik revolution as a model for radical transformation in America had serious side effects. Communists had trouble coming out of their hyper-revolutionary dream world of being American Bolsheviks and back to the real world of the 1920s. They often reverted to arguing ceaselessly among themselves about Russia or inventing slogans which sounded as if translated from Russian. Even radical art began to look Russian: Somewhat experimental at first, then by the later 1920s increasingly heavy. Communist intellectuals by this time emphasized "proletarian culture," an intelligent idea of working class people expressing themselves, but too often vulgarized into visions of large-muscled, virile-looking male workers who lacked only enlightenment to burst their integuments and inaugurate socialism. The old socialist and Wobbly sense of irony, mocking the bosses but also the "backward" worker who cooperates in his own exploitation, almost disappeared. So did the modernist covers of 1920s radical magazines like the *New Masses* and its Yiddish counterpart, *Der Hammer*.

Radical or avant-garde modes of expression had also been swallowed up by a distinctly American phenomenon. The quest for "docu-

Private Collection

20th anniversary Communist party banner.

Courtesy: Bruce Rubenstein

Hugo Gellert created this 1924 presidential campaign poster in a style reflecting the martial spirit of the early communist movement.

mentary" expression could be traced back at least to Walt Whitman and the desire to document the workaday lives of ordinary citizens as the basis of democratic possibility. By the early 1930s, widespread disillusionment with bohemianism and the artistic experimentalism of the 1910s-20s threw designers of radical publications and posters, along with more formal artists, back to an enhanced view of reality, especially the reality of lower-class life. A primitivist or reductive element in Communist class orientation had never pointed toward any other possibilities.

On the political and economic fronts, American communists had several opportunities for breakthroughs to large audiences of ordinary Americans. With around 20,000 members and perhaps five times that many followers in the ethnic and intellectual communities, they could rally their forces in a concentrated way for particular campaigns, in at least some important parts of the country, from New York to the Upper Midwest to California. They could reach out beyond these limits by filling in for a passive and conservative American Federation of Labor.

For instance, Communists led dramatic strikes of hard-pressed textile workers in Passaic, New Jersey, Gastonia, North Carolina and New Bedford, Massachusetts in 1926 and 1928. Only Communist-led unions had the courage (or naivete) to believe successful strikes against wage reductions possible in a declining industry and among largely uneducated workers. Bold tactics seizing opportunities for publicity and well-organized support campaigns to keep strikers and their families from

Both, photo and courtesy: Harold Freeman

Courtesy: Bruce Rubenstein

May Day events always offered a gala occasion, especially when socialists and communists shared the streets cooperatively.

Earl Browder, symbol of the Popular Front, seen by a popular Italian-American cartoonist and labor leader, Fort Velona.

William Z. Foster seen here, c. 1910, near the beginning of his always stormy career. A leading figure in American Communism during the 1920s, he was subordinated to Earl Browder, reportedly on Moscow's orders, during the 1930s.

A typical "patriotic" Popular Front pamphlet arguing that Lincoln faced in his time a crisis similar to that faced by the Communist Party of the 1930s, and a rousing song with a similar message.

Photo and courtesy: Alex Buchman

Leon Trotsky and Farrell Dobbs in Mexico, 1938. A symbol of the international Left's opposition to Stalin's rule and American Communist obeisance, Leon Trotsky directed his forces in the United States. Dobbs, a hero of the 1934 Teamsters' Strike in Minneapolis-St. Paul, was an important leader of the American Trotskyist movement.

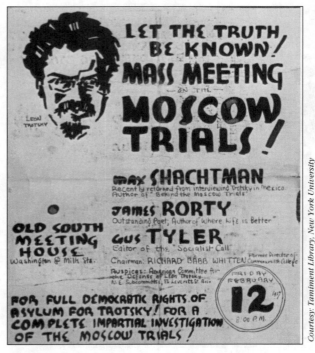

Courtesy: Tamiment Library, New York University

Trotskyists held public meetings denouncing Stalin's "frame up" of loyal Bolsheviks during 1936-39.

starvation, kept the strikes alive. If nothing could salvage victory against overwhelming odds, at least the communists tried, as they did similarly in the coal fields and scattered other spots.

Behind these industrial efforts, local communists created networks of support in the fraternal and cultural societies of immigrant groups. Like the socialists before them, but with growing sophistication, Jews and Finns established circuits of theatrical groups with sometimes high standards or at least wide community participation. They had set up summer camps for thousands of their children to learn the immigrant language anew, enjoy healthy exercise, and be propagandized (or educated) about the real America. Skillful chorale directors employed the latest techniques to create a powerful sound from ordinary working people. Beautiful magazines with keen cartoonists and funny as well as serious writers appeared. In communities with lower levels of activity, like the Greek, Lithuanian and Hungarian, communist newspaper editors spoke to the day-to-day life of immigrants in what seemed a very cruel, indifferent society. Left institutions made immigrants feel "at home," and offered hopes of a democratized homeland.

At the end of the 1920s, Communists had also begun to organize Harlemites to protest high rents and slum conditions of their apartments, and to urge the formation of community networks like the Harlem Tenants Union for further collective action. These campaigns had little effect at first, beyond simply exposing the terrible condition of housing for blacks. But like the early drives for industrial unionism, they helped convince community residents that they could address their plight – and that Communists, unlike nearly any other whites, honestly meant to help them.

When Communists worked in black neighborhoods, they slowly discovered that the African-American churches might be their best allies, and when they carried on lonely protests against U.S. "gunboat diplomacy" (like the brutal U.S. Marines' invasion of Nicaragua in 1926, quelling revolt and murdering the national hero, Augusto Sandino), they found white Christians by their side. *The World Tomorrow*, a Christian Socialist magazine, was the magazine of pacifist Devere Allen, former Y.M.C.A. leader Kirby Page and the network around the anti-war Fellowship of Reconciliation. Deeply impressed by the example of Indian leader Mohandus Gandhi, the *World Tomorrow* editors sought to show other American Christians that racism, poverty and oppression were not God's way and should be alleviated by positive remedies, nonviolently if possible.

Because communists represented Russia in most American eyes, because they disguised their presence in some reform movements, because they often used incomprehensible language and fought most bitterly among themselves, they remained alien to American life in the 1920s. One final round of internal purges in which large chunks of Communist leaders were expelled for questioning Moscow's authority convinced close observers that American Communism could not be democratic. And yet — the rank-and-file communist *engaged* in struggle when no one else seemed to dare; and communists had unceasingly predicted the economic collapse which came in 1929. The stock-market crash, and the Great Depression that followed, seemed compelling truth that the twenty thousand or so Communists had *something* to contribute to American life.

For college age and younger activists, especially around New York City, Communism could be an all-encompassing way of life with May Day events, an Epiphany of faith and determination (and a good way for boys and girls to meet each other). By the later 1930s when peacetime membership peaked at 55,000 (with perhaps ten times that many in affiliated or influenced labor and

Private Collection

The noted philosopher, self-defined democratic socialist and champion of participatory democracy, John Dewey, chaired a commission to investigate accusations brought against Leon Trotsky during the Moscow "Frame Up" Trials.

Courtesy: Morris Library, Southern Illinois University, Carbondale

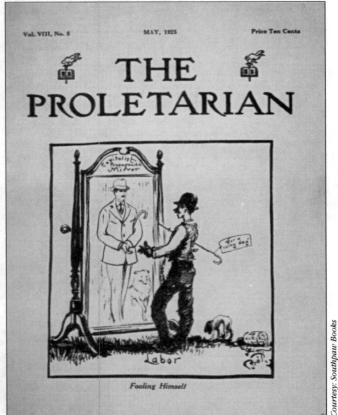

Courtesy: Southpaw Books

The first split-off from the Communist movement (expelled in 1920), the Proletarian Party maintained its own movement and publication for decades. The small Socialist Labor Party ran its own candidates and distributed literature for decades. It frequently attacked the Communist movement for misrepresenting socialist ideas.

cultural organizations), Communist leaders such as Earl Browder were practically respectable public figures. Continual fund-drives taxed members and supporters severely but many willingly sacrificed their own small incomes for their party.

Communist compromises with liberalism and their leaders' indifference to internal party democracy, as much as Communist support of the increasingly tyrannical regime of Joseph Stalin, set off Leftwing opponents. The old Socialist Labor Party maintained itself in "splendid isolation," restricting its activities to propaganda and election campaigns, and to attacking the communists. The Proletarian Party, a Detroit-based group of self-educated working people expelled from the Communist movement at its inception, carried on educational activities and helped form industrial unions. Small anarchist groups also proliferated, with the exiled German intellectual Rudolf Rocker their most estimable personage (although a gentile, he taught himself Yiddish to become part of the largest ethnic unit within anarchism).

More serious opposition emerged from organizations of former communists. Followers of 1920s Communist leader Jay Lovestone, expelled from the Communist party in 1928 during a dispute over international politics, soon captured important union locals in the garment industry, published their own intelligent weekly paper, and hosted the "New Workers School" in New York decorated with a famous mural by Diego

Courtesy: Tamiment Library, New York University

Diego Rivera's mural series, "A Portrait of America," at the New Workers School, with staff and students in the foreground. Later, the mural was disassembled.

Norman Thomas

Rivera. The American followers of Leon Trotsky, who were expelled the previous year, played an even more important role by leading teamsters and by rallying liberal American opposition to the Moscow Trials of longstanding Bolsheviks in terror-ridden Russia of 1937-39. Trotskyists also flayed the Communist shift to the "Popular Front" against Fascism in 1935 when communists eased their attack upon the colonialism still holding millions of non-whites in Asia and Africa (and American imperialism acting similarly in Latin America), as Stalin sought allies against Hitler. The beloved Franklin Roosevelt — as Trotskyists, Wobblies and socialists often reminded Communist sympathizers — had set his New Deal upon the preservation of capitalism, not the expansion of democracy; he could end the experiment at any moment, and probably would at the outbreak of war. Likewise, even the best of the new industrial unions, swearing support to Roosevelt, could themselves become bureaucratic imitations of the A.F. of L. conservatism.

NORMAN THOMAS

"Mr. Socialism" to two generations of Americans, Norman Thomas was also and perhaps better named "the conscience of America." He earned steadily less voter support in his candidacies for president after his high-point in 1932. But through his commanding courage and personal resolve, he earned respect bordering on public reverence.

Born in 1884, Thomas came from a family of ministers. His father, grandfather and great-grandfather had been Presbyterian clergy, and Thomas almost automatically graduated from Princeton and ordained at the Union Theological Seminary in 1911. He experienced his political moment of truth a few years later. A ministry in the slums taught him about human misery and the stupid brutality of World War One drove him toward pacifism. A budding Christian Socialist, Thomas joined the Fellowship of Reconciliation, worked with anti-conscription organizations and the National Civil Liberties Bureau, predecessor to the American Civil Liberties Union, to support war resisters.

In 1918, Thomas officially left the clergy and entered the Socialist Party just as it neared factional chaos and near-collapse. By 1921, most young radicals had transferred their enthusiasm to the Communists or simply dropped out of organization activity. Moving into a virtual vacuum, Thomas became editor of the fading daily newspaper, the *New York Leader,* and he joined the liberal *Nation* magazine as an associate editor. In 1924, he began his long career as a socialist candidate, running for governor of New York. From the beginning, he attracted prominent liberal intellectuals — notably professors and clergy — and aging (especially Jewish) socialist loyalists.

During the 1920s, Thomas also commenced his life as champion of labor and public guardian of civil liberties. Entering the desperate struggle of mill workers in Passaic, New Jersey in 1926, he boldly led a mass meeting defending strikers. Thomas faced down police who arrested him for "rioting" (the law would later be overturned in another victory typical for Thomas). By the 1930s, he was confronting Mayor Frank "I Am the Law" Hague of Jersey City, emerging beaten but morally triumphant; travel to the south, risking life and limb to defend multi-racial sharecroppers; and taking part in innumerable defense committees, including a key role in the Socialist Party's own Workers Defense League.

Thomas, the perennial candidate for office, was also the Socialist Party's greatest political asset. In 1925 and 1929, he took on the political corruption of the New York mayoralty, winning even some prominent conservatives to his side. His 1928 campaign for the presidency garnered few votes, but boosted the flagging Socialist party with prominent endorsements and Thomas for President Clubs. He reached his apex with the 1932 campaign, the grandest socialist personal performance since Debs' 1912 effort (Debs had been in prison in 1920) and along with LaFollette's 1924 run, the finest radical campaign for the presidency after 1920. Thomas Clubs proved especially popular on college campuses, where some straw votes showed him running ahead of Franklin Roosevelt. His supporters felt bitterly disappointed at the actual count of slightly less than 884,781 votes (no doubt some thousands had been "counted out"). Most Americans seeking change through the ballot box had obviously voted for Roosevelt.

And they would continue to do so in increasing numbers, marking Thomas' political doom. Thomas ran a vigorous 1936 campaign, complaining that the Democrats had carried out the Socialist platform "on a stretcher." But prominent socialists deserted to the New Deal camp. His less than 200,000 votes showed that the time had passed. Still, his subsequent campaigns invariably brought public and press attention to socialist ideas, and brought real benefits to the surviving Socialist Party locals. In 1940, he staged a great campaign against U.S. entry into war, warning correctly about the permanent military-industrial complex which would be the inevitable result (nevertheless, he supported military action against the fascist powers). In 1948, he again attracted considerable attention (and 140,260 votes) by positioning himself between Harry Truman, spokesman of the emerging military-industrial complex, and Progressive Party candidate Henry Wallace, whom Thomas believed insufficiently critical of Soviet policies.

Thomas had still less luck in leading the Socialist Party. He supported youngsters against the bureaucratic union leaders who ruled the party in the early 1930s, but his supporters splintered. When conservative socialists based in the garments trade labor bureaucracy left the Party in 1936, they took with them some of the major surviving institutions, such as the Rand School and radio station WEVD. Deprived of this last measure of support, Thomas attempted repeatedly, in the 1940s and 1950s, to revive the party. In the end, hardline supporters of the Vietnam War took it away from him, and killed its chances for recovery during the 1960s-70s. Still, Thomas offered moments of moral leadership to disarmament and anti-Vietnam war movements in his final years, and his personal example to those, like Michael Harrington, who would seek to assume his mantle in future socialist organizations.

Trotskyist leader James P. Cannon on vacation, c. 1946, with the phrase penned on the back of the photograph, "A picture of a man and a dog at peace with their own consciences." This photo was mounted on the wall of the Socialist Workers Party headquarters in Minneapolis/St. Paul until the office closed a few years ago.

Illustrations by Fritz Eichenberger marked the unique "look" of the Catholic Worker.

Private Collection

Courtesy: Southpaw Books

Launched by former socialist and wobbly Dorothy Day, and utopian reformer Peter Maurin, the Catholic Worker appealed for voluntary, religious solutions as members opened up refuge houses and farms to the homeless.

DOROTHY DAY

The most important religious radical of her time, Dorothy Day spanned twentieth radical labor history from the Industrial Workers of the World to the United Farm Workers and political history from the Socialist party to the anti-Vietnam War movement. Today, she is a serious candidate for Sainthood.

Born in 1897 and raised in Chicago, Day gathered ideas from the books of anarchist Peter Kropotkin. At the University of Illinois, she enrolled in the Socialist Party, and following graduation, talked herself into a $5/week job at the socialist New York *Call*. She found herself in the exciting swirl of Greenwich Village bohemia, a member of the *Masses* editorial staff — guest-editing the very issue that the federal government found "subversive" enough to put the regular editors on trial. She joined the *Liberator*, successor to the *Masses*, gaining respect or notoriety as a prominent woman reporter of strikes and other events.

After the birth of a child out of wedlock, her latent spirituality revived dramatically. The Catholic Church, then utterly conservative in political and social issues, nevertheless seemed to her the church of the poor, and the church of religious mystery. She privately debated her role until 1932, when she met the French-born Catholic radical and sometime soap-box orator, Peter Maurin. He persuaded her to adopt his combination program of urban houses for the poor, farming communes and Christian discussions. As an alternative to secular socialism or communism, these ideas stressed personal action, change in the individual and voluntary cooperation.

On Mayday, 1933, they distributed the first issue of the *Catholic Worker* at a penny a copy. Covering social issues of the day like unemployment and labor conditions, the *Catholic Worker* urged the progressive encyclicals of various Popes, and did it best to ignore the conservative (or pro-fascist) sentiment of powerful clergy. Urging "reconstruction of the social order," the *Catholic Worker* was banned from some churches and Day forbidden to speak in their diocese. Yet Day and her fellow activists continued to speak out for improved social conditions and against war (including World War II, the Korean War and the Vietnam War). Determinedly faithful to the Gospels in her own way, Day sometimes criticized the Church for its failures to live up to them.

The "hospitality houses" or centers for the poor backed up words with good deeds. *Catholic Worker* residents in these houses adopted voluntary poverty, living as well as reciting Peter Maurin's invocation that "the shirt on your back belongs to the poor." Here, more than anywhere else since the day of the I.W.W. headquarters, the wayfarers were treated not as clients or misfits but as decent people down on their luck. More than forty such houses opened by 1940, more than two hundred internationally in the years to follow, many of which remain centers for the homeless to this day. Less successful, the farms Maurin planned never became agrarian centers of cooperative life akin to the monasteries of vanished times, but rather survived as rural centers for the poor.

Day's influence upon following generations was felt, first of all, in the non-violence movements of civil rights and disarmament. Preaching a moral lesson in winning over those who disagree, even violently she did much in particular to inspire the post-communist (and non-Marxist) peace activists of the 1950s and early 1960s. Catholic Workers led by Day herself openly refused to participate in the civil defense air raid drills occurring across the nation. By 1983, American bishops' pastoral letters accepted her teaching of pacifism as a legitimate choice for Catholics, singling her out with Martin Luther King, Jr. as personal examples of non-violent courage. Still, she felt compelled to hold her editorial tongue toward those institutional leaders like Cardinal Francis Spellman and later Cardinal John O'Connor who zealously backed McCarthyism and the Cold War arms build-up, urged American soldiers into war against the Vietnamese, and meanspiritedly attacked the efforts of American feminists and homosexuals.

Secondly, Day had inspired a handful of young Catholic idealists, including Michael Harrington and Father Daniel Berrigan, who would go on to great moral leadership (often in defiance of Church directives). Beyond this, she had engaged a wide American public in a dialogue over moral values about wealth, war, peace and poverty. Curiously, although a devoted follower of one of history's least democratic institutions, she had also helped to revive the philosophy and practice of anarchism as a way of thinking and of living after the Cold War.

Communists are ribbed for their Russo-centric mentality, and the rich for thinking that William Z. Foster's 1932 manifesto, Towards Soviet America, *is about travel. From Otto Soglow,* Wasn't the Depression Terrible? *(1934)*

Anarchists maintained an active press with only a few thousand sympathizers; their most famous editor and essayist was Rudolph Rocker.

The Story that was **NOT** in the Headlines!

THE REAL REASON WHY CHAMBERLAIN
CAPITULATED TO HITLER AT MUNICH

HEAR

THE EXCITING LECTURE!

by

*World-Famous Journalist and Labor Leader; author of
"World Revolution," "A History of Negro Revolt,"
"The Black Jacobins."*

C. L. R. JAMES

ON

"TWILIGHT OF THE BRITISH EMPIRE"

As a front-line labor leader and journalist, C. L. R. James has played a leading role in the mass movements rocking the Empire.

He is one of England's foremost orators . . . uniquely equipped to tell you where tottering Britain is heading.

FIRST TIME IN AMERICA!

Auspices: Local New York, Socialist Workers Party — 4th International
116 UNIVERSITY PLACE

WEDNESDAY, NOVEMBER 30th at 8 P.M.

IRVING PLAZA - - - Irving Place and 15th Street

Admission 25¢

Read the SOCIALIST APPEAL

375

As Popular Front Communists abandoned anti-colonialist causes to focus on the dangers of fascism, Trotskyists and Christian Socialists took up the slack. C.L.R. James, author The Black Jacobins, *is hosted by Trotskyists on his first United States lecture tour, 1939.*

Communist headquarters at the high tide of revolutionary expectations: Union Square, 1932. Photograph by Charles Rivers.

Courtesy: Tamiment Library, New York University (Charles Rivers Collection)

Young Radicals

Little Lefty

The Young Radicals

One of the greatest successes of the "Old Left" was with young people. Beloved parents or grandparents, uncles and aunts — especially among the immigrant groups — guided children toward leisure activities, language training, and participation in "adult" work like strike support or parades, which in turn established friendships and social reinforcements for precocious political Leftism. In tiny islands of radicalism, like the cooperative housing on Allerton Avenue in the Bronx, children grew up thinking (they later claimed) that Big Bill Haywood was a national hero and May Day a national holiday. Most others simply dated their first pals, boyfriends or girlfriends, enjoyed encounters with nature and unique political excitement. Especially among Jews but others as well, this total involvement often led to the lifelong use of a non-English second language and to empathy for different cultures. It could also lead to future appearances before a Congressional investigating committee of the 1950s for the presumed crime decades earlier of leading a nature hike or enrolling in a Yiddish singing group.

The Young People's Socialist League, until 1920 the strongest radical youth group, reached 10,000 members in around 150 cities before severe government repression and division along factional lines fractured the organization. It had mostly devoted itself to education and recreation before turning to mobilization against United States involvement in World War One. After 1920, the Y.P.S.L. rebuilt slowly, peaking around 1932 with the campaign of Norman Thomas for President. Thereafter, it distinguished itself in neighborhood activities against militarism and war, while an allied student group, Student League for Industrial Democracy, carried out similar activities at colleges and universities. After further divisions, it

In the early days of the Communist movement, the Daily Worker *distributed many European translations and socialist children's books.*

Courtesy: Southpaw Books

Workers Children School series. Dozens of progressive Yiddish summer camps and day schools (held after public school several times per week) used these volumes as curricula. Mayr Alefbays (upper and lower left) taught Yiddish grammar and political ideals for very young readers. This sample page reads, "This is Papa/This is Mama/This is Marsha and Emma/Papa goes to the shop/Marsha and Emma go to school." In We Learn and Struggle (top row center, and right side), for second year readers, a sample reads "Mary was born in a wooden house. The house always showed the hardship of a worker's day. Mary carried suffering and hardship in her breast. And stories of workers struggles she swallowed with childish cheer." "Joseph's Dream" included the lines, "All doors closed/All windows closed/On a bed Joseph dreams/On the streets a night sleeps."

remained a small group behind Thomas, devoted to peace until Pearl Harbor, then known best for assisting conscientious objectors and pacifist groups like the Fellowship of Reconciliation.

The Communists, who drew the loyalty of many pre-1920 "Yipsels" (as the Y.P.S.L.ers were known), formed the Young Communist League in 1922. Mostly the children of first or second-generation immigrant radicals, the Y.C.L.ers distributed the *Daily Worker,* visited strike scenes, and at great risk to themselves organized young people to support strikes in far-away textile towns and coal mining zones. During the Depression, the Y.C.L. blossomed to perhaps 10,000, throwing their energy into frenzied attempts at organizing the unemployed, and often bloody confrontations with police and thugs during "hunger" marches on city halls.

From the middle 1930s, a more relaxed approach encouraged youth leisure activities, including neighborhood clubs, sports and musical groups. Turning from "revolution" to anti-racism and anti-fascism, the became a vanguard of democratic impulses on many scenes including the racial integration of sports, prompting allies like novelist Sinclair Lewis, sportswriter John R. Tunis and basketball coach Nat Holman to write for their publications. The New York area Young Communist League alone had perhaps 12,000 members. The Young Communists joined industrial union organizing campaigns, delegations of the American Student Union, Youth Against War and Fascism and the American Youth Congress and many activities of the youth branches

Courtesy: Faye Itzkowitz

Children at Camp Kinderland in 1935 unfurl banners calling for unity against fascism.

By the middle 1930s, youth movements celebrated their own holidays, and demanded jobs. International Youth Day is celebrated here in Ulmer Park, Brooklyn. Once a popular ethnic gathering site, the former park is now covered by high rise apartments.

Magazines for older children and teens increasingly treated sports, especially during the 1930s. Note the interracial sub-themes.

of the International Workers Order's allied ethnic associations.

The youngest radicals, the Young Pioneers, were organized during the 1920s to provide political education and experience for primary schoolers. Membership consisted mostly of children of Communist Party members. In 1934, the Young Pioneers were merged into the Junior Section of the International Workers Order. Strongest among Jewish working class communities of the East (and Chicago) and Finnish communities of the upper Midwest, the Young Pioneers actually conducted political campaigns against child labor, the Boy Scouts, and racial segregation of urban swimming pools and for such public programs as free school lunches. [Plate 60]

Jewish Socialists and Communists conducted Yiddish schools, stressing secular Judaism and the tradition of "classic" Yiddish authors like Sholem Aleichem. Dozens of schools, most of them in the New York area, provided supplementary education on afternoons and weekends for thousands of children (many of them frustrated at being forced to attend more classes). Their classes stressed the history of socialism and class struggle, but by the middle 1930s turned increasingly toward Jewish identity and its preservation. Children joined their teachers on picket-lines in various struggles. Meanwhile, some of the most talented Yiddish writers, such as Moshe Nadir and Chaver Paver, turned to writing children's books, sometimes illustrated by famous Jewish artists.

Some of the happiest moments of Left childhood took place in summer camps such as Camp Unity in Beacon, New York and Camp Kinderland, in various

שוואַרץ אוז ווייס

פֿון יעקב קרעפֿליאַק

Courtesy: Southpaw Books

A Yiddish-language book for older children, Black and White *by Jacob Kreplick, published in 1939, typically teaches racial empathy.*

Itche Goldberg, leading Yiddish pedagogue for Jewish children from the 1930s to the present, has played a central role in the Yiddishe Kultur Farband (YKUF), founded during the upswing of progressive Jewishness in the late 1930s. Goldberg today edits Yiddishe Kultur, *journal of the YKUF. From* In Dienst fun Folk *(1949).*

locations and now located in Tolland, Massachusetts. Here, children played, learned modern dance from noted choreographers, attended some classes (especially in Yiddish), and listened to some of the outstanding musicians of the nation including Paul Robeson, legendary bluesman Leadbelly (Huddie Ledbetter), Woody Guthrie and Pete Seeger. Many adults looked back on these summers as their happiest times of childhood friendship and self-discovery.

May Day Parade, Union Square, New York City, 1940, exalted the integration of big league baseball into a major political issue. (IWO) Demonstrators wear the uniforms of their own International Workers Order (IWO) leagues. From In Dienst fun Folk.

Photograph and Courtesy: Harold Freeman

Summer Camp was one of the most important experiences of 1930s radical youth. Assembly Hall, in Beacon, New York, a Young Pioneers Camp, is the scene of summer adventures with an ardent political flavor.

Go On Your Vacation To One of Our

PROLETARIAN CAMPS

Information for all four camps can be obtained at
32 Union Square, Room 505; Tel. STuyvesant 9-6332

CAMP KINDERLAND

HOPEWELL JUNCTION, N. Y.—All registrations for children
must be in office one week in advance at 143 East 103rd St.—
Children of 7 years or over are accepted—Registration for
adults at 32 Union Square—Rates for adults $17 a week

CAMP NITGEDAIGET BEACON, N. Y.

Boats leave for the camp every day from West 42d Street Ferry.
GOOD ENTERTAINMENT   DANCES AT THE CAMP

CAMP WOCOLONA   MONROE, N. Y.

Take 23rd St. ferry, Erie Railroad, to Monroe, N. Y.
A return ticket for the camp is only $2.60
CAMP WOCOLONA IS BEAUTIFUL AND MODERN
New bungalows with hot and cold showers, 4 tennis courts, field
for play and sport, culture, dance, music.
Rates $21.50 per week—TUUL members: $17.50
Camp Phone: MONROE 89

CAMP UNITY   WINGDALE, N. Y.

Autos to Camp Unity leave from 143 East 103rd Street at 9-10
every morning, Fridays at 9-10 A. M. and 6:30 P. M., also
2 P. M. every day. Saturdays at 9 A. M. and 4 P. M.
Sundays at 9 A. M.

For information about any
of these four camps— Call Stuyvesant 9-6332

*Children spend summer weeks at Camp Kinderland and other camps and meet famous personalities such as Paul Robeson during
the 1930s. Of the various Left youth camps, only Kinderland has survived (now relocated in Tolland, Massachusetts).*

Courtesy: Friends of Camp Kinderland

Paul Robeson at Camp Kinderland. Photography, Ben Itzkowitz.

PAUL ROBESON

If he had been white — people said at the time of Robeson's greatest fame — he might have been president. Instead, this famed athlete, concert singer, and fighting progressive experienced a political martyrdom, perhaps the most famous victim (after the Rosenbergs) of America's Cold War.

Born just before the turn of the century, Paul Robeson was the son of an escaped slave who had taken a divinity degree and become a Presbyterian minister in Somerville, New Jersey. Young Paul sang in church choir, did well in school, and entered Rutgers University at seventeen. There, the only black in his class, he earned among the highest grades, won elocution contests, starred in football (twice reaching All-American status), track, basketball and baseball. Intending to practice as a lawyer, he turned gradually toward a stage career.

By the middle 1920s, he became a star, dominating the stage with his audacious acting and his marvelous voice — perhaps only the second black man (after Charles Gilpin) to be accepted as a serious actor on the American stage. In many productions, in the United States and Europe, he received rave notices. By contrast, his movie career was a terrible disappointment, as he felt utterly denied to act in his own way.

But he triumphed most of all on the concert stage. He sang in many languages, usually folk songs including many with a political message. His version of "Ballad for Americans," sung first in 1939, became a sort of second national anthem in wartime. An international star, he became more famous in more parts of the world perhaps than any American figure save Franklin Roosevelt.

When he devoted himself to fighting for Black rights and fighting the Cold War, he lost everything but his courage. Robeson called for an end to colonialism abroad, segregation at home, and an end to the arms race and Cold War. By the end of the 1940s, he was barred from public performances, his records taken off the shelves, his concerts sometimes the inspiration of racist rioting, his passport taken away. In response he founded *Freedom* in 1950, a leftish black newspaper, with the collaboration of W.E.B. DuBois among others. By this time, health problems and depression practically ended his career. He died, after a final concert tour and many years of isolation, in 1976.

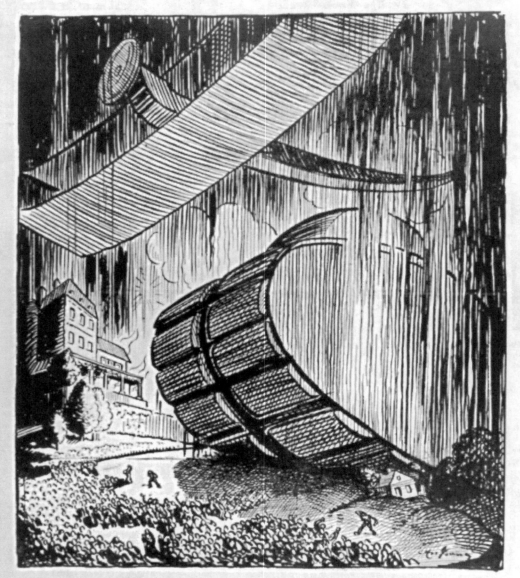

Left movements of young people during the early 1930s emphasized resistance to militarism and imperialism, in city neighborhoods and summer camps.

Depression Struggles

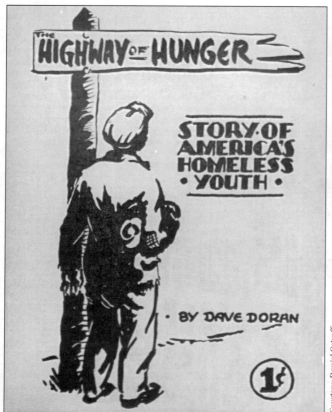

Rally on the steps of Utah State Capitol. Salt Lake City, January 29, 1931.

Depression Struggles

Seldom remembered today as the "Red Decade," the 1930s brought the largest ever number of Americans close to radicalism after the 1910s and before the 1960s. But it did so in often curious, even nonradical ways. The Depression lowered expectations for millions, even while it made them irate at the economic system which had failed them. The rise of Adolf Hitler seemed to push back hopes for dramatic change until the terrors of fascist oppression and the threat of world conquest could be defeated. Communists offered to many sympathetic Americans a vision of security, and to many artists a bridge between the America they saw before them and the democratic traditions they believed in.

For a moment in the early 1930s, the Socialist Party seemed poised to make a dramatic comeback. Socialists enjoyed a mild revival of municipal socialism, with officials elected in some Wisconsin towns, including Milwaukee, and in sections of Germanic Pennsylvania. By 1936, it had been derailed by a leftwing-moving New Deal, and splintered hopelessly.

Christian Socialists went on their own way. Organized in groups like the Church League for Industrial Democracy, the Fellowship of Socialist Christians and the Methodist Federation for Social Service, they vigorously support-

Radicals publicized the plight of the vulnerable, while police threatened demonstrators and President Herbert Hoover pleaded for calm. From the Labor Defender, *c. 1931.*

ed unions, civil liberties, and civil rights for minorities. The most important agitator among them, Claude Williams, founded a Peoples Institute for Applied Religion to reinterpret the Bible for religiously-oriented social activists. The most prestigious, Reinhold Niebuhr, proclaimed a highly intellectual doctrine for a future post-capitalist, cooperative age.

In the early 1930s, young radicals drifted toward the Communist party and to mass movements in which communists played significant, sometimes controlling roles. For instance, rent-strikes spread across New York's blue collar boroughs, especially intense in the Bronx, Brownsville and Williamsburg, with Communist-linked Jewish women in the leadership. Elsewhere in the country, "Johnny, go get a Red!" was said to be the frequently-heard plea of a mother, especially a black mother, to a child when her family faced eviction. Communists organized whirlwind demonstrations, often moved furniture back into apartments and compelled landlords to negotiate extensions.

Similarly, the communist-led Unemployed Councils, the socialist-led Workers Alliance and the independent Unemployed Citizens League threw themselves into action for the depression's victims. These groups demanded that local

Courtesy: Ben and Beatrice Goldstein Foundation

Radical artists of many styles and interests assailed the greed of the system which starved ordinary people. Jacob Burck a frequent Daily Worker cartoonist, used the familiar Masses *crayon style, below left; Hugo Gellert's style had evolved from a fanciful non-realism of his days at the* Liberator *to a rather grim realism. From Burck,* Hunger and Revolt *(1934); Gellert,* Capital in Lithographs *(1933), below right; and Gellert, "The Boss," silkscreen, c. 1932, upper right.*

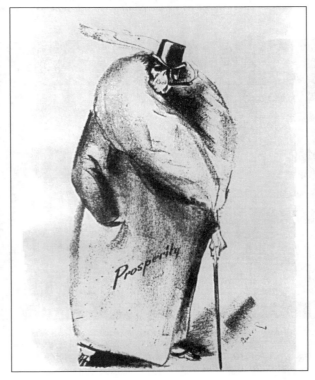

Both, Private Collection

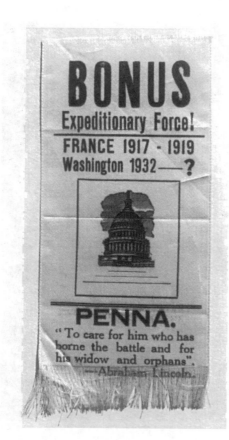

Private Collection

Courtesy: YIVO Institute

Yiddish-speaking workers in New York May Day and Unemployment Demonstration, 1932.

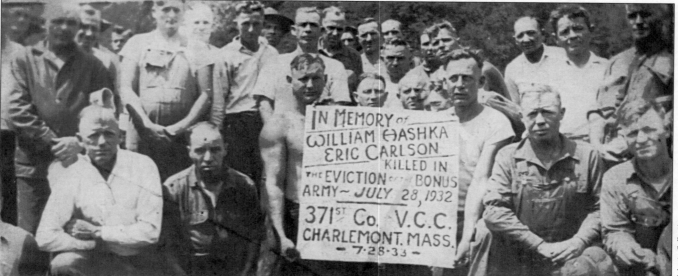

Private Collection

This rare photo names martyrs of the Bonus Expeditionary Force, official designation of the "Bonus Army," which rocked the nation's capitol in 1932; the ribbon suggests the rationale. The idea of the "industrial army" was recalled from the 1890s movement, and constituencies ready to march appeared spontaneously in many places. Socialists and Communists, however, worked vigorously to build a support system and to provide food and lodging for marchers passing through town.

Demonstrations by the unemployed on Boston Common, c. 1935.

A meeting of the Illinois Workers Alliance, Springfield, Illinois, c. 1935.

Paul Andreas Rasmussen, national secretary of the Workers Alliance of America (center back) and its president, Herbert Benjamin meet with others at W.A.A. headquarters in Washington, 1936.

Franklin D. Roosevelt's New Deal had carried out the socialist platform "on a stretcher," Norman Thomas quipped. The League for Industrial Democracy was an educational arm of the Socialist Party.

authorities increase welfare aid to families, supported local strikes, and launched occasional marches on Washington. Never much more than a series of ad hoc mobilizations, the unemployed groups did much to create a national demand for New Deal legislation like Social Security.

Among the most successful radical political campaigns of these days was Upton Sinclair's run for governor of California on the EPIC ("End Poverty in California") program in 1934. The famed socialist novelist won the Democratic Party primary but faced an assault by businessmen, California newspapers, and even Hollywood film moguls who compelled stars to appear in anti-Sinclair rallies or lose their jobs. Defeated despite his nearly 900,000 votes, Sinclair remained in the public eye, spokesman for a recovery program which somewhat resembled Franklin Roosevelt's "Second New Deal" of massive works projects and old age pensions.

Socialists had some luck in electing further local candidates, but all these had been defeated by 1940 except Mayor Jasper MacLevy of Bridgeport, Connecticut, and even MacLevy was censured by the state Socialist Party for the conservative character of his mayoral rule. Communist candidates had virtually no success in their own electoral campaigns, although they played a key role in advising and supporting many candidates for local and state offices, particularly in New York, Illinois, Michigan, Minnesota and California. [Plates 55-56]

But most of the radical   struggles

involved direct action and organizing for unions and social movements. Inter-racial initiatives showed socialists and communists at their most courageous, as the Americans who would risk life and limb to bring divided groups together. The Southern Tenant Farmers Union, organized by Tennessee socialist H.L. Mitchell and others, never successfully created a large-scale industrial body. But it led share-croppers and small farmers in parts of the South, from the middle 1930s to early 1940s, against conditions of virtual serfdom. It roused enormous sympathy from Northerners, and popularized a handful of fighting tunes such as "Roll the Union On."

Communists also conducted a wide spectrum of inter-racial activities, from political support for Harlemites to sharecroppers' and steelworkers' campaigns in Alabama to the National Negro Congress and Southern Negro Youth Congress. These two latter groups, influential respectively in urban neighborhoods and among southern black intellectuals, did much to create the background and leadership of the later civil rights movements. They led short-lived unions of Mexican-American farmworkers in California during the 1930s, successfully organized Filipinos in various West Coast unions and encouraged the formation of Congress of Spanish Speaking Peoples, made up mostly of Mexican immigrants in southern California. They also participated in the struggles of east coast Asians, especially the Chinese-American laundry workers of New York.

The Communists had another, distinctly different role during the Depression. The "Second New Deal" of the Roosevelt administration brought to power a wide spectrum of reform-minded intellectuals, many of them deeply committed to racial equality and the defeat of fascism. By the late 1930s, Left programs and activists had gained respect and support of some of these New Dealers, some in very high office. They also gained a favorable hearing from Eleanor Roosevelt, especially on racial matters. From the State Department to

End Poverty In California (EPIC), a political campaign led by veteran socialist author Upton Sinclair, won the state Democratic Party's nomination and almost captured the governorship in 1934.

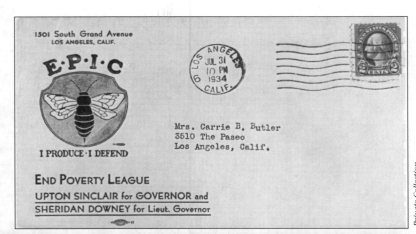

the Works Progress Administration and Tennessee Valley Authority, a friendly voice could be heard for assistance and cooperation, if often quietly spoken.

Three Socialist Mayors

JASPER McLEVY
Mayor of Bridgeport

J. HENRY STUMP
Mayor of Reading

DANIEL W. HOAN
Mayor of Milwaukee

Courtesy: Robert Millar

Several of the socialists elected to local office in the 1930s.

Courtesy: Museum of American Political Life, Neigher Collection

Courtesy: Bridgeport Public Library, Historical Collections

The Bridgeport Post *comments on socialist Jasper McLevy's election as mayor of that city in 1934; McLevy marches in a Fourth of July parade, 1930s.*

A 1930s Socialist party heavily influenced by Christian Socialism put forward many women candidates.

"Socialism" in the New Deal. Alger Hiss, later accused of spying (but convicted on dubious evidence only of deceiving Congress) represented a sympathetic ear to radical causes within the Roosevelt administration. Aubrey Williams, head of the National Youth Administration, was later a prominent leader of the Southern radical movement.

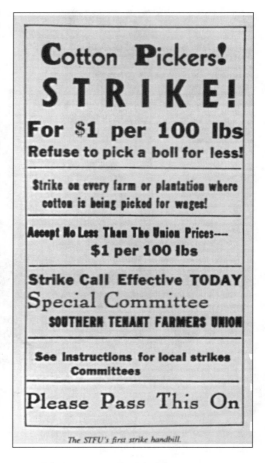

A collage of Southern Tenants Farmer Union material including (top left) the organization's logo; (middle left) its founder H.L. Mitchell in 1938; (bottom left) troubador-organizer John Handcox (who wrote "Roll the Union On"); (top right) the SFTU's first strike handbill; and (bottom right) an emblem created by Rockwell Kent during the centennial of Arkansas statehood in 1936.

Both, Private Collection

Private Collection

The vision of racial equality was among the most controversial of communist ideas. The League of Struggle for Negro Rights, succeeding in 1930 the earlier communist-led American Negro Labor Congress, was succeeded in turn by the National Negro Congress in 1935.

African-American educational leaders and entertainment celebrities rallied to the Communist-led interracial movement. Unlike its predecessors, the National Negro Congress urged racial integration and was influential in many cities.

Courtesy: Marge Frantz

Jane Speed's Bookshop with the proprietor in Birmingham, Alabama represented a brave current of Leftism in the repressive South.

Courtesy: Marge Frantz

The League of Young Southerners, some of its prominent members seen here in 1940, included future communist leader James Jackson (seated at far right) and Christian socialist author James Dombrowski (seated, second left).

Luisa Moreno, leader of the Congress of Spanish Speaking Peoples, and later a deportee, victim of the McCarthyite blacklist.

Courtesy: Southern California Library for Social Studies and Research

Courtesy: Renqui Yu

A progressive Asian-American movement grew strong in New York's Chinatown, especially after the Japanese invasion of China in 1932.

INEZ MILHOLLAND BOISSEVAIN

WHO DIED FOR THE FREEDOM OF WOMEN.

Although Alice Paul was both a leader and inspiration to the radical edge of the woman suffrage movement in its final phase, Inez Milholland Boissevain was its charismatic icon. Until her death in 1918, a victim of anemia and overwork, she often appeared astride a large white horse at the head of suffrage parades.

Official Program WOMAN SUFFRAGE Procession

Washington D.C. March 3, 1913

Color Page — 25

Many labor leaders and martyrs are pictured on these buttons.

Industrial Unionism

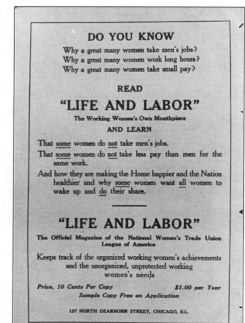

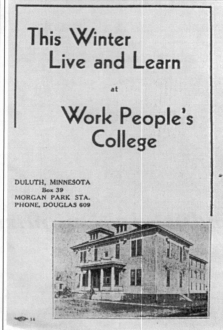

The Work People's College, in Duluth, Minnesota, an I.W.W.-related institution, taught future Finnish-American union activists valuable skills. Educators of the 1920s-30s in such institutions as Brookwood Labor College offered similar lessons and supplied valuable contacts among progressive unionists.

LIFE and LABOR BULLETIN

Covering the Activities of the National Women's Trade Union League and Some
Happenings in the Labor Movement

PUBLISHED BY

THE NATIONAL WOMEN'S TRADE UNION LEAGUE of AMERICA

311 South Ashland Boulevard, Chicago

| Vol. II | AUGUST, 1924 | No. 12—Serial No. 24 |

STATE LEGISLATURES and WORKING WOMEN

By FLORENCE P. SMITH

Forty-three state legislatures met in 1923, and thirteen have met in 1924. But the acts of these legislative sessions in so far as they directly affect working women can be counted on the fingers of two hands. By no means, however, does this indicate any lack of activity on the part of the women in the states and their organizations, for their record is one of incessant and tireless effort to improve conditions for the millions of women workers throughout the country by tightening up existing laws or by passage of new laws.

Progress Made

Nor does this mean that aside from the educational value of legislative campaigns there have been no definite gains. For instance, with the reactionary and deplorable behavior of New York and Illinois, where political maneuvering and the organized opposition of manufacturing interests have repeatedly prevented legal reduction in the hours of work of women, compare the success of Rhode Island, Wyoming and Wisconsin in stepping out of the ten-hour category. In Rhode Island the persistent campaign of

and Arizona advanced its statutory minimum from $10 to $16. An amendment to Minnesota's minimum wage law provides that publication of orders in one daily newspaper in each city of the first and second class, 20 days before the order becomes effective, its prima facie evidence of the existence of the order. In other words, an employer is not relieved of responsibility to comply with the law because a copy of the order fails to reach him through the mails.

Massachusetts has acquired no new laws, but has refused persistently to backslide. Again this year as last bills to repeal the 48-hour law and the minimum wage law were defeated. In fact, repeal of the hour law has been attempted at each session of the legislature since the passage of the law in 1919. Another bill this year asked for suspension of the law for four years and another sought to remove the night work restriction for textile mills. An attempt to repeal the minimum wage law resulted in postponement of the bill for consideration at the next legislature.

While in New York attempts at legislation regulating hours or wages of women were unsuccessful, there was created in 1923

The Life and Labor Bulletin, of the National Women's Trade Union League, helped educate women workers to organize and also urged Congress to enact protective labor legislation.

The socialist colony of Llano, which began in California in 1914 and moved to rural Louisiana in 1917, served as the base for Commonwealth College, which trained labor organizers during the 1920-30s.

Industrial Unionism

Communists had done best in 1920s unions where they could concentrate their strengths without confronting equally powerful enemies. In one dramatic effort, Communist unionists created the Furriers Union, which succeeded in bringing together Greeks, Jews, Hungarians and others against employers who customarily relied on the Mafia to protect them against unionization. Furrier leader Ben Gold, beloved by his rank-and-file, was an open Communist (and later, a Yiddish short-story writer) who won his members a forty hour week and other benefits among the best in the garment industry. The mostly socialist-led garment unions meanwhile retreated, some purging their troublesome communist members. Competition and acrimony among the radicals damaged feelings all around.

Across much of the rest of industrial America, where immigrants worked without benefit of unions, Communists established shop networks and local shop newspapers, publicized local grievances like dangerous conditions and urged industrial organization. No other political group carried on this kind of work with such determination and reliable local contacts.

Elsewhere, the industrial union idea survived a difficult period through labor educational institutions, like the small handful of labor colleges. Toward the end of the 1920s ethnic communists began newsletters and agitation in large industries urging unionization. Leftwing unions led many of these struggles from the late 1920s to the early 1930s, although none were too strong enough to form permanent bodies.

Throughout most of the early 1930s, labor organizations were so hard-pressed by the unemployment of potential members that only a series of almost desperate strikes took place against drastic reductions in pay. In 1934, a burst of direct action showed that many ordinary Americans believed labor organization could turn society around, and that many were willing to risk their lives for the union. In Minneapolis and St. Paul, Minnesota, a dramatic mass strike of workers supported truck drivers. In Toledo, Ohio, radicals allied strikers with the unemployed to win a major labor victory at an auto-supplies company, Auto-Lite. Across New England and parts of the South, tens of thou-

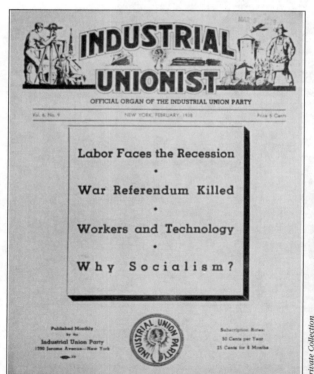

Private Collection

Small political groups like the Industrial Unionists (an SLP splitoff in Pennsylvania) could sometimes play a large role by organizing local workers during the early and middle 1930s into independent unions. Ironically, the rise of the radical-influenced C.I.O. eclipsed the small groups' influence.

Courtesy: Scott Molloy

Anne Burlak, National Secretary of the Communist-led National Textile Union (and the youngest woman trade union official in the United States) speaks to a crowd in Pawtucket, Rhode Island, in 1934.

Courtesy: Minnesota Historical Society, and "Max Sterling" (Mark Sharron, seen lower left).

(Top) The Minneapolis General Strike of 1934 brought Teamsters into the heart of radical unionism and young Trotskyists into the center of Teamsters activism. At the "Battle of Bulls' Run," May 21, 1934, police fled truck drivers and their supporters; (bottom) youngsters from New York joined the activities.

A.J. MUSTE

The great pacifist leader of the American Left, Abraham Johannes Muste was among the few radicals in the Cold War era whose activities had never been associated with communists or anti-communists.

Born in the Netherlands in 1885, Muste came to the United States with his parents as a child, and was raised in a strict Calvinist environment in Michigan. Trained for the Dutch reformed ministry, this son of a skilled furniture worker attended Union Theological Seminary along with Norman Thomas. He was drawn to urban work and to the anti-war Fellowship of Reconciliation, ending his ministerial career.

Briefly, he became an important labor leader. Guiding the Lawrence, Massachusetts, textile strike of 1919, he rose to the apex of the young but vital Amalgamated Textile Workers of America. As the A.T.W.A. failed, he turned to lead the recently formed Brookwood Labor College in Katonah, New York and to the avid workers' education movement of the 1920s. From that base, he challenged the conservative, exclusionary unionism of AFL president William Green. Muste's allies formed themselves into the Conference of Progressive Labor Action (C.P.L.A.), which played an important role in the unemployed movement and especially the 1934 Auto-Lite strike in Toledo, Ohio. Reformed into the American Workers Party, the "Musteites" merged with the Trotskyist movement and then merged again into the Socialist Party, losing their identity and most of their original members.

Muste himself turned away from Marxism to pacifism, and emerged publicly as director of the Fellowship of Reconciliation during the 1940s. Among other accomplishments, the FOR sponsored the early Congress of Racial Equality (CORE) which played a crucial role in the civil rights movement before being taken over by conservative nationalists.

Muste's movements of triumph came after his official retirement. In his seventies and older, he led antinuclear civil disobedience, helped found the popular pacifist *Liberation* magazine, and paved the way for the anti-Vietnam War movement. In lagging health but morally determined, Muste died shortly after returning from a visit to Vietnam to publicize the massive suffering caused by United States bombing of civilian targets.

sands of textile workers struck, riots broke out and governors ordered out the National Guard. Most impressive, though, was a longshoremen's strike in San Francisco, where a dockside union drive had brought the deaths of three workers and then a city-wide general strike with a massive parade. The city's rich reportedly fled to the hills of Oakland, and San Francisco became a "union town." Without radicals, these various struggles and their success would have been unthinkable.

Unionization of major industries now lay almost inevitably ahead, perhaps the most democratizing force in American social life during the Depression years. When the leaders of the recently-formed Committee for Industrial Organization divided from the conservative American Federation of Labor in 1936 and dubbed themselves the Congress of Industrial Organization, the gates opened wide to well-funded organizing drives in major industries. A year later, sitdown strikes erupted across the country, the most dramatic one in Flint, Michigan, where radicals provided the autoworkers logistical support. Employ-

Vincent Dunne, an important organizer of the Minneapolis strike, and a major Trotskyist. Two other brothers were also important Trotskyists and a third, William F. Dunne, was a leading Communist and for a time editor of the Communist Party's Daily Worker.

Workers! Brothers!

YOU KNOW THESE THINGS:

That we are striking for decent wages and Union recognition.
That the bosses forced us into this strike by breaking their pledge.
That they rejected the Haas plan which the Union accepted.
That the Citizens Alliance is out to smash us and all Unions.
THAT IN THE LAST THREE DAYS SCAB TRUCKS HAVE BEGUN TO MOVE UNDER THE PROTECTION OF THE MILITIA CALLED BY GOV. OLSON!

Local 574 is not going to tolerate the movement of scab trucks!

Are you going to stand idly by and see the State Militia help run scab trucks? Are you going to stand idly by and see the Citizens Alliance entrench itself even more deeply in its despotic rule?

A vigorous protest against the activities of the Militia must be made at once. Join us, workers, brothers, in a gigantic

Mobilization Rally!
Tonight at 8 o'clock
ON THE KNOLL
AT THE PARADE GROUNDS

Auspices: Strike Committee of 100; Local 574

ers often fought back fiercely, using private militias, legal injunctions against picketing, sensational newspaper charges against "reds" and police "red squad" harassment of known radicals. Communists, socialists and assorted radicals usually kept a low profile, emphasizing the economic issues involved and workers' quest for greater industrial democracy. By 1940, about half of all industrial jobs were unionized, with vast improvements in wages, conditions, and benefits.

The dozens or hundreds of Leftwing local, regional and national labor leaders provoked an expectable response from conservatives. Leftwingers like the make fun of (and organize against) the Hearst press. But the hatred whipped up the papers owned by William Randolph Hearst, the rage of corporate leaders, the racism and the anti-Semitism hurt radical causes badly. How badly, they would learn after World War II when union conservatives, business, and political leaders succeeded in "purging" unions of the dissidents, the very idealists who had made the great union victories possible in the first place.

The San Francisco General Strike of 1934 laid the basis for the International Longshoremen's and Warehousemen's Union and the Maritime Federation of the Pacific, on display here during a 1939 Labor Day parade.

Less remembered 1934 clashes, like this struggle against strikebreakers in Portland, Oregon, showed the scope of labor mobilization.

Dynamic, Australian-born Harry Bridges (center), founder of the I.L.W.U., dominated Westcoast and Hawaiian maritime activities, surviving a decades-long threat of deportation.

Mary Heaton Vorse, a feminist and leading labor journalist of the 1910s-30s, had covered the Lawrence Strike of 1912, the 1919 Steel Strike and served as publicity director of the 1926 Passaic, New Jersey textile strike before she arrived in Harlan County, Kentucky, in 1931 to cover miners strikes (and was expelled from the state by vigilantes). The publicity techniques she developed were used by labor activists for decades. She reported on CIO struggles throughout the heroic later 1930s. In later years she remained a battler for civil liberties, herself continually pursued by the F.B.I.

The "red" union which preceded the CIO-chartered National Maritime Union, the M.W.I.U., had few successes but opened the path to East Coast industrial unionism in shipping.

Heywood Broun. The avant garde newspaperman caricatured here in the New Masses, *helped guide the formation of the Newspaper Guild.*

Courtesy: Walter Reuther Library of Wayne State University

Private Collection

Cafeteria Workers Parade Badge for May Day, 1937, New York City. A notoriously radical group of employees in parts of the New York trade since at least the 1890s, cafeteria workers spent much time with the unemployed, often not charging them for food.

Private Collection

General Motors Sitdown strikers made history in Flint, Michigan. Artist records the strike's significance in the New Masses.

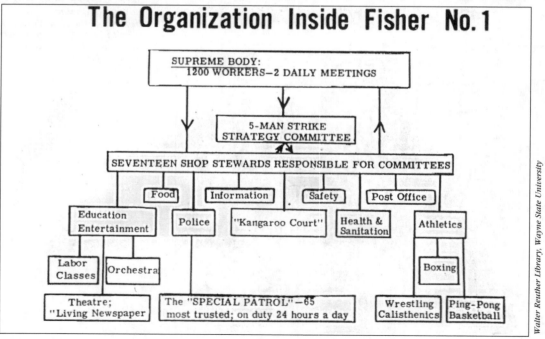

The Organization Inside Fisher No. 1

```
              SUPREME BODY:
           1200 WORKERS—2 DAILY MEETINGS

                    5-MAN STRIKE
                 STRATEGY COMMITTEE

  SEVENTEEN SHOP STEWARDS RESPONSIBLE FOR COMMITTEES

        Food      Information      Safety      Post Office

  Education                                  Health &
  Entertainment    Police    "Kangaroo Court"  Sanitation     Athletics

  Labor                                                       Boxing
  Classes   Orchestra

  Theatre;        The "SPECIAL PATROL"—65         Wrestling    Ping-Pong
  "Living Newspaper"  most trusted; on duty 24 hours a day   Calisthenics  Basketball
```

A strikers' chorus sets the mood for the industrial union drive. Their organizational devotion is shown here.

Genora Dollinger Johnson, leader of General Motors Women's Brigade, assembles a family picketline, while the iconographic mother figure mourns a family loss. Artist Maxo Vanca, a Croatian immigrant from the middle 1930s, was commissioned to paint a series of murals in the St. Nicholas Church of Millvale, Pennsylvania, which he completed by 1941. His "The Immigrant Mother Raises Her Sons for Industry," was painted in 1937. Depicted mostly as strike supporters and family members rather than strikers themselves, Depression era women figured often in labor images.

Courtesy and photo: Harold Freeman

Courtesy: Transit Workers Union

Courtesy: Southpaw Books

Irish-American nationalist and secret communist Mike Quill guided the Transit Workers Union of mostly Irish-American workers through a tumultuous era of organization and strikes, frequently directing action at the street level and offering fiery anti-fascist, anti-racist oratory. Here he passes a sandwich to one of his striking followers.

Cartoonists and union activists directed much energy toward the Hearst newspaper empire, and the anti-labor, anti-Roosevelt policies of its chief, William Randolph Hearst, who is targeted during this National Youth Day parade in 1936.

Private Collection

A characteristic anti-communist pamphlet of the period, issued by the United States Chamber of Commerce.

In Seattle of 1939 and Honolulu of 1940, Japanese-Americans and Filipino workers found union support through the Communist-led International Longshoremen and Warehousemen's Union.

Courtesy: I.L.W.U. Archives

Courtesy: Museum of American Political Life

A late 1930s demonstration in Chicago mixes labor messages with a variety of other themes.

Private Collection

Sardonic cartoonist M. Zipfel cast a skeptical eye at Roosevelt as the savior of the "little people."

Anti-Fascism and the Popular Front

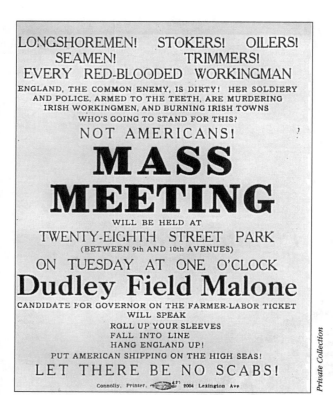

LONGSHOREMEN!   STOKERS!   OILERS!
SEAMEN!   TRIMMERS!
EVERY RED-BLOODED WORKINGMAN
ENGLAND, THE COMMON ENEMY, IS DIRTY! HER SOLDIERY
AND POLICE, ARMED TO THE TEETH, ARE MURDERING
IRISH WORKINGMEN, AND BURNING IRISH TOWNS
WHO'S GOING TO STAND FOR THIS?
NOT AMERICANS!
MASS MEETING
WILL BE HELD AT
TWENTY-EIGHTH STREET PARK
(BETWEEN 9th AND 10th AVENUES)
ON TUESDAY AT ONE O'CLOCK
Dudley Field Malone
CANDIDATE FOR GOVERNOR ON THE FARMER-LABOR TICKET
WILL SPEAK
ROLL UP YOUR SLEEVES
FALL INTO LINE
HANG ENGLAND UP!
PUT AMERICAN SHIPPING ON THE HIGH SEAS!
LET THERE BE NO SCABS!

Connolly, Printer.   2004 Lexington Ave

Private Collection

Irish-American demonstrators add their own imperial enemy, England, to the list of the oppressive states of Europe.

Courtesy: Andy Landsman

Courtesy: Walt Whitman Odets

RIFLE RULE IN CUBA

CARLETON BEALS
AND
CLIFFORD ODETS

Courtesy: Southpaw Books

Who Killed Carlo Tresca?

CHI UCCISE CARLO TRESCA?

Con prefazioni di
ARTURO GIOVANNITTI
e **JOHN DOS PASSOS**

TRESCA MEMORIAL COMMITTEE

Private Collection

In the midst of his most creative period, playwright Clifford Odets led a committee to Cuba to investigate the Batista government's persecution of artists and intellectuals. Carlton Beals, a noted American journalist, wrote widely on Latin America from the 1930s to the 1950s.

Anarchist Carlo Tresca, former I.W.W. leader, in later years was a leading Italian-American anti-fascist and publisher of the anarchist weekly Il Martello. He was assassinated in 1943, presumably by gangsters.

Anti-Fascism, Popular Front

A shift in Communist Party policy also helped make radicals more respectable in the public eye. By 1935, the rise of Hitler compelled Communists to re-evaluate their expectation of revolutionary conflict. Instead, they leaned toward support of all "democratic" and anti-fascist forces, looking to an uncertain transition from capitalism to a cooperative society.

Actually, determined anti-fascism had earlier beginnings. Among Italian-Americans of the 1920s, socialists and communists, but especially anarchists determined not to let the Fascists get a popular foothold in the United States (despite the support of Mussolini by the most circulated Italian-American commercial newspapers). Carlo Tresca, once the famed strike leader of Lawrence, Massachusetts, turned toward building anti-fascist sentiment until assassins ended his life in 1943. Hungarian-Americans including the former *Masses* artist, Hugo Gellert, had likewise campaigned against their homeland's Horthy government, later an ally of the Nazis. Individual radicals publicized the abuses of less-known dictators oppressing their people with tacit U.S. support, like the Batista regime in Cuba.

In 1936, American Communists abandoned vigorous campaigning for their own presidential candidates, or even working for the creation of an independent national third party, and supported Franklin D. Roosevelt's re-election. They did help create, however, a significant third party movement in New York State. The American Labor Party (A.L.P.) formed mainly by Jewish socialist unionists and by communists in order to elect labor candidates while supporting Franklin Roosevelt on an independent ballot line. The A.L.P. quickly adopted Italian-American radical Vito Marcantonio as its most charismatic fig-

Private Collection

Communist Joseph Figueredo led the anti-fascist Portuguese Alliance from New Bedford, Massachusetts, during the 1930-1940s.

Courtesy: Edwin Rolfe Archives, University of Illinois

Communist poet Edwin Rolfe (seated right center, with beret) and his Lincoln Battalion comrades in Spain, 1938.

Rolfe (right) and his friend Ernest Hemingway, safely back in New York City, review stills for the forthcoming film, For Whom the Bell Tolls.

Activists tried to neutralize the pro-Fascist and pro-Franco sentiment of Catholic authorities through special appeals.

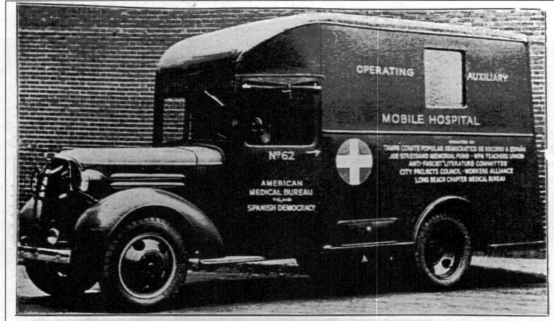

The Operating Auxiliary, one of four parts of the $50,000 mobile hospital unit to which Local 453 members donated $1,200 in memory of Joe Streisand. The unit, in addition to the above, consists of trucks with X-ray apparatus and oxygen tanks and two bullet-proof ambulances.

As anti-fascists from all walks of life organized committees and fund-raising efforts, some groups designated funds for ambulances. Hundreds of thousands of ordinary Americans marched in support parades. Author Howard Fast would later be jailed for refusing to hand over names of those who gave funds to purchase an ambulance.

The Spanish Civil War was an extraordinarily popular cause, especially for those who feared for their own relatives in part of Europe threatened with Fascism.

Borrowing language from Spain, "No Pasaran" became the rallying cry for various support groups in the United States.

ure. Representative of East Harlem's Puerto Ricans and Italians and a protege of New York's Mayor Fiorello LaGuardia, Marcantonio regularly contested Republican or Democratic party primaries in his Congressional career (1934-36 and 1938-50), while ferociously defending labor and radical causes. Communists supplied many of the foot soldiers for his campaigns, seeing him correctly as an aggressive proponent of egalitarian, multiracial democracy (and a reliable supporter of the Soviet Union).

Communists meanwhile helped create a milieu much larger than party members, including intellectuals, scientists, artists, immigrants and their children, all united by anti-fascism and hopes for a more democratic culture in America. Difficult as it was to imagine by the McCarthy Era of the 1950s, several of the most famous scientific figures in the United States, including Harvard's Walter B. Cannon and Princeton's E.G. Conklin, were proud to be part of the Popular Front. At its fringes, in the anti-fascist organization with strong leftwing input, could be found many other notables of American life, from anthropologist Ruth Benedict to theologian Harry F. Ward; from Detroit Tiger infielder Red Rolfe to photographer Margaret Bourke-White and stripper Gypsy Rose Lee. These people and celebrities like them were not often Communists themselves, but shared for a time the widespread conclusion that without the rank-and-file Communists' enthusiasm and talent for publicity, the anti-fascist, anti-racist and pro-labor message could not possibly go out nearly as fast or as far.

The rebellion of Spain's fascists against its elected government in 1936 signalled to many the opening phase of another world war, unless the spread of fascism could be halted. International brigades volunteered and fought heroically, while the Roosevelt government temporized (in fear of losing Catholic supporters) and the fascist states of Germany and Italy poured arms into Francisco Franco's offensive. Here again, and despite many contradictions of means and ends, Communist support was crucial for both Spanish hopes and for American culture.

The Abraham Lincoln Battalion of 2800 volunteers was not the only U.S. contingent. Socialists and Trotskyists supported the Debs Brigade, a unit of a few hundred Americans, raising money and public consciousness about Spanish non-communist revolutionaries. But most of the attention went to the "Lincolns," with full and zealous Communist support (at least sixty percent of the volunteers were Communist party members, and altogether disproportionately Jewish). From labor and religious meetings to star-studded Hollywood gatherings, the publicity and fund-raising machine went into high gear. Americans learned more about fascism and its dangers here than any other source before American entry into World War Two.

This Yiddish monthly featured many illustrations by Jewish artists on the threats of fascism.

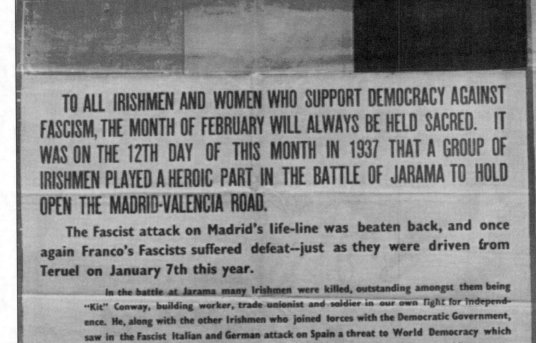

TO ALL IRISHMEN AND WOMEN WHO SUPPORT DEMOCRACY AGAINST FASCISM, THE MONTH OF FEBRUARY WILL ALWAYS BE HELD SACRED. IT WAS ON THE 12TH DAY OF THIS MONTH IN 1937 THAT A GROUP OF IRISHMEN PLAYED A HEROIC PART IN THE BATTLE OF JARAMA TO HOLD OPEN THE MADRID-VALENCIA ROAD.

The Fascist attack on Madrid's life-line was beaten back, and once again Franco's Fascists suffered defeat--just as they were driven from Teruel on January 7th this year.

In the battle at Jarama many Irishmen were killed, outstanding amongst them being "Kit" Conway, building worker, trade unionist and soldier in our own fight for independence. He, along with the other Irishmen who joined forces with the Democratic Government, saw in the Fascist Italian and German attack on Spain a threat to World Democracy which should not only be answered by Spaniards, but by all who stand for Liberty and Democracy.

Irishmen are still in the ranks of Spain's Republican Army, and in this month of February we join with them in paying tribute to those brave men of our Nation who have fallen in the battle to save Republican Liberty.

Demonstrate your loyalty to the cause of Democracy by demanding that our Government establishes proper diplomatic relations with the Spanish Republican Government and declares its support for that Government's right to buy arms to defend Spain against foreign Fascism.

With the Spanish People let our Answer to Fascism be:

NO PASARAN

An Irish-American angle.

Yiddish poet-painter Maurice Kish left a vivid portrait of fascism as seen by this artist.

Culture

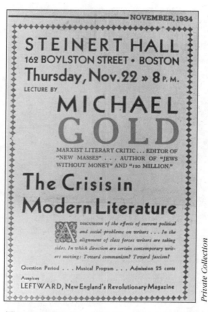

Private Collection

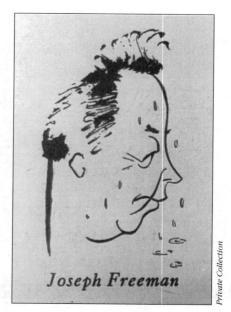

Private Collection

The New Masses *and its editors proclaimed a new "proletarian literature" and a proletarian theater in the early 1930s, with critics Michael Gold and Joseph Freeman playing leading roles. Here, Gold is featured at a John Reed Club event in Boston.*

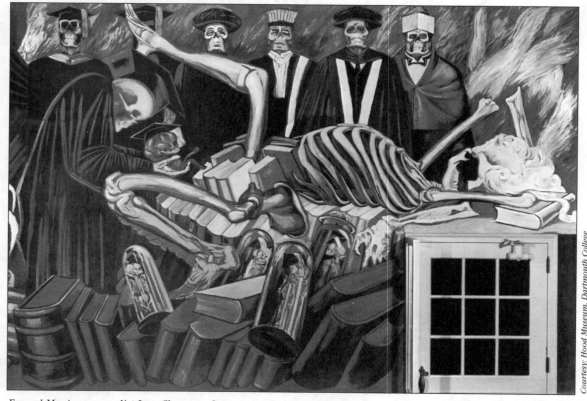

Courtesy: Hood Museum, Dartmouth College

Famed Mexican muralist Jose Clemente Orozco, invited to paint a fresco for Dartmouth College, composed "The Epic of American Civilization: God and the Modern World," 1932-34, with this final, uncompromising panel about the misuse of scientific knowledge and of the very search for learning.

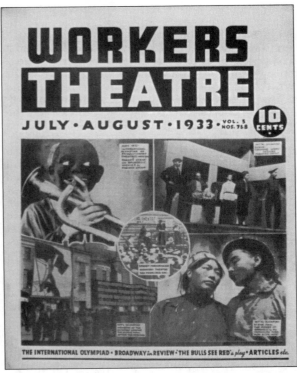

Left theatrical magazines rallied popular support for controversial plays and union organizing.

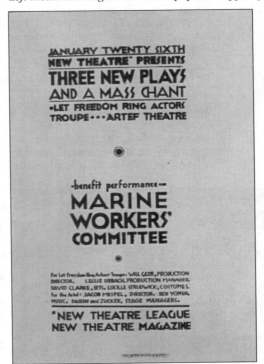

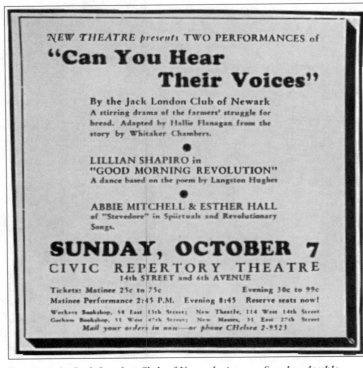

One of many contemporary theater benefit showings for union causes; the Jack London Club of Newark stages a Sunday double performance.

CLIFFORD ODETS

One of the most important American playwrights of any era, Clifford Odets captured the slice-of-life Jewish lower classes of the 1930s with their mixture of resentment, resignation and hopes. Despite his long decline from a promising youth, he has remained a premier dramatist of class and social themes.

Born to a slum home in the early years of the century, Odets dreamed of becoming a poet. Late in the 1920s, he wrote two unproduced radio plays and began acting in the left-influenced Group Theater. Several years later, he began writing plays, and in 1935 won a prestigious Left prize for "Waiting for Lefty." This strike drama, performed in union halls and even at mass rallies across the country, captured the language and spirit of contemporary labor upsurge and made him instantly famous. "Awake and Sing," written two years earlier but produced in 1935 to great acclaim, was one of Odets' most haunting dramas, of Jewish family life in the Depression. "Paradise Lost," produced the same year, was his own favorite play, full of characters with hopes that they could rise above the unhappiness of the day. In their expressive anticipations, they reminded theatergoers of Walt Whitman's poetry (and Odets named his son Walt Whitman Odets).

Odets buried his creativity by going to Hollywood. Although he wrote several other important dramas (like "The Big Knife," about disillusionment with Hollywood success), he despised the creative limitations. Not even "Deadline at Dawn" (1946), a brilliant murder mystery and one of the most interesting movies of the day, seemed worthy of his talents.

Called before the House Un-American Activities Committee, Odets became a reluctantly cooperative witness, suffering terribly for his actions. Among the films made before his death in 1963, "The Sweet Smell of Success" once more reminded viewers how well Odets could capture the soul-deadening, morally corrupt side of the American success story.

Cultural Movements

Artists friendly to the Popular Front therefore entered the Roosevelt-initiated Works Progress Administration arts program to draw some of the most famous murals on the walls of post offices and community centers. Young, radical theatrical people like playwright Clifford Odets training themselves for Broadway and Hollywood wrote and acted out themes of anti-fascism and working class (mostly ethnic) neighborhood life. They reached wide audiences through the W.P.A.'s Federal Theater. In Hollywood, radicals led the formation of stage unions and created films like Lillian Hellman's anti-fascist *Watch On the Rhine* (1943). Musical masters, including Aaron Copland, designed choral performances illustrating anti-fascist, pro-democratic themes, or like Marc Blitzstein composed popular music with protest sentiments and vernacular speech. Radical novelists including Richard Wright, Nelson Algren and Jack Conroy wrote stories of the unheard ordinary people, while noted literary figures like Erskine Caldwell, William Saroyan, Ernest Hemingway and Dorothy Parker enlisted themselves and their talent in Popular Front causes.

Many of these artists, by the late 1930s, dedicated themselves to expressing basic democratic qualities in American culture, often by portraying them in American history. So unthreateningly patriotic was composer Earl Robinson's "Ballad for Americans" (including verses about Paul Revere and George Washington) that the Republicans could adopt it for their 1940 convention! Others managed to find a balance, offering pictures of America as it might be if its own ideals were realized.

By this time, progressive artists of all kinds from the local union-newsletter cartoonist to the internationally-trained painter to theatrical set-designers and even sculptors had tried out themes related to labor. If unionization

Courtesy: Southpaw Books

Edited by Missouri novelist Jack Conroy and others, the Anvil *and* New Anvil *published many working class writers. Conroy's motto was "We Prefer Crude Vigor to Polished Banality."*

Courtesy: Abel Meeropol Collection, Boston University

Clifford Odets' play, Waiting for Lefty, *toured the nation in the middle 1930, here in Evanston, Illinois, often used during local strikes to build enthusiasm and popular support.*

was the most elemental democratic impulse of the age, in many ways artists tried to convey the drama of the strike moment, the dynamic power of the machine in human hands, and the vision of a better America recreated by a democratized production. The desire for documentation made itself felt on all sides. The Federal Theater, for instance, presented the "Living Newspaper," an imagined people's press come alive through actors. Artists lucky enough to be hired by the Works Progress Administration to create murals and friezes tried to show tenements, sweatshops, schools, farms and factories with real faces and bodies. "Proletarian" novelists and simply realistic novelists, often derided for their attempts to create imaginary radical middle Americans, strained to catch the sounds and look of their subjects. Some of them, like Nelson Algren, Jack Conroy, Fielding Burke, Thomas Bell, Richard Wright and James T. Farrell, succeeded brilliantly.

But the quest for realism also tended to slide off into the artists' own training or predilections, and what work seemed to respond to a burning political need or could be made available to the widest audience. Among the American Artists Congress figures who determinedly endorsed leftwing positions, famed artists like Max Weber, Louis Lozowick (who occasionally drew covers of Communist publications), Ben Shahn and Raphael Soyer worked far from documentary modes on most of their projects. The W.P.A. muralist, commanded to create a stylized work of Americana for a local post

The Communist-led John Reed Clubs brought many important new authors into view, including Edward Newhouse, Richard Wright (lower left) and Nelson Algren (above). You Can't Sleep Here *tells the story of one man's experiences in shantytowns and of his rise to fame as a militant labor organizer.*

Courtesy: Southpaw Books, Others, Library of Congress

E.Y. "Yip" Harburg (right), the radical lyricist for The Wizard of Oz *and author of the famous early 1930s song "Brother, Can You Spare a Dime?" is seen here with collaborator Fred Saidy in 1944, when they collaborated on* Bloomer Girl, *a musical about dress reformer Amelia Bloomer and nineteenth century ideas of women's emancipation.*

office, frequently fell back upon the heavily gendered (and increasingly unrealistic) version of the family with its members etched from sexual stereotypes. The idealistic quest for democratic harmony in a world threatened by fascism offered other impulses or temptations.

Very often, artists adopted stylized versions of the American mythology from Pilgrim to proletarian, including the conquering of the West (with Indians and Mexican-Americans strangely absent). But like E.Y. Harburg, who wrote "Brother, Can You Spare a Dime" in 1931, or Woody Guthrie who offered songs of lost highways for defeated people, they also helped create a vision of America in which the radical was not a stranger but someone who helped ride out the disappointments and disillusionments of the age.

By offering images of a diverse nation, with many different cultures, Popular Front artists strived most uniquely to improve public attitudes towards minorities of every kind, especially racial ones. Communists and their allies promoted black folk music, but they also promoted folk-style music with a political cutting edge. Woody Guthrie, who had for a time a column in the Communist *Daily Worker,* was the living legend of a truly popular Popular Front. Young Communists ferociously advocated radical integration of sports, winning admiration from Detroit Tigers third baseman Red Rolfe to boxer Joe Louis and other greats.

Every creative political effort was undercut, in the long run, by the political compulsion of Communists to defend Russian state collectivism and its tyrannical Joseph Stalin as a model society and a model ruler. By the late 1930s, when Stalin put his political opponents on public trial and killed thousands, the terrible truth had become clear to almost everyone else who bothered to analyze world affairs. Communists were a bulwark against Fascism, willing to lay down their lives to fight its advance, as thousands had already in the Spanish Civil War. But their political solutions for America were vague, continually shifting, and above all unconvincing.

Then again, the more "American" the Popular Front became, the less its artists and intellectuals concerned themselves with attacking

Leading literary figures in the Congress of American Writers, Erskine Caldwell, Malcolm Cowley and Granville Hicks lent Communist forces prestige, but abandoned the Popular Front camp after the Hitler-Stalin Pact in 1939.

the economic system's weaknesses and inequalities. New Deal reforms did not end the Depression and mass unemployment, which remained very high in 1939; only the war and defense spending did that. When Hitler and Stalin signed a non-aggression pact in 1939, and Communists returned to themes of class conflict, urging Americans to resist the drift toward war, even with Fascism, they met a disbelieving public.

Courtesy: Sam Robert

Langston Hughes with other writers at a Workshop Meeting of the Labor Poets of America, New York, 1937, Sam Robert is reading here. Jewish poet Aaron Kramer, not yet sixteen, can be seen at the right of Hughes's cigarette.

Courtesy: Eric Gordon

Radical composer Marc Blitzstein strove to set to music the American language as spoken. Among his social commentary and political satire were "Cradle Will Rock," a 1936 musical about a steel town; a World War II orchestral piece, "Freedom Morning;" the musical "Juno" (1949) based on Sean O'Casey's "Juno and the Peacock;" and the uncompleted "Sacco and Vanzetti" commissioned by the Metropolitan Opera. He is best remembered for his musical adaptation of Berthold Brecht and Kurt Weill's "Three-Penny Opera," which ran for seven years on Broadway and is now a standard in operatic repertoires.

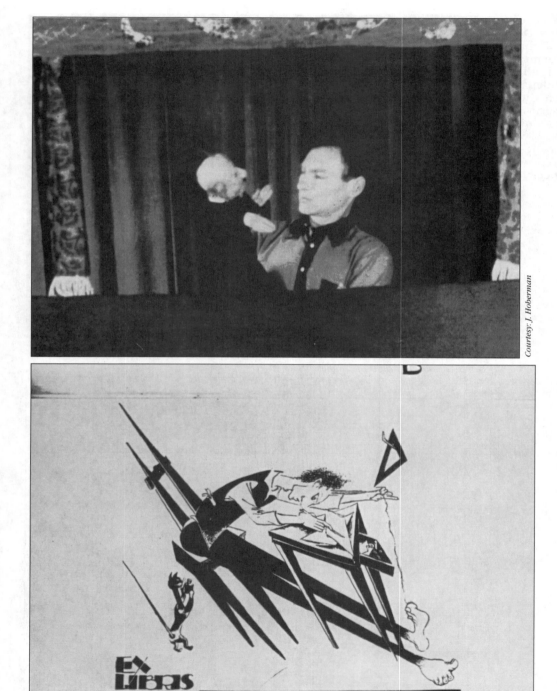

Artist-illustrator Yosel Kotler, along with artist Zuni Maud, organized "MODIKOT," the only Yiddish Marionette show, with many Leftwing skits. A still from a rare film of Modikot is shown above. Kotler was also one of the chief modernists in Yiddish book illustration. This drawing is taken from Muntergang *(1937).*

The "Futurians," a radically inclined circle of young science fiction writers, New York, 1938. Among the later notables: first row, third from left, Isaac Asimov, to his left, Donald A. Wolheim; second row, third from left, Frederick Pohl; top row, on left, Cyril Kornbluth.

Silhouette of H.P. Lovecraft by Perry (1925)

Horror story writer H.P. Lovecraft, inventor of a chilling popular literary mythology and leading author for Weird Tales, *was a self-described "Norman Thomas socialist." His stories have been adapted for television episodes and several films and his name was borrowed by a rock group.*

Lillian Hellman — author of the screenplays for Little Foxes, *the lesbian drama,* These Three, *and the anti-fascist classic,* Watch on the Rhine — *was a leading anti-fascist, married to Marxist mystery writer Dashiell Hammett.*

The New Masses *milieu included for a time the leading figures of the jazz world, African-American and white alike.*

Donald Ogden Stewart

Donald Ogden Stewart, a talented screenwriter (co-author of script for The Philadelphia Story, *among others), was a leading Hollywood leftist.*

Portrait of Elizabeth Hawes by Mary Morris Lawrence, 1941. Hawes wearing her suspender slacks and soft "Pussyfoot" shoes.

Portrait of Elizabeth Hawes in her Studio by Mary Morris Lawrence, 1941

Elizabeth Hawes, Left activist, author and avant-garde fashion designer, in 1941. Hawes designed clothes to be comfortable and to downplay the gender differences of male and female wear. By the 1960s-70s, many of her innovations had become standard wear. Photography: Mary Morris Lawrence

Anti-War to Anti-Fascist Mobilization

Courtesy: Harold Freeman

Student anti-war demonstration at Brooklyn College, a hot spot for radical agitation.

Anti-war to Anti-fascist mobilization

The struggle against militarism had been central to younger and older activists of the early 1930s, those who remembered the pointlessness of the First World War and those who would almost certainly fight in a second one. From Spring, 1936 to Spring, 1939, a half-million collegians (or half the entire national student body) alone mobilized in strikes against war. They sought, as many future student movements, aid to education rather than government support for R.O.T.C. programs (then mandatory on many campuses), racial equality, and bargaining rights of student employees. During the Spanish Civil War, the anti-war fervor

Courtesy: Peace Collection, Swarthmore College

Pacifist and veteran Christian socialist intellectual Jessie Wallace Hughan publicized her program during the 1930s.

Courtesy and Photo: Harold Freeman

A New York demonstration in 1933, mixes anti-war with anti-fascist themes.

and pacifist sentiment weakened; Communist students and their supporters shifted to anti-fascism, leaving socialists and religious radicals increasingly isolated.

This picture mirrored the larger one. By the later 1930s, Americans were deeply divided about the future of their own nation and its proper place in the world. The economic downturn or "Roosevelt Recession" of 1938, the pace of management-labor conflicts and the fear of U.S. military involvement underlined the tensions. Republicans captured Congress for the first time in a decade, and boosted the Dies Committee, which "investigated" subversives by holding local hearings to intimidate unions, civil rights and other radical activists of all varieties. On the other hand, more than half of the Congress of Industrial Organizations members polled in 1940 agreed that major corporations should be taken out of private hands and given over to some form of industrial democracy — a type of socialism.

Radicals disagreed sharply with each other about U.S. international obligations and many were simply unsure. Mass demonstrations and May Day parades often revealed contradictory impulses, against the capitalists as the war-makers and against the fascists as destroyers of civilization. Those who remained adamantly anti-war insisted quite rightly that war would bring about the militarization of American society, a false and perverse solution to unemployment and a permanent devotion to the god of war, with factories turning out devices to destroy the world and its people. Those who leaned in the other direction thought or hoped that a great crusade against fascism would democratize society from the bottom up.

Courtesy: Library of Congress

Charles Beard, the nation's foremost historian and a bitter opponent of the American drift toward war.

Often the differences broke down along ethnic and regional lines. Oldtime socialists, many from the Midwest or Southwest, rejected the idea of support for another "Imperialist War." Oscar Ameringer, the beloved socialist leader who edited the *American Guardian* from Oklahoma City, Oklahoma, almost until his death in 1942, refused to buckle under. But most of the descendants of European immigrants, with their relatives already or potentially stranded in war zones, wanted Hitler destroyed above all else.

Norman Thomas and his now small Socialist Party led a peace crusade, warning that American interventionism

Eugene Moy at the China Daily News. *Leftwing editor surveys current European news.*

would end all hopes of a transition to democratic socialism. Many black radicals, painfully aware of the punishment suffered by European Jews and others, nonetheless concluded that they should be given more democracy at home before being asked to fight for it abroad. A. Philip Randolph organized a giant March on Washington in 1940, cancelling it only when Roosevelt agreed on major reforms in federal policies. *El Congresso del Pueblo de Habla Espanola* (The Congress of Spanish Speaking Peoples), a radical group of Mexican-Americans in Los Angeles and the Southwest, took a similar tack as they protested anti-alien legislation, police brutality, lack of low-cost housing and public education for their people.

The Hitler-Stalin Pact of 1939 threw Jewish radicals particularly into confusion and many Communist supporters among intellectuals into despair and revolt. During the next eighteen months when Communists denounced war preparations and sought to work with isolationists and pacifists, the political groundwork they had labored hard to create was cut from under them. Anti-radical

A. Philip Randolph led the March On Washington (MOW) Movement which threatened a national demonstration in 1941 if President Roosevelt did not improve conditions for African-Americans. Roosevelt issued Executive Order 8802, banning discrimination in defense industries and establishing the Fair Employment Practices Committee. Randolph relented, but MOW had created a bridge from 1930s struggles to future civil rights activities. Photography: Gordon Parks

Courtesy: Library of Congress

Courtesy: Renqui Yu

government committees staged hearings to dramatize their highly inflated charges of communist "infiltration" of the New Deal. Several leaders of the Communist party were arrested on passport violations; known Communist college teachers were fired in New York state; and blocs of anti-communist union conservatives began pressing for ouster of the "reds." Most of the conservative (and liberal) schemes to eliminate radical influences were tried out briefly. They would be put into full operation after the war.

Radicals who remained against the war were reduced to a brave handful. Even Norman Thomas painfully reconciled himself to the war effort by 1942. A few traditional Left organizations like the Socialist Labor Party, and a few new ones like the Trotskyist-oriented Workers Party (a potent group of Trotskyists, young intellectual Irving Howe among them, made up mainly of young Jews), reiterated the traditional "revolutionary defeatism" rejecting support of even an "Imperialist war fought under democratic slogans." They reached restless workers in war plants, but had little influence otherwise.

The Communists came back astonishingly after the Japanese bombing of Pearl Harbor and the German invasion of Russia swept away previous political reservations to all-out attacks on Fascism. Russian Communism and its supporters now became the Western democracies' best allies in the world, despite suspicions on each side. The defeat of Hitler's armies by almost unbelievably heroic Russian resistance at Stalingrad was widely believed to have turned the tide in the war. The millions of dead and suffering Russians had, in effect, sacrificed themselves so that relatively few American soldiers would have to die in Europe.

American Communists and their Communist allies in virtually every ethnic group and most of the important unions engaged furiously in war support work. In Hollywood, Screen Actors Guild leader Ronald Reagan allied himself with dozens of other stars and hundreds of bit writers and

THE FINAL ACHIEVEMENT OF COMMUNISM'S "UNITED FRONT." Introducing the Fuehrer Joseph Adolph Stalinhitler.

KOMMUNISTISEN "YHTENÄISYYDEN" HUIPPUSAAVUTUS. Natsikommunismin korkein johtaja Joseph Adolph Stalinhitler.

(Finnish war cartoons Raivaaja 1940)

Veteran Finnish-American cartoonist K.A. Suvanto saw the tyrant in Stalin during the Hitler-Stalin Pact. Trotskyist cartoonist "Carlo" (Joseph Cohen) offered a "Third Camp" way out of the mess.

Courtesy: Michael Karni and the Center for Socialist History

The New Deal, Since Its Very Inception, Has Given Encouragement and Aid to Subversive Elements in the United States

Here are the FACTS:

STALIN'S RED RUSSIA RECOGNIZED

One of the first acts of Roosevelt's Administration was recognition of Soviet Union., subsequently rapist of Finland and Baltic Republics, signer of the bloody non-aggression pact with Hitler, co-conqueror of Poland Every Communist revolutionary in the United States cheered President Roosevelt's recognition action which gave Soviet Russia respectability in the family of Nations.

DIES' COMMITTEE FRUSTRATED

From the beginning the Dies' Committee to Investigate Un-American Activities has been hampered by Administration opposition and indifference. Chairman Dies accused Secretary of Labor Perkins and Secretary of Interior Ickes of "a well planned campaign of misrepresentation, sarcasm and ridicule."

"FELLOW TRAVELERS" IN HIGH POSTS

Says Democratic Mr. Dies: "Communists have risen high in the government and hold important key positions." Publication by the Dies Committee of a list of 563 Federal employees, members of the Communist organized League for Peace and Democracy, was denounced by President Roosevelt as "sordid."

MRS. ROOSEVELT AND AMERICAN YOUTH CONGRESS

Mrs. Franklin D. Roosevelt has sharply criticized the Dies' Committee and openly championed the Communist led American Youth Congress, entertaining its leaders in the White House. Early this year Mrs. Roosevelt called a meeting at the home of Edward J. Flynn, Tammany boss of the Bronx and now Chairman of the Democratic National Committee, to raise funds for the Youth Congress, branded a Communist Front by the Dies Committee.

EARL BROWDER, COMMUNIST, NEW DEAL SUPPORTER

Earl Browder, convicted Communist Party secretary and now its nominee for President of the United States, told the Dies Committee Communists unanimously supported the policies of President Roosevelt and the New Deal, including the Supreme Court Packing Bill. "The tradition against a third term must be set aside," said Earl Browder.

MME. PERKINS AND HARRY BRIDGES

So lax was the administration of the immigration and deportation laws by Secretary of Labor Perkins, the administration was COMPELLED to transfer these functions to the Justice Department. Mme. Perkins consistently refused to deport Harry Bridges, West Coast radical labor leader and agitator. The House of Representatives voted 330 to 42 to deport Bridges unconditionally. The bill remains on the Senate Calendar awaiting action.

F.D.R. VETOES ALIEN DEPORTATION BILL

President Roosevelt vetoed a bill for the deportation of aliens engaging in espionage and sabotage on the ground the legislation was "unnecessary and superfluous." Do the families of the 47 dead and more than 200 injured in the Hercules Powder Plant explosion agree?

WHITE HOUSE OPEN TO COMMUNISTS

The White House latch has been lifted for known radicals and Communists when Democratic governors, members of Congress and other Americans have found the President "too busy" to see them. David Lasser, former head of the Communist organized Workers' Alliance, a delegate to the Moscow Twentieth Anniversary of the Russian Revolution, at the Alliance's expense, frequently has conferred with the President and described his reception as "very cordial." Aubrey Williams, former deputy WPA Administrator and now National Youth Administrator, has lauded the Workers' Alliance—called the moments spent with Lasser "the most memorable of my life." Herbert Benjamin, Secretary of the Alliance, a confessed Communist, testified before a House Committee that the Alliance was the result of four years of Communist Party effort.

RADICALS ON N.L.R.B.

David J. Saposs, former chief economist of the National Labor Relations Board, was censured by the Dies Committee for his "Communist views." Congress subsequently refused funds for Saposs' department. The Board continued his employment by giving him a new title. Edwin S. Smith, N.L.R.B. member, was on the Dies' list of American League of Peace and Democracy members. In 1938 Smith went to Mexico to attend the International Labor Congress which voted to ally itself with the Second Internationale.

CLEAN OUT RADICALS   ELECT WILLKIE-McNARY

Distributed by REPUBLICAN NATIONAL COMMITTEE, Washington, D. C.

Courtesy: Museum of American Political Life

Conservatives bitterly attacked Roosevelt for his acceptance of radicals and near-Communists at the White House and in federal agencies, 1940. Photography: Steven Laschever

technicians in Communist-led campaigns to support the Allies. A few like horror film star Bela Lugosi actually headed movements, in Lugosi's case the Hungarian American Council for Democracy. Some Communist groupings, specifically the Greeks, directed the homeland anti-Nazi offensive from New York; others, like Slovenians and Croatians backing Marshall Tito's anti-Fascist resistance in Yugoslavia, provided the crucial bridge between Western allies and postwar leaders. Tragically, the win-the-war spirit prevented Communists (like the great majority of Americans) from protesting the incarceration of Japanese civilians and the legalized theft of their property. It also prompted Communists to support the federal prosecution of the Trotskyists in Minneapolis, with who were charged with violating the Smith Act. In a few years, Communists themselves would be tried on the same act.

Among intellectuals, the Left presence was yet greater. A circle of radicals including

Communists champion anti-fascism after the German invasion of Soviet Russia. Boxing champion Joe Louis, not especially political-minded but close to the sympathetic Daily Worker *sports editor, Lester Rodney, was easily one of the most popular Americans of his time. Otis Hood ran a typical wartime Communist political campaign in Massachusetts in 1943.*

Private Collection

future New Left philosopher Herbert Marcuse entered the Office of Strategic Services, predecessor to the Central Intelligence Agency, where they helped map out anti-fascist resistance. A handful of top scientists sympathetic toward Russia, including Robert Oppenheimer, were leaders of the Atom Bomb (Manhattan) project. Fine artists such as Ben Shahn created propaganda posters for the Office of War Information. Communist screenwriters such as John Howard Lawson turned out such classic anti-fascist war films as *Action in the North Atlantic* (1943). Most other American radical art emphasized the themes that the government mandated, production for war and victory of humanity over the Nazi beast.

This participation gained many new friends for leftwing causes, respect especially for the Communists' and their allies vigor against anti-semitism and racism. But the costs were also heavy. The wartime economic boom profoundly changed American life in many ways. Millions relocated, either mobilizing in the armed forces or taking jobs in defense industries. Away from home, soldiers often dreamed of escaping their blue-collar neighborhoods entirely rather than uniting neighbors to tackle landlords and industrialists. At work, formerly rural folk, southern blacks and whites along with women, came into unions which had grown suddenly more bureaucratic — even those led by Communists. Industrial union leaders for the first time saw themselves as respected public figures rather than scruffy radicals. Management agreed with the "dues checkoff," by which union dues came

Courtesy: Ben and Beatrice Goldstein Foundation

Courtesy: Southpaw Books

Wartime communist graphics such as this William Gropper cartoon, above, typically mixed anti-fascism with a traditional May Day call to action (and appeal for a Second Front, which Churchill and Roosevelt accepted with no haste and great reluctance). Fred Ellis added the Communist message which many working people refused to heed in the rising tide of strikes, 1943-45.

Leftists' efforts to bring the emerging horrors of anti-Semitic persecution and the approaching holocaust to public attention were widely ignored or given low priority by most Americans. So were heroic Jewish resistance, such as the Warsaw, Poland, Ghetto Uprising of 1943.

directly out of the pay-check, and unions had more incentive to discipline the work force.

Franklin Roosevelt's public burial of "Dr. New Deal" for "Dr. Win the War" met total Communist approval. At the peak of their influence, Communists agreed with the prosecution of anti-war union dissidents, and with the cruel relocation of Japanese-Americans into prison camps. They also dissolved organizations, like the Congress of Spanish Speaking People, crucial for defending populations under fresh attacks like the Los Angeles "Zoot Suit Riots" of 1943 by racist G.I.s on Mexican teenagers.

As the war ended, radicals felt a brief surge of confidence. The ideals of democracy had, after all, triumphed in the world. *The House That I Live In,* a short film feature written by radicals and featuring Frank Sinatra, played widely in theaters, emphasizing popular hopes for an end to racism and other hatreds that presumably had no place in anti-fascist America. Leftwing artists drew portraits of brotherhood achieved, in realistic but not stilted formulae. The Congress of American Women, enrolling notable women reformers, anthropologists and descendants of the woman suffrage crusade's famed leaders, quickly rose to a membership of a quarter-million. Organizing against businessmen's extreme post-war price-hikes and against the return of violent racism, and arguing for equal pay and public child-care centers for women, they prefigured the women's movement of later decades.

Radical-oriented civil rights activists meanwhile reorganized themselves in the south, mobilizing such influential figures as Martin Luther King, Sr., and a generation of younger and more radical black youth to press for integration. Jewish radicals founded dozens of schools for the survival of Yiddish after the Holocaust had killed millions of speakers of that language. Envisioning the advance of the two historically oppressed groups together, Jewish and African-American leftists stressed the importance of unity and of combatting regressive nationalists in both camps.

Otis Hood used this collection box during his wartime gubernatorial campaign.

Private Collection

Leader of the American Slav Committee, Milwaukee socialist Leo Krzycki joined other anti-fascists from Eastern Europe in supporting victory for the Allies. Drawing by caricaturist Saul Raskin who had been drawing socialistic cartoons since his days at the Groysser Kundes. From the Amalgamated Clothing Workers convention program of 1940, Convention Stitches.

Private Collection

The Seaman's Union of the Pacific supported the war effort but refused to ban strikes or accept government control of ship discipline.

Courtesy: Washington State Historical Society, Special Collections

Artist Maxo Vanka's "Battlefield," 1944, refused optimistic portraits of victory over Fascism. Zuni Maud, cartoonist for the yiddish Morgen Freiheit, was more optimistic that all the evils of the world could be swept away.

From V-J Day to McCarthyism

William Gropper

A Bronx women's consumer's group, 1947. Skyrocketing shop prices and greedy landlords prompted tenants' groups, usually led by women, to challenge rent laws in many cities.

Heavily organized by the Left, Hollywood film studio unions faced overwhelming resources, redbaiting and government spies (probably including future president Ronald Reagan) in their 1945 strike.

From VJ Day to McCarthyism

The Cold War killed these dreams and many others, but only after a period of uncertainty when it seemed things could go either far Left or Right in America and the world. President Harry Truman, following Franklin Roosevelt's tragic death in office, immediately resolved to "get tough" with America's former Russian and many other anti-fascist allies. Insisting on a world open to U.S. leadership, he approved the use of atomic bombs on Japanese civilian populations and asserted an American monopoly on atomic power. During his administration, Washington also refused to agree to independence for Vietnam, protected rightwing dictators, forbade West Germans to introduce public control of industries, and directed massive "dirty tricks" campaigns against Communist electoral campaigns in Italy and elsewhere. Russia's Joseph Stalin, obsessed with national security and even more indifferent to democratic procedures, ordered Eastern Europe closed to non-Communist competition.

Together, Truman and Stalin along with their respective bureaucracies would crush the hopes of European socialists and communists for a post-war united Europe with people's governments, a democratic model for the world. But they did not succeed without a struggle. At home, a post-war strike wave larger than any in U.S. history gave labor one more chance to reshape American life. Refusing to accept wild price increases and the return of high unemployment, unionists set off a half-dozen city-wide "general strikes" (often opposed by Communists but supported by other radicals) and big industrial conflicts of auto, steel and other workers. Wages for these workers raced upward, promising rewards for those who fought back against the wealthy classes. A dramatic strike by the studio unions of Hollywood in 1945 was beaten back, in no small part by anti-communist and anti-Semitic attacks that predicted worse to come.

Ordinary Communists and other radicals registered a determined enthusiasm despite much in-fighting and disorientation among the political leaders and a growing sense of unease or leftwing protest at the authoritarian governments created in Eastern Europe after the Red Army's conquests. At the neighborhood level, Communists and their allies determined to retain wartime price guidelines, mounting an especially intense effort in New York. Congressman Vito Marcantonio and the American Labor Party embraced the issue, publicizing it furiously in the first major political effort to defeat gouging landlords.

Some of the creative zeal could be seen best in the world of art and culture, with the launching of new magazines like the artistic *Mainstream* or the radical-run *Hollywood Quarterly,* the first significant film magazine in the nation. A handful of Communist-leaning filmwriters and directors, for instance, contributed decisively to the creation of *film noir,* perhaps the most artistic genre of American films ever created. Others added social films on themes that Hollywood had hardly ever covered: working class life, the struggles of non-whites and women for equality, the criminal conduct of business and the persistence of anti-semitism.

Folk singing also took off as a major musical form. Concerts by Paul Robeson helped boost the appeal of young and older black singers, for instance, from Leadbelly to Josh White. The Almanac Singers, featuring young Pete Seeger, enjoyed best-selling hits, while a host of other radical talents, including Burl Ives, sang regularly and often wrote the songs for fund-raising functions. Even the gathering of folk music archives and the audience for previously unknown rural singers owed much to radicals' fieldwork (Folkways Records' founder, Moses Asch, was the son of the famed progressive Yiddish author, Sholem Asch) and to the zeal of left-

Courtesy: Scott Molloy

Amid sharp labor struggles and briefly renewed hopes for a national labor party, popular artists elaborated in this unique comic book their ideas of labor's own culture and promise of a democratic society.

Courtesy: Benjamin Harris

Jefferson School advertisement

Courtesy: Howard Fast

Many Communists, including author Howard Fast, envisioned a widening struggle for socialism in America. Artist Rockwell Kent created this cover (New York: United May Day Committee, 1947).

RAYA DUNAYEVSKAYA, C.L.R. JAMES, GRACE LEE

A trio of unique radicals, the three led a small political-intellectual group in the 1940s-50s with a large intellectual impact continuing to the present.

The most famous, C.L.R. James, was born in Trinidad, became one of the earliest English-language novelists of the Caribbean, and moved on to Britain in the 1930s. There, he helped found the African anti-colonial movement, wrote the masterful Caribbean history *The Black Jacobins,* opposed Stalin, and became a beloved cricket reporter for the *Manchester Guardian.* Switching his base to the United States in 1939, he toured and wrote for the Trotskyist movement. Expelled from the country in 1953, James returned in 1969 as an *eminence grise* of Pan-Africanism, an important cultural critic, and a philosophic inspiration of New Left intellectuals.

Raya Dunayevskaya, a Russian-born Jewish intellectual active in the 1920s Communist party, joined James in forming the "Johnson-Forest Tendency." This group perceptively argued that Russia had become a "State Capitalist" society, and insisted that only democratic struggle from the lowest ranks of American society could revive the American Left. Committed to a humanist Marxism, they translated sections of Marx's *1844 Economic Philosophical Manuscripts,* then virtually unknown. Breaking with James and Lee, Dunayevskaya formed the group "News & Letters," still in existence, and published many books in philosophy and politics.

Grace Lee, daughter of a prominent Chinese restaurateur, took a Ph.D. in philosophy from the University of Chicago, and entered the Left as one of the very few Asian-American intellectuals. She later married the black automobile workers, James Boggs, and with him led many community movements in Detroit. Surviving her former political partners, she continues to be active in the 1990s.

Courtesy: Grace Lee Boggs

Three Unique Rebels: Raya Dunayevskaya, C.L.R. James, and Grace Lee.

Courtesy: Socialist Party National Office

In the late 1940s, radicals won some of their last third-party victories, the socialist Frank Zeidler, who captured the Milwaukee mayoralty and held it until 1960. He later ran for president on the Socialist Party ticket.

wing audiences for "folkies," old and young.

Non- and anti-communist radicalism also enjoyed an extended honeymoon. An anarcho-pacifist spirit fed the new Congress of Racial Equality and many of the first sit-ins against racial segregation. An array of new magazines including Dwight Macdonald's *Politics* made an impression upon disillusioned G.I.s in particular. Small but militant Trotskyist groups pressed for internal union democracy where Communists had chosen the bureaucratic route, and made their arguments for a world democracy free of Stalin and Truman alike. Even the socialists had some success. After the failure of a radical coalition to create an anti-capitalist and anti-communist groundswell, Norman Thomas regained a position of respect if not many votes with his 1948 presidential campaign. A handful of local socialists held or recaptured a familiar office, notably the mayorality of Milwaukee, Wisconsin.

But dark clouds overshadowed all this activity and enthusiasm. A Republican Congress passed the Taft-Hartley Act over Truman's veto, thus legally forbidding such familiar labor tactics as boycotts, mass picketing and sympathy strikes that had made industrial unions possible. The vast military build-up and the president's supercharged rhetoric of confronting Communism meant the end of hopes for a different America in a more peaceful world – unless the wave of reaction could be turned back. Supporters of the Popular Front and a broad spectrum of American liber-

Courtesy: Benjamin Harris

Communists maintained a modicum of optimism in the Age of the Atom. Meanwhile, pacifists of the Congress of Racial Equality (CORE) staged a Journey of Reconciliation to Moscow, April, 1947. Participants included folksinger Bayard Rustin, sixth from left, later an advisor to Dr. Martin Luther King, Jr.

Courtesy: War Resisters League

WOODY GUTHRIE

The best-known and best-loved folk singer of the century, Woodrow Wilson Guthrie cut through turgid theories and dull political institutions with a simple, clear social message and a catchy tune. Never more than an adequate musician himself, in the thousand songs he wrote over twenty years he shaped the way future generations of politically rebellious musicians approached the world and saw themselves in it.

Born in 1912 to a tragedy-ridden Oklahoma family, Woody Guthrie saw his father go broke and his mother sent to a mental asylum. He drifted with the people he would write his songs about, hoboes and itinerant working people down on their luck or driven by wanderlust. As a teenager from a musical family, he began playing in local hillbilly bands, then drifted west with the "Oakies" (or "dust bowl refugees") to California where he chose music over migrant labor.

Guthrie made his mark on the Popular Front-oriented Los Angeles station KFVD, and this vague but important connection proved decisive to his career. Protest songs like "Do Re Mi," historical-political ballads such as "Pretty Boy Floyd" or "1913 Massacre," existential tales like "Roll On Columbia" and "So Long It's Been Good To Know You" won wide audiences for their colorful use of details and their often whimsical ambiance. With "This Land Is Your Land," he acutely identified and captured the New Deal idealism of the later 'thirties, the widespread hope to realize through cooperation and shared cultures a possibility of freedom deep in the American experience.

Not an intellectual in the ordinary sense of writing books or lecturing, Guthrie read newspapers carefully and kept his responses in overflowing notebooks. As he interacted with working people of many different kinds, singing to them or protesting with them, he acquired an instinctive anti-racism. He worked closely with black singers, wrote the touching ballad "Deportee" about Mexican-American migrant labor, and he rejected prejudices of other kinds. His last mother-in-law was a noted Yiddish poet and he spent much time in his later years around aging immigrant Jewish radicals, who (like many of their children who grew up hearing him sing in their "progressive" summer camps) loved him ferociously.

He went public in a political way at the end of the 'thirties, writing a column ("Woody Sez") for the *Peoples World,* the west-coast communist daily, and performing for leftish Hollywood fund-raisers. In 1940, he moved to New York, where he immediately emerged as a central figure in the nascent "folk song movement." Recording *Dust Bowl Ballads* commercially, he worked with the Almanac Singers (featuring the young Pete Seeger) and at times appeared on network radio. World War II gave him a patriotic mission, for the first and only time: he entered the armed forces, wrote the popular recollective volume *Bound for Glory,* and reached the verge of real commercial success.

Politics and personal life pulled him back. He felt uncomfortable in the role of a respectable citizen, and his drinking, carousing and woman-chasing ruined him for the straight life. On the other hand, he consistently refused to bend his lyrics to Tin Pan Alley formulas, and the Cold War ended his success. Union militancy disappeared, Leftwing officials were purged or entire unions swallowed up, and thereby his main paying constituency dramatically narrowed. "People's Songs," an institutional entity for leftish music, including his, closed in 1949 due to anti-communist pressures.

He could not have escaped his own physical collapse in any case. By 1952, Huntington's Chorea rendered him helpless, and he spent fifteen years in depression and decline before his death. By that time, his admirers and imitators included Bob Dylan (who, like many, visited Woody in the hospital), Phil Ochs, Joan Baez, Tom Paxton, Utah Phillips, Judy Collins, and Peter, Paul and Mary — to say nothing of Woody's son, Arlo. By extension, even Bruce Springsteen felt the Guthrie touch. So would topical singers into the foreseeable future, and audiences who have never seen the sentimental film biography, *Bound For Glory,* with Peter Carradine, or his son's offbeat classic, *Alice's Restaurant.*

Photograph and courtesy: Seema A. Weatherwax

Woody Guthrie raised money for the Hollywood strikers of 1945.

als, from New Deal thinkers to Hollywood stars like Katherine Hepburn, turned to former Vice President Henry Wallace, who had been driven out of Harry Truman's cabinet. Activists of labor's Political Action Committee which had played an important role in the re-election of Roosevelt in 1944 urged Wallace to run against Truman, who had quickly gained the backing of "Cold War" liberals. Wallace, an idealist and mystic, had great popular appeal in his vision of a peaceful world, but a tendency toward political ineptness. Early polls showed him winning more than eight million votes. But the Progressive Party, launched early in 1948, was doomed by Cold War tensions, by the vitriolic campaign of the commercial press, and by the overwhelming fear of former Roosevelt voters that no one but Truman could retain for them the government benefits won in the New Deal. By election day the campaign had almost collapsed, and only voters in the Bronx and parts of California had voted heavily for the noted dissenter.

Worse than all this, conservative political offensives and communist defenses of Russia had eroded basic hopes for democratic social change coming out of the Depression. America was richer, more powerful as a nation than ever before. But its claim to power rested on military preparedness, on a scale never before imagined except by radical critics. Billions of dollars spent on armaments and soldiers stationed at home and abroad had been diverted from programs to deal with growing social problems of poverty and race. The United Nations,

Photograph and Courtesy: Richard Partlow

Courtesy: Harold Leventhal

Folksingers Vern Partlow and Burl Ives, Pete Seeger and the Almanac Singers, carried the political message of world peace and cooperation, c. 1945, while they renewed the national memory of beloved people's music.

Courtesy: Irwin Silber

Folksay Group in rehearsal for "Tomorrow Is Good Morning," c. 1948. Communist-leaning youngsters sought to create art forms in the American genre; folksong impresario Irwin Silber even "called" Leftwing square dances. While never popular, the dance forms echoed New Deal themes and reflected the choreography of Oklahoma *by former Group Theater member, Agnes DeMille.*

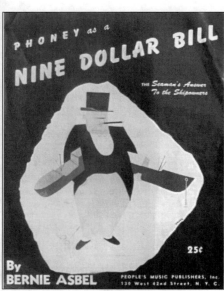

Courtesy: Bernie Asbell and Southpaw Books

Bernie Asbell and Pete Seeger singing Asbell's "Phony as a Nine Dollar Bill" at a meeting of the Greater New York City CIO Council during the 1946 maritime strike. In the background Ewart Guinier (father of Lani Guinier) can be seen.

meant to bring the world together, became another arena of conflict for world control. American Communists and their supporters had failed to elaborate a vision of a different America, closer to its historic ideals.

Working class Jewish poetry enthusiasts gathered at Camp Lakeland, New York in 1949. Poet Aaron Kramer is at center. Above him, in white smock and braids, is Leah Schaefer, widow of the famed Yiddish choral composer Jakob Schaefer.

The prestige of liberal, labor and entertainment world supporters disguised the weakness of the progressive Citizens of America and the new Progressive Party to meet the manipulated and sensationalized charges of disloyalty. Among labor, the Longshoremen and Warehousemen's Union was one of the few willing to resist pressures against supporting the 1948 Wallace campaign.

The Hollywood contingent was the one of the Wallace campaign's highlights. Actress Katharine Hepburn and Robert Kenny, Progressive Party Chairman (and legal aide to persecuted Hollywood writers) are shown here at the founding 1948 convention. Photograph by Otto Rothschild

Courtesy: Museum of American Political Life

journey to Israel
by Congressman Leo Isacson
illustrated
with photographs
from
the Palestine
front

Both, Private Collection

Leo F. Isaacson, the only Progressive party Congressional victor (in a special election, early in 1948), represented the mixture of Left politics and Israel support sought by his Bronx constituents. Leftwing Jewish unions such as the Furriers Union donated large amounts to the new state of Israel.

Mike Quin (pseudonym of William Paul Ryan), a prolific and popular
West Coast radical journalist, poet and detective novelist, is shown
here with his family shortly before his 1946 death from cancer. He was
often compared with Tom Paine.

Courtesy: Southpaw Books

A bemused Alger Hiss eyes the verbal sparring between his counsel Lloyd Paul Stryker
and Assistant U.S. Attorney Thomas F. Murphy (later a New York City Police
Commissioner) before Judge Samuel Kaufman. William Sharp, "Trial of Alger Hiss,"
pen and ink, 1949.

Courtesy: The Ben and Beatrice Goldstein Foundation

While brilliant young playwright Arthur
Miller (top) assailed the spread of
McCarthyism, the young novelist
Normal Mailer (bottom) renounced
capitalism and communism, seeking
some third route out of the world's
mess. From Morris U. Schappes, Jews in
the United States.

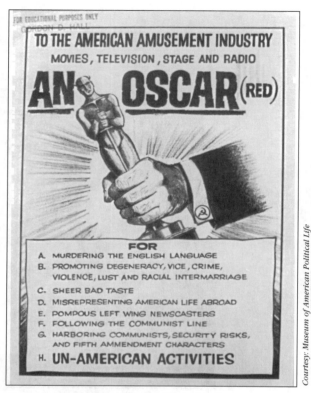

Conservative Attack on the Hollywood Left.

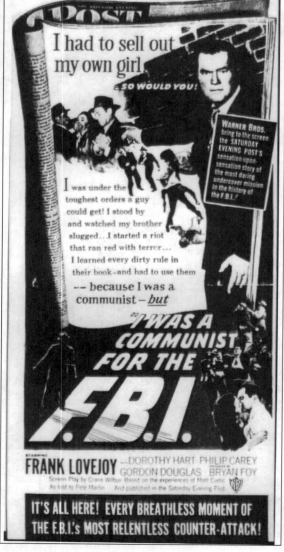

Hollywood also made a series of anti-communist films. None were box-office successes.

Politics of Race

HALL OF JUSTICE

Photo and courtesy: Phil Stern

In 1942, a frenzy of anti-Mexican publicity followed a mysterious murder near a Los Angeles quarry called Sleepy Lagoon. Police conducted a drag-net, beating up and eventually indicting nearly two dozen men, all but one of them Mexican-American. The Los Angeles Left took up the case vigorously, as led by lawyer George Shibley. After their conviction by an all-Anglo jury, an Appeals Court overturned the verdict. In this picture, captured by a photographer later known for his famed portraits of stars such as Marlon Brando, the defendents return to freedom, an historic moment for Mexican-Americans. The notorious "Zoot Suit" anti-Mexican riots had shortly followed the original arrests, and the 1980s play Zoot Suit *recalled the series of incidents.*

The Politics of Race

By 1950, it had become clear that W.E.B. DuBois was right: race was the great dividing line of the twentieth century. Franklin Roosevelt's New Deal had brought radicals into the system part-way, but at the expense of softening some of their criticism of the administration's political alliance with the Democratic party "Bourbon" (or racist) Southern politicians and its unabashed support of both Latin American dictators and their U.S. investors. Harry Truman, under great pressure from Democratic liberals, enforced integration of the armed forces. But nearly all the rest of Truman's policies at home and abroad conveyed the determination to hold onto white (and American) rule of a mostly non-white world population. Fatally weakened by their support of Stalin and by the spreading waves of repression, American Communists nevertheless launched an impressive campaign for racial equality in the larger society.

Some of the forgotten moments occured among minorities less concentrated and numerous than African-Americans. Although repressed and their leaders deported, radical Mexican-Americans found solace in legal victories against repression and in the formation of low-key groups as the Community Services Organization, out of which the next generation of activists (notably Cesar Chavez) emerged. Chinese-American activists, buoyed by the revolution in their homeland, waxed relatively strong until repressed during the Korean War. In Hawaii, the International Longshoreman's and Warehouseman's Union won a major 1946 strike on the sugar plantations which significantly improved the lives of Japanese-American workers. A series of persecutions followed in Hawaii, too. Among still other groups, such as Filipinos, radical unionists and writers found a support system to sustain them through difficult times.

But most emphasis had been placed upon winning rights for the black community. From a publicity point of view among African-Americans themselves, personalities from W.E.B. DuBois to Langston Hughes, youngsters Harry Belafonte, Ruby Dee and Ossie Davis, put themselves on the line (and willingly suffered) because they recognized no better allies in America. Many others, like bebopper Dizzy Gillespie, singer Billie Holliday and actor Canada Lee, were on the fringes of Left-oriented movements for equality, and caught in the "blacklist."

In organizational terms, the Civil Rights Congress was most impressive. Formed through a 1946 merger of the International Labor Defense, National Negro Congress and the National Federation of Constitutional Liberties, its ten thousand members specialized in defending African-American radicals. Chapters in New York, Detroit, Seattle, San Francisco and Los Angeles included many future mainstream civil rights leaders,

With the publication of America is In the Heart (1946), leftwing labor activist and sometime editor, Filipino immigrant Carlos Bulosan became known briefly as a leading America author. Blacklisted and his health broken only a few years later, he died penniless but not forgotten.

Courtesy: Oscar Campomanes

The Christian socialist gospel of interracial peace and a "New Earth" illustrated by Biblical citations was the political message of Claude and Joyce Williams, white radicals in the South from the 1930s to the 1970s.

Courtesy: Southern Exposure magazine

As the Left fell victim to persecution and collapsed internally, race equality became its key domestic issue. W.E.B. DuBois emerged as one of its great personalities.

Private Collection

W.E.B. DuBOIS

The most influential black intellectual of the twentieth century and one of America's most important historians, DuBois was also through his long life a father of Pan Africanism, a leading organizer of African-American institutions, and a foremost intellectual of the Left.

Born in 1868 of free black parentage in Great Barrington, Massachusetts, DuBois grew up in poverty but spared the customary racist treatments of the contemporary society. After two years at Fisk University — DuBois's introduction to the black southern world — he went on to graduate cum laude from Harvard. Studying in Berlin (where he sometimes attended socialist rallies), he returned to receive a PhD from Harvard. His dissertation, "The Suppression of the African Slave Trade to the United States of America, 1638-1870," was a precocious classic, the first in the Harvard Historical Series. After a teaching job at Wilberforce University, he was commissioned by the University of Pennsylvania to study black Philadelphia, resulting in the classic sociological treatise *The Philadelphia Negro: A Social Study* (1899).

During his long tenure at Atlanta University, beginning in 1897, DuBois began to assess the complexity of black consciousness in light of stubborn segregation and rising racial violence. A series of essays published in the Atlantic Monthly appeared as *The Souls of Black Folk* (1903), a wide-ranging commentary on black religion and culture, and on the color line as the great unresolved problem of the dawning century. At this point DuBois began to move toward radicalism, cooperating in the formation of the Niagara movement (which led to the N.A.A.C.P. a few years later) and reading socialist books. By 1907, he declared socialism the "one great hope of the Negro in America," a few years later actually joining the Socialist Party and contributing to *The New Review,* a socialistic intellectual journal

DuBois edited the influential NAACP magazine, The *Crisis,* from its beginning in 1910, and it became his primary vehicle as his public reputation declined during the 1920s. The Depression radicalized him economically, that prompted him to write *Black Reconstruction,* an epic treatment of American slavery, the Civil War, Emancipation, Radical Reconstruction and regression in racist America. He established that slaves and ex-slaves, empowered by their cultural background and the religious faith, had mightily changed the face of the nation and posed America's destiny, race empire (and finally, self-destruction) or equality and redemption. Although highly critical of American Communists, DuBois shifted subtly to accept Russian opposition to colonialism as the most valid expression of the white world.

After the Second World War, DuBois devoted himself to anti-colonial and anti-Cold War activities. For this, he suffered the persecution of threats, cancelled engagements, and the loss of his passport. He received more than 200,000 votes as candidate of the American Labor Party for Senate in New York. Increasingly alienated from life in the Cold War US, DuBois accepted an offer of citizenship in Ghana in 1961, determined to complete the "Encyclopedia Africana." He died two years later, the encyclopedia unfinished but the magazine *Freedomways* (with his wife, Shirley Graham DuBois, in control) fairly launched upon a distinguished career as the cultural-political voice of the African-American radicals.

such as later Detroit Mayor Coleman Young. In their time, the Congress took on such cases as that of Willie McGee, Mississippi truckdriver accused of raping a white woman when a husband discovered an extramarital affair. In the organization's last days, hounded by government persecution, it still managed to mobilize protests against the lynching of Emmett Till, a black Chicago teenager who was lynched on a trip to Mississippi when he reportedly got "fresh" with a white woman. The C.R.C. also published *We Charge Genocide*, a massively reprinted document detailing crimes of American race bias. In all these cases, the Congress managed to embarrass the U.S. government abroad, and for that reason it was vigorously persecuted.

The Council on African Affairs and National Negro Labor Congress had similar political ties and met similar persecution. The N.N.L.C. sought to compel every union to adopt a model clause promising fair practices. The C.A.A. supported anti-colonial movements in Africa, assisting them with information and fund-raising. Sadly, even liberal labor leaders (such as Walter Reuther of the United Auto Workers) ordered members to refuse cooperation. In its first constitution, the AFL-CIO outlawed ties with Communists but not segregated locals. Mainstream labor had lost its ideals. Likewise, liberals shunned the African National Congress which the C.A.A. ardently supported, thus justifying the continuation of U.S. support for the South African apartheid regime decades longer.

Whites willing to risk their lives for civil rights in the South frequently had such ties. Carl and Anne Braden, two journalists at the *Louisville Times*, fought legal cases, bought a home for a black family, and faced charges of state sedition as well as federal "investigation." They went on to train activists, fight the House UnAmerican Activities Committee, and guide the influential integrationist Southern Conference Educational Fund (S.C.E.F.). By the 1950s, former communists who continued to work on specific issues while refusing to support the Soviet Union stood on high ground because by contrast, nearly all the anti-communists had stood so low. A young Martin Luther King, Jr., attending graduate school at Boston University, was said to read the *Daily Worker* because no other paper had such sympathetic coverage of black struggles.

Independent, non-communist radicals had their own difficult row to hoe without any existing support system for their work. Some locally influential figures such Grace Lee Boggs and her husband James Boggs (a black automobile worker) exerted themselves within civil rights activity by virtue of their background in the Trotskyist movement and by their force of personality. Veteran labor organizer H.L. Mitchell moved his little Southern Tenant Farmers Union into the meat-cutters union, also pioneered the support campaign for California farm-workers unionization, and

HEAR HENRY WALLACE

- PAUL ROBESON
- FRANK KINGDON
- ENTERTAINMENT

CONVENTION HALL - 34th below Spruce
Friday, September 19—8:00 P. M.

auspices of PCA

TICKETS ON SALE NOW AT PCA, 1831 CHESTNUT STREET
LOcust 7-4313
.65, .90, 1.30, 2.00, 3.00 TAX INC.
(ALL SEATS RESERVED)
Progressive Citizens of America

(Above) Some of Henry Wallace's most exciting campaign moments came from his courageous embrace of African-American causes and political leaders like Harlem minister and later Congressman, Adam Clayton Powell, Jr. (Below) Paul Robeson was an early supporter, shown here with Congressman Vito Marcantonio at the 1948 Progressive Party national convention.

POWELL & WALLACE AN INTEGRATED TICKET

even organized southern fishermen and sugar-cane workers. Myles Horton and others of the Highlander Research and Educational Center in Monteagle, Tennessee, originally a labor college of the 1930s, simply encouraged those interested in an integrated society to work and educate themselves together. Future civil rights leaders Rosa Parks, Fannie Lou Hamer and Stokely Carmichael were among the more prominent students. Whatever their affiliation, these radicals had played a vital role in questioning not only American racial practices but also the values that made such practices possible.

New York's Chinatown Left, shortly before the victory of the Chinese Revolution and the swift repression of its American-based Asian supporters.

in defense of
NEGRO RIGHTS

BENJAMIN J. DAVIS
FORMER CITY COUNCILMAN OF NEW YORK

Testifies in

the Trial of

the Communist

Twelve at Foley Square

15 CENTS

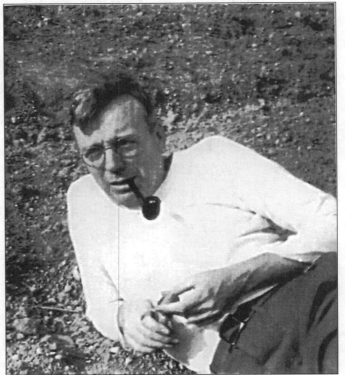

Twice elected to the New York City Council (1943-47), civil rights lawyer and open Communist Benjamin Davis was indicted on the Smith Act in 1948 and later served a term in prison. Communist Rob Hall directed Southern strategy until McCarthyism made most of the Left racial activity in that region impossible.

Courtesy: Stephen Deutsch

Leadbelly (Hudie Ledbetter) and Josh White, two of the most dynamic leftish folk singers in 1945. Photo by Stephen Deutsch.

Courtesy: Kim Chernin

Little Kim Chernin, daughter of Los Angeles Left leader Rose Chernin, leads an anti-discrimination demonstration in 1946.

Further Reading

Paul Buhle, *C.L.R. James: The Artist as Revolutionary* (London: Verso, 1989)

Martin Bauml Duberman, *Paul Robeson* (New York: Alfred A. Knopf, 1988).

Barbara Foley, *Radical Representations: Politics and Form in U.S. Proletarian Fiction, 1929-1941* (Durham: Duke University Press, 1993).

Gerald Horne, *Communist Front? The Civil Rights Congress, 1946-56* (Rutherford: Farleigh Dickenson Press, 1987).

Maurice Isserman, *Which Side Were You On? The American Communist Party During the Second World War* (Middletown: Weslyan University Press, *1983*)

Robin D.G. Kelley, *Hammer and Hoe: Alabama Communists During the Great Depression* (Chapel Hill: University of North Carolina Press, 1990).

Charles Larrowe, *Harry Bridges: The Rise and Fall of Radical Labor in the U.S.* (Westport: Lawrence Hill, 1972).

Robbie Lieberman, *My Song Is My Weapon: People's Songs, American Communism, and the Politics of Culture, 1930-50* (Urbana: University of Illinois, 1989).

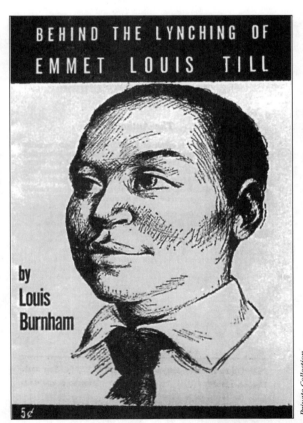

Private Collection

The lynching in 1955 of 14 year old Emmet Louis Till by Mississippi vigilantes for whistling at a white women became a national sensation and a cause celebre for the faltering Old Left. Author Louis Burnham was an editor of *Freedom, a Harlem Left paper published by Paul Robeson and predecessor to *Freedomways.

Courtesy: Aaron Kramer

Jewish American writer Aaron Kramer wrote frequently, from adolescence onward, poems about African-American themes of oppression and freedom. His oil portrait is by Alice Neel.

Josh White's music and his political commitments made him a favorite of leftwing folk music fans.

George Lipsitz, *A Rainbow at Midnight: Class and Culture in the Cold War* (N. Hadley: Bergin & Harvey, 1980).

Harold Meyerson and Ernie Harburg, *Who Put the Rainbow in the Wizard of Oz? Yip Harburg, Lyricist (Ann* Arbor: University of Michigan, 1993)-

Marlene Park and Gerald E. Markowitz, *Democratic Vistas: Post Offices and Public Art in the New Deal* (Philadelphia: Temple University Press, 1984).

Nancy Lynn Schwartz, *The Hollywood Writers' Wars (New* York: Alfred A. Knopf, 1982).

Renqui Yu, *To Save China, To Save Ourselves: The Chinese Hand Laundry Alliance of New York* (Philadelphia: Temple University Press, 1992).

Carl and Anne Braden, an extraordinarily brave Southern couple who frequently risked imprisonment to support racial integration, seen here at Carl's "conspiracy" trial in 1954.

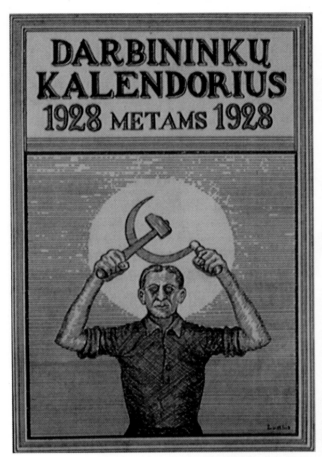

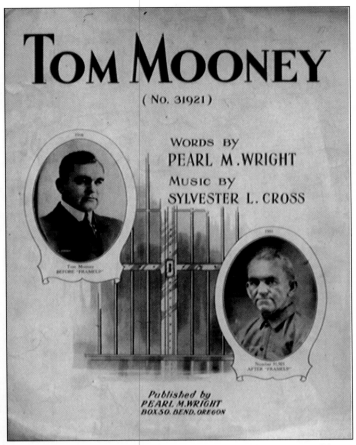

Popular proletarian culture. Lithuanian-American workers' calendar sold door-to-door in blue collar neighborhoods by various ethnic radical groups affiliated with the Socialist Party, Socialist Labor Party and Communist Party. These calendars added American holidays, May Day and other revolutionary holidays to traditional ethnic Saints Days, and gave viewers a different selection of popular folk or radical art each month. For generations their sale served as a major fund raising mechanism.

Sheet Music, "Tom Mooney (No. 31921)," 1932: "The great world war was calling men from factory and field...It's bread not bullets people need and might does not make right..." Chorus: "Now he's growing in prison..."

All, Private Collection

Nicola Sacco and Bartolomeo Vanzetti.

A rare piece of folk art by anonymous members of the National Maritime Union: Eglomise painting with added butterfly wings, c. 1940.

"A JOYOUS LAUGHTER-FILLED EVENT!" — CBS-TV

LAST YEAR'S **LONGEST RUNNING OFF-B'WAY HIT!**

Lorraine Hansberry's

TO BE YOUNG, GIFTED & BLACK

Adapted by
ROBERT NEMIROFF

Original Production Directed by
GENE FRANKEL

"AN EXTRAORDINARY ACHIEVEMENT! It is a whirl of probing, celebrating, hoping, laughing, despairing and moving on...a thrust of spirit...so brilliantly and tenderly alive."
— Nat Hentoff, N.Y. TIMES

"MAGNIFICENTLY AMUSING" "SUPERB!"
— NEWARK NEWS — Los Angeles TIMES

"A TRIUMPH!" "WONDERFULLY MOVING"
— N.Y. POST — Clive Barnes, N.Y. TIMES

"MARVELOUS!" "BEAUTIFUL THEATER"
— James Baldwin in ESQUIRE — WALL STREET JOURNAL

"SHE STANDS AS THE ULTIMATE BLACK WRITER FOR TODAY"
— Julius Lester, VILLAGE VOICE

"MIRACULOUS—one marvels at the range!"
— THE VILLAGE VOICE

"THE WORDS AND IMAGERY OF A BLACK O'CASEY"
— THE GUARDIAN

"A MILESTONE!"
— TIME MAGAZINE

"The Finest Stage Work in New York... YOU MUST SEE IT!"
— Emory Lewis, THE RECORD

FINE ARTS COUNCIL, BOWKER AUDITORIUM
FRIDAY, SEPT. 25th, 8:00 P.M.
SATURDAY, SEPT. 26th, 2:30 P.M. & 8:00 P.M.
Reserved Tickets: U. Mass. undergrads: $1.50
Grad. Students & other Students: $2.00 Faculty/Staff: $2.50 Others: $3.00
Fine Arts Council Box Office, 125 Herter Hall. Phone: 545-0202

Production of a play by Lorraine Hansberry, brilliant young playwright and militant activist (later, an important lesbian influence). Her best known play, Raisin In The Sun, *was later adapted for the television show* Good Times.

Progressive activist Jessica Mitford, later author of The American Way of Death, *poses here before a Civil Rights Congress poster supporting Southern black victim, Willie McGee.*

Chapter Five
Past, Present and Future

Lisa Lyons

Against the Cold War

"Bits" Hayden, "The Mugity Wumpus" (from Mike Quin, On the Drumhead)

Against the Cold War

Social movements after the World War Two bore superficial resemblances to their predecessors, with some of the same political organizations mobilizing veteran activists. But the character of the crises facing the nation and also the perceptions of how a better society might look steadily reshaped the contours of American radicalism. An imagery often scarcely recognizable to the world of the 1920s-30s grew around and through radical circles.

By the 1960s if not before, old issues faded. The activities or consciousness of industrial workers no longer seemed the key for radical hopes; the giant state apparatus once idealized in Communist states or the New Deal had meanwhile become increasingly repugnant. But arms proliferation, race hatred, and American rulers' unending need for enemies to threaten and resources to swallow, all intensified the world wide crisis in the environment. The terrifying spread of poverty, wars and plague-like diseases undercut the old confident belief in progress, and the fixed belief that only Communism obstructed a happier world order. These phenomena together also cast doubt on the twentieth century radicals' familiar recipes and recalled instead the distant origins of radicalism and the first utopian visions of a new world. The newer utopians tried to supply remedies for ailments and at least hopes for a real cure. A stern idealism also dictated a modern political-artistic expression: documentation of and protest against the intolerable.

Widespread revulsion at the use of the atomic bomb on the civilian populations of

Peekskill Concert Demonstration, September, 1949.

Courtesy: Indiana University Archives

Hiroshima and Nagasaki had initially roused artists, intellectuals and moral figures to the dread prospects of future warfare. A small group of war resisters, veterans of American prisons in the 1940s, created the Committee for Nonviolent Revolution in 1946. Dave Dellinger, Jim Peck and Ralph DiGia merged their organization in 1948 with Peacemakers, a radical pacifist group started partly by the Rev. A.J. Muste. The Catholic Worker group, which continued to run dozens of "hospitality houses" for the homeless, also committed itself to ending the boundless preparation for war. These groups and old-time Wobblies repeatedly attempted to enter U.S. missile bases non-violently so to reveal, in a deeply personal way, the insane logic of so-called military security.

Famed intellectuals also spoke out against the use of atomic bombs and their monopoly by the United States. Lewis Mumford, America's leading architectural critic and one of its first important environmentalist writers, authored a radical manifesto, "Gentlemen, You Are Mad!" demanding that all weapons and relevant information be turned over an international agency which would dispose of bombs and ensure that atomic weapons would never be used again. Many leading scientists, including several who had worked on the Manhattan Project, heartily agreed. They launched the *Bulletin of Atomic Scientists* to warn against the growing dangers, and helped to draft legislation that would have made scientists morally responsible for the consequences of their action on the human population and the environment. They condemned the Truman administration for protecting military decision-making and the profits of the military-industrial complex from effective criticism by a vast new security apparatus.

By the later 1940s radical artists prepared their own response to the Trumanized society. Politicized bohemians of the San Francisco Bay area answered the crazed rationalism of the welfare-warfare state with their own brands of anti-war and anti-

Los Angeles demonstration against Repression, 1951, led by Emil Fried (later the key founder of the Southern California Library); and New York City labor demonstration against the Red Scare, c. 1950.

authoritarian logic. *Circle* magazine connected Andre Breton and other French surrealists in exile with a young San Francisco poet, Philip Lamantia, who would himself become a leading figure in the reorganized American surrealist movement of the 1960s-90s. Surrealists preached freedom of artistic activity from realist aesthetics and from Communist politics, but also stressed their own commitment to anti-capitalist aspirations. *Circle's* final 1948 issue characteristically announced the existence of a "New Writers Group" which insisted

> There is a struggle going on or the minds of the American people. Every form of expression is subject to the attack of reaction. That attack comes in the shape of silence, persecution and censorship: three names for fear. In the face of this fear, the writer can speak. We believe in the possibility of a culture which fights for its freedom, which protects the economic interests of its workers in all fields including the arts, and which can create for itself new forms and new voices, against reaction and threat of war...
>
> We will function politically...will work to open up new channels of expression...

The Hollywood Ten and their families on the eve of the writers' departure to prison.

Courtesy: State Historical Society of Wisconsin

This kind of perspective was a precursor to the formation of the Beat Generation, a few years later. It also informed the anti-war Bay Area coalition which formed KPFA, America's first listener-sponsored radio station. This broadly experimental station had plenty of jazz, poetry readings, Native American folklore, and anarchist conversation against the state and militarism. By encouraging the emergence of a nation-wide Pacifica radio network, it provided a bridge to an anarchistic, avant-garde art scene that would soon help to reshape American radicalism. From another musical angle, Los Angeles rhythm 'n blues drummer Johnny Otis became one of California's most popular disk jockeys, militantly interracial and politically radical. The public concerts he put together, regularly threatened with closure by local authorities, offered an advanced look at the energy that black-based music could give a later generation of interracial and politically active youngsters.

Meanwhile, the Hollywood Left had provided another sort of conceptual or artistic bridge between American radicalism and American popular culture. The investigations and successful intimidation of movie studios and their employees by the House

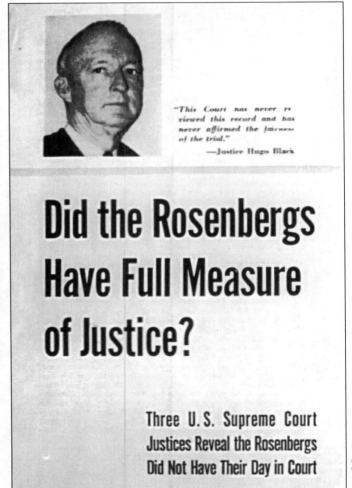

The Rosenberg Case.

Howard Fast addresses Veterans of the Abraham Lincoln Brigade, an important political source of identity for thousands of ageing radicals.

UnAmerican Activities Committee and Dies Committee after World War Two steadily chilled artistic freedom. In late 1947, Congress cited ten screenwriters for an unwillingness to cooperate with the investigation; by 1950 the "Hollywood Ten" faced prison sentences. Studios formally blacklisted all those who would not purge themselves of Communist ties (and those who refused to testify against their old friends). Lionel Stander, Zero Mostel, Sam Jaffe and a host of writers, musicians and assorted technicians were driven from the industry for decades. Dozens of politically challenging projects were never realized, and hundreds of the most talented people in every aspect of moviemaking, from *film noir* detective stories to documentaries to comic animation, lost heart in the grinding repression that followed.

A BLACK WOMAN SPEAKS . . .

OF WHITE WOMANHOOD

OF WHITE SUPREMACY

OF PEACE

A Poem by BEULAH RICHARDSON

PRICE 25 CENTS

Courtesy: Southpaw Books

Activist poet Beulah Richardson bringing together radical perspectives in the early 1950s; she was later deported.

HOWARD FAST

The most prolific radical author of the century, Howard Fast, is also one of the most versatile and most politically committed intellectuals on the modern scene.

Son of a factory worker in New York, Fast was a literary prodigy. Dropping out of high school, he published his first novel before he turned twenty. Unlike Upton Sinclair, the writer whose work Fast's most nearly resembled, Fast turned at first almost exclusively to the historical novel form. His epics of the Revolutionary War period, including *Citizen Tom Paine* (1941), reached a wide audience with a message remarkable for its skillful telling and for his sensitive handling of native peoples (so often treated indifferently by radical authors of this period seeking to revive democratic-national themes). His *Freedom Road* (1944), a novel of the Reconstruction era, contained one of the strongest statements of African-American emancipation outside W.E.B. DuBois *Black Reconstruction*. Still other novels of the period included several on victims of legal oppression, including *The Passion of Sacco and Vanzetti* (1953). He also wrote a first-person attack on vigilante violence, *Peekskill, U.S.A.: A Personal Experience* (1951).

Fast, operating with apparently limitless energy, kept a political career going alongside his literary one. He joined the Communist Party in 1943, when he was not quite thirty years old, and played a prominent part in many public events, from the lecture and banquet circuit to political campaigns (including a run for Congress on the American Labor Party ticket). Insiders and radical youngsters knew him best, perhaps, as a sometime teacher of the American novel at New York's Jefferson School.

The House UnAmerican Activities Committee pressed Fast in 1950 to provide the names of all those who had contributed funds to the hospital which he had aided in its care for Spanish Civil War veterans. Refusing, he accepted a prison sentence of three months. As an author, he now faced a publishers' blacklist. He launched his own company, Blue Heron Press, publishing his own remarkable historical saga of a slave uprising, *Spartacus* (1951). Rendered into a film script and produced by Kirk Douglas, it broke the Hollywood blacklist (even if final cuts maimed the radical message intended by Fast) and made Fast's career as a scenarist. In later years, he returned to the best-seller list as an author, penning detective fiction, biographies, science fiction and a highly-successful novel, *The Immigrants* (1977), the first of a connected series of works on the American family in twentieth century conflicts, eventually made into a two-part film for television.

Private Collection

All others, photo and courtesy: Frank Wilkinson

Key civil libertarians: (top left) pamphlet by former labor journalist Harvey O'Connor; (top right) prominent experimental educator Alexander Meikeljohn; (bottom right) Carey McWilliams, editor of The Nation; *(bottom left); Dr. Otto Nathan, executor of Alfred Einstein's estate, at the far left, together with Frank Wilkinson and Carl and Anne Braden.*

Across American society generally, the repression was still worse. Harry Truman's Executive Order 9837 of 1947 barred Communists, fascists, other totalitarians and anyone guilty of "sympathetic association" with them from government employment. The "test" quickly spread to private employers, aided by the F.B.I., city police "Red Squads," conservative newspapers and local vigilantes. If government firings identified prominent radicals, "Second stage" McCarthyism by private employers made it difficult for radicals to remain politically active or even lead normal lives. Joseph McCarthy, merely the most notorious of Congressional investigators, was far less important than the dozens of others like him, both Democrats and Republicans, conservative and liberals, building their careers and earning large fees by identifying supposed subversives. Perhaps 10,000 people in all lost their jobs.

Millions of Americans were intimated through threats of various kinds, from job threats and expulsion from America (if they were born abroad) to jail terms if they refused to testify against former friends. On a day-to-day basis, they struggled to cope with whispering campaigns instigated among neighbors and office-mates by the F.B.I.

Courtesy: Museum of American Political Life

With little chance of drawing many votes, the Progressive Party continued campaigning in 1952 for civil liberties and against the Cold War. Here, Bay Area lawyer and presidential candidate Vincent Hallinan addresses a crowd.

or local police "Red Squads" supposedly carrying out confidential investigations. The emerging leaders of labor movement, increasingly eager to cooperate with government demands that they "purge" suspected radicals, expelled several of the most militant and most interracial bodies of the Congress of Industrial Organization. Under these conditions, the wartime tendency toward bureaucratization was quickly completed. Unions generally abandoned their old crusading image and gradually lost their social influence, preparing their irreversible decline during the decades ahead. Rebel idealists remained active in many sectors of labor, rowing against the tide. But they could not restore the old momentum.

The Hiss and the Rosenberg cases topped off the era. Alger Hiss, a high-ranking New Deal official well-known to be sympathetic to the Left, was accused of passing State Department documents to the Soviet Union. His accuser, the mentally unbalanced former Communist Whitaker Chambers, admitted to giving perjured testimony against Hiss and the first trial ended in a hung jury. But the Cold War political climate permitted Richard Nixon, a freshman Republican Congressman from California, to make a name for himself by attacking the Democratic Party for supposedly harboring traitors. Producing a dossier of secret "new" evidence (later revealed to be Bureau of Standards material available at public libraries), Nixon dramatized his charges and prepared his candidacy for Vice-President in 1952. Hiss, convicted of perjury rather than spy charges, served forty-four months in prison. He has continued to maintain his innocence.

Engineer Julius Rosenberg, fired from his government job for allegations of Communist Party membership, was arrested on spy charges in May, 1950 of giving the Russians the secret for the atomic bomb. Ethel Rosenberg, a Brooklyn housewife and sometime political activist, was also arrested, along with Morton Sobell, a college classmate of Julius'. After a brief trial in which doubtful evidence was offered and (it was later learned) the F.B.I. coached witnesses, Judge Irving Kauffman sentenced the

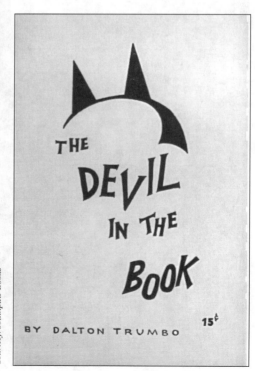

Courtesy: Southpaw Books

A leading Hollywood Red speaks out on the issues of repression. Published by the California Emergency Defense Committee, c. 1951.

Rosenbergs to death, preposterously blaming them for the Korean War. A world-wide campaign for clemency convinced three Supreme Court judges to grant a stay, but the full Court denied the stay. Tens of thousands gathered for a vigil. Protesters pointed especially to the anti-Semitic framing of the case, a warning against Jewish "disloyalty" (meaning: rejection of U.S. foreign policies). Ironically, Stalin was also prosecuting Jewish intellectuals for similarly imagined crimes against the Soviet state. [Plates 85-86]

The Rosenberg defense helped bring to life a vigorous civil liberties movement in the face of intimidation directed at lawyers willing to take controversial cases. The National Lawyers Guild, badly persecuted, was itself named as "subversive"; a National Emergency Civil Liberties Committee, launched in 1951 to fill the gap, combined notable New Dealers with radical journalists and brave academics. Eventually it helped halt Congressional witch-hunts, overturn wrongful convictions and end the kind of

Courtesy: Constitutional Liberties Information Center

"Verdict First, Trial After." Dorothy Healey, Southern California Communist Party chair, conferring with her attorney John J. Abt before HUAC hearing. Abt, a former New Deal official, was a prominent defender of witch-hunt victims.

★ PATRIOTISM *against* McCARTHYISM

PRICE 1¢

Courtesy: Southpaw Books

Robert Thompson, New York Communist Party chair and an officer in the Abraham Lincoln Battalion, is shown here being decorated for valor during World War II. He was later sentenced to seven years in prison for violation of the Smith Act.

"Thought Police" and other anti-HUAC pamphlets. Haplessly, the Left sought to fight back against McCarthyism with reasoned arguments.

Courtesy: Ruth Adlard MacLennan Uphaus

"Chapter and Verse": former CIO "Bishop" and a socialist leader in New Haven, Connecticut during the 1930s, the Rev. Willard Uphaus cites religious interpretation against racism and repression during the McCarthy Era. For decades, he and his wife Ruth Adlard Uphaus directed the World Fellowship camp in New Hampshire.

travel restrictions the government placed upon prominent dissidents. In the dark years only a handful of independent publications including the *Progressive*, the *Nation* and the *Guardian* stood forcefully against the witch hunt.

Even in these dreadful years of political repression, radicals continued to have an effect. Hollywood writers, for instance, helped rework the critical themes of popular culture and aesthetics. Writer and sometime director Abraham Polonsky's *Body and Soul* (1947) and *Force of Evil* (1948) were exquisite renditions of greed and of racial division under capitalism. Polonsky was the real Clifford Odets of the big screen, many believed. As the Blacklist fell across Hollywood, Polonsky switched to television, authoring scripts for *You Are There* (historical recreations with frequent anti-McCarthyite references) and as some of his colleagues wrote for *The Phil Silvers Show* (the first major interracial sitcom and perhaps the most iconoclastic show of the era). Ring Lardner, Jr., imprisoned for contempt in 1950, moved to England and wrote for *Robin Hood,* the classic anti-authoritarian television program. A host of other radical writers slipped into the substrata of cinematic SciFi, producing cult films with an ecological subtext, such as *Creature from the Black Lagoon* (1952), or worked in Westerns, creating some of the first pro-Indian (and anti-Custer) films. By rehearsing the "progressive" aesthetics of mass entertainment during the 1940s and 1950s, they showed how to get a message across, although usually at a considerable artistic cost.

Meanwhile, continuing nuclear tests in the Pacific renewed sentiment against the bomb, now increasingly organized around the "fallout" issue. The pacifist Fellowship of Reconciliation circulated petitions against all atomic testing, and an Albert Einstein-Bertrand Russell appeal of July, 1955, brought together prominent scientists world-

Traditional pacifists of the Catholic Worker *group and prominent atomic scientists joined in the struggle to halt or slow the arms race.*

wide to call for an end to the nuclear arms race. The same year, the National Committee for a Sane Nuclear Policy formed (socialist psychologist Erich Fromm dubbed it with the acronym SANE) and published the first of many full-page newspaper advertisements in the *New York Times* pleading for the abandonment of nuclear testing. Within a few years, in 1959-60, two thousand New Yorkers actively protested the official Civil Defense drill (to prepare for atomic war) and the Student Peace Union led "Ban the Bomb" rallies on many campuses. Shed of past Stalinist associations, the peace movement rose further, this time on a massive scale.

An "Old Left" anti-war movement hardly survived the Progressive Party's 1948 presidential campaign debacle. Remnants of the Progressives led opposition to the U.S. role in the unpopular and massively destructive Korean War. But revelations of Stalin's execution of Jewish intellectuals began to surface in the early 1950s, demoralizing the now-small American Communist Party. In 1956 Premier Nikita Khrushchev, confirmed these rumors to a tumultuous 20th Soviet Congress, adding mountains of evidence to the suspected enormity of Stalin's crimes. The same year, Russian troops marched into Hungary to crush a workers' uprising. American Communists reeled, sought to reform their party — and then in large numbers abandoned it for dead.

Courtesy: Oregon State University Libraries

Historian William Appleman Williams, an independent socialist who traced the rise of Empire and pleaded with Americans to come to terms with their own legacy. His book, The Tragedy of American Diplomacy *(1959) was inspiration to a new generation of radicals.*

Peace groups like the National Council on American-Soviet Friendship, which had flourished during the Second World War, withered under attacks from the federal government. Not even distinguished religious peace leaders, like the Rev. Willard Uphaus, could escape legal threats of persecution for their association with it.

The shift of political forces helps explain the changing symbols from radical transformation to civil liberties and survival. But this shift explains little about the iconographic pathos of the McCarthy Era. From the purge of the labor movement and the orchestrated campaign of intimidation-by-investigation to blacklistings of homosexuals to the almost incredible pain of the support movement for Julius and Ethel Rosenbergs, the artistic description of the witch hunt is memorable almost a half century later. The dignity and poise, under fire, of so many personalities and organizations or movements is the key to the relevant image. Here and there the expectation of an impending American fascism fed a supercharged artistic sense of martyrous destiny, a sensibility clearest in Communist and near-Communist images. But such garishness is amazingly slight. Instead, the emerging political aesthetic is both understated and modernized: this fearful moment is the not last stage of the "Old Left" but the first stage of the cultural sensibility ahead.

Courtesy: Paul Richards

Women Strike for Peace, an important group independent of any Left affiliation and successfully resistant to government repression, demonstrate with great publicity in 1962. Photograph by Harvey Richards

Civil Rights to Black Power

Civil Rights to Black Power, 1955-65

The "Old Left" played an essential role in the civil rights revolution, first by preparing the way through courageous action and then by providing sage strategic advice and political (as well as financial) support. The F.B.I.'s "war" on civil rights, with infiltration, legal persecution and continued public attack on brave local activists and leaders, was partly based on Director J. Edgar Hoover's unabashed personal racism. But F.B.I. operatives also observed what those sympathetic often noted, that the willingness of radicals (and unwillingness of others) to risk career and even life for the sake of minorities sustained the alliance. Leading African-American intellectuals were understandably unconvinced that their people would ever see real justice in a capitalistic system.

The role of radicals in the post-World War II South proved especially important, because civil rights activity there often involved great physical danger. The Southern Negro Youth Congress, which had significant influence among educated younger southern blacks for a few years, was driven out of existence after a major 1946 conference in Columbia, South Carolina demanded full civil rights, an immediate end to segregation, support of Third World independence movements and the elimination of nuclear weapons. But the Southern Conference Educational Fund, established in 1946 for the expressed purpose of eradicating segregation, had a stronger connection with prominent national liberals. Aubrey Williams, former leader of the New Deal National Youth Administration, was S.C.E.F.'s president for nearly twenty years; Eleanor Roosevelt, Williams's trusted friend and ally, defended it against red-baiting attacks from conservatives and Cold War liberals of the Arthur Schlesinger, Jr., variety.

In Monteagle, Tennessee, the Highlander Research and Education Center, led by socialist Myles Horton, had served since the 1930s as adult-education school, activist training center and progressive locus for poor people enriching their cultural roots by engagement and dialogue with each other. Surviving a steady stream of attacks from the state of Tennessee, the Ku Klux Klan, the F.B.I. and the Internal Revenue Service as well as congressional investigating committees, Highlander became a crucial advanced guard on civil rights.

From the North, radicals from a variety of backgrounds formed local community movements for racial equality. Because liberals sharply limited their support and influence to issues of equal housing and job opportunities, radicals carried the weight of education and agitation around deeper social questions of concentrated wealth and poverty. Their deep sincerity, their neighborhood contacts and their belief in the inter-racial possibilities of America carried them naturally toward leadership of the swelling currents.

Courtesy: Frank Wilkinson

Martin Luther King, Jr., with Frank Wilkinson at a reception at Morehouse College, 1960, just before Wilkinson surrendered to authorities to begin a jail sentence for contempt of Congress, i.e., refusing to cooperate with the House UnAmerican Activities Committee.

The Left could still claim the loyalty of leading intellectual and cultural figures in African-American life. After Paul Robeson openly stated that African Americans should not fight in any wars against Communism, his passport was confiscated in 1952 and America's leading black performer effectively banned from domestic stage appearances for twenty years. W.E.B. DuBois, for a half century the most important American Black thinker, was so stung by the post-World War II racism that he turned to Communists and their allies. He worked with Robeson at the Council on African Affairs, preparing Africa's liberation from colonialism, and in 1950 (at the age of 82) ran for congress from New York on the American Labor Party ticket, receiving more than 200,000 votes. In return, he was quickly made another noted victim of Cold War hysteria and persecution. Likewise, C.L.R. James, a revolutionary bitterly opposed to Communist policies, was expelled from the United States in 1953 on a passport violation.

But the U.S. Supreme Court's Brown vs. Board of Education decision in 1954 gave new life to black radicalism. Integration had become the law of the land, but it remained for radicals to lead the campaigns to realize that law in practice. The Rev. Martin Luther King, Jr., who came to prominence as leader of the Montgomery bus boycott, had in graduate school been a casual reader of various Marxist and Left publications and a scholar of Karl Marx's favorite philosopher, G.W.F. Hegel. Rosa Parks, whose refusal to yield her seat to whites had launched the boycott, was herself trained at Highlander Folk School and had longtime ties with the Southern Conference Educational Fund.

King held his political cards close to his sleeve. Several of his key advisors and many of his important followers had longstanding radical connections, but King restrained himself from making openly anti-capitalist statements until near the end of his life. He often confided to aides (and black intellectuals in particular) that he considered himself a socialist. These connections and sentiments did not

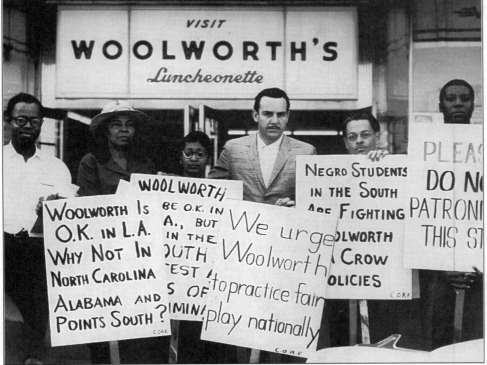

Both, Courtesy: Johnny Otis Collection

Disk jockey and Rock 'n Roll star Johnny Otis joins the lunch counter sit-ins in Greensboro, North Carolina, in 1960, and around the same time meets with Langston Hughes, whom Otis often acknowledged as his inspiration.

Highlander Folk School
Monteagle, Tennessee

The School for Southern Union Members
Endorsed by Leading Labor Unions

SUBJECTS: *What Southern Union Members Need to Build Their Unions!*

STEWARD TRAINING—The job of handling grievances: writing them up, preparing your case, presenting the grievance.

UNION PROBLEMS—Developing more union leaders — Building up attendance at meetings · Contract study — Negotiations — Union administration.

PARLIAMENTARY LAW and PUBLIC SPEAKING — Practice speaking — Presenting ideas clearly in union meetings — Rules of running a meeting — Setting up committees.

UNION HISTORY AND LABOR ECONOMICS — The story of the American Labor Movement — The fight for full employment and higher wages. — How corporations and monopolies work. — Anti-union weapons.

POLITICAL ACTION—Importance of 1946 election — Get-Out-The-Vote programs. Setting up union and community political action organizations.

LABOR LEGISLATION—The National Labor Relations Act — Social Security Laws — State Workmen's Compensation Laws — Current Bills labor is interested in, both federal and state. — Anti-Labor legislation.

PUBLIC RELATIONS—Working with Community Groups. — Use of Newspapers and Radio.

FALL TERM
Sept. 15-29, 1946

SPECIAL PROGRAMS will demonstrate how to build interest in union meetings. These programs will include union films, forums on current events, dramatic presentations of union problems, singing, and special speakers.

A center of civil rights education and a religious-based socialism from the 1930s onward, Highlander Folk School was a crucial institution for the movements of racial integration.

Highlander was also a natural target for redbaiting.

"prove" that King was a communist, as J. Edgar Hoover often insinuated in the government campaign to destroy the civil rights leader. They did suggest once more that black protest leaders turned instinctively to radicals for ideas and assistance. At the local level the alliance was usually more specific, older generations quietly supporting and tutoring new ones on the tactics of creating alliances and confronting the race codes of capitalism. [Plates 88-89]

Beyond the bus boycotts and the moral crusades of Dr. King lay the 1960 sit-ins at lunch-room counters where blacks could not be served, voting registration campaigns in dangerous Southern counties, and Northern campus campaigns to support Southern work. These events excited idealistic Americans of all races. The Student Non-Violent Coordinating Committee, which organized or led many of the movements, arose from student enthusiasm and unabashed radicalism. Against the advice of more cautious black leaders, S.N.C.C. openly cooperated with radical groups and made no secret that many of S.N.C.C.'s most courageous white activists were children of Communists or socialists. Like Andrew Goodman and Michael Schwerner, murdered in Mississippi, they were also likely to be Jewish. Indifferent to Russia, which seemed by this time another white world power, S.N.C.C. supporters were attracted to Cuba's romantic guerrilla hero Che Guevara or to African and other Third World revolutionaries. Stokely Carmichael, the charismatic S.N.C.C. spokesman born on the West Indian island of Trinidad, articulated a perspective of "Pan Africanism" or Black world solidarity across all borders. This was Black Nationalism.

Malcolm X, a former railroad worker and imprisoned petty criminal, made himself a foremost black radical. Enrolled in the Nation of Islam, or "Black Muslims," a sect with roots in the Garvey movement of the 1910s-1920s, Malcolm emerged from jail a brilliant speaker and skilled intellectual synthesizer. He gave a sense of race pride to black listeners burdened with great rage but limited education. Overnight, he had become a leading political personality. His lawyer, longtime Left activist Conrad Lynn, helped guide Malcolm's self-education toward the works of another great black intellectual, C.L.R. James.

After a trip to Africa in 1964, Malcolm X broke with the Nation of Islam, allying himself to civil rights radicals and Marxists. Martin Luther King, Jr., whom Malcolm had often attacked as overly moderate, issued a welcome to his former critic. A new Organization of Afro-American Unity (O.A.A.U.) emerged with Malcolm at its head. F.B.I. Bureau Director Hoover issued a command to disrupt or destroy the movement. Only a few months later, assassins gunned Malcolm down at New York's Audubon Ballroom. The trigger man came from a Muslim Mosque reputedly infiltrated by F.B.I. agents. *The Autobiography of Malcolm X*, co-authored by Alex Haley, later the screenplay author of television's *Roots*, became one of the best-read books of the 1960s. Its vivid recollections returned once more in Spike Lee's 1993 epic film *Malcolm X* — but minus the hero's late-life Marxist connections.

The African-American response to the assassination of Malcolm X, and to that of Martin Luther King, Jr., in 1968, was the outbreak of ghetto rebellions across most major American cities from 1965 to 1970. First in Watts, the one of biggest

Courtesy: Paul Richards

Julian Bond, young civil rights leader and later a Georgia state legislator, is today a prominent historian. Photo: Harvey Richards

Courtesy: State Historical Society of Wisconsin

Tom Hayden, in Newark Community Union Project (N-CUP), a Students for a Democratic Society local organizing venture.

Courtesy: Library of Congress

Ella Josephine Baker, shown here with leaders of the National Association for the Advancement of Colored People during the 1940s.

ELLA JOSEPHINE BAKER

A civil rights activist for fifty years, Ella Josephine Baker made her mark not so much as a public figure but as an activist, grassroots organizer, and guide to young politicized generations seeking their own way.

Born in North Carolina shortly the turn of the century, Baker grew up in a lower-middle class family, daughter of a waiter on a Chesapeake steamship. Her maternal grandfather, a former slave, a minister and community leader, was known for defying whites. Her mother tutored the children on speech, preparing Ella Baker as a debater. Not surprisingly, Baker graduated at the top of her class at Shaw College, a black school. She then moved to New York and quickly got in touch with the Left, attending many debates and demonstrations without joining any group. In 1930, she helped found, and directed, the Young Negroes Cooperative League which aimed to help blacks survive the Depression. By the middle 1930s, she coordinated a consumer education program of the Works Progress Administration in Harlem, and wrote for several African-American publications.

Her organizing talents and wide contacts served her well. In 1938, Baker became a field secretary for the N.A.A.C.P. (five years later, she rose to national director of branches). She often clashed with organizational officials' focus on a strictly legalistic strategy, seeking to make the N.A.A.C.P. more directly engaged in campaigns for racial equality and social justice. Among her foremost accomplishments, she helped train a generation of future civil rights leaders.

By the time that civil rights movement rose to national renown, Baker had long since resigned from the N.A.A.C.P. staff and organized other movements, including Parents Against Discrimination in Education. A trusted advisor to Martin Luther King, Jr., she traveled to Atlanta in 1957 to head the Crusade for Citizenship, a voter rights arm of the Southern Christian Leadership Conference. Struggling once more to de-centralize authority and empower ordinary activists, Baker recognized the student "sit-ins" as a potential turning point. A conference that she organized led to the formation of the Student Non-Violent Coordinating Committee (S.N.C.C.) and the historic "freedom rides" through the south. In turn, her work deeply influenced "Freedom Summer" and the launching of the Mississippi Freedom Democratic Party.

Closer to the end of her life, she joined the staff of the radical Southern Conference Education Fund, still later took action against the Vietnam War, and for the liberation of Africa from its neo-colonialist legacy. A generation of civil rights insiders knew how important she had been to many struggles; those outside rarely guessed.

Correspondence

To recognize, report and   serve the New Society

Wonder Where The
Young Folks Went
See Page 3

Vol. 6—No. 2   Detroit, Michigan, February, 1962   73   10c a Copy

Courtesy: Grace Lee Boggs

Correspondence, *a Detroit newspaper, featured stories about civil rights struggles north and south.*

Private Collection

The political agenda of the Civil Rights movement emphasized leaders and sometimes diminished the importance of rank-and-file participation. But the 1963 March On Washington was an emblematic event for ordinary people to organize, meet each other, and celebrate the strides made forward.

explosions of energy and conflict; then in Newark and Detroit, causing the most extensive property damage of any riots in U.S. history. Protesting inadequate public facilities (Watts, in Los Angeles, had no hospital and virtually no public transportation), police brutality and the general climate of prejudice and discrimination, these events had no main instigators or leadership. Yet radicals of all kinds worked frantically to educate the public about the civil insurrections, to provide assistance to victims, and to create, where possible, political alternatives to the existing system.

"Black Power" was the slogan of the day, adopted by S.N.C.C. and then made the operative ideology of the Black Panther Party for Self-Defense. Founded by two former students at Merritt College in Oakland, California, the Panthers were inspired by Malcolm X and determined to monitor the police who harassed and threatened community organizers. Essentially a paramilitary group merging Marxist and black nationalist impulses, the Panthers appealed to angry youths avowedly willing to die rather than go on living in submission. The organization also published *The Black Panther,* one of the best-read and certainly the most radical national newspaper of the African-American community. Among its editors was David DuBois, adopted son of W.E.B.

The Panthers had a short and bloody history. Men with violent and poverty-stricken backgrounds, they were easy targets for the federal COINTELPRO program which targeted their movement for disruption and destruction. In April, 1968, Oakland police invaded a residence of Panthers, killing the treasurer of the party and wounding leader Eldridge Cleaver. In September, Huey Newton, another key leader, was imprisoned on charges following a struggle and a shoot-out with Oakland police. In December, Chicago police entered a Panther apartment after midnight, and executed the unarmed local leaders in bed. By the end of the sixties, 28 Panthers had been killed outright and hundreds imprisoned on dubious charges — the most concentrated, violent repression of any political group in American history. Most of the remaining strength of the Black Panthers went into legal defense campaigns. When the Black Nationalist movement re-emerged in the 1970s, it was noticeably less radical and more purely racial.

Black radicals of every kind had successfully challenged white America to live up to democratic claims, propelled passage of the 1965 Civil Rights Act by Congress, and encouraged colleges to instate the most aggressive programs ever developed for recruiting minority students and encouraging black (also Chicano and Asian) scholarship. But, trapped by circumstances, black radicalism also tended often to collapse back in upon itself and implode the troubled personal backgrounds of its sometime heroes, like the fallen Black Panther leaders who returned to drugs or became garish conservatives. Worse, the black community had been deprived of its greatest leaders. Still worse, the rapid recovery of warfare-welfare liberalism allowed power-brokers in the Democratic Party, the labor movement and other traditional liberal institutions to deny remedies for centuries of wrongdoing by joining conservatives to insist that all minority radicals were now the real racists. "Freedom" was redefined downward from a great vision of a new society into the narrow vision of individual access to money, material goods and career opportunities. The next great interracial opportunity for a democratic leap forward awaited another day.

The progression of radical images, through the various civil rights and Black Power movements, is relatively easy to follow. From black-and-white handshakes to gun-wielding black male images marks only one dimension. The steadiness of white radicals' empathy marks another, changing less than the liberals imagined when they applauded civil rights demonstrations and then blamed the black family for urban poverty. White radicals took their lumps, sometimes from those whom they had taken for friends; but they made no mistake about the repressive intentions of business and the state. Publicists and documentarists using cameras, canvases and utterly vernacular media such as buttons, thus converged upon

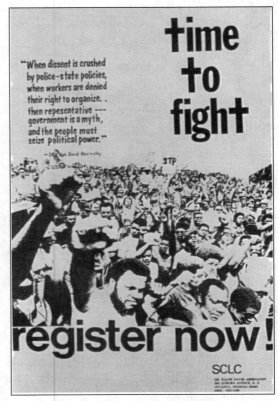

Originally a moderate vehicle for Martin Luther King Jr.'s campaign for racial integration, the Southern Christian Leadership Conference became radicalized (as did King himself), supporting the direct action of sit-ins and street demonstrations as well as voter registration drives.

common tasks. African-American political activity represented a long history of American society at large, a history which demanded recuperation and reinterpretation; black rage spoke for a deep resentment that often struck out mistakenly at wrong symptoms, but at its lucid moments transcended race and summed up a weariness at the sheer hypocrisy of a self-proud and self-involved nation.

Courtesy: State Historical Society of Wisconsin and Private Collection

Mississippi's Freedom Democratic Party contested white state rule. At the 1964 convention of the Democratic Party, delegates of the M.F.D.P. refused to accept the compromise of token representation offered them by New York Congressman Allard Lowenstein.

James Foreman's militant pamphlet, published by the Students for a Democratic Society.

Student Andrew Goodman (bottom) was martyred with James Chaney and Michael Schwerner in Neshoba County, Mississippi, June 21, 1964. Historian and popular orator Howard Zinn (top right) taught at Morehouse College in Atlanta, influencing future leaders of civil rights movements, before shifting to Boston University.

Illustration from a voter registration manual, Holmes County Chapter of the Mississippi Freedom Democratic Party, 1967. Drawing: Susan Lorenzi

Paul Robeson, his health shattered by 1965, had the respect of historical-minded activists in the new civil rights generation, although many young people hardly knew his name. Clifton DeBerry, Trotskyist and Black Power supporter, represented the new militance.

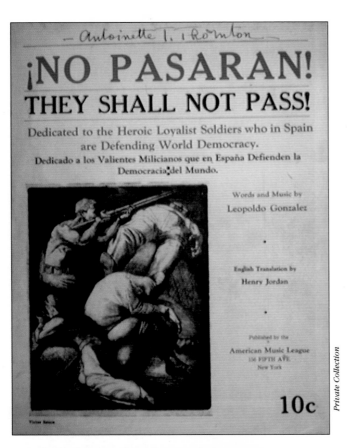

Sheet music and print: a sampling of material related to the vast array of publications, cultural activities and assorted American activity supporting Loyalists in the Spanish Civil War.

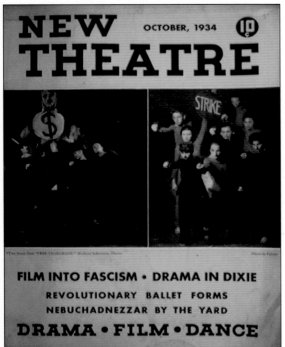

Popular publications of leftist theater repertory groups show a broadening of themes and approaches as the 1930s progressed. Workers Theater was succeeded by New Theater *and that by* Theater and Film, *which folded in 1937. Many of the outstanding artists of that day and later could be read or seen in the pages of these magazines.*

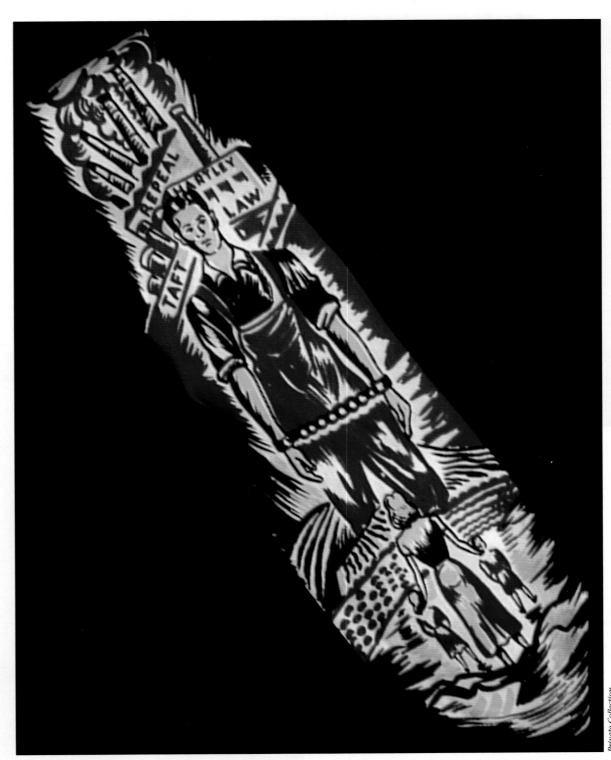

This necktie symbolizes an unhappy story for American radicals. The Taft-Hartley Act, passed by Congress over President Truman's veto in 1947, was considered a "slave labor act" by unionists. It barred unions with elected Communist leaders from using the mediation functions of the National Labor Relations Board. Many leaders disavowed their loyalties, but the AFL and CIO expelled all known Communist-led unions. A later Supreme Court decision dismissed the oath, but trade union momentum had been stopped cold, never to revive at the same pace. The Lion Cravat Corporation, c. 1948.

NEW LEFT NOTES

SDS · 1608 W · MADISON · CHICAGO · ILL·

VOLUME 2, NUMBER 27   let the people decide   JULY 24, 1967

NEWARK RIOTS – NCUP VIEWS

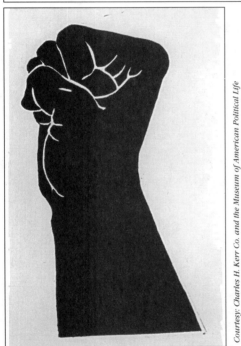

Courtesy: Charles H. Kerr Co. and the Museum of American Political Life

New Left Notes, *weekly newspaper of the Students for a Democratic Society, reports on the Newark Uprising. The stylized upraised fist was a symbol of black defiance and white radical support.*

Private Collection

Dick Gregory button and dollar bill. Gregory's humor and well-publicized fasts were an important contribution to the Civil Rights movement.

THE CRUSADER

NEWSLETTER

ROBERT F. WILLIAMS, Publisher   — IN EXILE —

VOL. 9 — No. 4   **MARCH 1968**

REACTION WITHOUT POSITIVE CHANGE

The short hot summers of '65, '66 and '67 came and went leaving the imprint of discontent and rebellion in their wake. As a result of the growing turmoil of these past summers, the power structure is reacting out of hysteria and is brutally applying the laws of the jungle as a solution to long standing social problems. The power structure reacts hysterically violent out of fear of any challenge to its authority and

Rev. Robert F. Williams, a prominent black minister, went into exile in Cuba and elsewhere after defending African-American armed self-defense against white violence.

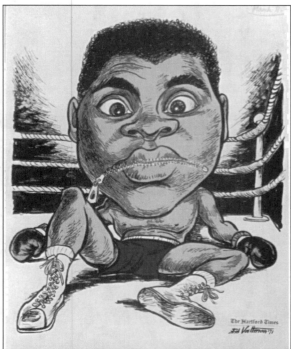

Muhammad Ali was a symbol of black militance and a target of resentment by many conservatives. Pulitzer Prize winner Edmund Valtman comments on his censure by the World Boxing Federation, in the Hartford Times, *March 11, 1971. Photo by Daniel Rosenberg*

Courtesy: Southern California Library

Whites offered political support for black radicals through electoral efforts like the Peace and Freedom Party.

Private Collection

Perhaps in a bid for national recognition, the California-based Peace and Freedom Party chose two nationally known figures as its White House nominees.

Photo and Courtesy: Richard Quinney

Defense of black political prisoners became a primary issue with the "dirty tricks" and legal attacks of the FBI, local "Red Squads" and state attorneys general on activists.

The martyred George Jackson, a federal prisoner and eloquent writer for the Black Panther Party, killed by San Quentin guards in 1971, is commemorated in the Black Panther.

Black Panthers Bobby Seale and Erica Huggins were the chief defendents charged with murder and finally exonerated in federal court in New Haven, Connecticut. The trial attracted great publicity.

Pursued and prosecuted for providing legal assistance to George Jackson, Communist historian Angela Davis became an international cause celebre. Drawing by Peggy Lipschutz.

Black workers took the leadership in local labor struggles of Detroit, through the League of Revolutionary Black Workers and in many short-lived coalitions. Their movement was quelled by the "downsizing" of the U.S. workforce.

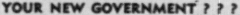

INDEPENDENCE AND SELF-DETERMINATION
United African Descendant's
People's Republic
PROVISIONAL GOVERNMENT
Prime Minister
Al Sultan Nasser Ahmad Shabazz

Have You Registered for Your
Citizenship Certificate in
YOUR NEW GOVERNMENT ? ? ?

Get off of
your Knees
you Noble
African
Descendants
People
and Act
Like Men -
You can
Accomplish
what You
Want!

"Says Al Sultan"

Al Sultan says: "Because of the African Descendants People's Evolution, There must be a revolution. since there must be a Revolution, there must also be a Revolutionary Party. The force at the core, leading our cause forward is the Ad Nip Party. The theoretical basis guiding our thinking is Black Nationalism. Without a Party built on Black Nationalism Revolutionary Style, it is impossible to lead the Block Masses of People to self determination and independence. Without the efforts of the Ad Nip Party. without Black Nationalism as the mainstay of Black People. The African Descendants can never achieve independence and liberation, or industrialization and modernization of a country of their own."

The Ad Nip Party is the core of leadership of the whole Black People. Without this core the cause of independence cannot be victorious. We must have faith in the Black masses and we must have faith in the Party. These are two cardinal principles. If we doubt these principles we shall accomplish nothing. It is up to us to organize our people. That which is not organized is not Civilized. The enemy will not perish of himself. The Party must carry the revolution through to the end.

JOIN THE BLACKGUARDS AND GUARDRETTES
BROTHERS AND SISTERS

911 Fillmore Street   San Francisco, CA. 94117
Phones: (415) 567-0268 – 346-9813

With the failure of radical politics, black nationalist styles and sentiments flourished in many parts of the African-American community.

Survivors: Ruby Dee and Ossie Davis, stars of stage, screen and television for more than three decades, did countless benefit performances for progressive causes and put themselves on the line for interracial movements.

Artists & Writers Revolt

THE "BEAT" LEFT

San Francisco, for a century an unusually literary and "wide open" town in many ways, gave birth during the 1940s-50s to an avant garde of poet, publishers, politicos and others who helped redefine American radicalism. In the decade or so after World War II, they published literary "little magazines" with a political kick, held poetry readings (with jazz backgrounds), and performed on listener-funded radio station KPFA.

A landmark development took place in 1953, when City Lights Bookstore was founded by poet Lawrence Ferlinghetti. Immediately, it became a gathering spot for anti-war artists, and with the coffee houses nearby, a center of poetic intensity. City Lights Books published Allen Ginsberg's *Howl and Other Poems* in 1956, to great public acclaim (for a year the publishers were attacked by legal authorities, who finally gave up after inadvertently setting a legal precedent that later allowed the publication of *Lady Chatterly's Lover* and *Tropic of Cancer*).

Among the avant-gardists many had sustained political connections. Ferlinghetti himself was an important poet and activist against the militarization of Americanization society. Diane DiPrima, granddaughter of an Italian anarchist, is easily the most important of the women "Beat" writers, an anti-war poet whose *Revolutionary Poems* in the later 1960s crossed the generation gap to thousands of young people. In later decades, poet-novelist Ishmael Reed founded the Before Columbus Foundation, a multicultural literary project with many Asian-American, Chicano and other radical participants. Nancy Joyce Peters, co-director of City Lights Books during the 1980s-90s, joined Philip Lamantia in the revival of the surrealist movement and publication of the journal, *Free Spirits*.

City Lights Bookstore when it opened in 1953 and in a 1982 reunion of bohemians around poet and City Lights founder Lawrence Ferlinghetti. Nicaraguan poet and Liberation Theologian Ernesto Cardenal is in the center with Ferlinghetti.

Artists and Writers Revolt

"Culture" had never been absent from the radical movements, and was often a defining feature of radical personalities. But never until the 1960s did culture occupy an unquestioned equal status with economics and politics. The youthful nature of the rebels had much to do with this development. But the continuing redefinition of what radicalism meant to society and the individual was central as well.

Cultural radicals often adopted an imagery intended to shock, to awaken America's sleeping conscience or simply to announce the presence of a new uncensored generation. Even when the political romanticization of Third World revolutionary movements, for instance, seemed to evoke an exotic force of total negation, artists at every level nevertheless attempted to rework existing popular cultural images, to play off current styles and advertising.

Diane DiPrima, leading female poet of the Beats, is seen here in 1986. Photo: Sheppard Powell

Courtesy: Diane DiPrima

Sweeping innovations demonstrated, ironically, that American radicals had turned to familiar images of all kinds to envision better, less destructive ways of living.

Outside the little bohemias in the major cities, cultural breakthroughs could be felt earliest in the popularization of radical-minded folk music. Echoes of Woody Guthrie continued in many singers, including the young and (as of 1962) still virtually unknown Bob Dylan. Idealistic youngsters yearned for a different life, for a world without war or racism, for more numerous and varied sexual experiences and soon for recreational drugs. The "Ban the Bomb" movement on a few campuses helped identify the likely political dimension, if not yet the various cultural possibilities. So did the appearance of local coffee houses, following an old Italian- and Jewish-American tradition of bohemian space with room for political conversation.

The broadening of a radical cultural-political milieu followed the rise of the civil rights and anti-war movements, and gave political meaning to a technological developments in the printing trade; especially tabloid newspapers with inexpensive "short runs" of 5,000 copies or less. In 1964, Art Kunkin, a former secretary to C.L.R. James, began publishing the *Los Angeles Free Press.* Within four years, around five hundred similar newspapers had taken their chance with local readers, achieving circulations ranging from a few hundred to many thousand each. Generally four to eight

Photo and Courtesy: Diana Davies

Bob Dylan, nee Bobby Zimmerman, from Hibbing, Minnesota, visited Woody Guthrie in the hospital, sang on street-corners, and became a bohemian-radical idol by the early 1960s.

pages, they reported what the commercial newspapers suppressed or misreported, from the escalating war in Vietnam to the deep culture clash between young people and their elders to the expanding networks of peace mobilization.

The "undergrounds" were revolutionary not only in content but even more so in form. Poems or single illustrations spread across entire pages, collages of various kinds replaced the wire service photo, and local illustrators (supplemented by reprints of many favorite artists with national reputations) had a field day. In many ways, the underground press thereby democratized illustration and layout of the radical publication generally. Veteran surrealist painter Jean Miro, among others, recognized the importance of the development, a mirror to the appearance of the *Masses* during the 1910s if not in fine art terms then in sheer proliferation of energetic and liberating image-making.

Among the most remarkable features was a rebirth of comic strips, far and away the most popular style of art in the U.S. for several generations. Walt Kelly's *Pogo* had already hinted at themes soon adopted, combining iconoclasm with a child's version of the world. *Mad Comics* under editor Harvey Kurtzman had during the early 1950s guided his artists as they lampooned McCarthyism and brilliantly dissected the commercialism of television, newspapers and comic art itself. But it was Gilbert Shelton, an Austin, Texas, history graduate school dropout (also friend of Janis Joplin) and sometime greeting card illustrator Robert Crumb who set the new pace of strips appearing in the underground press, and the new underground comic books first launched in 1968.

Courtesy: Ring Lardner, Jr.

Courtesy: Moberly Area Community College, Conroy Collection

(Left) Ring Lardner, Jr., one of film's finest writers, won Oscars for co-authoring the scripts for Woman of the Year *and* M*A*S*H *but was blacklisted for decades in between. (Photo by Mitzi Trumbo.) (Right) Jack Conroy, one of the most admired "proletarian" authors of the 1930s, remained active for a half-century as a midwestern leftwing speaker and writer.*

Ron G. Davis, founder of the San Francisco Mime Troupe, performing in "The Dowry" in Washington Square Park, San Francisco, in 1962, as Brighella from the Commedia dell-arte. *The Mime Troupe became an effective agit-propaganda group around anti-war activities in the later 1960s, and has survived as the most political-minded theatrical group in the nation. Photo: Erik Weber*

These comics (or "comix," as they were styled) mocked society's morals and manners, bemoaned the loss of earlier commercial styles, and generally tried to stretch the comic medium to its stylistic limits. On the explicitly radical-political side, *Radical America Comics* (published by Paul Buhle's *Radical America* magazine and edited by Gilbert Shelton) set a pace followed by ecological, feminist, and anarchist comics among others.

Feminists, here as in every other sphere of cultural activity, increasingly charted their own course. An older generation of distinguished poets, novelists, and illustrators recognized among young women the emancipatory urge they had only been able to evoke earlier among scattered individuals, and with often overwhelming opposition. Younger feminist artists took their creative options for granted and rejected the limited options usually open to them – even within many of the radical movements. The feminist rage but also the dignity, the explosive creative energy created still another radical press. Unlike the underground press itself, which was heavily harassed by government agencies and after 1972 dwindled into a commercialized "alternative" press, feminist outlets survived for a long time with their politics largely intact. Gay and lesbian culture, determinedly always at the cutting edge, had noted flashes of promise at the few open windows of an often fetid culture. Here and there

Literary counterparts of Black Power activists, younger poets Amiri Baraka (nee LeRoi Jones, center) and E. Ethelbert Miller (right) walk with cultural activist James Early on the Howard College campus in 1979. Photo: Nathaniel Harris

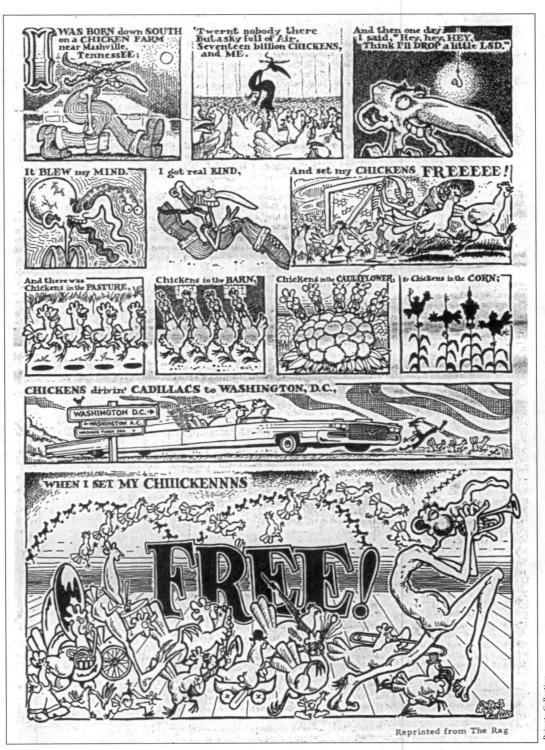

Gilbert Shelton drew comic figures such as the Furry Freak Brothers that made him famous for unique forms of political and social satire. From the underground newspaper Connections *(Madison, Wisconsin), 1967.*

feminist, gay and lesbian efforts exerted subtle influences upon mainstream popular culture in comic strips, television films, documentaries, feature films and even advertising. Too often, the radical edge had been dulled in the process.

Meanwhile, at the summit of media culture, echoes of older and newer radical currents could also be felt. The Hollywood blacklistees who survived often made a late-life comeback. Martin Ritt, blacklisted during the McCarthy Era as an actor, went on to direct *Sounder, Norma Rae* and the *Molly Maguires*. Walter Bernstein, scriptwriter for the *Molly Maguires*, also wrote such films as *Fail Safe, The Front,* and *The House on Carroll Street*. A spectrum of other 1960s-90s films and television which used anti-racist themes, was critical of big business, friendly to labor and protective of the environment. These efforts owed a great deal to the Hollywoodites' repressed and rediscovered tradition. Younger generations had their own unique contribution to make, from the inspired political television of the *Lou Grant* show and *Crime Story* to films like *China Syndrome, Missing, Silkwood* and *Wall Street* which addressed nuclear power and nuclear wastes, U.S. policies abroad, and the perpetual greed of the system's rulers, respectively. *Daniel* and *Matewan*, recalling the story of the Rosenbergs and the memory of militant labor, signalled that the process of collective memory would continue, even in the face of a sometimes far-rightward tilt in contemporary American politics. John Sayles, *Matewan*'s director, offered the best personal evidence in film after film that radical-realist styles of the past had a definite future.

Courtesy: Rudolf Baranik

Angry Arts, a political movement of mostly New York artists, is represented here by the work of Rudolf Baranik, Lithuanian-born abstractionist, former leftwing journalist and longtime activist. Baranik here reinterprets Picasso's "Guernica," in the depiction of the torture of war's civilian victims.

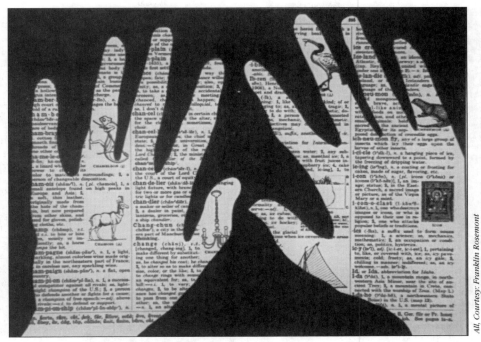

Collage by Franklin Rosemont.

An I.W.W. publication of the 1960s directed by youthful Surrealists.

A Surrealist manifesto.

Courtesy: Lorraine Perlman

Collage artist, writer, translator, printer and anarchist activist Fredy Perlman was an inspiring Detroit figure of the 1970s.

Private Collection and Courtesy, Jeff Goldthrope

Inspired by British-based Punk Rock, rebellious American musicians and artists forged new avant-garde styles in the 1980s. Some Left magazines publicized "Rock Against Racism," a political movement. Other activists tied punk themes into local events. "End of the World's Fair," a punk carnival was held in 1984 in San Francisco's Dolores Park.

MAC BIRD:
Expose him?

Illustrations by Lisa Lyons for Barbara Garson's play, MacBird, *widely performed Macbeth-style satire of Lyndon B. Johnson's accession to power.*

Generations of the Hollywood Left: Lionel Stander, the original "Hollywood Red" and Ed Asner, former president of the Screen Actors Guild, representing several generations of Hollywood progressives at a civil liberties commemoration sponsored by the Southern California Library in 1991.

The music goes on. Richard Flacks, a founder of SDS in the early 1960s, today is a disk jockey for a long-running show of protest music on the student-run radio station of the University of California-Santa Barbara. Photo: Wilfred Swalling

Vietnam

R. Crumb

Vietnam

The War in Vietnam was the longest armed conflict in American history. It was also, apart from the Civil War, the most divisive. It did not create the new radicalism of the 1960s, and in fact its effects may have destroyed the radicals' visions of constructive change. But it shaped a generational experience, of revulsion at military-technological overkill or science gone mad in chemical warfare and attacks on civilian populations. It effectively summed up a "Culture of Death" against which protesters tried to create or at least imagine a "Culture of Life." It propelled people from virtually every sector of American life, military personnel to grade school students, to raise their voices in calling for a halt to the carnage.

The newer peace movement began where the older peace movement left off. Its first voice was lyrical and anarchistic, the magazine *Liberation,* founded in 1957 by pacifists and socialists including Reverend A.J. Muste and urban theorist Paul Goodman, with the support of Lewis Mumford and others. Closer to the traditions of the 1948 Henry Wallace Progressive Party but unhierarchical in its structure and operation, Women Strike for Peace was founded in 1961, while a radioactive cloud from Russian atomic tests passed over the U.S. Concerned about the effects on children, and the prospects of nuclear war, more than 10,000 women in sixty cities abandoned kitchens and workplaces in an unprecedented one-day protest. Like *Liberation*, W.S.P. blamed both sides in the Cold War and excused neither: "No Tests — East or West" was their first major slogan.

By emphasizing powerful *men's* responsibilities for war, W.S.P. was able to legitimize its criticism of the Pentagon, and to brush off an attack from the House

The Free Speech Movement of Berkeley, University of California, 1965.

UnAmerican Activities Committee in 1962. "The quest for peace," W.S.P. insisted, was now "the highest form of patriotism." Newspaper headlines commented satirically on the latest witch-hunt, PEACE GALS MAKE REDHUNTERS LOOK SILLY. By 1963, then at its peak, W.S.P. had grown to perhaps half a million women. It lost steam with the signing of a test ban treaty that same year, but quickly reoriented around the war in Southeast Asia by emphasizing that the people of Vietnam were not the enemy, putting forward the slogan "Not Our Sons, Not Your Sons, Not Their Sons," and counseling young men about the draft. By 1970, W.S.P. had done much to place its own legislative chairperson, Bella Abzug, into Congress.

The wider Vietnam War protest began in 1963, as the South Vietnamese government began to disintegrate and went on a rampage of violence against its own citizens. Notoriously corrupt and kept in power only by U.S. support, the ruling Catholic clique was vehemently opposed by Vietnamese Buddhists. When Mme Nhu — wife of the head of the secret police and herself notorious for jeering the self-immolation of protesting Buddhist monks as "barbecues" — visited several U.S. campuses, crowds booed or carried signs. Only her sponsorship by the extreme "hawk," New York's Francis Cardinal Spellman, prevented embarrassing outbursts at Catholic colleges.

In 1964, President Lyndon Johnson escalated the military campaign that John F. Kennedy had begun. The number of U.S. servicemen in Vietnam reached 20,000 for the first time. In May, rallies against the war were held in New York City, San Francisco and several other cities, with crowds of a few hundred to nearly a thousand. An aged Norman Thomas was the main speaker in New York. Johnson ran for re-election by portraying his Republican opponent Barry Goldwater as hungry for war (Goldwater had threatened to use atomic weapons in Vietnam) and himself as a peace advocate. Activists wore buttons that read "Part of the Way with LBJ," a satire on the Democrats' official "All the Way with LBJ" slogan. Johnson won an overwhelming victory.

But protests exploded in 1965, when the promises of a search for peace turned out to be lies. In August, 1964, U.S. gun-ships cruising the shore of Vietnam claimed they had been fired upon. Using this pretext, President Johnson sent the first bombing raid on North Vietnam, and convinced Congress to pass the "Tonkin Bay Resolution," which many congressman later believed a deception and a guise for further escalations. Only two senators and one congressman voted against it. The Students for a Democratic Society (S.D.S.), a mildly socialistic group with historic roots in the pre-1920 Inter-Collegiate Socialist Society, called for a march on Washington during the Spring. Johnson began a major escalation of bombing in February, planning to salvage the unpopular South Vietnamese government through massive doses of U.S. military firepower. Tens of thousands of Americans were shocked into action.

The Bay Area and especially the Berkeley campus of the University of California had seen intermittent protests since 1960,

Courtesy: the Fifth Avenue Peace Parade Committee

Abraham J. Muste, an elder saint of the anti-war movement, seen here in his last years.

when a crowd of several thousand demonstrated against a local appearance of the House UnAmerican Activities Committee. In 1964, former civil rights activists in the South along with other kinds of campus clubs and societies, demanded political rights, especially the right to use university facilities for civil rights support work. The administration, with the inept assistance of campus and local police, provoked a peaceful confrontation which suddenly found civil rights activist Mario Savio addressing a hastily-gathered crowd from the top of a student-surrounded police car. The Berkeley "Free Speech Movement" with months of student strikes and demonstrations established the climate for university protest across the nation. Students could take stands on political issues, but they often linked those demands to campus issues, making them more real to fellow students. Berkeley became the natural organizing center for the Vietnam Day Committee of 1965.

Vietnam Day, May 21-22, 1965, attracted wide attention and large crowds in several locations. Novelist Norman Mailer addressed the Bay Area demonstrators memorably, challenging Johnson and predicting what was to follow:

Courtesy: Paul Richards

The use of napalm (jellied gasoline) bombs dropped indiscriminately upon Vietnamese civilians horrified many Americans, prompting demonstrations at factories making napalm. Photography: Harvey Richards

If we wish to take a strange country away from strangers, let us at least be strong enough and brave enough to defeat them on the ground. Our marines, some would say, are the best soldiers in the world. The counter-argument is that native guerrillas can defeat any force of a major power man-to-man. Let us then fight on fair grounds. Let us say to Lyndon Johnson, to monstrous Secretary of Defense Robert McNamara, and to the generals on the scene, "Fight like men. Go in man-to-man against the Vietcong. Call off the Air Force. They prove nothing except that America is coterminous with the Mafia. Let us win man-to-man or lose man-to-man, but let us stop pulverizing people whose faces we have ever seen." But, of course, we will not stop, nor will we ever win man-to-an against poor peasants. Their vision of existence might be more ferocious and more determined that our own. No, we would rather go on as the most advanced monsters of civilization, pulverizing instinct with our detonations, our State Department experts in their little bow ties, and our bombs.

Only listen, Lyndon Johnson, you've gone too far this time. You are a bully with an Air Force, and since you will not call off your Air Force, there are young people who will persecute you back. It is a little thing, but it will hound you... They will go on marches and they will make demonstrations, and they will begin a war of public protest against you which will never cease. It will go on and on and it will get stronger and stronger.

That public protest on a near-massive scale had already begun, with a demonstration in Washington on April 17 of a then-amazing 20,000 people, mostly students. Folk singers Judy Collins and Joan Baez, along with Senator Ernest Gruening, were the most famous figures on the platform. The protest had spread in an entirely different way, on the same day as the Berkeley events, with "Teach-Ins" at dozens of campuses. Sympathetic professors analyzed the war, especially the dubious government arguments for continuing the conflict. As the teach-ins continued into April, 1965, observers received another shock: 24,000 U.S. troops invaded the Dominican Republic, ostensibly to rescue a few dozen U.S citizens but actually to prevent a legal election from taking place freely. The State Department, which had planned to send in "Truth Teams" to refute the academics' criticism of them, gave up after one try. The Vietnam invasion was no exception or "mistake," as older radicals reminded young people, but part of a consistent historical pattern. Horror stories of C.I.A. activities around the globe gained new credence and large audiences through the underground press and even mainstream outlets.

Demonstrations continued to grow from 1966 through 1970, responding to continued escalations and rising casualties in Vietnam, the continuing draft calls to young men but also in response to the growing self-confidence of the "Movement" to make a difference in American life. The number of college students eager to demonstrate their dissent impressed the media and other observers, whether positively or negatively. Americans had never seen anything like it. But the diversity of other protesters added crucial elements of meaning.

There were, for instance, the anti-war personalities. Abbie Hoffman, former civil rights activist and founder of a craft store for Mississippi poor people's products, staged an event at the New York Stock Exchange in 1967 when he and his friends created chaos by hurling dollar bills from the visitors' gallery. Later that year he organized the first "Be-In," or peaceful, celebratory conclave of peaceniks, in Central Park. Dozens of these followed over that spring and summer. Founding the Youth International Party ("Yippies," more of a press release than an organization), he led a Festival of Life at the Democratic Party Chicago convention of 1968 and nomi-

Courtesy: Southpaw Books

From its founding in 1957 until its close almost a quarter century later, Liberation *magazine was a major voice for pacifism. Choosing non-violent resistance, its editors broke in 1965 with liberals who wanted U.S. forces to remain in Vietnam until successful completion of peace negotiations.*

nated a pig ("Pigasus") for president. Hoffman was fun, and continual copy for the newspapers.

Jane Fonda, daughter of actor Henry Fonda and well-known for her sexy role in *Barbarella* among other films, became "Hanoi Jane" in the eyes of her opponents. With former S.D.S. theorist (and future California state representative) Tom Hayden, she toured Vietnam to survey American bombs' damage, and conducted a U.S. tour opposing the war. Donald Sutherland, Paul Newman and Joanne Woodward, Robert Redford, Marlon Brando, Barbara Streisand and many other stars also expressed their absolute opposition to the war. Less glamorous but more respected than Jane Fonda, the "Baby Doctor" Benjamin Spock, a longtime crusader for peace, became the outstanding senior personality at peace rallies. Only Martin Luther King, Jr., who announced his opposition to the war in 1965, had earned more personal admiration from ordinary Americans.

But the most famous anti-war radical was neither an intellectual nor a film personality, but a sports champion: Muhammad Ali, reputed by many to be the best in the history of boxing (or as he put it "I'm the greatest.") Drafted in 1967 but converted to Islam, he refused, declaring "No Viet Cong ever called me 'Nigger.' " He had his crown taken away (much as Paul Robeson had been stripped of his audience), and Ali

This Oakland Induction Center demonstration in 1967 typified "direct action" against the war. Photo: Harvey Richards

Courtesy: Paul Richards

was denied fights for the likely best three years of his career. He gamely spoke at many anti-war rallies. He later regained the championship and stayed too long, unable to make up for lost time.

Below the celebrity level, groups like the Vietnam Veterans Against the War deepened the public perception of grass-roots opposition. From 1968, radical activists had opened coffee houses around military bases with entertainment and counseling (and unofficially, sometimes also marijuana) for servicemen. Almost fifty local newspapers sprung up, many written largely by G.I.s themselves, with titles like POW (its motto, "Every GI is a Prisoner of War") and *All Hands Abandon Ship.* Out of these activities and the growing disillusionment of G.I.s stationed in Vietnam grew a movement that rattled military brass — boldly uniformed veterans at the front of anti-war demonstrations, many in wheelchairs, some of them burning their citations and attempting to give back their medals. Ron Kovic, hero of the later film *Born In The USA,* was among the most famous. A group of more anonymous G.I.s changed their military life insurance policies to make the Black Panthers the beneficiaries.

The demonstrations culminated in Spring, 1970, after President Nixon had ordered an "incursion" (invasion) of Cambodia, setting off the collapse of the neutralist government and propelling the murderous Khmer Rouge to power. Millions demonstrated, National Guardsman fired on Kent State University demonstrators, killing four students (two of them only bystanders). Mississippi state police

The underground press typically mocked symbols of advertising as part of a society of war. From a particularly well-designed Madison, Wisconsin, paper.

fired wildly at students of all-black Jackson State College, killing more. Shock waves rolled over the nation.

En route to military defeat, U.S. forces showered more than a million acres of Vietnam with the herbicide "Agent Orange," defoliating and poisoning huge zones (and planting long-term hazards in G.I.s who were also exposed to the compound). Unknowingly or indifferently, the unprecedented scale of chemical warfare helped trigger environmental consciousness in social movements to come. In 1971, Nixon's "Vietnamization" program in effect abandoned America's clients. After still more murderous bombing, the Peace accords were signed, Saigon fell and the war was over.

Radicals, at the head of the anti-war column, had won their greatest victory since the organization of industrial unions, or perhaps since the freeing of the slaves. But what had they won? George McGovern, anti-war candidate for the presidency in 1972, was trounced by President Nixon. Nixon in turn was so caught up in the web of government conspiracy developed during the war that his crucial errors inspired the Watergate burglary and his fall into ignominy. But Democrat Jimmy Carter, who came to the presidency in 1976, had been an avid supporter of the war, and a vigorous proponent (after 1977) of an unprecedented military buildup. The "Vietnam Syndrome" nevertheless remained, more psychological than political but still a presence in American life. Not even the 1991 Gulf War, with easy victory over an unpopular foe, could restore blind faith in military adventures. That much had been accomplished by the friends of peace.

Vietnam also inspired an enormous output of artistic energy, more photographic in character perhaps than any event since the Second World War. The need to document the small gatherings of protesters growing into ever-larger crowds and finally

Student groups point to corporate connections and war complicity of the universities. The W.E.B. DuBois Clubs were a small outgrowth of the Communist Party, with strong interracial programs but little influence upon the New Left.

throngs inspired self-made camera artists like Harvey Richards, who stayed close to youthful demonstrators until mainstream television news teams gained the courage to do likewise. The anti-war posters of the day, often collages of horrifying battle scenes and strident demands for peace, reinforced the message that real people were dying in Vietnam and that Americans needed to look beyond the government-constructed images of a patriotic crusade against Communism. The next generation of documentary photographers, such as Ellen Shub, set for themselves the historic task of going beyond the increasingly glib "protest photos" circulated by the wire services, of following the irreducible diversity of progressive public expression, and capturing the individuality of the actors who made up the various crowds and gatherings, commemorations, demonstrations and celebrations, massive or intimate in size and character. In doing so, the photographers like the poster makers had indeed created a new art.

STRIKE FOR THE EIGHT DEMANDS STRIKE BECAUSE YOU HATE COPS STRIKE BECAUSE YOUR ROOMMATE WAS CLUBBED STRIKE TO STOP EXPANSION STRIKE TO SEIZE CONTROL OF YOUR LIFE STRIKE TO BECOME MORE HUMAN STRIKE TO RETURN PAINE HALL SCHOLARSHIPS STRIKE BECAUSE THERE'S NO POETRY IN YOUR LECTURES STRIKE BECAUSE CLASSES ARE A BORE STRIKE FOR POWER STRIKE TO SMASH THE CORPORATION STRIKE TO MAKE YOURSELF FREE STRIKE TO ABOLISH ROTC STRIKE BECAUSE THEY ARE TRYING TO SQUEEZE THE LIFE OUT OF YOU STRIKE

Harvard Strike Poster Spring 1969

Courtesy: Charles H. Kerr Co.

A student Strike poster becomes a form of art, at Harvard in 1969.

ESTABLISHMENT SOCIOLOGY KEEPING COOL IN A TIME OF SOCIAL CRISIS

'...BUT YOU SHOULD HAVE SEEN RODNEY BITING THE COP IN THE CALF...
AND HE NEVER LET GO!'

Courtesy: Lisa Lyons and the Museum of American Political Life

Berkeley cartoonist Lisa Lyons uses Picasso motif to poke fun at neo-conservative intellectual (and former socialist) Seymour Martin Lipset, a vitriolic opponent of the antiwar movement and of student activists in particular; Hartford Times *cartoonist Edmund Valtman offers his similarly conservative view of student protest.*

The most notorious and influential "black list."
Artists, musicians, entertainer, writers and scientists
were named along with their presumed un-American
activities. Counterattack also issued a monthly
newsletter. American Business Consultants; New
York, 1950.

May Day, 1951. Furriers union war veterans seek
to answer McCarthyism and the blacklist with
raw loyalty to Marxist and working class
traditions.

A family of civil libertarians: Roger Baldwin, a founder of the American Civil
Liberties Union, and his nephew William Preston, leading historian of repression
and a founder of F.O.I.A., Inc. (named for the Freedom of Information Act).

Color Page – 49

Courtesy: Southpaw Books

A colorful addition to personal stationary.

'Fight the Red Menace'; one card in a set of 48 subtitled 'Children's Crusade Against Communism' and issued by the Bowman Gum Co. in 1951. Shown here is a 'great American city' following a Reds's atomic attack.

Courtesy of the artist

"The Embrace," one of a series of paintings by Janet Walerstein Winston depicting the Rosenbergs in jail; oil on canvas, 1984.

Hugo Gellert's artwork, which had grown more and more stylized since his youthful Masses days, adorns the cover of a pamphlet by civil libertarian (and historic Communist leader) Elizabeth Gurley Flynn, c. 1952.

"Appeal of the Scientists," by Irving Fromer, referred to a worldwide Albert Einstein-Bertrand Russell campaign in 1955 calling for measures of survival in the atomic age. Charcoal on canvas.

Harry Belafonte was one of the most influential Black artists of the Civil Rights movement. He served as a negotiator for Martin Luther King, Jr., during King's frequent stays in jail, raised funds through concerts and participated in freedom marches.

"Young Blacks," by Robert Templeton, offered the new generation a view of young African-American leaders emerging out of the Civil Rights movement. Oil on canvas.

Collection of lapel buttons displaying events and personalities around the Black Power movement.

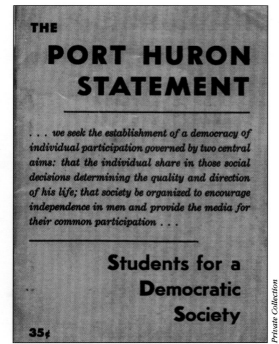

The Port Huron Statement, the basic political document of Students for a Democratic Society, was drafted by Tom Hayden among others and published in 1962. It stressed the importance of "participatory democracy" and launched the radical student movement of the 1960s.

Civil Rights issue of Studies On the Left, *the first of the "New Left" journals. Its leading figures included James Weinstein, Saul Landau, Tom Hayden, and historian Eugene Genovese.* Freedomways, *successor to Paul Robeson's newspaper,* Freedom, *was the leading African-American publication of the 1970s-80s, with contributors ranging from Ruby Dee and Alice Walker to John Killens, Lorraine Hansberry, Derek Walcott and C.L.R. James.*

Courtesy: Michael Rossman and the Aouon Archive

Poster stressing the importance of "Community Control," a popular demand of the African-American community for restraint of police behavior. Produced in Oakland, 1970s.

Courtesy: Maurice Jackson

Maurice Jackson, elected delegate to the Constitutional Convention for District of Columbia statehood in 1981. Jackson was the only Communist to have gained elective office since the 1940s.

Photo and Courtesy: Diana Davies

Phil Ochs, one of the pioneering political musicians of the younger folksinging generation, played hundreds of benefit performances and kept activists hopeful.

Private Collection

The third "underground" comic to be published and the first political one, RADICAL AMERICA COMIX was edited by Gilbert Shelton, creator of the "Fabulous Furry Freak Brothers," and distributed as a 1969 issue of Radical America, edited and published by Paul Buhle.

Courtesy: Charles H. Kerr Co.

Surrealist dancer Alice Farley continued the tradition of Isadora Duncan into the 1970s-90s.

Courtesy: Harvey Pekar

Harvey Pekar, who would later appear on (and be banished from) the Letterman Show for denouncing General Electric for its military-industrial connections and ownership of the NBC television network, began publishing the multi-ethnic, blue collar Cleveland American Splendor in 1976.

Courtesy: Spain Rodrigues and Jay Kinney

Back page of Subvert Comics, *1970, written and drawn by Spain Rodriques, one of the most politically-minded artists during the 1960s-90s; and cover of* Anarchy Comics, *1980, edited by Jay Kinney and Paul Mavrides. Both comics are highly satirical of the traditional ideas of revolution as well as of the system that anarchists strike to replace.*

Color Page — 56

ON THE WALL

#2

DON'T GET BUSTED TWICE

Two people were arrested on Wells Street Sunday for putting up "Handwriting" They posted the paper without taking any special precautions. Charges were disorderly conduct— *released on bond.*

When you go out to post the paper, don't go at night. If you knew the city, *or under less-militarized conditions,* it might be easier or safer to hang paper then; here, given the instructions under which cops are operating, it should be suicidal. You could be "mistaken for a looter" and shot. And it could go harder on you without bystanders around if you're caught.

During the day, though, keep off main streets— Wells, Clark, North, et cetera are all heavily patrolled, and the traffic on those streets is so thick that you often can't spot approaching squads.

Side streets, with much less traffic, give you a lot more time.

The faster the method you use for sticking them up, the safer you'll be.

Both thumbtacks and paste seem to take a long time. (Wide) packing tape is quicker. Staple-guns are ideal if you can get them (!).

The people on the streets of the community took a great interest in the paper. As soon as it was posted, groups gathered around to read it. This kind of medium is really good for getting real news around the city in the most immediate way, and making it clear what's going down.

Be careful, though, when you're posting "Handwriting".

The Red Squads in all major cities have briefed the cops here on activists from their areas.

DON'T GET BUSTED TWICE, NO MATTER WHAT FOR!

Be cautious, but remember that the point of caution is not to stay innocent, but to stay active. Good guys don't get caught.

NEWS MEDIA

Their newspapers/TV/radio talk about news blackout in Chicago right now. *Media blackout: no live TV outside the Convention, rumors about no mobile trucks or cameras allowed in the streets and all the other choking "restrictions" that go with "security"* Cronkite and Severeid compare Chicago with Prague. Cool. *See something about not having covered real USA before, naked power.* Liberals outraged— talk of defying restrictions and all that jive; see the power we've lived with all along being used against them for the first time maybe. *Truth is in the air. They may, finally, have petty reasons— these professional men with their professional working arrangements and relations and deals getting fucked over— but still,* the truth we knew all along is in the air.

What do we think? Many things:

(1) That the news blackout in Chicago isn't surprising. It is only a logical extension of the concentration camp that Chicago has become. More than that, Chicago and USA have always been concentration camp/armed garrison,

only revealing themselves concretely to many people in certain situations. So there's nothing surprising in all this, only confirmation.

(2) That this situation is dangerous for us. Direct TV eliminated, less liberal outrage against the mercenary *violence of the pigs, or the manipulated fear of National Guard/Regular Army faced with their own people. No record, no cameras— we're in the street and the pigs are all around us. Got to watch your ass and lay good plans. Black* is up against it all the time. Got to begin to practice for the time when we don't have *much liberal space to move in.*

"Liberal outrage": wasn't ever much to count on; was unhealthy to protect *ourselves with. We're learning not to beg,* so we act accordingly.

(3) That we ought to think about possible *relations with the established media during this Chicago time.*

There is no "free access to information" in USA and there never has been. *There is* "free access" for those who pay: who agree, who are "objective", who play the right games. But now, Chicago/Daley and

ruling *structures local and national have* hampered "free access" even to those paying members of the club who have always played the game acceptably. The stakes were high enough this time. (Why ?)

OK. So repression has been extended— probably just for this week— to another group in the society. As they feel that weight we got something to talk to them about. *When people feel the heat we know about—* the truth about USA— then you can start to talk.

Could talk about media organization alot. How it's broken up into parts: boards and presidents, liberal program directors and front men, union crews. Each one another problem, each one situated differently in the society. But there isn't time to talk about that now. We got things to do.

The main thing. You're going to see TV and reporters on the streets, in Movement centers, wherever there's any action. They're going to come to you. And we can move on them, we can push; because right now the truth about USA is all oozing up through the asphalt. Not soft/subtle/sly obsequious talking, but a hard line. How are they going to put-up now?

BLACKOUT

SATURDAY NIGHT FIGHTS

The cops and the Yippies held field maneuvers Saturday night in Old Town in preparation for the big confrontation Sunday. The cops, and the motorists on North Wells, lost.

The confrontation started about 10:30 p.m. when pigs began massing on the east side of Lincoln Park, apparently ready to charge if the singing, chanting crowd didn't split by the 11 p.m. curfew. Teams of plainclothes cops in nervous *survival* groups of six to eight circulated on the fringe of the crowd, while SDS and Yippie people tried to figure out what to do.

Suddenly a police van moved into the crowd, and the pigs busted one Yippie. The crowd lost its cool for a minute, kids began to run, but soon settled down to moving slowly out of the park to the west.

But the pigs weren't prepared for what happened next: The crowd split, only to re-form a few minutes later on North Clark, and began streaking straight toward North Wells, the main drag of Old Town, Chicago's attempt at a West Village. (One smaller group lined up on the sidewalk, facing a line of advancing cops, shouting "Red Rover, Red Rover, send Daley right over!")

Traffic was heavy on North Wells, *and in five minutes the crowd, joyfully circulating through and down the middle of the lines of stalled cars, had everything at a total standstill.* Yippies and SDSers quickly passed out all their NLN and began shouting "Stop the Democratic Convention." *The motorists seemed puzzled, amused;* only a few honked. Crowds soon massed on the sidewalks from the cafes, and many young kids with McCarthy stickers joined

the street mill-in. No cops at all showed up for half an hour.

The only cops to arrive hit the main intersections and split up the crowd, a few of whom quickly shot down side streets to re-form on North Wells several blocks up. The cops busted one or two Yippies at the intersections, but were unable to deal with the main Yippie crowd, which would melt into the sidewalk crowd as pigs appeared near them.

The Yippies suffered from their disorganization, and only a few were together enough to systematically outflank a few of the pigs at the main intersections. But the possibility of successful traffic tie-ups in an area where other crowds made heavy busts impossible was proven. The streets of Old Town belonged to us Saturday night, and it wasn't just rhetoric.

On The Wall, *SDS wallposter created for the tumultuous 1968 Democratic Party convention in Chicago.*

Soldier-protesters and Vietnam Veterans Against the War, California, early 1970s. These demonstrations dramatized, as perhaps no others as well, that only the upper levels of the military establishment continued to support the war In Vietnam. Photography: left, Tony Velez; right, Harvey Richards

Courtesy Harvey Richards and Tony Velez

Mock 'Search and Destroy' mission, by New Jersey Vietnam Veterans Against the War. Photography, Tony Velez

The cases of these soldiers at Fort Hood and Jackson became major media events. Ted Richards' "Dopin' Dan" cartoon strip was popular with soldiers themselves.

Courtesy: Fifth Avenue Peace Parade Committee

"Flowers for Graves" and "In the Teeth of War," New York City demonstrations against the war in the 1960s.

Courtesy: Marge Frantz

Courtesy: Fifth Avenue Peace Parade Committee

The famous and the obscure: Poet Allen Ginsberg leads New York anti-war demonstration. Emma Gelders Sterne, founder of the San Jose Peace Center during the 1950s is arrested for draft board obstruction in 1965.

Courtesy: Women Strike for Peace

Women Strike for Peace declares its solidarity with the women of Vietnam, c. 1970.

Courtesy: Anita Hoffman

Abbie Hoffman meets a friendly crowd after being accused of conspiracy, in the aftermath of the demonstrations at the 1968 Democratic Party convention in Chicago.

ABBIE HOFFMAN

Clown prince of the 1960s radical movement, Abbie Hoffman responded insightfully to the problem of being heard in the age of the mass media. He offered young people provocative ideas — some of them silly or thoughtless, but many of them helpful — to put their own imaginations to work in protest against the Vietnam war and the militarization of American culture.

Born in 1936 in Worcester, Massachusetts, to a lower middle class Jewish family, Hoffman was thrown out of high school for a fight with his English teacher. But he went on to Brandeis University, then unique for its radical teachers. He graduated in 1959, a devotee of Abraham Maslow's psychology of self-transformation. Soon after, Hoffman became active in the civil rights movement, and a few years later in the movement against the War in Vietnam. Struck by the rebellious energy of young people, he created an identify for himself as the foremost cultural rebel, radical wiseguy and unpredictable activist. In 1967, Hoffman and his friends threw dollar bills from the visitors gallery into the New York Stock Exchange, inviting chaos and ridicule of money-madness.

That summer, Hoffman organized "be-ins" at Central Park, a descendent of the civil rights "sit-ins" but without any express purpose except for young people to "be" (have a picnic, smoke marijuana, play musical instruments and sing or dance) together. In October, as 50,000 demonstrators surrounded the Pentagon to protest the War, Hoffman led a playful chant to lift the building from its foundations and "exorcise" its obvious evil from the American spirit. While oldtime radical politicos regarded Hoffman as an embarrassment and his self-publicization as an affront to the difficulties of political mobilization, Hoffman seemed to bring out crowds that no one else reached with any political message.

His followers were "hippies," a name supplied by the angry "hipsters" or low-class bohemians who regarded intellectuals and middle class teens with suspicion and disdain. On New Year's Day, 1968, Hoffman and his side-kick Jerry Rubin proclaimed themselves "Yippies," or members of the (largely imaginary) Youth International Party, *i.e.*, politicized hippies. Their street mobilizations led up to the "Festival of Life" in Chicago during the 1968 Democratic Party convention. While official candidate Hubert Humphrey proclaimed his enthusiasm for continuing the Vietnam War and police clubbed protesting delegates along with street kids, Hoffman nominated the porker "Pigasus" for president and invited arrest by scrawling a four-letter word on his forehead.

Hoffman helped discredit Cold War Democrats in the eyes of many observers, although Richard Nixon seemed the immediate political beneficiary of the chaos he stirred. Prosecutors charged Hoffman along with other activists as the "Chicago Seven." During the trial, Hoffman claimed to be the illegitimate son of Judge Julius Hoffman and cursed him in broken Yiddish for selling out Jewish morality. Hoffman beat the rap and wrote several very popular books including *Revolution for the Hell of It* (1967), *Steal This Book* (1971) and *Vote!* (1972). Arrested on drug charges, he spent a decade "underground," much of it as an environmental activist, emerging in the 1980s as a seasoned anti-war veteran. His suicide in 1989 did not surprise his friends, who knew that he had suffered from severe depression most of his adult life.

Photography and Courtesy: Diana Davies

Pete Seeger and Tom Paxton singing at an anti-war rally in Washington, D.C., late 1960s.

AN

INTRODUCTION

OUR STRUGGLE IS JUST COMMENCING

Courtesy: Charles H. Kerr Co.

INSTANT NEWS SERVICE

1703 GROVE, BERKELEY   841-6480
COURTESY: PEOPLE'S PRESS SYNDICATE

| Special Issue No. 1 | Page 1 | Sunday, May 25, 1969 |

CHEMICAL WARFARE IN BERKELEY

"... CS should not be used in a training or field exercise area where it may drift downwind into civilian communities..." - From Department of the Army Field Manual 21-48.

THERE ARE FIVE KINDS OF CHEMICAL RIOT CONTROL AGENTS USED IN BERKELEY IN RECENT MONTHS, AS CAN BEST BE DETERMINED BY PERSONS TREATING THE INJURED: 1) CS TEAR GAS, 2) CN TEAR GAS, 3) NAUSEA GAS, 4) BLISTER GAS, AND 5) MACE.

This article discusses the ways each agent is dispensed, its properties, its symptoms, treatments and protection. The article is based on an interview with Chuck McAllister, coordinator of the medical first aid groups in Berkeley and member of the Medical Committee for Human Rights (MCHR).

===== GENERAL STATEMENTS =====

Be aware that the police are using some canisters that blow up in your hand when you try to pick them up... Do NOT use vaseline for any gas because gas adheres to vaseline and causes more severe burning; vaseline CAN be used for mace, which is a liquid (see below)... A rubber gas mask is an ideal protection against any gas EXCEPT nausea gas (see below)... Wet paper towels can be used for breathing more easily with any of the gases... Surgical masks, which are good protection against the two tear gases (CS and CN), can be picked up at the Free Church, 2200 Parker, or from a medic... Do NOT rub your eyes after being gased or maced but DO carry and use eye drops... Do NOT try to get gas or mace off your face with soap because it might run and get in your eyes, irritating them further... THE LONG-TERM EFFECTS OF GAS AND MACE ARE NOT KNOWN.

| CS TEAR GAS |

CS gas is the form of tear gas which has been so widely used this quarter during the People's Park crisis. The first known use in Berkeley was in the last days of the Third World Liberation Front (TWLF) strike last quarter when it was sprayed from pepper fog machines. Prior to that time, it is believed that only the milder tear gas, CN, was used.

Dispensing. The gas comes in various kinds of canisters, in plastic grenades, in pepper fog machines; it is also sprayed from helicopters.

Properties. CS is a very heavy, potent tear gas which contains burning and nausea agents, in addition to normal tear gas agents. CS, along with blister gas, is a fat soluble gas with a peppery smell.

Symptoms. Harrassing sting, nausea, reddened exposed area, burning feeling, tears, runny nose, tightness, coughing, and in some cases sneezing.

Private Collection

An SDS Pamphlet marks the Left's optimism at the end of 1970. A local bulletin issued in Berkeley warns against the force likely to be used on demonstrators.

Private Collection

Anti-war images old style. An often reprinted cartoon of the middle 1960s from a famous iconoclastic magazine published by Paul Krassner (a close friend of comedian Lenny Bruce) places the planet as female victim.

A feminist celebrity against the Vietnam War: Jane Fonda speaks out at Columbia University, 1972. Photograph by Charles Rivers.

Courtesy: Robert F. Wagner Archives, New York University (Charles Rivers Collection)

Movements of Liberation

R. Crumb

Movements of Liberation

The movements of "Life" against death were given the name "Liberation": Black Liberation, Brown and Red Liberation, Women's Liberation and Gay Liberation, to name only several with roots in the 1960s. Behind the slogans, these movements and others hinted at something larger than "freedom" described as political participation; something more like emancipation from the collective burden of social pressures and prejudices, allowing free individual as well as group expression.

Mexican-American (or Chicano) movements first demonstrated the multiplicity of the anti-racist struggles. Cesar Chavez, leader of a dramatic grape boycott and of the United Farm Workers, symbolized and even personified, for a time, a larger community movement. Others caught the public eye only briefly outside the Southwest. The Crusade for Justice (founded in Colorado by poet-boxer Corky Gonzalez), *El Partido de la Raza Unida* in Texas, and the 1966 seizure of former Indian land in New Mexico by the *Alianza Federal de Mercedes* also marked a new day. So did the high-school strikes or "Blowouts" of Chicano youths against the War in Vietnam. And so did the engaged and increasingly radical sympathy of many priests, nuns and Catholic lay people for Mexican-Americans' plight.

The Chicano movement in turn helped ignite two other key developments at the very end of the 1960 and early 1970s. A new generation of Asian-Americans, historically among the most quiet and therefore most endangered minorities, took both to the streets and to scholarship of "people's history" to assert themselves. Like other minori-

It hurts to see our offices destroyed, but the power of our UNION can never be destroyed. The heart of our movement is LIBERATION, and it is in the love of liberation that we are reborn...

CESAR CHAVEZ

Courtesy: Abner and Mimi Diamond

A larger-than-life figure almost equal to that of Martin Luther King, Jr., Cesar Chavez symbolized the Chicano political coming-of-age. Drawing by Peggy Lipschutz.

ties, they felt compelled to defend their communities and also challenge the traditional ruling groups which had historically collected federal patronage in return for keeping the communities quiet. Over the long run, cultural activities more than political ones defined the main moves of radicalized Asian-Americans, but occasionally groups of them played key roles (as in the Jesse Jackson's 1988 nomination campaign).

More spectacularly, Indian rights activists combined to battle police brutality and to demand better opportunities on and off the reservations. In 1969, mostly younger, urban-raised Indians occupied Alcatraz Island in San Francisco Bay, a dramatic move. Three years later, a national caravan dramatized the "Trail of Broken Treaties" and ended in an occupation of the Bureau of Indian Affairs. Documents captured during this occupation revealed mismanagement and massive corruption. The American Indian Movement (A.I.M.) seized world attention when it assisted the Oglala Sioux at the Pine Ridge Reservation to oppose strip mining in the Dakotas. A massive military task force directed from the White House, including armored personnel carriers and Phantom Jets, subsequently staged the largest-scale attack on any domestic "enemy" since the Civil War. In the resulting fire fight, two F.B.I. agents died and A.I.M. leader Leonard Peltier was arrested for murder. Suppressed evidence, coerced or false wit-

Courtesy: Paul Richards

The example of the mostly Chicano grape workers inspired Filipino agricultural workers into action in Delano, California. This photo of Dolores Huerta is one of the most famous images of agricultural workers' struggles. Photos: Harvey Richards

Parts of the Catholic Church including many priests supported the Chicano crusade for social justice, while others resisted progressive stands. Meanwhile, farm workers issued their own publications.

nesses and a fabricated murder weapon marked his trials. The F.B.I. has stubbornly refused to open 6,000 pages of secret testimony, but Amnesty International has cited an "admittance of guilt" by the Bureau in the death of 66 Lakota citizens. In July 1994, supporters staged a 3,800 mile Walk for Justice and rallied at Washington's Lafayette Park to demand amnesty.

Federal efforts broke the back of A.I.M. as they did the Panthers, through a remarkable combination of harassment, surveillance and frame-ups engineered by agents infiltrating the movement. But a new sense of empowerment was backed up by legal claims to traditional lands, many of them repatriated in the courts during the 1970s-80s as a consequence of earlier direct action. During that time, leaders of Indian peoples and frankly left-wing intellectuals like Ward Churchill asserted their role as the original American environmentalists, with their own distinct philosophy of conservation.

Young and mostly white middle class Americans developed during the 1960s another, very different notion of liberation. The philosopher Herbert Marcuse's famous volumes, *Eros and Civilization* (1955, reissued 1966) and *One Dimensional Man* (1964) made him what *Time* magazine called the "guru of the New Left." He successfully identified repressive structures within modern society in general, not merely in the economic system. Cerebral youngsters determined to break out of the dominant structures looked to his writings for guidance.

Many identified these changes first of all with the "sexual revolution" which freed men and women from many traditional constraints. It was born contradictorily, from a combination of newly available birth-control technology (especially the "pill"), relatively prosperous and leisured young people, and an all-out advertising campaign for consumer products predicated on the nexus of youth and eroticism. Things changed rapidly with the blossoming of campus and near-campus neighborhood "Youth Culture," in which anti-war sentiments, marijuana and relatively casual sex (or serial monogamy) seemed concomitant if not interchangeable. The underground press characteristically presented political messages in heavily coded sexual terms.

The anarchist-minded Detroit rock group MC5, which helped launch a small "White Panther Party," for instance, sought to base itself on working class youth by playing up the message of "sex, drugs, rock 'n roll" as the appealing, popular answer to the conservative patriotism and business values of the over-30 crowd. Other enthusiasts of youth culture attempted to present a softer picture of sweet-eyed innocents at "be-ins" or teenage girls placing flowers in the barrels of National Guard rifles. Yet even here the sexual aspect was never entirely missing. The hippie girl as "Earth Mother" of the renewed utopian colony or "commune" evoked images of pastoral simplicity, unfettered by the sexual norms of her mother's generation.

Such images gibed poorly with a generation of young women better educated and entering work-roles more ambitious than any before them. Like the anti-draft struggles that cast women into "support" roles (one S.D.S. slogan of 1965: "Girls Say Yes to Boys Who Say No"), the hippie roles seemed demeaning to many women. By 1966-67, a handful of women with a strong background in the southern civil rights movement (where black and white women, lacking the prestige of their male counterparts, nevertheless ran local offices and frequently made key decisions) began to speak out. Borrowing terms from black liberation, they called their budding movement "Women's Liberation."

These women from the New Left styled themselves against radical men who had oppressed them, the society at large, and also against the liberal feminist movement. Betty Friedan, author of *The Feminine Mystique* (1963) had helped organize the National Organization for Women, urging political action at the highest national levels. In fact, on the urging of Women's Bureau head (and former radical labor organizer) Esther Peterson, President Kennedy created the President's Commission on the Status of Women, and in 1963 Congress passed the largely symbolic Equal Pay Act, as well as establishing Title VII of the 1964 Civil Rights Act with the formal if nominal illegalization of discrimination in employment. But these measures made little actual impact on most women's lives. Besides, women's liberation movement enthusiasts wanted an open, egalitarian tendency utterly opposite the stiff bureaucratic workings of NOW and the federal government.

Instead, the women's movement was based in highly localistic activities and in "consciousness raising" (or CR) groups, which described the process of collective truth-seeking among women talking among themselves about their lives and relationships. Sharing problems that most had seen as individual, they came to new understandings and often the determination to take action. Writer Carol Hanisch coined the phrase "the personal is political," to break down the artificial barriers between "personal" life and "political" activity. From courthouses to workplaces to bedrooms, they insisted, the sources of power had to be confronted and could be confronted by determined women. They dramatized that sensibility through protests at the 1968 Miss America pageant in Atlantic City, crowning a sheep and hurling into a "freedom trashcan" the objects of "female torture" including cosmetics, hair sprays, girdles and copies of *Ladies*

Private Collection

Ironic commentary on a traditional anti-communist slogan, by an Indian activist. From Ramparts Magazine, *1970.*

WILLIE FRANK

Involved nearly a century for the cause of his Nisqually tribe in the state of Washington, Willie Frank, Sr., died in 1983 at the age of 104. His father, Klckesuh, had been present at the signing of the Treaty of Medicine Creek in 1854 and fought in "Leschi's War" the next two years against its provisions. Their rebellion brutally suppressed, the Nisqually gained better reservation privileges. In 1887, as the reservation Nisqually were declared American citizens, young Qu-lash-qud was sent to live at a Catholic boarding school and he changed his name to Willie Frank. He returned at the turn of the century, to care for the dwindling and diseased tribe. In 1915, as soldiers illegally enlarged a nearby military base, Frank used his share of a financial settlement to buy a homesite. He quickly made it the center of continuing resistance: "Frank's Landing."

By the middle 1930s, he joined with others in establishing a new self-government under the Indian Reorganization Act. Repeatedly, he fended off government efforts to keep the Nisqually from catching salmon off-reservation, and he rebuilt the tribe from a virtual point of disappearance. In 1961-62, the media declared a "new Indian war" had broken out in the region. By that time, he guided the formation of the Survival of American Indians Association (S.A.I.A.) with Frank's Landing as its headquarters. A central figure in the 1970 documentary film, "As Long As the Rivers Run," Willie Frank built a school to teach children Indian ways. At his death, Seattle activists declared that "Grandpa" had taught Chicano and African-American activists to share and protect natural resources.

Willie Frank Soto.

Courtesy: Roxanne Dunbar Ortiz

Leonard Peltier, frame-up victim from a federal shoot-out against the Oglala Sioux and leaders of the American Indian Movement at the Pine Ridge Reservation in 1973, remains America's foremost political prisoner.

YOUNG LORDS PARTY
13 POINT PROGRAM
AND PLATFORM

TENGO PUERTO RICO EN MI CORAZON

YLP

THE YOUNG LORDS PARTY IS A REVOLUTIONARY POLITICAL PARTY FIGHTING FOR THE LIBERATION OF ALL OPPRESSED PEOPLE

1. WE WANT SELF-DETERMINATION FOR PUERTO RICANS, LIBERATION ON THE ISLAND AND INSIDE THE UNITED STATES.

For 500 years, first spain and then the united states have colonized our country. Billions of dollars in profits leave our country for the united states every year. In every way we are slaves of the gringo. We want liberation and the Power in the hands of the People, not Puerto Rican exploiters. QUE VIVA PUERTO RICO LIBRE!

2. WE WANT SELF-DETERMINATION FOR ALL LATINOS.

Our Latin Brothers and Sisters, inside and outside the united states, are oppressed by amerikkkan business. The Chicano people built the Southwest, and we support their right to control their lives and their land. The people of Santo Domingo continue to fight against gringo domination and its puppet generals. The armed liberation struggles in Latin America are part of the war of Latinos against imperialism. QUE VIVA LA RAZA!

3. WE WANT LIBERATION OF ALL THIRD WORLD PEOPLE.

Just as Latins first slaved under spain and the yanquis, Black people, Indians, and Asians slaved to build the wealth of this country. For 400 years they have fought for freedom and dignity against racist Babylon. Third World people have led the fight for freedom. All the colored and oppressed peoples of the world are one nation under oppression. NO PUERTO RICAN IS FREE UNTIL ALL PEOPLE ARE FREE!

4. WE ARE REVOLUTIONARY NATIONALISTS AND OPPOSE RACISM.

The Latin, Black, Indian and Asian people inside the u.s. are colonies fighting for liberation. We know that washington, wall street, and city hall will try to make our nationalism into racism; but Puerto Ricans are of all colors and we resist racism. Millions of poor white people are rising up to demand freedom and we support them. These are the ones in the u.s. that are stepped on by the rulers and the government. We each organize our people, but our fights are the same against oppression and we will defeat it together. POWER TO ALL OPPRESSED PEOPLE!

5. WE WANT EQUALITY FOR WOMEN. DOWN WITH MACHISMO AND MALE CHAUVANISM.

Under capitalism, women have been oppressed by both society and our men. The doctrine of machismo has been used by men to take out their frustrations on wives, sisters, mothers, and children. Men must fight along with sisters in the struggle for economic and social equality and must recognize that sisters make up over half of the revolutionary army: sisters and brothers are equals fighting for our people. FORWARD SISTERS IN THE STRUGGLE!

6. WE WANT COMMUNITY CONTROL OF OUR INSTITUTIONS AND LAND.

We want control of our communities by our people and programs to guarantee that all institutions serve the needs of our people. People's control of police, health services, churches, schools, housing, transportation and welfare are needed. We want an end to attacks on our land by urban renewal, highway destruction, and university corporations. LAND BELONGS TO ALL THE PEOPLE!

7. WE WANT A TRUE EDUCATION OF OUR AFRO-INDIO CULTURE AND SPANISH LANGUAGE.

We must learn our long history of fighting against cultural, as well as economic genocide by the spagiards and now the yanquis. Revolutionary culture, culture of our people, is the only true teaching. JIBARO SI, YANQUI NO!

8. WE OPPOSE CAPITALISTS AND ALLIANCES WITH TRAITORS.

Puerto Rican rulers, or puppets of the oppressor, do not help our people. They are paid by the system to lead our people down blind alleys, just like the thousands of poverty pimps who keep our communities peaceful for business, or the street workers who keep gangs divided and blowing each other away. We want a society where the people socialistically control their labor. VENCEREMOS!

9. WE OPPOSE THE AMERIKKKAN MILITARY.

We demand immediate withdrawal of all u.s. military forces and bases from Puerto Rico, VietNam, and all oppressed communities inside and outside the u.s.. No Puerto Rican should serve in the u.s. army against his Brothers and Sisters, for the only true army of oppressed people is the People's Liberation Army to fight all rulers. U.S. OUT OF VIETNAM, FREE PUERTO RICO NOW!

10. WE WANT FREEDOM FOR ALL POLITICAL PRISONERS AND PRISONERS OF WAR.

No Puerto Rican should be in jail or prison, first because we are a nation, and amerikkka has no claims on us; second, because we have not been tried by our own people (peers). We also want all freedom fighters out of jail, since they are prisoners of the war for liberation. FREE ALL POLITICAL PRISONERS AND PRISONERS OF WAR!

11. WE ARE INTERNATIONALISTS.

Our people are brainwashed by television, radio, newspapers, schools and books to oppose people in other countries fighting for their freedom. No longer will we believe these lies, because we have learned who the real enemy is and who our real friends are. We will defend our sisters and brothers around the world who fight for justice and are against the rulers of this country. QUE VIVA CHE GUEVARA!

12. WE BELIEVE ARMED SELF-DEFENSE AND ARMED STRUGGLE ARE THE ONLY MEANS TO LIBERATION.

We are oppose to violence - the violence of hungry children, illiterate adults, diseased old people, and the violence of poverty and profit. We have asked, petitioned, gone to courts, demonstrated peacefully, and voted for politicians full of empty promises. But we still ain't free. The time has come to defend the lives of our people against repression and for revolutionary war against the businessmen, politicians, and police. When a government oppresses the people, we have the right to abolish it and create a new one. ARM OURSELVES TO DEFEND OURSELVES!

13. WE WANT A SOCIALIST SOCIETY.

We want liberation, clothing, free food, education, health care, transportation, full employment and peace. We want a society where the needs of the people come first, and where we give solidarity and aid to the people of the world, not oppression and racism. HASTA LA VICTORIA SIEMPRE!

Proclamation of Puerto Ricans in the Young Lords Party, influential in Chicago and New York during the early 1970s.

Home Journal. (Contrary to newspaper reports, no bras were actually burned.)

Feminist newspapers, magazines and pamphlets added a fresh spirit to American radicalism. Periodicals with titles like *It Ain't Me Babe, Off Our Backs* and *No More Fun and Games* published sprightly manifestoes, ample poetry and lots of male-directed humor. *Oob* appealed in its first issue for women to "oppose and destroy the system that fortifies the supremacy of men while exploiting the mass for the profit of the few" (adding, defensively, that "our position is not anti-men but pro-women.")

Feminists also addressed current political issues. A "Jeannette Rankin Peace Brigade," named after the congresswoman who voted against U.S. entry into both world wars, formed the first all-women section of a major Washington demonstration in 1968. Twenty thousand rallied in New York, and thousands more across the country, on the fiftieth anniversary of the passage of the woman suffrage amendment, demanding round-the-clock childcare centers, abortion on demand and equal opportunity. Socialist feminists, many active in the several dozen "Women's Liberation Unions" around the country, sought to interpret the ways traditional or New Left socialist ideas of class and race oppression would have to be modified or transformed to encompass women's experience. The lively dialogue helped frame Women's Studies courses and curricula in colleges and universities, but many women's groups themselves disintegrated with the political retrenchment of the late 1970s and early 1980s.

Gay Liberation had a different, more complex connection with American radicalism. The first important homosexual-advocacy group, the Mattachine Society, was founded in Los Angeles in 1951 by Harry Hay and several other American Communists. Mattachine arose in response partly to the severe anti-homosexual climate of the early 1950s, as hundreds of homosexuals were dismissed from federal employment, while the FBI along with the Civil Service Commission and the Post Office, tracked down potential offenders. But Hay and others intended more than a civil liberties organization. Their manifesto urged a "new pride...in participation in the cultural growth than social achievements of...the homosexual minority." After authorities seized the Mattachine Society's magazine, *One,* more conservative elements took over the organization. But in a sense, gay radicalism had been launched.

The growth of openly homophile groups, institutions and neighborhoods as part of the "sexual liberation" sentiment of the late 1960s reintroduced a rappochment between gays and radicals. Some feminists claimed "Feminism is the Theory, Lesbianism is the Practice," and sleeping with men was a way of affirming the power of the system over everyone's lives. Gay men and lesbians increasingly formed their own contingents at anti-war demonstrations, and for-

The beloved philosopher of eros, Herbert Marcuse was a favorite author of the 1960s. Photo by Isolda Ohlbaum.

mulated the slogan "Gay is Good" following "Black is Beautiful" as an emblem of pride rather than pleading for society's acceptance.

The Stonewall Riot of 1969, a crowd counterattacking the usual police harassment at a Greenwich Village gay bar, is considered a turning point of militancy. The election of San Francisco city supervisor Harvey Milk in 1977 (Milk was later murdered by a homophobic city official) holds similar symbolic significance for gay electoral politics. Milk's political successor, Harry Britt, was a prominent figure in the socialist movement nationally. By the 1970s and 1980s, radical or avant-garde publications like the *Village Voice* boasted of their large gay readership. The fight against demonization of AIDS victims and for a cure, as well as the continuing fight for full civil rights of homosexuals, became radical causes that Democratic presidential candidate Jesse Jackson adopted enthusiastically in 1988, and liberals increasingly accepted into their platforms. The twenty-fifth anniversary celebration of Stonewall in 1994 brought perhaps a quarter-million to Manhattan for an unforgettable display and restatement of the movement's radical aims. Its remarkable array of images, like the gay and lesbian movement itself, could not be returned to the closet.

Courtesy: Lee Baxandall

Bohemianism of the early 1960s renewed the vision of sexual liberation. Brecht translator and playwright Lee Baxandall joins future feminist historian Rosalyn Baxandall on a Paris jaunt in 1960.

Youth Culture of the later 1960s merged at points with political commitment. West Coast Socialists hurried to keep up with the excitement.

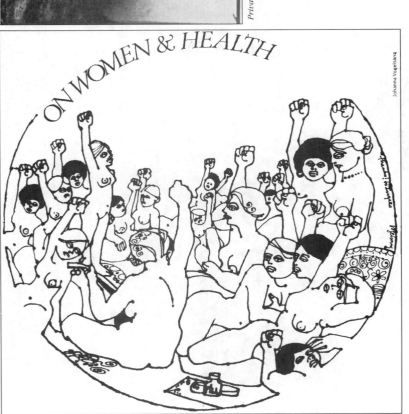

Sometimes called the "New York Times of the women's movement," and published from 1970 to the present, Off Our Backs *offered a central perspective of American feminism. It also offered a sharp criticism of male-centered "youth culture."*

Young Boston enthusiasts of Women's Liberation, Judith E. Smith and Noel Jette, c. 1973.

Courtesy: Annette Rubinstein

Literary critic and editor Annette Rubinstein has been an important intellectual in the Left for fifty years.

Courtesy: Photo and credit, Richard Bermack

Tillie Olson, a promising young writer in the 1930s proletarian literature movement, brought a literary heritage of the Left to feminist readers.

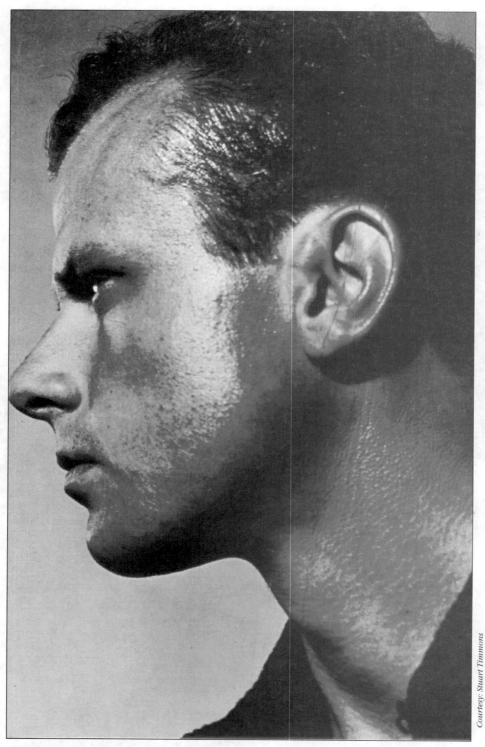

Courtesy: Stuart Timmons

Harry Hay, a founder of the Mattachine Society and a Communist during the 1940s and early 1950s, carried a Left messsage into the gay movement. He has remained an important progressive figure in Los Angeles. Photo: Le Roi Robbins

The International Socialists published their own Gay newsletter from Berkeley, seeking to bridge the political gap and to educate socialists.

Photo and Courtesy: JEB

"Ladies Against Women" sparked a variety of satirical feminist demonstrations against Far Right nuttiness during the 1980s.

Photo and Courtesy: Ellen Shub

Photo and Courtesy: Ellen Shub

Two popular singers on the Left. Holly Near (left), progressive musician and lesbian activist in concert in Boston, for a nuclear free future, October, 1982. Tracy Chapman (right), folksinger and activist in concert in Boston, 1994.

Maggie Kuhn, a founder of the dynamic Gray Panthers movement for senior citizens, died in 1995.

Female CETA employees demonstrate at New York City's Department of Employment, Lower Manhattan, 1980, against discrimination in employment programs.

Courtesy: Marge Frantz

Liz Roettger, senior Gay supporter, California 1980s.

Supporting Movements Abroad

"Phasers on 'kill,' Mr. Spock!"

Lisa Lyons

Supporting Movements Abroad

The support movement which arose in the later 1950s and developed over the course of the 1960s-80s is related to previous impulses of radical anti-racism and anti-imperialism, but also different in certain fundamental ways. It has, first of all, been directed mainly, if by no means entirely, toward the Americas, toward peoples held under the thumb of U.S. clients rather than the victims of European fascism. It has also been "faith based" more proportionately than any previous radical movement since abolitionism. More uniquely yet, it has been powered or assisted by radical factions, such as the Maryknolls and sections of the Jesuits, within a mostly conservative-dominated American Catholic community. And it has involved the "temporary migration" or tours of political duty by thousands of U.S. citizens abroad through various peace, human rights and rebuilding projects in Central America, Haiti, Mexico and a scattering of other locations.

The support movement for South Africans began as early as the 1940s and found various movements and organizations to carry on. American churches, civil rights activists, and many progressive artists aided the struggle that the persecuted radicals of the McCarthy Era, like W.E.B. DuBois, had done so much to launch. By the 1960s-70s, more liberal organizations took up the challenge, as anti-apartheid activists insisted upon a boycott of South African athletics and divestment of corporate and university funds. By the 1980s, TransAfrica, led by Randall Robinson, added pressure to sanctions. Still, for decades the U.S. State Department and the Central Intelligence Agency (and many other Cold War strategists, including leading officials of the A.F.L.-C.I.O.) had bitterly opposed the African National Congress. Indirectly supporting the apartheid government and its proxy wars against the A.N.C.'s allies across Southern Africa, at an enormous cost in human lives, they compelled humane observers to take opposing and radical positions.

Nelson Mandela's visit in 1992 to the United States excited mass enthusiasm and grudging acceptance of his great moral role. With the end of the Cold War, the long struggle took another turn, and even Americans who had despised the ANC now claimed to have aided him into democratic leadership of a transformed nation. Radicals had played a major part in compelling America to live up, after generations of delay, to some of its stated ideals.

The Latin American- and Caribbean-oriented movement began during the 1950s with support for exiled Cubans

Courtesy: Van Pelt Library, University of Pennsylvania

Waldo Frank, literary modernist and unconquerable romantic, wrote important books on Latin American life and culture from the 1930s-50s. He was, near the end of his life, an important early, if critical, supporter of Fidel Castro's Revolution. Seen here c. 1920.

who prepared to overthrow the dictator Fulgencio Batista. Congressman (and Reverend) Adam Clayton Powell, Jr. from Harlem, who had been active in support of Henry Wallace, made himself a spokesman for these progressive Cuban-Americans. After Fidel Castro and his supporters toppled Batista and the U S. government made noises about arming a counter-revolution, a Fair Play for Cuba Committee took shape as an amalgam of progressive Cuban-American and various American radicals. The organization itself was conducted largely by the Socialist Workers Party (dogged loyalists of Leon Trotsky's political legacy). Conservatives' accusations of treason and persecutory investigations by congressional committees crushed the F.P.C.C. shortly after the failed Bay of Pigs invasion and the Cuban missile crisis.

For most of the decade, progressive political energies on international affairs focused on Vietnam. But Caribbean immigrants and others protested the U.S. invasion of the Dominican Republic in 1965 to prevent a fair election, and the North American Congress on Latin America (N.A.C.L.A.) opened its doors in 1966 with the quiet support of major Protestant denominations.

The politics of Vatican II meanwhile reinforced those Latin American bishops who complained at the suffering of their peoples and who rejected State Department and CIA plans to crush radicals. The Missioners of the Maryknoll Fathers, thrown out of Guatemala for favoring the anti-government forces, became a key early force for the practice and theory of Liberation Theology. The Maryknolls' press, Orbis, went on to publish some of the most important radical books of the 1970s-90s.

Puerto Ricans living in the United States also publicized the colonial condition of their homeland, sometimes with impressive support for independence (Jane Fonda, Holly Near and even a young Geraldo Rivera spoke at a Madison Square Garden independence rally in 1974). The Puerto Rican Solidarity Committee, whose National Board included Ella Josephine Baker, Rev. Benjamin Chavis (later a controversial Director of the N.A.A.C.P), and poet-activists Corky Gonzales and Amiri Baraka became for a time a vital national movement.

The U.S.-guided overthrow of the Allende government in Chile in 1973 with a fascistic bloodbath of civilians, and the rise of right wing "death squads" in the U.S.-backed regimes of Guatemala, El Salvador and Nicaragua prompted another range of support activities. The overthrow of U.S. client Anastasio Somoza in 1979 and the emergence of a revolutionary Nicaraguan government solidified strategies aimed at both congressional lobbying and direct aid to embattled peoples. Committees by the dozens visited troubled Central America to see for themselves the conditions of the poor. A large variety of organizations raised funds and volunteers to build schools and provide various types of assistance, from food to medicine. As many as two thousand local groups brought hundreds of thousands of people into action during the 1970s-80s.

The electoral loss of the Sandinistas (under

Courtesy: Radical America

C. Wright Mills, radical sociologist, wrote Listen, Yankee! *(1962) about the U.S. role in Cuba, shortly after the failed Bay of Pigs invasion.*

massive U.S. military and economic pressure) and the end of the guerrilla war in El Salvador brought new strategies and problems for U.S. support movements. Now they had to find new ways to assist groups struggling for a political role in the post-Cold War climate. The plundering of natural resources by international corporations, for instance, and the expanded use of U.S.-manufactured pesticides, pointed to the importance of defending village women's demands for a clean environment. The threatened extermination of Indian peoples guilty only of occupying valuable oil lands recalled shadows of the Holocaust. In Mexico and Brazil, popular radical parties made up of workers movements, with the backing of women's movements and environmentalists, faced powerful U.S. interests. The need for regional solidarity among radicals and the growing presence of Latin Americans in the United States brought the first glimmerings, by the middle 1990s, of the configurations yet to come. American radicals took up their positions against U.S. business and intelligence agencies' support of political repression, toxic exports, and deforestation.

Haiti and Chiapas already pointed toward the post-Cold War future and to the radicals' response. When U.S. trained military leaders overthrew Haitian President Jean-Bertrand Aristide and C.I.A. officials declared him unfit to return, it seemed yet another, extremely familiar incident in history of the Caribbean basin ("the American lake"). But Aristide, although bitterly opposed by Vatican conservatives, was himself a formidable spiritual force for Liberation Theology in the region. And this time, hundreds of thousands of new immigrants to the United States — Haitians speaking their

Courtesy: Harry Magdoff

Harry Magdoff and Paul Sweezy. *Editors of* Monthly Review, *forefathers of Third World support movements and among the most important American Marxist intellectuals of the 1950s-90s.*

own Creole language, and numerous if deeply impoverished in various cities — felt toward their nation's legitimate leader as U.S. socialists had felt toward Eugene Debs. Support demonstrations, lobbying, and the work of radical religious organizations kept the spirit of religious and secular solidarity alive. Longtime American backers of the A.N.C. added an important an-ti-racist element in support of Haitians, the first slave people to successfully overthrow New World rulers. No one knew what the future held for the Haitian immigrant community or for the explosive Caribbean island.

Similarly in Chiapas, among the Indian peoples of Mexico, a long history of abuse climaxed in the reverse of land reforms and the dread promise of the North American Free Trade Agreement (N.A.F.T.A.) era with its wholesale replacement of subsistence farming with a vast, toxified agribusiness. A carefully articulated armed uprising in 1993, after the era of guerrilla warfare had presumably ended, recalled the persistent energy hidden in long-repressed cultures. American radicals would learn, if they were wise, how to understand the sources of these energies as the newest but also very old voices of the Americas. For the moment, they scrambled to make first-hand information available and to assist the embattled peasants in every way possible.

Courtesy: Van Gosse

American students return from Cuba and Albert Mahan speaks at an airport press conference, August 14, 1964. The support movement for the Cuban Revolution helped to create a basis for a genuinely New Left. Photo: Jamie Huberman

Courtesy: Southpaw Books

A protest against US troops invading the Dominican Republic in 1965 in order to prevent the legal election of a left-leaning nationalist, Juan Bosch.

In this process they would be educated in every sense by the new patterns of inter-locking culture and language spreading with the growing diaspora. Radical leaders from Latin America and the Caribbean were no longer strangers or mere occasional visitors to U.S. shores. Radical journalist and former Shakespeare teacher Tim Hector from the impoverished little island of Antigua, for instance, not only made frequent speaking tours to the United States but had a significant portion of the readership there for his weekly Caribbean newspaper, *The Outlet*. Similarly, calypso music and costumes, long a major folk art of the Caribbean and the avenue for political content, could be seen and heard in Brooklyn-based festivals each year, just as reggae and salsa had become a permanent part of the national music scene. Famed radical calyp-sonians Black Stalin and Chalkdust, like Jimmy Cliff and Bob Marley in another era, had many thousands of devoted fans and careful listeners here. In the same sense, Hector's columns on Caribbean politics, art, music and sports events and the *Outlet's* revelations of a C.I.A.-linked regional drug trade were part of the weekly lives of immigrants and scholars. People like him helped unify the radicals of the Americas.

The visual possibilities introduced by wide contact with Latin peoples in particular had a marked impact upon the entire range of radical iconography. A large number of key artists and poster-makers in previous movements had also been born abroad and maintained a lively interest in artistic impulses of their homeland (usually Eastern Europe). But rarely had previous artistic groups reorganized themselves in U.S. cities (as several groups of Latinos did in the Bay Area, for instance) with the intent of

Courtesy: Roxanne Dunbar Ortiz

Collage photo of Roxanne Dunbar, a leader of the Women's Liberation Movement and a supporter of Vietnam's National Liberation Front, 1968. Collage: Jean Louis Brachet

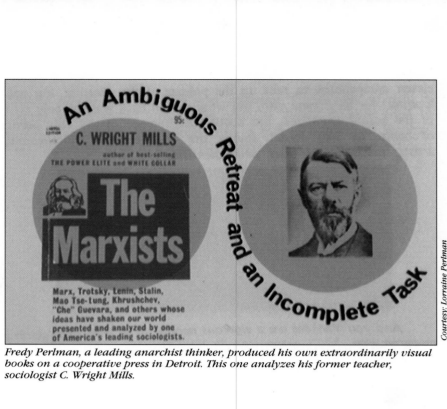

Courtesy: Lorraine Perlman

Fredy Perlman, a leading anarchist thinker, produced his own extraordinarily visual books on a cooperative press in Detroit. This one analyzes his former teacher, sociologist C. Wright Mills.

Private Collection

A selection of lapel buttons displaying slogans and touting organizations opposed to the War in Vietnam. The green center button is probably the earliest.

The struggle around the International Hotel in San Francisco's Chinatown rallied the Asian-American New Left, at its peak during 1970-1972, to fight for their neighborhood and struggle for their own unique identity.

Women's Liberation sheet music, 1970.

Wendell, *a comic written and drawn by progressive gay activist Howard Cruse, the editor of* Gay Comics, *the first of the genre.*

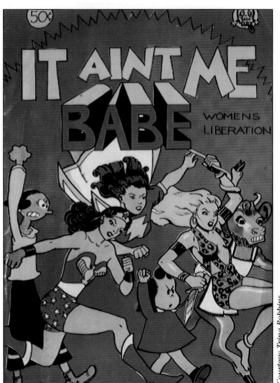

Two notable covers of "underground comix" produced by women artists and editors. It Ain't Me Babe *(1970), was the first of the genre and was the brain-child of Trina Robbins (daughter of a prominent Yiddish-language cultural and labor activist).* Tits and Clits Comix #3 *(1977), is part of a series of avowed sexual explorations of women's experiences and interests.*

The "Divest Now" poster from the Fireworks Multimedia
Collective (San Francisco and Los Angeles) in 1985 was
strictly literal in its message.

This educational comic commemorates the victims of
U.S. global policy and in particular the suffering of
children (seen through their own art).

Noam Chomsky, the foremost radical critic of U.S. foreign policy
during the 1960s-90s, has one of the most controversial writers
on international issues anywhere. Father of "generative
grammer" in linguistics, he transformed himself from an Ivory
Tower intellectual to a kind of underground figure of resistance,
despised by the Establishment while adopted by political rock
groups as the basic sources of accurate information.

developing political and popular graphic materials specifically based upon homeland traditions.

The revolution in poster-production at the end of the 1960s seemed perfect for the needs of this new generation, and the swift rise in Latin populations gave the poster makers many opportunities for commercial work. Indeed, for the first time in American radical history the creative output of poster-makers probably exceeded the pace of organizing and in some measure made up for the organizational weaknesses of contemporary Left politics (where small groups furiously attempted to compete with each other for political space) and a stagnant ideology. This development reflected, too, the changing role of the printed publication within lower class sympathizers of Left causes. In past generations, the printed word had been the great unifier, and the daily or weekly newspaper the heart and soul of the radical immigrant movement. In the television generations with disintegrating public school systems, the word ceased to have this kind of magic. Newspapers and newsletters continued to have an irreplaceable importance. But music and pictures carried a larger part of the message.

Radical or revolutionary versions of modernism had been seen on a small scale as early as the middle 1960s in magazine covers of *IKON* and assorted avant-garde publi-

Fund-raiser event poster, Bay Area. Produced anonymously in 1968, this poster was expressive of black cultural nationalism but nevertheless influenced in design of lettering and image by contemporary rock-dance posters.

Photo and Courtesy: Ellen Shub

During the 1980s, local networks of activists provided sanctuary for victims of U.S.-sponsored governments in Central America. Federal authorities often attempted arrests and sometimes succeeded. "Estella," Salvadorian trade unionist fleeing from persecution, gives testimony, April, 1985.

cations in sympathy with current Cuban artwork. Puerto Rican political art, in a distinct but parallel trend, shaped the similarly modernistic agitational images of the *Independistas* in New York and Chicago. The movements of the 1980s multiplied the number of available images a hundred-fold and emphasized a folk-art element in composition but especially in the use of vivid colors. Partly the work of newer immigrants and partly of sympathetic Americans, this work drew heavily upon traditional designs of Latin American peasant societies, themselves undergoing near-revolutionary change. For perhaps the first time in radical art since the nineteenth century, Christian themes of suffering and redemption could be restated directly in images of crosses and crucifixion of martyrs.

Conrad Lynn, civil rights attorney (and former lawyer for Malcolm X), was a keen critic of the imperial mind. Here, he reads between the lines of the neo-conservative Commentary *magazine, on* Paper Tiger Television, *produced by Deedee Halleck for syndicated cable showings.*

Courtesy: Paper Tiger Television

Courtesy: Robert F. Wagner Archives, New York University (Charles Rivers Collection)

Demonstration for democracy in Chile, 1973, after the Central Intelligence Agency and the U.S. State Department arranged the military overthrow of elected president Salvatore Allende. Photograph: Charles River.

Michael Harrington, former Catholic Worker and author of The Other America *(1962), was later in his life a leading figure in the Socialist International. The S.I.'s strongest member parties were in Western Europe and one of its weakest in the United States, Harrington's own Democratic Socialists of America. Pictured here in 1975 with (and photograph courtesy of) Anne Lipow.*

Witness for Peace demonstrations symptomized the spiritual influences on the Left. This one, in 1984, marked perhaps the apex of Liberation Theology's political influence within the U.S.

American Indian activist William Means and Nobel Prize winner
Roberta Menochu, supporters of international human rights movement.

Photo and Courtesy, both: Roxanne Dunbar

Brian Willson: His legs ripped off in a California demonstration to prevent shipping of
military equipment to US-supported thugs in Central America, Willson becomes a symbol of
self-sacrifice during the 1980s.

Healing the Spirit

Healing the Spirit, Healing the Earth

The collapse of social movements during the 1970s left an enormous emotional vacuum in the lives of hundreds of thousands of idealists. Their hopes of changing American society in a fundamental way had been thwarted. They had helped to halt the U.S. war on Vietnam and thereby saved hundreds of thousands of lives. They could not stop what intelligence agencies called "low intensity conflicts," murderous wars from Latin America to Africa to Asia which took no American lives and evoked little popular interest. Many activists felt discouraged or simply exhausted. But some sought new ways forward.

The most important, by far, was environmentalism. The dominant socialistic movements of the 1920s-40s, organized labor and the Communist Party, had by and large lost interest in the visions of nature that previous radicals had believed to be the hope of cooperative society. However, at the fringes of the radical movements, another spirit had survived. Local activists, for instance, had been quietly engaged in projects to defend working people and the poor from hazardous dumps and to defeat or restrain the misdirected commercial "development" which turned green space into concrete nightmares.

Meanwhile, the publication of a famed radical-conservationist text, socialist Aldo Leopold's *Sand County Almanac* in 1949, dramatized the long-standing efforts of two socialists, Benton MacKaye and Robert Marshall, for a radicalized conservationism. They criticized what Marshall called "civilization remote from nature, artificial, dominated by the exploitation of man by man," and hailed "the freedom of the wilderness." Marshall's *Arctic Village* (1933) was a best-selling recollection of a year in the Alaskan mountains and the happiness of the people that he encountered. His *The People's Forests* (1933), the first classic of socialist conservationism, demanded the socialization of wilderness to protect it from the depredations of private greed. MacKaye and Marshall joined in 1935 with two collaborators to create the Wilderness

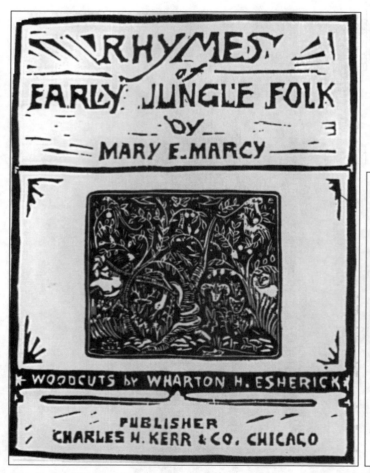

Noted artist Wharton Esherick drew the cover and woodcut illustration for Mary Marcy's Rhymes *(Chicago: Charles H. Kerr Co., 1919).*

Society, dedicated to protect the "wilderness environment as a serious human need rather than a luxury and plaything." The presence of conservationists within the New Deal helped legitimize the sentiment, largely missing in government since at least Theodore Roosevelt's day.

The radical cutting edge of the conservationist movement represented for decades by the Wilderness Society had historical ties to nature and hiking groups formed by immigrant radicals earlier and adapted for their children's generation. The Nature Friends of America, for instance, had been founded in the 1910s by German-American socialists, and continued to purchase land for Camp Midvale in New Jersey. By 1940, Nature Friends camps grew up in Connecticut, Pennsylvania, Illinois, Wisconsin and California; a larger variety of people joined. Only those with "fascist convictions" were explicitly excluded from Nature Friends, but in practice hiker-members supported a wide spectrum of radical causes from labor to civil liberties. Hard hit by McCarthyism, their visitors trailed and harassed by F.B.I. agents, these camps barely survived, mostly by eliminating direct political ties.

A few lone critics such as Scott and Helen Nearing also advocated and acted out their own "back to the land" movement, emphasizing vegetarianism and organic foods. A former socialist and Communist intellectual, Scott along with Helen removed himself from New York to Jamaica, Vermont, later moving on to Harborside, Maine. The two created showplace organic farms, with extensive maple sugar orchards, for thousands of summer visitors. Their very popular work, *Living the Good Life* (1954), went through several printings and Scott Nearing continued liv-

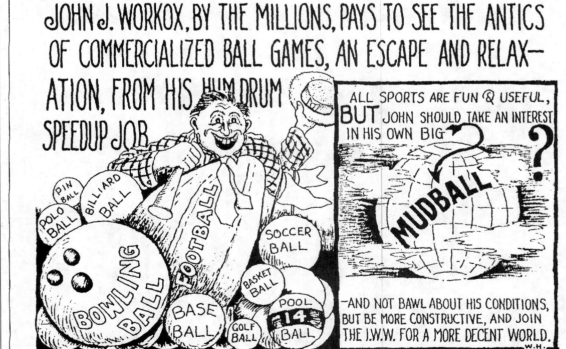

Other Wobbly and anarchist publications foresee attacks on the planet.

ing his model until his death in 1983 at age 100. He survived long enough to see a considerable segment of society drawn to his ideals, if not able to live the simple life themselves.

The 1962 publication of best-seller *Silent Spring* by Rachel Carson, the first woman to gain a high-level position in the U.S. Fish and Wildlife Service, dramatized for a new generation the dangers of pesticides, and encouraged investigations into varied dangerous practices of manufacturers. Science fiction novels of ecological destruction, especially Ursula LeGuin's *The Word for World Is Forest* (1968) found other terms to describe the life-effacing activities and mind-set of destroyers. LeGuin's fellow science fiction writer (and radical), Philip K. Dick, luminously described in various works such as *The Three Stigmata of Palmer Eldritch* a future world so eviscerated that people took drugs to hallucinate life at a stage of lesser destruction.

During the later 1960s, when social movements of all kinds gained steam, traditional environmental societies rapidly took on new meaning. The Sierra Club, a mountaineering society based on the West Coast, quickly expanded from a few thousand members to more than 100,000 by 1970 and a half million by 1980. Glossy Sierra Club books presented readers with a visit to the man-made hell of environmental destruction and local clubs took up issues ranging from overcutting of surviving countryside green space to the many forms of pollution.

Criticism of thoughtless city and suburban planning also took on new dimensions as the fuller results of highway expansion and neighborhood destruction became clearer. The radical critic-philosopher Lewis Mumford had, since the 1930s, urgently

Ansel Adams' "Sermon On the Mount," c. 1935. Photograph by Cedric Wright. Copyright by the Trustees of the Ansel Adams Rights Trust. All Rights Reserved.

THE ANTEATER'S UMBRELLA

A CONTRIBUTION TO THE CRITIQUE
OF THE IDEOLOGY OF ZOOS

"...the ostrich, the deer, the jerboa, etc., will come and join forces with man as soon as his company becomes attractive to them, which it can never be in the civilized order!"

—Charles FOURIER

It is not without significance that the animals in zoos are *captured* and brought against their wills to this, the penitentiary of the instincts. The contemptible slavery that man too readily tolerates and allows to dominate human existence provokes an immediate revulsion, a profound disdain, a cataclysmic resistance among these animals of grace and savagery. It is only through the technological brutality of science in the service of oppression that the living are forced into a suspended death, in which dreams are deprived of the future they call forth, and sleep itself crumbles against the bars of destruction.

Here, in the zoo, in this place of hypnotic fascination, human beings come to see *their own instincts* caged and sterilized. Everything that is intrinsic to man, but smothered by capitalist society, reappears *safely* in the zoo. Aggression, sexuality, motion, desire, play, the very impulses to freedom are trapped and displayed for the alienated enjoyment and manipulation of men, women and children. Here is the harmless spectacle in which everything desired by human beings exists only to the degree that it is separated from the reality of human existence. The cages are merely the extensions of the cages that omnipresently infest the lives of all living beings. Here the animals are placed in the unnatural habitat of a society unnatural to life itself.

The incandescent speed of cheetahs, the desperate prowling of leopards, the celestial fever of black swans, the immaculate laughter of seals, the absent-minded tumbling of marmosets, the cabalistic brooding of owls: these veritable emblems of grandeur are imprisoned, severed from the past and the future and turned into empty shells of a previous joy. All that has been natural and a source of pleasure, for animals, has been converted into the performative slavery of a zoological bastille. Ability has been made the toil of suffering.

The condition of slavery automatically poses the question: *What are the prospects for liberation?* It hardly needs to be stressed that the very notion of the revolutionary transformation of the relations between men and beasts is all but *unthinkable* today. And yet, in the great myths of the American Indians and ancient African cultures, in the writings of certain thinkers of rare genius (Charles Fourier, Alphonse Toussenel, John Ruskin), *in the tradition of so-called "accursed" poetry* and in a remarkable popular tradition that extends at least from Mother Goose to animated cartoons, from *The Musicians of Bremen* to *The Call of the Wild*, it is possible to perceive at least some faint glimmers of the immense possibilities in this domain. One must heed, too, the invulnerable signals through the flames by the animals themselves: A few years ago, for example, the polar bears at Brookfield Zoo, after heavy rains flooded their lair, swam across the moat, broke into a concession stand and frolicked about as they consumed thousands of marshmallows. . . .

If enslavement begins with men, it must end with the simultaneous liberation of men and animals from the yoke of commodity fetishism and narcissistic effusions. The brutal confinement of animals ultimately serves only to separate men and women from their own potentialities, and to make them victims of their own insidious barbarity.

It is the reality of dreams that necessitates the reintegration of man and animals in everyday life. In the realization of its deepest desires, humanity will achieve what it has always sought: a universe of the incredible.

The Surrealist Group

Drawings by Leonora Carrington

Latter day Wobblies, the Chicago surrealists attack human attitudes toward "wild" animals.

Courtesy: Dorothy Day Collection, Marquette University

Into Dorothy Day's old age, both she and the newspaper paper that she guided remained in the thick of the fight against poverty and war. From 1955-61, Day repeatedly led non-violent disobedience against mandatory civil defense drills for atomic warfare. Insisting she was acting as a good Catholic (even while New York's bishops eagerly endorsed McCarthyism and the arms race), she came to be seen almost as a saint by the time the Vietnam War drew to a close.

advocated an economic regionalism which would make for self-sufficiency and maximize renewable fuel sources rather than dependency on oil and, later, atomic power. His classic 1936 work, *Culture of the Cities,* reprinted and joined with newer Mumford volumes like *The Pentagon of Power* (1961) urged readers to fight their way clear of the military-industrial state and create sustainable communities. Anarchist Murray Bookchin developed his own pioneering critique of urbanism and technological destruction from the 1950s onward, founding the Institute for Social Ecology in 1974 and completing his own magnum opus, *The Ecology of Freedom,* in 1982.

For many new enthusiasts of environmentalism or "ecology," a term popularized in the later 1960s, "Earth Day" in 1970 was simultaneously a fulfillment and a denial. Official recognition of the day by Richard Nixon's administration and even sponsorship by Coca-Cola along with other corporations (many involved, themselves, in environmental destruction) seemed to demonstrate widespread acceptance of the 1964 Wilderness Act as a shared social value. On the other hand, the continued destruction of wetlands and forests suggested that the celebration was little more than a public relations effort to hide real corporate intent.

The formation of Greenpeace in 1971 met the sense of defeat and despair with a vigorous, dramatic campaign of non-violent, direct action to save whales, seals, dolphins and other species under attack from the ships of various nations. A public educated by the television specials of Jacques Cousteau, among others, responded to Greenpeace's financial and political appeals, making the organization the most powerful with radical connections in the 1980s and early 1990s. It even opposed the Gulf War on environmental grounds and consequently lost many supporters.

Yet more militant than Greenpeace was Earth First!, founded in 1980 by Edward Abbey, novelist and author of a cult book, *The Monkey Wrench Gang* (1976). The style of Earth First!, mixing direct action, poetry and cartoons, reminded many of the old Industrial Workers of the World, and indeed a badly-reduced I.W.W. itself virtually merged with the environmental organization. Agitational pamphlets like the *Li'l Green Song Book* (a play on the title of the Wobbly classic, *Little Red Songbook)* humorously explained the need for the recreation of nature by blocking environmental destruction in any (peaceful) way possible. Hundreds of local groups, oriented more towards lobbying and community action, sought to link together environmental dangers with racial and economic discrimination against the poor, and opposed government placement of waste dumps and toxic waste incinerators in minority neighborhoods.

For other activists, younger and older, the growing crisis of the planet suggested something larger missing from the equation. During the 1960s, Martin Luther King, Jr., had preached a theology or ministry of preciousness of all human beings regardless of status. Prelates from Brazil to Central

Courtesy: Eric A. Gordon

In his later years, famed radical composer Earl Robinson turned to environmentalism and his own version of Liberation Theology.

Courtesy: Robert F. Wagner Archives, New York University (Charles Rivers

Ruth Messenger, Borough of Manhattan President and noted feminist progressive, denounces the introduction of nuclear weapons to New York's harbor, 1988. Photograph by Charles Rivers.

America and parts of Mexico increasingly preached a sort of religious socialism with a heavy dose of environmental concern for the indigenous peoples endangered by exploitative economic development.

Liberation Theology, the doctrine of these prelates, had many followers in the United States including nuns, priests, lay followers of the Catholic Church, liberal Protestants and even a handful of Jewish progressives. These people played an especially important role in rallying support for people's movements attacked by the repressive, U.S.-financed regimes and guerrilla armies of Central America. "Witness for Peace" placed thousands of volunteers in potential line of fire of the Nicaraguan contras (one volunteer was murdered on an agricultural project), while sanctuary activists protected in their homes and churches the refugees from countries such as Guatemala and Honduras. The Christic Institute, an outgrowth of these religious-radical projects, initially exposed the connections leading to the Iran-Contra Hearings. On the fringes of Liberation Theology, an ecologically-oriented "Creation Theology" enjoyed wide backing — and suffered persecution by powerful conservatives who had reasserted their authority through Pope John Paul II's generally rightward-leaning appointments.

It was not difficult for artists of various kinds to find or create images of devastation: Oil-soaked seabirds, factories churning out toxic wastes along with profits, end-of-the-planet scenarios of the last tree or the last clean drink of water could be seen widely by the 1980s-90s. Artists struggled to find possible antidotes in hopeful images and did not see them in the folksy "progress" visuals of the New Deal, for instance, or of recent industrial society in general.

Photo and Courtesy: JEB

ACT-UP demonstration in Washington, D.C., 1988, demands action against spreading disease.

In the face of competitive society's sheer propensity for self-destruction, crusaders for a better, different, more cooperative world seemed more and more like their distant political ancestors, the utopian visionaries. At the dawn of the seventeenth century, philosopher-mystic Jakob Böhme had asked in his *Aurora* "to whom shall I liken the Angels?" and answered,

> to little children who walk in the fields in *May*...and make use of the beautiful heavenly flowers for their play or sport in their *senses*, and make beautiful garlands, and rejoice in the delicious pleasant May of *God*.

This was a Mayday with more meaning after the fall of Communism, with the new generations of children facing their future in a world where the particulars of twentieth (and even nineteenth) century radicalism had fallen away but the singular truths remained.

Lewis Mumford, philosopher of city life and the environment. Murray Bookchin, a notable environmentalist since the 1950s is author of The Ecology of Freedom *(1982) and a founder of the Institute for Social Ecology.*

Photo and Courtesy: Richard Bermack

Scott and Helen Nearing. Practitioners and prophets of the Simple Life, organic farmers in Maine.

Photo and Courtesy: Ellen Shub

Direct action at Seabrook Nuclear Power Plant, Seabrook, N.H., May, 1980. "It Won't Be Built!" vowed nuclear protesters, and although defeated they made their point. Many planned facilities were never built, as the high costs and dangers became increasingly clear.

"Underground" comic artist R. Crumb relocated to Winters, California in the Yolo Valley and worked for several years with one of the most ecology-oriented alternative newspapers, Winds of Change.

Courtesy: Ursula LeGuin

A foremost feminist author and the daughter of a famed anthropologist, Ursula LeGuin has offered readers pictures of other worlds or imaginary earth societies with cultures starkly different from our own.
Artist: Henk Pender

Photo and Courtesy: Richard Quinney

Peter Schumann's Bread & Puppet Theatre, active from the 1960s to the present, has specialized in open-air events, especially demonstrations, using puppets and masks of all sizes including very large, often mounted on poles.

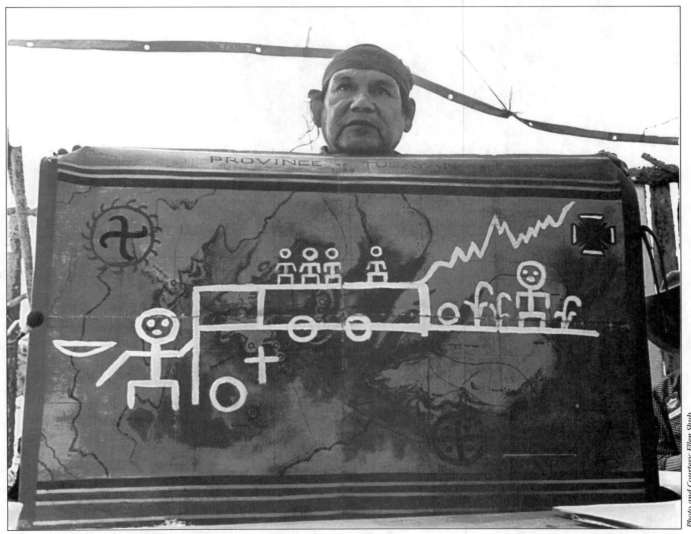

As federal officials pitted Hopi and Navaho Indians against each other in a sophisticated land grab for minerals, Hopi Spiritual Elder Thomas Benyacka explained tribal philosophy which tells of the need to prevent the "gourd of Ashes" from again falling to the earth, and of our current choice between chaos and destruction, or corn and survival in peace. Speech given at the International Black Hills Survival Gathering, South Dakota, July, 1980.

Courtesy: Marge Piercy

Marge Piercy, famed feminist poet-novelist and long-time resident of Cape Cod, has written often on ecological themes.

Rethinking the Radical Past

R. Crumb

E.P. THOMPSON

Edward Thompson, born to a British father and an American mother, was the most influential Anglo-American radical historian of the 1960s-70s as well as an inspiration to anti-war activists everywhere.

A prominent British war veteran and Communist, Thompson taught workers' education in the late 1940s and 1950s, and found time to write a famed biography of England's socialist poet-laureate, William Morris. Thompson and his friends broke with the Communist Party in 1956, and set out to create a New Left, the first in the U.S. or the U.K. Thompson himself helped lead the great "Ban the Bomb" Movement of mass marches. he also began writing labor history. In 1963 he brought out the epochal *Making of the English Working Class,* which reshaped the historical scholarship of a generation.

Thompson's works took the stress off blind economic forces in history and placed it upon people's own lives, especially the daily existence of ordinary working people. His tours of the U.S. deeply influenced young scholars trying to relate history to their political beliefs, and encouraged the historical recovery of many of the individuals and movements in this book.

In later years, Thompson wrote influential books on subjects ranging from the "security" state apparatus to the poet-artist William Blake. He personally led European Nuclear Disarmament (END) which opposed both capitalist and communist governments. His death in 1993 marked the end of an era for historians and peace activists.

E.P. Thompson.

Courtesy: Dorothy Thompason

Rethinking the Radical Past

During the 1960s-80s, the study of history had the kind of prestige that writing novels and writing about novels used to have for radicals during the 1920s-50s. Leading intellectuals proposed that rethinking the past would make a better future possible. Labor history, black history and women's history, quickly followed by Chicano and gay history, attracted many scholars and thousands of students eager to understand themselves and their traditions in some new, more sympathetic way. A new and radicalized social history, mainly the study of past lower classes, their lives and culture, seemed to promise a way to rethink the possibilities of democracy. At times, the enthusiastic discussions of "public history" in museums, exhibits, documentary films and other public presentations seemed to create a social movement with far-ranging potential.

One wing of historical reconsideration began with the journal *Studies On the Left* in 1959, published by a circle of young radicals on the University of Wisconsin campus of Madison and inspired by the fearless historian William Appleman Williams.

David Montgomery, America's premier labor historian and himself a former shop-floor militant, shown here with Peter Rachleff (far right), a St. Paul, Minnesota labor historian and fellow labor activist.

Oral history became by the 1970s-80s well known as a major means for reanimating living memories of radicalism: (top) Paul Buhle interviews Don Chase, youthful protestor against the 1926 U.S. invasion of Nicaragua and later a minister in a progressive San Francisco parish. Photography, Richard Bermack. (Lower left) Ed Sullivan interviews former Brooklyn College instructor Henry Klein, dismissed in an academic freedom case and later from New York City schools by the notorious Rapp-Coudert Committee. Photography, Lawrence Klein. (Lower right) Studs Terkel, radical radio talk show host and author of many oral histories of life in America.

James Weinstein, the predominant editor of the journal, formulated a political perspective. The Socialist Party of Eugene Debs's day had been the keenest and most important American radical movement of the century. But subsequent radicals including the Communists had been trapped by the corrupting power of liberal presidents and their administrations to hand out increased social benefits while strengthening the corporate control of society at large. In developing a firm critique of U.S. foreign policy, *Studies* also analyzed the capacity of American elites to manipulate world events to their own benefit and induce ordinary Americans to share reckless international crusades as the supposed price of freedom.

A second history-oriented journal, *Radical America*, began publication in Madison in 1967 with a rather different perspective. Not disparaging the Socialist party's accomplishments, *RA* hailed the I.W.W. as a predecessor to the Civil Rights movement and the 1960s mass protests, able to mobilize and inspire millions (even if it could hold onto a fraction of them in any stable organization) with its vision of ordinary people transforming society *through their direct actions.* Future historians from *Radical America's* circle turned from analysis of the elite toward the study of the lower classes, black history, women's history, gay/lesbian history and the history of popular culture. With a growing number of other young scholars, they used oral history techniques to discover a "hidden history" of radicalism buried away in the local experiences of ordinary Americans.

A broad rethinking had meanwhile begun among surviving elders of radical movements active from the 1910s or 1920s to 1950s. In memoirs and full-length autobiographies, dozens of former socialists, Communists, labor militants and radical pacifists assessed the strengths and limitations of movements to which they had devoted their lives. Sometimes young historians assisted

Private Collection

A very special Women's History issue of Radical America, *containing the essay, "Women in America Society" by Mari Jo Buhle, Ann D. Gordon and Nancy Schrom. Reprinted as a pamphlet, this served as a primary textbook for many women's history courses of the 1970s. In 1994 Nancy Schrom Dye became the first woman President of Oberlin College.*

Courtesy: Southern Exposure magazine

Southern radicals recovered their history through this unique magazine.

Courtesy: Nell Painter and Private Collection

Heroes of the South: (above) H.L. Mitchell made documentation of his historic Southern Tenant Farmers Union a later life's work; (below) former Birmingham Communist Hosea Hudson is the subject of an important biography by Nell Painter.

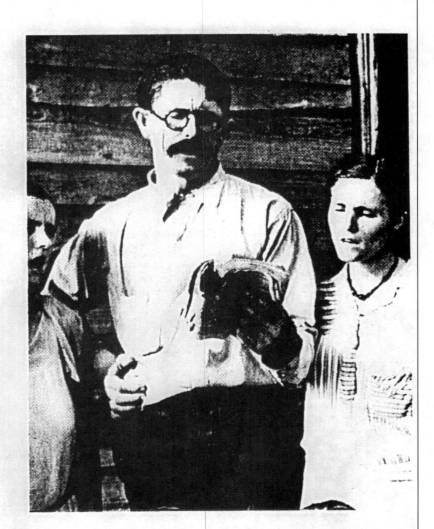

RELIGION

A Quarterly Journal of Critical Thought/Vol. IV No. 2

RADICAL

$2.50

HISTORY I: RELIGION AND LABOR

Claude and Joyce Williams, southern religious radicals of the 1930s-70s, remembered here.

Jewish Currents

$2.00
June
1993

McCarthyism and Jewish Fraternalism
By ARTHUR J. SABIN

Did the Rosenbergs Have to Die? Asks Amnesty International
By MARTINE HERZ

*The International Workers Order
by Rockwell Kent*

Children of the Intermarried   *By ELIZABETH PHILLIPS*
Jewish Fiction Sampled   *By ROGER B. GOODMAN*
The Sabbath and Jewish Secularism
By BENNETT MURASKIN

Courtesy: Gil Green

Courtesy: Morris U. Schappes

Living memories of the American Jewish Left. Jewish Currents *and its octogenerian editor, Morris U. Schappes, represented by the 1990s the Jewish Left still determinedly socialist after disillusionment with Russian Communism. Gil Green, a Communist youth leader of the 1930s, was for decades a chief personal source of radical history as well as one of the most beloved leaders of the "Old Left." Photo by Guy Schoichel.*

them by way of oral history, editing, or just moral encouragement. Nell Irvin Painter produced a history of former Birmingham steelworker Hosea Hudson and Theodore Rosengarten created the award-winning *All God's Dangers* (1974) an oral history of a radical Alabama sharecropper. The writers and editors of *Jewish Currents,* formerly a communist magazine, dealt continuously with the Jewish radical tradition. Former sharecroppers' leader H.L. Mitchell founded the "Historic Southern Tenant Farmers Union" to encourage the collection of 'ocuments and devoted his own last years to publicizing the importance of this unique moment of interracial, southern radicalism. Old-timers disinclined to write about themselves nevertheless opened their files and their memories to scholars, eager to receive an honest accounting of their accomplishments.

The political activity of the elderly themselves also leaped over the generations as a kind of living history, more noticeably after the movements of the 1960s had collapsed. Labor agitators of decades past addressed strike rallies, gay and lesbian movement pioneers evoked their generations' struggles while urging new advances, and octogenarian Jewish radicals assailed both the return of anti Semitism and the Israeli occupation of the West Bank. Here and there, veteran radicals were actually elected to public office with the enthusiastic support of campaign workers a half-century their junior. Altogether, and despite physical infirmities, these radical elders showed how to keep radicalism alive. It was an important lesson in the years to come.

By the 1980s-90s, enthusiasm for the social history of radicals had moved from the university to the community or rather to many different kinds of communities. Descendants of the Icarians, most of them still living in rural Illinois, met regularly to celebrate their shared legacy and add new information to it for public interest. The Shakers inspired a handful of little publications and craft-goods production, while caretakers ushered growing

Private Collection

Courtesy: James Weinstein

Historian-activists: Marxist scholar Hal Draper was a Berkeley librarian and historian of the Free Speech Movement; James Weinstein, author of Decline of Socialism in America, *was an editor of* Studies on the Left, *later founder-editor of the newspaper and magazine* In These Times.

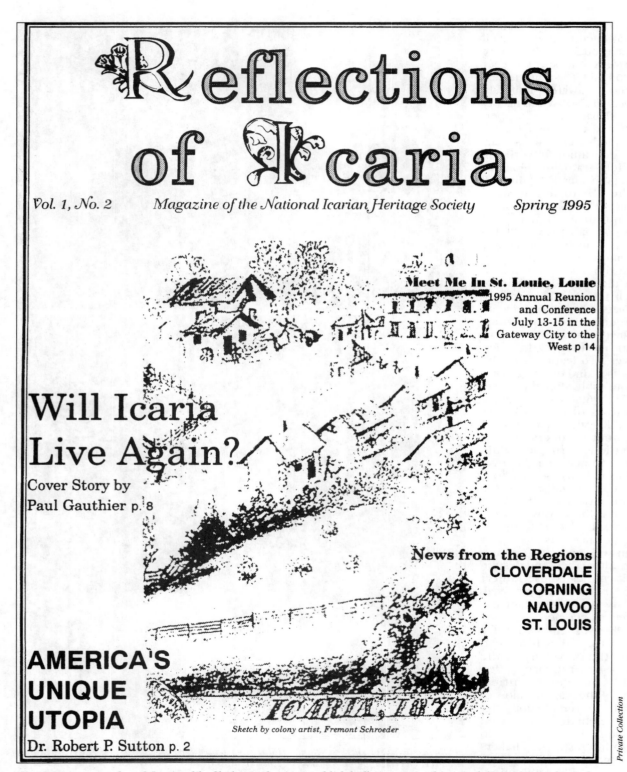

Reflections of Icaria

Vol. 1, No. 2   *Magazine of the National Icarian Heritage Society*   *Spring 1995*

Meet Me In St. Louie, Louie
1995 Annual Reunion
and Conference
July 13-15 in the
Gateway City to the
West p 14

Will Icaria Live Again?

Cover Story by
Paul Gauthier p. 8

News from the Regions
CLOVERDALE
CORNING
NAUVOO
ST. LOUIS

AMERICA'S UNIQUE UTOPIA

Dr. Robert P. Sutton p. 2

ICARIA, 1870

Sketch by colony artist, Fremont Schroeder

Private Collection

Utopianism remembered: Icarian like Shaker enthusiasts publish bulletins urging historical discussion and popular participation in commemorative events.

audiences through Shaker community museums. Feminists rallied to demand commemorative statues, plaques and other indications of historic significance. Environmentalists developed public history displays of past beauty destroyed by greed and bad planning. By the middle 1990s, labor history societies and community leaders had prompted the National Park Service to create "historical corridors" of preserved industrial zones, with the historic contribution of labor and the ethnic communities highlighted. Gay community history more than any other, perhaps, dealt frankly with the radical contribution. Most of the hard work in all these areas remained, predictably, local and anonymous. In much public presentation, moreover, the specific radical role often seemed disguised to slip by the gate-keepers.

Meanwhile, documentary films and their appearance on public television offered historians the possibility of more images and information on subjects ranging from American Indian society to Group Theatre, Depression struggles, McCarthyism, Civil Rights and gay struggles to the protests against U.S.-made disasters in Vietnam and Central America. Occasionally a feature film such as *Reds* (1983) even captured a bit of radicalism's particular story, or touched it with loving irony, like *The Big Fix* (1978) or *Radio Days* (1987), or seriously, as in Arthur Miller's 1993 television production, *American Clock*. In a curious way, the radical theme remained a large part of family history, especially Jewish family history, as if the "Old Red" had become a beloved if untrustworthy uncle of twentieth century experience. More, perhaps, could not be expected in a moment of acquisitive individualism and rightward-drifting national politics.

Courtesy: CINEASTE

Film magazine CINEASTE recalls the movie that broke the Hollywood Blacklist.

Courtesy: Eric Foner

Eric Foner, a noted radical historian, was the 1993-94 President of the Organization of American Historians.

Waiting for a cargo wench hook, in the 'tween deck of a South Korean sloop, c. 1980, Stan Weir was the real-life model for several of Harvey Swados's novels and short stories about a socialist rank-and-file worker. Weir later became the publisher of Singlejack books about the life-experiences of working people. Photo: Paul Hassell

Celebrating Liberation Theology, this design for a magazine cover by Jay Kinney (co-editor of Anarchy Comics) *offers a vivid interpretation of "God's people" martyred for their cause.*

Artist-illustrator Nick Thorkelson chose the "superhero" theme to illustrate the cover of a book of drawings from the pages of Dollars and Sense, *an ongoing radical critique of capitalism's economic unfairness.*

In the tradition of the great Mexican muralists, artist "Roberto" links global issues to minority needs in local elections. Produced in 1980.

"Peace Dove," by Ned Cartledge. This commentary on the Gulf War epitomized the folkish and individual nature of much artistic protest in an era of relative quiescence; acrylic on wood, 1990.

Sponsored by Local P-9 of the United Food and Commercial Workers in Austin, Minnesota. 18'x55', 1986. Artists: Mike Alewitz with Dennis Mealy and other striking meat packers. This mural was later destroyed by the order of U.F.C.W. bureaucrats.

Color Page – 69

"The Carousel" by Maurice Kish. Visual counterpart to a Yiddish-language poem by Kish about a magical night when the carousel horses of Coney Island break loose from their iron bars and prance happily in the waves. Oil on canvas, c. 1970. Kish was a self-taught painter, longtime factory worker and unionist, and in later years Chair of the Arts Section of the Yiddishe Kultur Farband. Reprinted from Cultural Correspondence.

Karl and Elaine Yoneda, mid-1980s. Activist Karl Yoneda's thoughtful memoir Ganbatte: Sixty Year Struggle of a Kibei Worker *(1983) confirmed him as a senior figure in the Asian-American labor movement and a pioneer Asian Marxist. Elaine Black Yoneda was a prominent Bay Area activist for decades.*

Oldtimers still in the thick of political life: Retired barbers union leader and 1922 textile strike organizer Luigi Nardella calls for a Providence, Rhode Island, crowd to send money to striking coal miners in 1978. Longtime Bay Area activist (and mother of singer Country Joe) Florence MacDonald was elected to City Auditor in Berkeley in 1975 (where she cut her own salary) and founded Berkeley Citizens Action, a key electoral coalition of the Left. Nardella Photo and Courtesy: Richard Quinney. MacDonald Photo and Courtesy: Richard Bermack

Toward the Future

Toward the Future

Radicalism of the 1990s permeates the far corners of American life without being able to overcome the enormous advantage of conservative funding and the firmly pro-business prejudices of the mainstream media and the major political parties. Radical strength can be found mainly in the diversity and localness of movements, but this factor has often made even successful activity almost invisible. The fall of communism, which should have freed radicals from the burden of state-sponsored tyranny calling itself "socialism," had the short-run effect of seeming to prove that nothing could possibly survive capitalism's overpowering influence. On the other hand, the coexistence of incredible luxury with worsening poverty, the shameless plunder of the planet's natural resources and the sheer ugliness of emerging commercial landscape made clear that the system "worked" by encouraging destructive greed.

The handful of noted radical heroes and their current roles might also provide persuasive evidence of something different, however. Among the most influential African-American intellectuals of the day, for instance, can be counted several outstanding radicals: Cornel West, black philosopher and ubiquitous lecturer who makes the strongest claims to democratic socialist credentials; Manning Marable, for a quarter-century the publisher of an African-American news-service and now Black

Courtesy: Karen Kubby

Karen Kubby, Socialist Party activist, elected member of Iowa City, Iowa, City Council, 1992.

Ward Churchill, Cree/Cherokee Metis activist, co-director of the American Indian Movement of Colorado and Marxist philosopher.

Studies director at Columbia University; and the novelist Alice Walker, well known to challenge black male as well as white prerogatives. Radicals also have their representatives in Congress, notably Bernard Sanders of Vermont (the first elected socialist since the 1920s), Ron Dellums of California and at least on many issues, Senator Paul Wellstone of Minnesota. At the state and local level they could boast dozens more, like Mayor Paul Soglin of Madison, Wisconsin.

The strength of the radical movements can be seen in mass rallies for any number of causes, including foreign policy adventures but also labor, African-American, women's, gay and lesbian issues, each capable of bringing tens or even hundreds of thousands to the nation's capitol or the streets of New York and San Francisco. This power to mobilize is more subtly exerted in the unmeasurable effort of citizens to work for a less racist, less class-ridden, less politically corrupt society capable of setting a genuinely good example — rather than today's apotheosis of waste and elite power-mongering — for a troubled world. Teachers, poets, trade unionists, environmentalists, computer experts and a thousand other kinds of skilled activists all have their own distinctive contributions to make to this process.

The same might be said, one-final time, about the images produced and replicated. Mixtures of realism and surrealism, photos and cartoons, humor and pathos surround the close observer in a hundred ways. We are not likely to see the aesthetic triumph of any one sign among these, nor the disappearance of any large historic tropes, although work in certain formats (like computer images) will certainly increase. We may look forward to a succession of imitation and exploration, so long as artists and craftspeople in very the maw of the system continue to think critically, and to dream.

Further Reading

Courtesy: Harry Kelber

Courtesy: Paul Andreas Rasmussen

Aged labor militants Harry Kelber (left) and Paul Rasmussen (right) continue the struggles of a lifetime. Kelber takes aim at labor bureaucrats in a stingingly critical newsletter, while Rasmussen rallies money for rank-and-file support of strikes. In October, 1995, labor reformers backed by Kelber and Rasmussen defeated the bureaucratic machine which had controlled the AFL-CIO for decades. Kelber photograph by Mark Lyon.

Patricia Bell Blawes, *Tijerina and the Land Grants: Mexican-Americans in Struggle for their Heritage* (New York: International Publishers, 1971).

Paul Buhle, ed., *Popular Culture in America* (Minneapolis: University of Minnesota, 1987).

John D'Emilio, *Sexual Politics, Sexual Communities: The Making of a Homosexual Minority in the United States, 1940-1970* (Chicago: University of Chicago, 1983).

Todd Gitlin, *The Sixties: Years of Hope, Days of Rage.* New York: Bantam Books, 1987).

Fred Halsted, *Out Now: A Participant's Account of the American Movement Against the Vietnam War* (New York: Monad Press, 1978).

Lawrence Lader, *Power On the Left* (New York: Norton, 1979)

Lucy Lippard, *Mixed Blessings: New Art in a Multicultural America* (New York: Pantheon, 1990).

Manning Marable, *Black American Politics* (London: Verso, 1985).

Amy Swerdlow, *Women Strike for Peace* (Chicago: University of Chicago, 1993)

Beating on doors at the Women's Pentagon Action, November 17, 1980.

Photo and Courtesy: Ellen Shub

America's favorite peacenik Joan Baez faces the future at a disarmament rally, June 12, 1982.

Ken Wachsberger, ed., *Voices from the Underground* (Tempe: Mica Press, 1993), two volumes.

Photography: Top and Courtesy: Ellen Shub; Bottom, courtesy: Abby Diamond

The chief enemy of human rights remains the military-industrial complex. (Top) Veteran activists David Dellinger and David McReynolds with Civil Defense at the Pentagon, 1980, (bottom) and New York's famed anti-nuclear demonstration, 1982.

Courtesy: Manning Marable, Cornel West and Orbis Books

Clockwise, Manning Marable, African-American intellectual; Cornel West, today's leading Black philosopher; James Cone, a leading historian of African-American theology.

The Apollo Theater, famed Harlem nightspot, greets Nelson Mandela on his visit to New York in 1992, one of the most enthralling events of the decade.

A demonstration in Phoenix, during 1988, to make Dr. King's dream come true.

The Caribbeanization of "American" Radicalism. By 2050, a majority of U.S. residents are expected to be from the Caribbean region or South America. Tim Hector, editor of the weekly Outlet *from Antigua, has many U.S. readers today. His own column, "FAN THE FLAME," mixes current political commentary with reflections on Shakespeare, cricket, calypso, and Caribbean literature.*

Humorous response by artists Jay Kinney and Paul Mavrides to public cynicism about politicians and big business. From Anarchy Comics *(1978).*

The CLASS STRUGGLE

New Socialist Game ⌾ Good Fun ⌾ Good Propaganda

This game is played in the same manner as the old-fashioned games of backgammon or parcheesi. There is a chart divided into a hundred unequal spaces, through which is a path winding up one column and down another, starting from Capitalism and ending in Socialism. The game is played with one die, and as many markers as there are players.

"The Whole Family Can Play It."

Every player in turn throws the die, and advances his marker as many spaces as are indicated by the number which falls uppermost. But here and there are spaces in which are pictures and inscriptions showing incidents in the class struggle. Those which are favorable to labor set the player ahead a certain number of spaces if the number he throws lands his marker on one of them; those favorable to capital set him back. Thus the game is full of suggestions helping young people to realize the opposing interests at play in the class struggle now going on.

Price, 25 cents; to stockholders, 15 cents, postpaid. Agents wanted.

CHARLES H. KERR & COMPANY, Publishers
153 Kinzie Street, CHICAGO

Board game designed by Marxist philosopher Bertell Ollman, and an earlier board game with the same name, c. 1912.

Courtesy: Bertell Ollman and the Charles H. Kerr Co.

Courtesy: Greenpeace

Above and opposite, Greenpeace expedition to southern Pacific Ocean to protest against Japanese whaling. Inflatable raft from MV GREENPEACE, opposite, is at the stern ramp of a Japanese factory ship as a harpooned minke whale calf is being hauled aboard, January, 1992. In 1995, Greenpeace launched similar direct-action protests against renewed French nuclear testing in the Pacific.

Courtesy: Mike Konopacki

Mike Konopacki, a favorite syndicated cartoonist of the 1980s-90s labor movement, offers a probable prospect.

Courtesy: Ralph Nader

Ralph Nader, a tireless crusader, has conducted muckraking journalism against automobile makers during the 1960s and has continued to be a major advocate of the public interest. Photo: Beverly Orr

Courtesy: Mike Rotkin

A progressive coalition took power in Santa Cruz, California, in 1981. Longtime city councilor Mike Rotkin, mayor during 1981-82, 1985-86 and returned to the mayorality in late 1995, is a rare American socialist repeatedly elected. A strong advocate of broader health-care, he meets here with senior citizens.

Courtesy: Bernie Sanders and Frank Wilkinson

Radical Congressional representatives: Independent socialist Bernie Sanders (Vermont), left, and Democrat Ron Dellums (California), upper left.

Demand for Tolerance: Lesbian and Gay Pride march, Boston, 1985.

Photo and Courtesy: Ellen Shub

Humorist Larry Bush offers hope in Babushkin's Digest, *1986.*

The next generation of radical comics artists now at work.

Endless tasks of opposition and satire: Pulitzer Prize winning cartoonist Art Spiegelman and Charles Burns offer their view of Washington demonstrations against the Gulf War.

Indexes

The uprising of the proletariat.

Artists marked with asterisk (*)
Color reproduction pages in boldface

Artists marked with asterisk (*)
Color reproduction pages in boldface

INDEX TO TEXT